Anders Cullhed and Lena Rydholm (Eds.)
True Lies Worldwide

True Lies Worldwide

Fictionality in Global Contexts

Edited by
Anders Cullhed and Lena Rydholm

DE GRUYTER

ISBN 978-3-11-055300-0
e-ISBN 978-3-11-030320-9

Library of Congress Cataloging-in-Publication Data
A CIP catalog record for this book has been applied for at the Library of Congress.

Bibliographic information published by the Deutsche Nationalbibliothek
The Deutsche Nationalbibliothek lists this publication in the Deutsche Nationalbibliografie;
detailed bibliographic data are available in the Internet at http://dnb.dnb.de.

© 2017 Walter de Gruyter GmbH, Berlin/Boston
This volume is text- and page-identical with the hardback published in 2014.
Cover image © Rosanna Rydholm, Stockholm
Typesetting: Meta Systems Publishing & Printservices GmbH, Wustermark
Printing and binding: CPI buch bücher.de GmbH, Birkach

♾ Printed on acid-free paper
Printed in Germany

www.degruyter.com

Preface

> Once upon a time, Chuang Chou [Zhuang Zhou] dreamed that he was a butterfly, a butterfly flitting about and happily enjoying himself. He didn't know that he was Chou. Suddenly he awoke and was palpably Chou. He didn't know whether he was Chou who had dreamed of being a butterfly, or a butterfly who was dreaming that he was Chou. Now, there must be a difference between Chou and the butterfly. This is called the transformation of things.
> *Zhuangzi*[1]

> Edward: I don't know if you're aware of this, Josephine, but African parrots, in their native home of the Congo – they speak only French.
> *All three stop to listen.*
> Josephine (amused): Really.
> Edward: You're lucky to get four words out of them in English. But if you were to walk through the jungle, you'd hear them speaking the most elaborate French. Those parrots talk about everything: politics, movies, fashion – everything but religion.
> *Taking the bait ...*
> Will: Why not religion, Dad?
> Edward: It's rude to talk about religion. You never know who you're going to offend.
> *A beat.*
> Will: Josephine actually went to the Congo last year.
> Edward: Oh, so you know.
> Screenplay from the movie *The Big Fish* (2003)[2]

Fiction and Fictionality ...

What is reality, or truth, and what is fiction? What purposes and needs does fiction fulfill in people's lives? People of all times and in all cultures have produced and consumed fiction in a variety of forms, not only for the sake of entertainment, but also to spread knowledge and to disseminate religious or political beliefs. Moreover, fiction has played a part in reflecting and shaping the cultural identity of communities, as well as the identity of individu-

---

[1] The philosopher Zhuang Zhou (Zhuangzi) lived approximately between 369 and 286 BCE. This is one of the most famous passages in the philosophical and literary masterpiece *Zhuangzi*, here in translation by Victor H. Mair in *The Columbia Anthology of Traditional Chinese Literature*. New York: Columbia University Press, 1994, 45.
[2] "The Big Fish," directed by Tim Burton, was based on a novel by Daniel Wallace. Quotation from John August's screenplay (Copyright © 2003 Columbia Pictures), http://johnaugust.com/downloads_ripley/big-fish.pdf (16 August 2013).

als, in the past and in the present. While all kinds of story-telling, literature, opera, theatre and art were major transmitters of fiction in past times, modern media – through radio, film and television up to our present computer games and virtual worlds – seem to fill an important function all over the globe. In today's global society, fiction enjoys an increasingly influential position, as part of our daily lives and as an incredibly profitable industry. In spite of its renown for lacking veracity ("lies and accursed stuff," as Henrik Ibsen famously put it), the apparent impact of fiction on peoples' values and ways of thinking, on opinions and life-styles, has led authorities in many countries to subject fiction to heavy censorship, both in the past and at present. So what does the power of fiction consist in? Why do we use and abuse it? In short: What is the function of fiction in human civilization?

In 2012, on the 16th–17th of August, a number of distinguished scholars gathered at the Royal Swedish Academy of Letters, History and Antiquities in Stockholm for the conference *Fiction in Global Contexts: History and Recent Developments*. The aim of this cross-disciplinary conference was two-fold: one strictly theoretical, to explore the concepts of fiction and fictionality as they are understood and implemented in various disciplinary contexts, and one pragmatic, to look into the uses of fiction in different cultures, in different forms, and from different epochs, both ancient and more recent. The organizers, Anders Cullhed (Professor of Literature at Stockholm University) and Lena Rydholm (Professor of Chinese at Uppsala University) wanted the conference to cover a broad range of interests, from ancient literature, art, opera, and theatre, to modern media, such as film or computer games/blogs. Another goal was to enable scholars from sometimes widely different academic areas or fields of interest, who would otherwise probably not have the opportunity to meet and exchange views, to take part in comparisons and discussions about topics such as: the nature of fiction; fiction and its relationship to "truth"; the demand for fiction; its function and uses; the development of fiction from ancient to modern times; different forms of fiction; fiction in social contexts or in a gender perspective; the view of and function of fiction in different cultures, and other related topics.

Owing to the overwhelming response to the conference, we were not able to carry out all our plans for this cross-disciplinary intercourse. We were obliged to single out certain aspects of fiction and fictionality, reflected in this volume, which covers the main part of the contributions to the conference.

... And Globalization

Globalization is often emphasized as something typical of our time. But in many respects, the global network has been growing for centuries. A specific characteristic of globalization in the 21st century, however, is that we are discussing questions globally and simultaneously. The two major causes of this development are the internet and that a number of political, religious and cultural issues (for instance, the subject of this volume) have been promoted from a national to an international level.

By all appearances, this overall dislocation of certain debates and topics from domestic to global contexts does not result in any cultural homogenization on a grand scale. Local religions and regional customs will prevail. What is emerging these days, at the beginning of the twenty-first century, seems to be a transcultural discourse in media, in politics, and at universities – a global agenda, as it were, with a number of items.

In addition, on an academic level, this development appears to be connected with a new interest in World History that emerged as a distinct discipline in the 1980s. In every ideological interpretation, history will inevitably play a role. It is the storage chamber from which arguments are regularly brought to bear on the issues of the present day. This gives World History a specific role in a period characterized by increasing globalization.

In 2008, a conference was organized in Istanbul, where leading Swedish scholars working on World History gathered, only one, however, from each discipline: one historian, one archaeologist, one sinologist and so on. The idea was to bring about long-term interdisciplinary and high-quality World History projects. This initiative was followed up by a conference in Stockholm to which younger scholars and postgraduate students were invited, in an endeavor to scan the total field of World History on a national level. A third step in this project was to organize three both international and more specialized conferences during the years 2012 and 2013: one on fiction (the outcome of which is documented in this volume), one on global trade and one on methodology in World History.

The Conference

Gregory Currie, Professor of Philosophy at the University of Nottingham, and Göran Malmqvist, Professor Emeritus of Sinology at Stockholm University and a member of the Swedish Academy, were our keynote speakers and have both contributed to this book. Currie, incidentally the author of one of the most influential works in the field of fiction theory, *The Nature of Fiction* (1990), kindly agreed to write the Afterword to the book, summarizing his impressions of the papers and discussions during the conference. The other eighteen distinguished contributors in this volume are Lars-Erik Berg (Professor of Social Psychology at the University of Skövde), Margalit Finkelberg (Professor of Classics at Tel Aviv University), Ming Dong Gu (Professor of Chinese and Comparative Literature at the University of Texas at Dallas), Mari Hatavara (Professor of Finnish Literature at the University of Tampere), Stefan Helgesson (Professor of English at Stockholm University), Fritz Peter Knapp (Professor Ordinarius Emeritus of Ruprecht-Karls-Universität, Heidelberg, and a member of the Academies of Humanities and Sciences in Heidelberg and Vienna), Christian Kupchik (poet, editor and translator from Buenos Aires), Stephan Larsen (Assistant Professor of Literature at Stockholm University), Gunilla Lindberg-Wada (Professor of Japanese Studies at Stockholm University), Torbjörn Lodén (Professor of Chinese Language and Culture, Stockholm University), Christina Nygren (Professor of Theatre Studies at Stockholm University), Anders Pettersson (Emeritus Professor of Swedish and Comparative Literature at Umeå University), Göran Rossholm (Professor of Literature at Stockholm University), Lena Rydholm (Professor of Chinese at Uppsala University), Marcia Sá Cavalcante Schuback (Professor of Philosophy at Södertörn University), Bo Utas (Professor Emeritus of Iranian Studies at Uppsala University), Wim Verbaal (Professor of Latin Language and Literature at the University of Gent), and Ayling Wang (Professor of the Academia Sinica, Taipei).

Acknowledgements

As outlined above, the conference was part of a series of international symposia within the framework of a Swedish research program on World History. It was organized by Janken Myrdal, Professor of Agrarian History at the Swedish University of Agricultural Sciences. This program, including the conference and the present volume, was financed by The Bank of Sweden Tercentenary Foundation (Riksbankens jubileumsfond). The Royal Swedish Academy of Letters, History and Antiquities kindly provided the conference facilities. We would also like to thank Polly Hsu, our conference secretary without whom the Stockholm symposium would have remained on the drawing-board, Michael Knight, our English language editor, Ljubica Miočević, who created the index of the book, and Rosanna Rydholm, our designer for the book cover.

Anders Cullhed, Janken Myrdal and Lena Rydholm

Contents

Preface —— v

Here, There – and Everywhere? Eastern examples

Lena Rydholm
Chinese Theories and Concepts of Fiction and the Issue of Transcultural Theories and Concepts of Fiction —— 3

Torbjörn Lodén
Literature as a Vehicle for the Dao: Changing Perspectives of Fiction and Truth in Chinese Literature —— 31

Gunilla Lindberg-Wada
Murasaki Shikibu and *The Tale of Genji*: Fate and Fiction —— 51

Fictional Spaces: Image, Language & Identity

Marcia Sá Cavalcante Schuback
The Fiction of the Image —— 67

Anders Pettersson
Linguistic and Psychological Mechanisms Behind Literary Fiction —— 83

Lars-Erik Berg
Photons of the Human Mind: The Fiction of Personal Identity —— 95

Live Fiction: Play & Performances

Ayling Wang
Interaction Between the Reader, the Critic and the Author: The Qing Dramatist Hong Sheng's Historical Play *Changshengdian* and Wu Yiyi's Commentary —— 111

Christina Nygren
Performing Life and Live Theatre: Fiction in Popular Performances —— 137

Fiction Past and Present: Historical Perspectives

Margalit Finkelberg
Diagnosing Fiction: From Plato to Borges —— 153

Bo Utas
Classical Persian Literature: Fiction, Didactics or Intuitive Truth? —— 167

Fritz Peter Knapp
Historicity and Fictionality in Medieval Narrative —— 179

Wim Verbaal
How the West was Won by Fiction: The Appearance of Fictional Narrative and Leisurely Reading in Western Literature (11th and 12th century) —— 189

Telling Tales: Narratology & Fictionality

Ming Dong Gu
Toward a Transcultural Poetics of Fiction: The Fusion of Narrative Visions in Chinese and Western Fiction Studies —— 203

Göran Rossholm
General Beliefs from Fiction —— 227

Mari Hatavara
Historical Fiction: Experiencing the Past, Reflecting History —— 241

The Frontiers of Fiction: Recent Developments

Stefan Helgesson
Unsettling Fictions: Generic Instability and Colonial Time —— 261

Stephan Larsen
Whose Magic? Whose Realism? Reflections on Magical Realism in Ben Okri's *The Famished Road* —— 275

Christian Kupchik
Confessions of the Hydra: Variations on the Concept of Fiction in Latin America —— 289

Coda: Fiction, Translation & Interaction

Göran Malmqvist
Fiction in Global Contexts: Translation, the Universal Language of Literature —— 301

Gregory Currie
Afterword: Fiction as a Transcultural Entity —— 311

List of Contributors —— 325

Index of Names —— 333

Here, There – and Everywhere?
Eastern examples

Lena Rydholm
Chinese Theories and Concepts of Fiction and the Issue of Transcultural Theories and Concepts of Fiction

Introduction

In our present globalized world, researchers in many fields explore the possibilities of creating transcultural theories and concepts within the humanities and social sciences. This paper deals with the issue of creating transcultural theories and concepts of fiction. I will be using mainly Chinese notions of fictionality, in a domestic as well as in a global context, to raise certain basic questions about transcultural theories and concepts of fiction. The paper begins with a discussion of the "nature" of fiction in the context of Western theories of literature, genre and fiction, followed by a discussion of Chinese theories of literature and fiction, in the past and in the present.[1] The paper ends with a discussion of three of the major problems related to the creation of transcultural theories and concepts of fiction. These are: the problem of the normative impact of Western paradigms on transcultural theories and concepts of fiction, problems concerning the ideological foundation of transcultural theories and concepts of fiction and, finally, problems related to the very "nature" of fiction when attempting to create transcultural theories and concepts of fiction.

What Is the "Nature" of Fiction?

Theories of fiction in the West abound, especially from the 20th century onwards. In this short paper, I will merely refer to a few theories that are relevant to my present view of the "nature" of fiction and that can assist me in explaining my way of dealing with this complex concept in the context of transcultural theories of fiction. I will also draw on certain theories and concepts of literature and genre for analogies. The concept of literature in many Western theories of literature in the 20th century, as proposed by René Wellek and Austin Warren, David Lodge and many others, is closely related to the

---

[1] Translations from Chinese sources into English in this paper were made by the author unless otherwise stated.

concept of fiction. (Harris 1992, 193) J. M. Cameron even claimed that "the making of fictions" is the purpose of literature.[2] In *Dictionary of Concepts in Literary Criticism and Theory*, W. Harris provides four explanations of the concept of fiction:

> 1. That which is feigned or invented in order to entertain and/or to instruct. 2. The previous sense as restricted to prose narrative. 3. That which is feigned or pretended as an agreed practical convenience. 4. That, feigned or invented, which comes to be believed. (Harris 1992, 99)

My discussion of fiction touches upon all of these aspects of fiction, with the exception that it is not restricted to narrative prose (point 2 above). In classical Chinese novels, prose narrative mixes perfectly well with interspersed songs and poems, as in novels in many other cultures. Therefore, a discussion of transcultural concepts of fiction should not be limited to prose narrative and could in fact involve many literary and popular fiction genres, although in this paper, I will mainly focus on discussing Chinese novels, novellas and short stories. However, when discussing the very "nature" of fiction, there is one basic prerequisite for its existence that we should not ignore. Regardless of whether a literary work is fiction in the sense of Harris's four definitions (cited above); and regardless of whether a fictional work is considered literary or popular; regardless of its relationship to a certain "reality" or "truth"; regardless of the form or medium it is expressed in; and regardless of the time, place or culture in which it was created, all works of fiction still share one inevitable prerequisite: they were all created *by someone*. They are created by human beings, based on a thought, an idea, a concept, an emotion, a dream, a fantasy, a vision or whatever in the creator's (or creators') mind. In this sense, fiction resembles literature itself, or literary genres for that matter. To draw on an analogy, Anders Pettersson, when discussing literary genres, just as John Searle does in his *Construction of Social Reality*, distinguishes two kinds of reality, the natural and the social:

> In one sense, genres do not exist: they have no material existence […] If human kind were to be wiped out while the rest of the world remained intact, neutrons and stones and stars would continue to be there – at least according to realist ontologies of various descriptions – but not literary genres. In another sense, however, literary genres do exist, the novel for example. […] So a literary genre like the novel possesses a social existence or, with perhaps a clearer formulation, ideas about such literary genre as the novel exist in people's minds. […] The mental or social mode of existence should not, however, be conflated with the material or natural one. (Pettersson 2006, 294–295)

---

[2] J. M. Cameron, "Poetry and Dialectic," in *The Night Battle*, London: Burns and Oates, 1962, 136–37, quoted in Harris 1992, 194.

Literary genres are mind-dependent. In Pettersson's view they exist as intellectual and social constructs. I believe the same can be argued about the "nature" of fiction: *Ideas about fiction exist in people's minds.* If mankind did not exist, neither would fiction. Since fictions are in essence intellectual and social constructs, our ideas about what fiction is may change at any time. Kendall Walton (1990) describes fiction as a kind of social activity, a game of make-believe played by author and reader. But to engage in a game, you have to know the rules. Reader and writer have to *share certain ideas about fiction*, that are the prerequisite to enable this kind of communication between author and reader to function. And these "rules of the game" apply in a specific culture, at a specific time, and among people familiar with them, and may change at any time. There are no limits to what fiction is, or should be, or could become in the future.

Shuen-fu Lin describes genres as "clusters of stylistic and thematic traits that a number of works hold more or less in common and that change irregularly over the course of time." (Lin 1994, 5) Fiction, in my view, can also be seen as a cluster of features of all kinds, intra-textual, inter-textual and extra-textual, that change irregularly over time, and in addition, vary in different literary cultures, depending on the ideas about fiction in people's minds. As opposed to the case in the natural sciences, we cannot, by means of empirical studies, uncover the basic laws of nature governing this process of transformation, of assimilation of new features and/or rejection of other features within these clusters, since there are no laws of nature that pertain to the concept of fiction.

The concept of literature is equally illusive: literature, literary genres and fiction all incorporate clusters of features that change irregularly over time and vary in different cultures. Definitions of the concept of literature through the ages have been based on intra-textual, intertextual or extra-textual factors and conventions, or different combinations of these. But from a most basic point of view, literature, just like literary genres and fiction, is mind-dependent. Created by humans, it is in essence an intellectual and social construct, based on ideas about literature that exist in people's minds. And people's minds are far from objective. J. A. Cuddon in *A Dictionary of Literary Terms and Literary Theory* about "Literature":

> If we describe something as "literature," as opposed to anything else, the term carries with it qualitative connotations which imply that the work in question has superior qualities; that it is well above the ordinary run of literary works. (Cuddon 1998, 472)

Literature is often awarded positive qualities, such as being creative, artistic, imaginative, original, aesthetically appealing and so on. Roman Jakobson gave us the concept of "literaturnost" (literariness), but it seems to be beyond us to create a scientific, all-encompassing definition for this term. As it turns out, it is just as difficult to define "literariness" as it is to define "literature" itself. In the end, what is "quality" in literature is inseparable from human values. Terry Eagleton explains:

> [...] the suggestion that "literature" is a highly valued kind of writing is an illuminating one. But it has one fairly devastating consequence. It means that we can drop once and for all the illusion that the category "literature" is "objective," in the sense of being eternally given and immutable. Anything can be literature, and anything which is regarded as unalterably and unquestionably literature – Shakespeare, for example – can cease to be literature. Any belief that the study of literature is the study of a stable, well-definable entity, as entomology is the study of insects, can be abandoned as a chimera. (Eagleton 2003, 9)

What is labeled literature, what is excluded from this concept, and what is considered the "nature," function and status of literature depends on ideas about literature in people's minds (in a certain culture and at a certain time), and this is obviously subject to human values and ideologies. What is considered to be the "nature," function and status of fiction is, in my view, subject to the same limitations, to the human values and ideologies in a certain culture and at a certain time shaping our ideas about fiction. This will be made clear in the following section describing the view of fiction in Chinese tradition, but the same applies to Western theories and concepts of fiction.

Ideological Orthodoxy and the View of Fiction in China

The first obstacle when discussing Chinese theories and concepts of literature in English has already been pointed out by James Liu.

> It is often impossible to draw an equation between a Chinese word and an English one with not only the same referent but precisely the same implications and associations, [...]. In fact, in Chinese there is no word that is the exact equivalent, in conception and scope, of "literature," as the word is commonly used in English today, but there are several Chinese terms that correspond more or less to it. (Liu 1975, 7)

The same goes for other key concepts in literary theory, such as literary genre, style and the like. As Ming Dong Gu points out: "'Fiction' is a Western concept. [...] The closest term to the Western idea of fiction in China is, of course, *xiaoshuo* in its modern sense, which refers to the short story, the novella and the novel in popular perception." (Gu 2006, 19)[3] Although both modern and

---

3 For a more thorough discussion of the concept of *xiaoshuo*, see Gu 2006, 19–21.

traditional forms of Chinese *xiaoshuo* mainly include the genres generally associated with fiction in the West, namely the short story, the novella and the novel (Cuddon 1998, 320), it is more problematic to apply modern Western concepts and theories of "fiction" to classical Chinese *xiaoshuo*, as this paper will show. Many forms of traditional Chinese *xiaoshuo* share features that differ remarkably from both their modern Chinese and their Western counterparts. The Chinese term *xiaoshuo* originally meant "small talk" or "lesser sayings," and this concept has had a history of development in many ways different from the concept of fiction in the West. As stated above, classical Chinese *xiaoshuo* are not limited to prose narrative, nor, as will be discussed in the following section, are they limited to the purely "invented," "feigned" or "pretended" in Harris's definition quoted above. (Harris 1992, 99)

The following two sections of this paper, dealing with theories of fiction in China, will of course not give an exhaustive account of all theories and concepts of *xiaoshuo* through the ages. In the first section, I will focus on describing theories and concepts of literature and of fiction incorporated in mainstream ideology, in pre-modern and modern times. In the second section, I will discuss some contemporary ideological trends that either have had, or may in the future have, an impact on the development of literary theories in China. I ask my readers to keep in mind the important distinction between Chinese mainstream *theories of fiction*, that is, views of fiction, and Chinese *fiction* itself, that is, fictional works, a topic further elaborated on by Torbjörn Lodén in this volume.

Ideological Orthodoxy and the Mainstream View of Literature and of Fiction in China in Pre-Modern and Modern Times

When the First Emperor unified China in 221 BCE, he realized the importance of unifying the script to control the empire through his administration. The bureaucrats of ancient China were trained in writing in a standardized literary language, *wenyan*, which enabled civil servants all over the empire to communicate regardless of spoken dialects. Confucianism became the state ideology in China during the Western Han dynasty (206 BCE–8 CE).[4] Through the ages, young men from families of civil servants or gentry were trained in the Confu-

---

4 Confucianism in China has not been a static and fixed entity, but has developed and assimilated traits from other schools of thought. Idema and Haft points out that already in the Han dynasty, a synthesis of Confucianism, Legalism, Taoism, and Mohism formed a "Central tradition" (a term used by Erik Zürcher), in which Confucianism was the core. (Idema and Haft 1997, 23–27).

cian Classics and other important works to pass the imperial civil service examination (abolished as late as 1905), in order to obtain a government post, to gain status, wealth and power. Only a small fraction of the population was literate, and, to a large extent, these were the government officials. Hence most writers were also at some point bureaucrats and vice versa. These bureaucrats'/writers' view of the function of literature was deeply rooted in Confucianism. James Liu has labeled this view: "The Didactic view: Poetry as moral instruction and social comment."[5] In the Preface to the Mao edition of the *Classic of Poetry* (*Shijing*), the oldest preserved collection of songs/poetry in China dating approx. from 1000–600 BCE, the "Confucian" view of the didactic function of poetry was established:[6]

> "Guan ju" is (a reflection on) the virtues of the Empress. It is placed at the beginning of the Feng section (of the *Shijing*); its purport is to influence (*feng*) the entire world in the rectification of the relationship between husbands and wives. The poem is as valid to the humblest dwellers of villages as it is of ceremonial use on national occasions. The word "*feng*" means "influence"; by extension it means "teaching" (*jiao*). Men are affected by influences, they are educated through teaching. [...] The former kings used poetry for the regulation of proper relationships between husbands and their wives, for the establishment of a sense of respect and loyalty for the old, for reinforcement of human bonds, for the amelioration of civilized life and for the removal of bad customs.[7]

The function of "songs/poetry" (*shi*) was to "influence" (*feng*) and to "teach" (*jiao*). Within the orthodox, "Confucian," didactic tradition, a concept of literature developed in which literature should be used for moral instruction: "Literature is a vehicle for the *Dao* [the (Confucian) way]" (*wen yi zai Dao*).[8] Moral instruction through literature became a prerequisite for a peaceful and harmonious society; literature served to legitimize state ideology, to preserve the hierarchic social, economic, cultural and political system controlled by the bureaucratic power elite of imperial China. The Confucian classics were

---

[5] Liu 1962, 65–69. In this book, *The Art of Chinese Poetry*, Liu also discusses some alternative views of poetry in China.
[6] As James Liu points out, orthodox Confucians would claim Confucius as their authority for their view of poetry as moral instruction, but judging from certain remarks attributed to Confucius in the *Analects* (*Lunyu*), his view of the function of poetry cannot simply be reduced to a didactic view (Liu 1962, 65–66).
[7] The anonymous "Mao shi xu" in Guo's edition (1999, vol. 1, 63). Trans. Wong 1983, 1–2. This preface has traditionally been attributed to Confucius' disciple Zi Xia [Pu Shang] (507–400 BCE), (Liu 1962, 66).
[8] As Liu points out, "Literature is that by which one carries the Way" is the most famous phrase used to describe that literature should be used for moral instruction, formulated by Zhou Dunyi (1017–1073), (Liu 1975, 114).

believed to contain all human wisdom, and history provided records of the ancient sage kings' and wise ministers' moral words and deeds for future rulers and officials to study and emulate. The Confucian Classics, the Histories, the Philosophers' works, certain forms of poetry such as *shi, fu* and the like, and various forms of prose essays and documents used in politics and administration, these genres were held in high esteem, since they were supposed to be used for moral instruction, to disseminate truth and wisdom and to provide examples of correct moral behaviour, deeds and sentiments. (Rydholm 2006, 52–110) Such a view of the function of literature naturally led to suspicion of "fiction" in the sense of that which is "feigned," "invented" and not true, and simply made up to entertain. The traditional Chinese *xiaoshuo* as a genre was considered to have evolved from myths, legends and folk tales, from "street talk and popular gossip" (*jietan xiangyan*), collected and put into writing by low-rank officials. In the bibliographic treatise ("Yiwen zhi") of *Hanshu* [The History of the Former Han Dynasty], Ban Gu (32–92) explained the humble origins and low status of the *xiaoshuo* genre:

> The school of small talk originates from the baiguan [office of low ranking]. It has been created out of the talk of the streets and the gossip from the alleys and what one has overheard on roads and pathways. Confucius said: "Also on the small roads there must be things worthy of consideration. When you have high-flying aspirations, you are afraid of [getting stuck in] the mud. That is why the prince does not devote himself to this." However, you may not let it be wasted. Also the petty information that you can receive in alleys and villages suffices to be written down and to be preserved, if there is a word worthy of being edited into an anthology. This is true also of the debating of wood-cutters and clodhoppers. (Ban Gu 1975, vol. 5, 1745, trans. Sommardal 1998, 138–139)

To a certain extent due to the low status of fiction, *xiaoshuo* were excluded from many influential anthologies and genre theories through the ages. No complete theories of fiction appeared in China before the late 19th century (Huang and Han 2000, vol. 1, 649), but ideas about *xiaoshuo* were expressed in prefaces to story collections and the like. Many early stories were accounts of anomalies and contained descriptions of exotic places, birds, plants, strange beasts and supernatural beings such as gods, spirits, demons and monsters. During the Six Dynasties (220 CE–589 CE), a distinguishable prose genre called "tales of the supernatural" (*zhiguai*) emerged and gained a certain popularity.[9]

---

9 DeWoskin 2000, 652. According to Huang and Han, tales about the supernatural (*zhiguai xiaoshuo*), gods and spirits, were closely connected with religious superstition: "Daoism and Buddhism in China bear the responsibility for the unfortunate religiosification of literature, but at the same time contributed to the development of the elements of romanticism such as imagination and fiction in literature." (2000, vol. 1, 18).

Editors of collections found material in written sources (histories, the Classics, biographies etc.) as well as in local popular legends, tales and rumors. (DeWoskin 2000, 652)

In the eyes of the orthodox Confucian bureaucrats who held a didactic view of the function of literature, that literature should contain truths and morally instruct, these "tales of the supernatural" were fabrications and spread superstition among the people. In the Confucian *Analects*, the supernatural is clearly not suitable for conversation: "The Master [Confucius] never spoke of the supernatural, superpowers, the abnormal, or spirits" (*Zi bu yu guai, li, luan, shen*).[10] Probably to a certain extent to avoid criticism from the orthodox Confucians, in the prefaces to story collections, the editors often claimed that the stories, myths and legends told were accounts of actual events, that they were a form of history or biography writing.[11] Although these claims were probably made to avoid criticism, there was indeed a close connection between history writing and "tales of the supernatural," and initially these tales were seen as "a degenerate branch of history." (DeWoskin 2000, 652) In ancient China, court historians were often also astrologers, in charge of interpreting signs and omens for the ruler to facilitate his governing, thus the recording of signs, portents and the like (in particular anomalous ones) were an important part of history writing. (Hu 2010, 543) In the bibliographers' classification system, "tales of the supernatural" were also placed in the category of "history" up to the early Song dynasty. (Hu 2010, 542)

A particularly interesting case is Gan Bao (d. 336), a court historian of the Eastern Jin dynasty (317–420), who became known as "the Dong Hu of the world of ghosts" (Dong Hu was a legendary historian praised by Confucius).[12] In the famous Preface to his collection of "tales of the supernatural," the *Soushen ji* (literally meaning "Records of searching for spirits" and variously translated as *In Search of Spirits* and *In Search of the Supernatural*),[13] Gan Bao claims to be using earlier written and oral sources "to make clear that the way

---

[10] *Analects*, 7: 20. Translation by J. Legge: "The subjects on which the Master did not talk, were – extraordinary things, feats of strength, disorder, and spiritual beings." (1970, 209) In translation by A. Waley: "The Master never talked of prodigies, feats of strength, disorders [of nature], and spirits." (1988, 127).

[11] For instance Guo Pu (276–324), in "Shan hai jing xu" [Preface to the Book of Mountains and the Sea] (Huang and Han 2000, vol. 1, 7–8), and Ge Hong (?284–364), in "Shenxian zhuan zixu" [Preface to the Biography of the Immortals] (Huang and Han 2000, vol. 1, 14–15).

[12] "Gan Bao" in *Jinshu* [History of the Jin Dynasty], *juan* 82. (Fang et al. 1974, 2150) Trans. Campany 1996, 147.

[13] A recent translation by K. J. DeWoskin and J. I. Crump was published as *In Search of the Supernatural: The Written Record*, Stanford: Stanford University Press, 1996.

of the ghosts and gods is not a fabrication" (*yi zu yi ming shendao zhi bu wu*).¹⁴ In other words, ghosts and spirits really exist. As Campany points out, this entire preface is included in Gan Bao's biography in *History of the Jin Dynasty*, and the preface was only added to *Soushen ji* by later editors; the preface should therefore be interpreted in the context of Gan Bao's biography. (Campany 1996, 146) In this passage in the biography of Gan Bao, it is stated that Gan Bao actually believed in spirits because he himself witnessed a couple of miraculous events (DeWoskin 2000, 652), one of these being the bringing back to life of his brother:

> [...] Bao's older brother once stopped breathing due to illness. For several days he did not grow cold, and later he regained consciousness and spoke of seeing the affairs of the ghosts and spirits of Heaven and Earth; he said it felt as though he were in a dream, and he did not know that he was dead.¹⁵

Now, such a miraculous event that Gan Bao witnessed may have been easily explained by modern medical science, but for people present at the time, it may have seemed no less than a miracle. Today, we can of course not prove beyond any doubt that Gan Bao believed in ghosts and spirits, but the entry in his biography and this preface indicates that it is quite possible that he did. Gan Bao's *Soushen ji* had a huge influence on the subsequent development of fiction and has in modern times been seen to mark "the birth of Chinese fiction." (Tian 2010, 202) Kenneth DeWoskin has described the influence of tales of the supernatural on subsequent fiction and drama:

> Early collections such as *In Search of Spirits* served as repositories of popular characters and plots, and provided a legacy of character stereotypes, plot devices (e.g. demon impersonators, celestial intervention) and favorite props (e.g. magical mirrors, stones, gems, and swords). It can be argued that the *zhiguai* tales established the degrees and kinds of supernaturalism and coincidence – in general, the canons of plausibility – that were tolerable in later literary fiction. (DeWoskin 2000, 652)

Tales of the supernatural were subject to censorship from early times. Zhang Hua (232–300) compiled and presented Emperor Wu with a huge collection of

---

14 Gan Bao, "Soushen ji xu" [Preface to In Search of the Supernatural: The Written Record], in his biography in *Jinshu*, juan 82 (1974, 2151), and in Huang and Han 2000, vol. 1, 20. In different translations: "to make clear that the way of spirits is not a fabrication" (Hu 2010, 551), "to show that the spirit world is no fabrication" (Tian 2010, 211) The expression *shendao* means "the way of the ghosts and gods" (*guishen zhi Dao*), according to Huang and Han 2000, vol. 1, 21, footnote 8. Campany also discusses two possible interpretation of *shendao* (1996, 149–150).
15 "Gan Bao," in *Jinshu*, juan 82, 1974, 2150. Trans. Campany 1996, 147.

400 fascicles of tales of the supernatural, anomaly accounts of all kinds based on miscellaneous written and oral sources: the *Treatise on Manifold Subjects* (*Bowu zhi*). According to Wang Jia (?–390), the Emperor's response was to quote the statement about Confucius not discussing the supernatural and abnormal (cited above), and then state that the *Treatise* would "startle and bewilder [the public] with things unheard of and unseen of, will scare and mislead the children, and upset the eyes and ears." (Wang 2000, vol. 1, 25) The Emperor subsequently ordered the removal of large parts of it, and the 400 fascicles of the work were cut down to ten; these ten fascicles were kept by the emperor in a box to be enjoyed in private in his leisure time. (Wang 2000, vol. 1, 25) This account illustrates the double standards of the cultural elite in ancient China, to publicly condemn the *xiaoshuo* and "protect the people" from it through censorship, while still enjoying collecting, reading (and writing) *xiaoshuo* themselves. Interestingly, even today, in a recently published edition of Gan Bao's *In Search of Spirits*, with translations of the tales into modern Chinese to reach a broader audience since modern readers cannot be assumed to read classical Chinese, the editors still feel compelled to denounce the supernatural content of the work. In the editors' preface ("Bianzhe de hua") to the Wanjuan edition of *In Search of Spirits* (*Soushen ji*), it is stated that there are certain "negative aspects" of the work, namely that it "excessively propagates superstition and spiritual thinking, and in addition a fatalistic viewpoint that should be rejected [...] but the major part of the content is still healthy and progressive." (Gan 2009, 8)

In the Tang dynasty (618–907), storytellers dwelled in the capital, many of them Buddhist monks telling Buddhist legends in verse or verse mixed with prose, to convert the audience. (Hsia 1968, 6–7) Their tales inspired the writers of short stories about gods, spirits, demons and strange love affairs called "tales of the strange"(*chuanqi*). This genre, which had its roots in the "tales of the supernatural" (*zhiguai*) in the collections by Gan Bao and others (Lu 2009, 46–47), was cultivated in *wenyan* by members of the literati and shared formal similarities with history writing. The authors still often claimed that the stories pertained to real people and actual events (history, biography), rather than admitting to writing fiction. (Idema and Haft 1997, 134–135)

The professional storytellers in the amusement quarters of the growing cities of the Song dynasty (960–1279) told stories about historical events, love affairs, martial arts heroes, supernatural beings and so on, keeping up the interest of the paying crowd by putting vivid exaggeration and imagination into their stories. The most famous classical Chinese novels (*xiaoshuo*) in printed editions from the sixteenth century, the *Sanguo yanyi* [Romance of the Three Kingdoms], *Shuihu zhuan* [Water Margin] and *Xiyou ji* [Journey to the

West], all drew their material from popular legends and story cycles told by professional story-tellers during the Song dynasty or earlier (Idema and Haft 1997, 198, 208), as well as from some historical sources, such as the dynastic histories. They all include, to a varying degree, supernatural and/or religious elements such as demons, monsters and spirits, people with abnormal strength or powers, Daoist recluses, Buddhist monks and others. These stories were written in the vernacular or in combinations of vernacular and literary language, of prose narrative mixed with poems. The anonymous *Jin Ping Mei*, variously translated as *The Plum in the Golden Vase* and *The Golden Vase* from the late sixteenth century was written in vernacular prose narrative mixed with so many songs and poems that C. T. Hsia called the novel a "poetic anthology within a narrative framework." (Hsia 1968, 169) This novel consists of an "easily summarized" main story plot interspersed with "a large number of borrowed stories" (Hsia 1968, 170), incorporating supernatural elements, such as ghosts, and a Buddhist reincarnation along with karma. This novel is most notorious for its pornographic descriptions and was officially banned well into the late 20th century. In modern times it has been praised by scholars as a break-through in Chinese narrative art, "a most important milestone in the transition of Chinese narrative from historicity to fictionality." (Gu 2006, 125)

The low status of *xiaoshuo* had several reasons. The genre had deep roots in an oral, popular tradition, in myths, legends, "street talk and popular gossip," tales of the supernatural and the like. These novels drew material from the storytellers' tales and were written in a vernacular heavily influenced by the storytellers' rhetoric and artistic devices. The storytellers told tales that were to a large part "feigned" and "invented" for the main purpose of vulgar entertainment and making money, not to fulfill the orthodox Confucians' didactic purposes of literature, that is, to convey truth, wisdom and moral instruction about the Confucian way. The *xiaoshuo* supposedly spread lies, sex, violence and superstition and were considered vulgar and immoral. But as mentioned above, this did not prevent the educated elite from collecting, reading and writing *xiaoshuo*.

In the eighteenth century, Wu Jingzi (1701–1754) wrote the famous satirical novel *Rulin waishi* (translated as *The Scholars*, literally meaning "The unofficial history of the literati"). Not including poems and being less influenced by the practice of storytelling, supernatural interventions and the like, this novel differs substantially from the sixteenth-century novels. The eighteenth-century masterpiece *Hongloumeng* (variously translated as *Dream of the Red Chamber*, *Dream of Red Mansions*, and *The Story of the Stone*), by Cao Xueqin (1715–1764), is considered to be partly autobiographical and has been praised for its strong element of psychological realism. (Hsia 1968, 246) It describes the economic and moral downfall of a wealthy and influential clan, an epic love story, and the life journey of the main character Bao Yu towards Buddhist enlightenment. It is written in the vernacular with poems that blend into prose narrative so well that they appear to have been written by the characters themselves. (Bergman 2005, 41) According to Ming Dong Gu, "*Hongloumeng* marks the completion of poeticization of fiction in Chinese history and is a poetic novel par excellence." (Gu 2006, 108) With the creation of *Hongloumeng*, Ming Dong Gu emphasizes, "Chinese fiction finally rid itself of the odium of lowliness and became a respectable literary art on a par with venerable lyric poetry and classical prose." (Gu 2006, 108) Another factor stressed by Ming Dong Gu is the "visible movement of Chinese *xiaoshuo* from historical narrative to pure fiction." (2006, 84–88)

I fully agree with Ming Dong Gu's description of the remarkable progress in the art of the classical novel that *Hongloumeng* represents. However, I do not think that "poeticization" or "fictionalization," or any other intrinsic qualities suffice to explain the rise in status of the novel as a genre. A major factor, in my view, is the change in ideological climate, a change in the ideas about the *xiaoshuo* in people's minds during the 20th century, when the novel's status rose to unprecedented levels. This required a "revolution in the realm of the novel" (*xiaoshuojie geming*), as in the famous slogan by reformist and literary critic Liang Qichao (1873–1929). This changed attitude towards the nature, function and status of the *xiaoshuo* is manifest in Liang's article "Lun xiaoshuo yu qunzhi zhi guanxi" [On the Relationship Between Fiction and the Government of the People], published in 1902 in the first issue of what is considered the first journal in China to specialize in publishing novels (with Liang as editor), *The New Novel* (*Xin xiaoshuo*):

> If one intends to renew the people of a nation, one must first renew its fiction. Therefore, to renew morality, one must renew fiction; to renew religion, one must renew fiction; to renew politics, one must renew fiction; to renew social customs, one must renew fiction; to renew learning and arts, one must renew fiction; and to renew even the human mind and remould its character, one must renew fiction. Why is this so? This is because fiction has a profound power over the way of man.[16]

For the reformists within the enlightenment movement, fundamental reforms in the political system were required to modernize China – its education, economy, science and technology – to be able to build a strong nation that could withstand the foreign aggression since the Opium wars of the 1840s. Liang

---

[16] Liang Qichao in the essay "On the Relationship Between Fiction and the Government of the People" from 1902. Trans. Gek Nai Cheng (Liang 1996, 74). Translation slightly modified.

Qichao blamed the traditional novel for virtually all of China's contemporary misfortunes: the corruption, the superstition, and the passive attitude towards foreign intruders could all be traced back to the "poisonous" thoughts spread by the traditional *xiaoshuo*. (Liang 1997, 286–287) Just like the bureaucrats of the past, Liang decided to use literature for education and "moral instruction." In that sense, Liang adheres to the traditional, mainstream didactic view of the function of literature, seeing novels as vehicles for a certain ideological content. But instead of viewing literature as a vehicle for the "Confucian way" (*wen yi zai Dao*), as discussed above, and using it to maintain the status quo, Liang wanted it to convey the ideas of the Enlightenment (*qimeng sixiang*); and he chose the *xiaoshuo* genre to bring about this major change in culture and society. The novel could and should save China. This opened up the scene for the development of a modern Chinese realistic and political novel, exposing and criticizing Confucianism and traditional culture and society.

One problem with spreading the messages of the reformists was the low level of literacy in China at the time. The use of the vernacular in literature increased rapidly, and after many debates, with Hu Shi as a major advocate for this development, the literary language *wenyan* was abolished in the educational system in favor of the vernacular (*baihua*). Hu Shi also claimed that the modern novel in the vernacular was not based on "imitating" the traditional *xiaoshuo* but rather became "true literature" (*zhen wenxue*), by describing contemporary society in a straightforward, realistic way.[17] There was an urge for realism in the novel and a critique against traditional Chinese literature in this regard, to a certain extent inspired by Western literature and literary theories. Guan Daru wrote that the major "shortcoming of the Chinese novel" was that it was not "realistic" as in the West; in his view, novels should "reflect society," and it was even against the very "nature" of the novel when writers were "facing the wall and fabricating [a content] out of nothing" (*xiangbi xuzao*).[18] Lu Xun, the great writer of the 20th century, versed in both the Chinese and the Western literary heritage, wrote *A Brief History of Chinese Fiction* (*Zhongguo xiaoshuo shilüe*) in the 1920s. Previously, in 1918, he wrote in the vernacular what has been called the first "modern Chinese novel," *A Madman's Diary* (*Kuangren riji*), inspired by Nikolai Gogol's *The Diary of a Madman* (1835). Lu Xun's novel is deeply satirical and critical of traditional Confucian values, culture and society. He wanted to change not only the political system but also the Chinese people's national character, *guominxing*. (Qian,

---

17 Hu Shi, "Wenxue gailiang qianyi" [A Discussion of Literary Reform], *Xin qingnian* [New Youth] 2.5 (1917), quoted in Guo 2008, 206.
18 Guan Daru, "Lun xiaoshuo" [Discussion of the Novel], in *Xiaoshuo yuebao* [The Novel Monthly Magazine], 1912, quoted in Guo 2008, 205.

Wu, Wen and Wang 1987, 5) Lu Xun also shared views similar to those of Liang concerning the didactic function of the novel.

> In speaking of "why I write novels" just like ten years ago, I still hold on to "the idea of enlightenment," and that it [the novel] must "serve human life," and even improve human life. I deeply detest those who call novels "leisure books," and in addition believe in "art for art's sake," seeing the novel merely as a new name for "passing time in a leisurely way." Therefore, I draw my material from the unfortunate people of a sick society; my idea is to uncover the symptoms of the disease and draw attention to finding a cure.[19]

Mao Zedong and the Chinese Communist Party continued in the same tradition of using literature as a didactic tool, as "a vehicle" for political ideology, for Marxism-Leninism. The Chinese Communist party took the politicization of literature to extreme levels, especially during the Cultural Revolution with its almost complete isolation from the West and report-like works on the class struggle. The Communist Party's literary policies also meant increased popularization, a return to developing domestic oral story-telling, drama and other forms that were more accessible to the illiterate farmers, with political themes and contents. (Li and Jiang 1999, vol. 1, 202–224) The importance of conveying a certain ideological/political message also led to the tendency to focus on content rather than form: to evaluate literary works (and their authors) based on whether they contained a politically correct content, rather than discussing formal, linguistic features or aesthetic merits.

To sum up, in my view, the unprecedented rise of the *xiaoshuo* genre's status in China in the 20th century cannot be explained solely by the maturing of the traditional *xiaoshuo* with regard to intratextual qualities such as "poeticization" and "fictionalization." Nor do I think that the elevation of the status of the novel was solely due to the influence of Western literature and literary theories in the early 20th century. It is rather a matter of a politicization of *xiaoshuo* with deep roots in traditional, mainstream Confucian ideology and literary theory. Reformists and politicians such as Liang Qichao and Mao Zedong, however critical they were of the culture and society of ancient China and of Confucianism, realized the potential of the *xiaoshuo* to "educate" and "indoctrinate" the public. They realized that the novel could effectively convey certain ideological/political messages and "influence" (*feng*) people. This was in essence consistent with a traditional "Confucian" view of the didactic purposes of literature, now applied to the formerly disdained genre of *xiaoshuo*.[20]

---

19 Lu, Xun, "Wo zenme zuoqi xiaoshuo lai" [Why I Write Novels]. Quoted in Qian, Wu, Wen and Wang 1987, 5.
20 Genres aimed at entertaining people, especially forms of oral literature and of popular entertainment, popular song lyrics, texts written in the vernacular (instead of *wenyan*), and/

Thus they changed the ideas about the *xiaoshuo* in people's minds in a way that actually conformed with traditional ideological orthodoxy, since it suited their contemporary political purposes.

Some Ideological Trends and Ideas About Literature, Literary Style and Fiction by Chinese Scholars Since 1978

Since 1978, China has opened up to the West in the realm of economy and trade but also to a large extent in the realms of culture and science. Politics takes much less precedence compared to the preceding period of the Cultural Revolution. Western literature and theories of literature have been pouring into China in translations of varying quality, along with books on Western philosophy, linguistics, rhetoric, narratology, fiction and so on. Western linguistic research, Russian formalism and structuralism initially inspired many Chinese scholars. With the diminished influence of politics in literary studies, the earlier focus on the political content of literary works alone shifted to the study of aesthetic aspects. Formal and linguistic features were now being incorporated into theories and studies of literature, literary genres, styles, and fiction. The recent scholarly freedom, relatively speaking, stirs emotions within writers and critics who have experienced the oppression during the Cultural Revolution, and who have suffered as a result of their works being judged by non-literary (i.e. political) criteria. Wang Meng describes his sentiments in the preface to a series of literary style (*wenti*) in the 1990s:

> I thank heaven and earth that it is finally acceptable to study literary style. At last, there are many scholars and specialists doing research within this field, and it is now possible for the publishers to publish such books. [...] Writers need to be understood and appreciated. This understanding/appreciation mainly concerns style. When a reader or critic admits that style exists in this world, it already makes one feel warm inside; if they also recognize the stylistic features of an author's work, then this simply makes one's eyes fill with tears. (Wang Meng 1999, 1–2)

This shift in ideology, allowing literary research based on literary criteria instead of simply political correctness, along with the openness towards West-

---

or with immoral content (love, eroticism), or fictional content, supernatural beings etc. would often be excluded from the functionalistic genre systems and anthologies created by the orthodox Confucian bureaucrats. The song lyric genre *ci*-poetry as well as *qu*-drama have also suffered neglect and contempt in the past for "shortcomings" in some of these areas. But just as the novel, these genres have gone through a similar process, gaining status with a change in theme and content that better fulfilled the didactic purpose of literature. (Rydholm 2006, 107–108).

ern scholarship, has led to an upsurge in new research on literature, genre, style, and fiction/*xiaoshuo* in China, as well as among overseas Chinese scholars. A large part of major works on fiction in recent decades will also be enumerated and discussed by Ming Dong Gu in this volume, and will therefore not be treated here.

The period after 1978 up to the 1990s is in some ways very similar to the beginning of the 20th century, when intellectuals and scholars in all fields were eager to learn from Western theories to modernize China, to develop Chinese society and its economy, science and technology. For a while, it appeared that Western theories could solve all of China's problems, even in the fields of the humanities and social sciences. After a period of isolation, scholars in every field were struggling to "catch up," applying Western theories and models, adopting Western paradigms, not only in the natural sciences but also in economics, foreign politics, media studies and literary studies. But in the 1990s, there was a reaction to this trend. Not only did the market economy not automatically bring democracy, but in many other fields within the humanities and social sciences it became increasingly clear that Western models did not fit Chinese reality. Western theories and models failed to incorporate the specific experience of Chinese history, its political system and its cultural heritage. Many scholars turned to Chinese tradition to search for a way to define a specific Chinese cultural identity in a globalized world. This led to an upsurge in interest in Chinese philosophy, in Confucianism as well as in Daoism. China could develop its economy and society in a "Chinese way" and become extremely successful in terms of economic power in the world, so there was obviously an alternative model, the "Chinese model," which could be applied to other fields as well. A Chinese model could integrate parts of Western theories but is expected to be rooted in Chinese history, society and politics, as well as in traditional Chinese cultural values and ideas. Hence there is "socialism with Chinese characteristics" (*you Zhongguo tesede shehui zhuyi*), "reform with Chinese characteristics," and many others. A quick Google search on the Internet shows that almost everything can have "Chinese characteristics" (*Zhongguo tese*): "microfinance with Chinese characteristics," "Legal precedents with Chinese characteristics," "Theory of rights with Chinese characteristics," "Human resource management with Chinese characteristics," and so on. This is not simply a matter of political or commercial slogans (or a sense of humour), it is a serious issue in research within many fields, for instance media and communication, as Hu Zhengrong and Ji Deqiang points out:

> Instead of seeing western paradigms as "advanced experiences" with universal values and applicability from a developmentalist perspective, Chinese communication scholars must first contextualize the theories that have been introduced and translated into Chi-

nese [...] Key concepts like journalism, communication, state, party, freedom, democracy, modernization, market, public spheres and globalization are fundamental components of current communication theories, yet less serious academic attention has been paid to the historical and social backgrounds where the concepts emerged and make sense. They are considered as common sense and can be used directly and without modification. (Hu and Ji 2013, 152–153)

In their article, Hu Zhengrong and Ji Deqiang point out the many problems connected with applying Western paradigms to Chinese reality and call for "a new paradigm in order to combine theory and practice on the basis of 'Chinese characteristics'." (Hu and Ji 2013, 148) The field of literary studies is not different in the sense that it follows the trends and shifts of ideology in the rest of society. Are Western theories of literature, genre, style, and fiction applicable to Chinese literature? Many scholars have come to the conclusion that to a large part they are not. Chinese literature has its own distinctive features and qualities as a result not only of the language, literary conventions or aesthetic values, but also from its deep roots in China's cultural, philosophical, political and historical background that neither Western theories nor terminology can completely cover. Literary scholar Zhang Yi aims to create a "Literary stylistics with Chinese characteristics" (*you Zhongguo tesede wenxue wentixue*) that can combine "modern Western" studies of linguistic style, stylistic theories and research methods with a "traditional Chinese" analysis of content and the impact of culture and society (Zhang 1996, 4–5, 9–11):

> Now we will establish a theory of literary stylistics with Chinese characteristics. On the one hand, we shall incorporate the excellent parts of traditional [Chinese] literary theory and modern Western theories of literary stylistics; on the other hand we shall struggle to overcome all kinds of shortcomings in both [...]. (Zhang 1996, 329)

What is the place of Chinese literature and literary theory in a globalized world? Should everything distinctively Chinese simply be reduced to a "special case" of Westerns theories or paradigms? Or is there something basically wrong with Western paradigms being unable to accommodate the Chinese experience? And why should not the West open up to Chinese literature and literary theories? Ming Dong Gu in his *Chinese Theories of Fiction*, written in English, introduces Chinese ideas and notions of fictionality through the ages, and furthermore aims "to construct a non-Western system of fiction theory in the context of the international fiction studies," and to "contribute to a paradigm shift in fiction studies." (Gu 2006, 10) This important work gives Western scholars within the field of literature a deeper understanding of Chinese fiction and fiction theory, and even presents, in my view, new perspectives on Western fiction and fiction theory, as discussed in the following section dealing with the issue of transcultural theories and concepts of fiction.

The Issue of Transcultural Theories and Concepts of Fiction

As has been stated above, theories of fiction are, in my view, essentially ideas about fiction in people's minds, and are therefore inseparable from human ideologies and values. In this section, I will discuss some problems related to the creation of transcultural theories and concepts of fiction. In the first part, I will discuss the problem of the normative impact of Western theories and concepts of fiction; in the second part, I will focus on the problem of the ideological foundation of transcultural theories, concepts and paradigms in general; and in the third and final part, I will discuss the problem of the "nature" of fiction in the context of transcultural theories and concepts of fiction.

The Problem of the Normative Impact of Western Theories and Concepts of Fiction

The first reason for my skepticism of transcultural theories and concepts of fiction has to do with the normative impact of Western theories and concepts. In the West in the past few decades, scholars within the field of literature, just as in many other fields, have started to "wake up" and to explore what globalization and increasing encounters between literary cultures mean for the writing of world literary history and the development of transcultural literary theories. In research programs such as the Swedish "Literature and Literary History in Global Contexts," scholars in the fields of several languages and literatures gathered to discuss the problem of the lack of knowledge of non-European literatures in the West; the Eurocentric-perspective of Western world literary histories of the past (and the little amount of space allotted to non-European literatures, if included at all); and the theoretical and methodological problems that occur when writing world literary history from a non-Eurocentric perspective, treating the different literary cultures on equal terms.[21] The four volumes of *Literary History: Towards a Global Perspective* published by the program in 2006 contain studies of the notions of literature and genre in different cultures and in different times, and elucidate literary encounters between literary cultures in modern times. In the second volume, Anders Pettersson warns against the danger of applying Western terminology to literary cultures in a global context:

---

21 See Gunilla Lindberg-Wada, "General Preface to the series *Literary History: Towards a Global Perspective*," in Lindberg-Wada 2006a, vol. 1, IX–XII.

Every description of something implies the use of some specific system of representation ultimately connected with purposes, values, and ways of viewing the world. Thus we cannot hope for a neutral, value-free system of transcultural literary-historical representation [...]. Even if we wanted to create a new terminology, we would have to employ these words and concepts [Western literary-critical vocabulary] in explaining it and agreeing on it. (Pettersson 2006, 303)

Pettersson also quotes Paul Jay warning of "the danger that globalizing literary studies will colonize world literatures for Western academic consumption by channeling them through its own normalizing vocabulary."[22] It is obvious that the very same dangers are present when trying to develop transcultural theories and concepts of fiction. That is the first reason for my doubts about transcultural or "universal" theories and concepts of fiction. If we look at many influential Western theories of literature, genre or fiction, they have had a huge normative impact even though the terms and concepts used in them (as James Liu, Ming Dong Gu many others have pointed out) do not readily apply to Chinese literature.

Influential Western theories of fiction, for instance Gregory Currie's *The Nature of Fiction* (1990) and Kendall Walton's *Mimesis as Make-Believe: On the Foundations of the Representational Arts* (1990), are difficult to apply to Chinese *xiaoshuo* for several reasons. One reason is the early practice by many Chinese literati when collecting stories, or even writing stories themselves, to claim that the stories were true and based on actual events, that they belonged to the genres of history or biography, even though they contained supernatural beings, miraculous events and the like. In this sense traditional Chinese fiction defies modern Western fiction theories by Kendall Walton and others since it is not really a mutual game of "make-believe." (Walton 1990) It is not really a case of "We are intended by the author to *make believe* that the story as uttered is true." (Currie 1990, 18) The author's intention is *not* that the reader "make-believe the text (or rather its constituent propositions)," as discussed by Currie (1990, 30–35). It is rather a case of the author inviting the reader to actually believe that the text is true, regardless of if the story or any of its constituent propositions are true, and in spite of the story and its propositions often being (at least by modern standards), blatantly feigned and invented. But that does not necessarily mean that the author is consciously misleading and deceiving the reader. The author might very well actually believe that the story is true himself. Historian Gan Bao, in his biography mentioned above, is reported to

---

22 Paul Jay, "Beyond Discipline? Globalization and the Future of English," *PMLA* 116 (2001), 41, quoted in Pettersson 2006, 302.

have believed in spirits and to have claimed that the supernatural stories in his *Soushen ji* were true. According to Tian Xiaofei:

> Although [*In Search of the Supernatural* has been] regarded in modern times as marking the "birth of Chinese fiction," in this period the recording of such tales was undertaken not as a literary endeavor, but rather in the spirit of chronicling true occurrences or at least preserving ancient documents for future generations. The language of such tales, which are never very long, is usually plain and straightforward, and their narrative pattern betrays a strong influence of the historian's style. (Tian 2010, vol. I, 202)

Other near contemporary writers were Buddhists or Daoists. Ge Hong (283–343) was a Daoist writer who compiled *Biographies of Divine Transcendents*. Tian Xiaofei describes its content and discusses the authors' intent (Ge Hong's and Gan Bao's):

> It [*Biographies of Divine Transcendents*] records the lives of more than a hundred figures from antiquity down to Ge Hong's own age who had obtained "transcendence" and become immortal beings with extraordinary powers. Despite its fantastic nature, it is important to bear in mind, in the context of Ge Hong's age and his personal belief system, that *Biographies of Divine Transcendents* was not intended as fiction but as a record of actual facts [...]. The same can be said of the historian Gan Bao's *In Search of the Supernatural* (*Soushen ji*). [...] In the preface, Gan Bao claimed that he had compiled this work from various written and oral sources to show that "the spirit world is no fabrication." In fact, much of the material in *In Search of the Supernatural* on omens and portents also appears in the dynastic histories. (Tian 2010, 211)

In Gregory Currie's words "We need to say that a work is fiction if (*a*) it is the product of a fictive intent and (*b*) if the work is true, then it is at most accidentally true." (Currie 1990, 46) But if the information discussed above, about Ge Hong, Gan Bao and their contemporaries, is correct, these authors had no "fictive intent" in Currie's sense. Chinese traditional *xiaoshuo* where the author claims the stories to be true, are by Currie's definition not fiction. At most, in Currie's terms, they can be labeled "pseudo-fiction," that is, works without "fictional intent," but that are obviously (by modern standards) not true, and therefore *read as if* they are fictional works. (Currie 1990, 37) In this way, if we apply Currie's theory of fiction to the ancient Chinese *xiaoshuo* (a procedure which he has by no means endorsed himself), traditional Chinese fiction is excluded from the realm of actual "fiction." If we apply Western theories, terms and concepts of fiction to traditional practices of writing Chinese *xiaoshuo*, they will not readily apply, since they were not based on studying Chinese fiction but modeled on Western fiction. Regardless of the author's intent, which in Gan Bao's case (or for that matter in the case of most writers) we cannot prove anyhow, and regardless of the readers' judgment through the ages on whether the content is fictional or not, the author's ambiguous "intent" has not, and still does not, intrude upon the reading and appreciation of traditional Chinese *xiaoshuo*.

Even though many modern Western theories of literature and fiction were not modeled on Chinese literature and were not intended to apply to traditional Chinese literature, they still have had a huge normative impact, on both Chinese and Western scholars discussing and evaluating traditional Chinese fiction in modern times. Ming Dong Gu has criticized the Eurocentric biases in some Western concepts of fiction used to evaluate Chinese fiction. Western critics/scholars have often tended to regard the idiosyncratic properties of traditional Chinese fiction as "limitations" or even "anomalies":

> I admit that Chinese fiction and fiction theory do possess some idiosyncratic features not found in Western fiction [...]. In fictional practice, traditional Chinese fiction displays these interesting features: fiction commentaries may be printed alongside fictional works; a narrator may intrude into his fictional work as he pleases; author, narrator, commentator, and reader may all appear in the same fictional work; the narrator may declare a patently untrue account as relating true events that have happened in life or history; realistic tales may be structured in mythical or supernatural frameworks; in largely realistic stories and novels, gods and fairies, ghosts and demons, fox spirits and animal spirits, may become true-to-life characters who participate in the affairs of the human world; in generic forms, a prose narrative may be intermingled with storytelling, lyric poems, and dramatic songs; in narrative focus, an insistence on total vision and faithful recording of dialogues and events may tend to give rise to the rhetorical foregrounding of conflicting points of view; an extended fictional work may be organized on an episodic structure that sometimes shows no obvious connection between episodes; and the narrative language may range from the most literary and archaic classicism to the most vulgar vernacular of the illiterate. By the standards of Western fiction theory predicated on mimesis and realism, most of these idiosyncrasies seem to be shortcomings or limitations. [...] due to the lack of a systematic study of the laws of Chinese fiction, few scholars have realized that those idiosyncrasies are not symptoms of narrative weakness but signs of fictional artistry [...]. I further contend that those idiosyncrasies are by no means shortcomings or limitations. They are characteristic features that grew out of the philosophical, social, cultural, and aesthetic conditions of a tradition and constitute contributions made by Chinese fiction to the general art of fiction. [...] most of them [the idiosyncrasies] are narrative ploys deliberately designed to advance the art of fiction, and some anticipate modern, modernist, and even postmodern techniques of fiction writing. (Gu 2006, 2–3)

Ming Dong Gu's critique of Western theories and concepts applied to Chinese fiction not only points to certain biases in Western research but in addition, renders new perspectives on Western literary fiction. The problem is not that Western scholars have developed theories of literary fiction that seem to apply to (at least parts of) Western fiction. The problem is rather that some scholars/ critics in the West and in China seem to have assumed that these theories are universal and should apply to fiction in all other literary cultures. They have even thought that if fiction in other cultures does not measure up to a Western norm, it is of lesser value, or "immature," or is caught in a developing stage towards *becoming* more like Western fiction, as if this was the universal goal of literary fiction. I do hope that Chinese fiction will not adapt to and merge into Western fiction and disappear. Nor do I wish for Chinese theories and concepts of fiction to merge into Western theories of fiction and vanish. Chinese literary fiction, traditional and modern, should be studied and discussed with regard to the specific features that are highly valued in Chinese literary culture, and these may be hard to distinguish and appreciate within transcultural theories and concepts. It is hard, not to say impossible, to create a concept on such a high level of generalization that it has universal claims without excluding something that is unique and wonderful about the fiction in different literary cultures. In my view, pluralism is far more preferable in the creation of fiction, as well as in fiction theory, than the creation of "universal" theories, concepts and paradigms.

The Problem of the Ideological Foundation of Transcultural Theories and Concepts

The second reason why I am skeptical of transcultural/universal theories or "paradigms" in literary studies has to do with their ideological foundations, regardless of whether they are Western, Chinese or other. In China, for instance, the initial absorbing and application of Western theories in the 1980s gave way to developing Chinese models to deal with Chinese reality, society, culture and so on that incorporated parts of Western theories in the 1990s. But the urge to define Chinese cultural identity in a globalized world, together with China's increased integration with and influence in the world, has in some circles also been coupled with nationalism rising to fill the void in political ideology as a legitimizing and uniting force. There is now an interest among some intellectuals and scholars to create Chinese theories and paradigms with universal claims (just as the West has done for centuries). One particularly influential Chinese model of world order with universal claims is the Tianxia system. It was promoted by a philosopher and researcher at the Chinese Academy of Social Sciences, Zhao Tingyang, in the bestseller *Tianxia tixi: Shijie zhidu zhexue daolun* [The Tianxia System: A Philosophy for the World Institution], published in 2005. Tianxia literally means "all under heaven," but Zhao's interpretation of this concept is based on what many Chinese scholars regard as misinterpretations of the concept of *tianxia* in the

Daoist *Classic of the Way and the Virtue* (*Daode jing*).²³ In his article "Chinese Visions of World order: Post-hegemonic or a New Hegemony" William Callahan describes how Zhao Tingyang creates a master narrative in which the Tianxia system is a superior system that can bring order into the chaos of the world brought about by the immoral and imperialist West. (Callahan 2008, 749–761) For Zhao, the world and all its peoples' best interests are not served by democracy, since this system is based on individual desires, but rather by a Confucian-Leninist elite that is observant of social trends; what people really desire, then, would be "order" rather than freedom.²⁴ Callahan describes how Zhao's Tianxia system is portrayed as an "all-inclusive" world order that is able to accommodate all peoples and all differences under heaven; it seems possible to abolish the self/other or friend/enemy dichotomy:

> The goal of the Tianxia system is "transformation" (*hua*) that changes the self and the Other, normatively ordering "chaos" by transforming the "many" into "the one" ([Zhao] 2005: 13). [...] Zhao (2005: 33) tells us that "Tianxia theory is a theory for 'transforming enemies into friends,' where 'transformation' seeks to attract people rather than conquer them." (Callahan 2008, 752)

In spite of critique in China from many scholars within the fields of history, philosophy and literature, this theory, as William Callahan shows, has had a huge impact on setting the agenda for the Chinese intellectual debate, especially within international relations (IR), but also on policy makers, and could easily be connected to the regime's political ambition to create a "harmonious world." (Callahan 2008, 756–759) Callahan concludes that "rather than guide us toward a post-hegemonic world order, Tianxia presents a new hegemony where imperial China's hierarchical governance is updated for the twenty-first century." (Callahan 2008, 749) If this philosophy were to become the mainstream ideological foundation of research within the humanities and social sciences in China, we might see the growth of literary theories and a paradigm in which literature once again becomes "the vehicle for *Dao*" (*wen yi zai Dao*), but with the *Dao* now being interpreted in a pragmatic way as a mix of Confucianism and Marxism-Leninism with Chinese characteristics. Such a paradigm would certainly not promote the development of free, creative thinking in research into literature and literary theories, but rather, once again, *transform the "many" into "the one."*

When I was working with the project group on literary genres within the program "Literature and Literary History in Global Contexts" (mentioned

---

23 William A. Callahan is criticizing Zhao's explanation of chapter 54 of Laozi's *Daode jing* (Zhao 2005, 62) in Callahan 2008, 753.
24 Callahan 2008, 752, discussing and quoting Zhao 2005, 19, 31.

above), it became obvious to us that it is not really possible to create a completely objective, scientific, all-inclusive, universally applicable genre grid with ready-made genre concepts to be simply applied when writing world literary history, no matter whether constructed from an emic or an etic viewpoint or from a combination of these. It is far more important to convey the diversity of genres and genre concepts in different literary cultures. And I think the same about transcultural theories and concepts of fiction. Transcultural or universal theories and concepts and paradigms may lock our thoughts into set models and patterns rooted in cultural biases or ideological orthodoxy and prevent free thinking and creativity. I have no wish to "unite everything under heaven," to create an all-encompassing hybrid Western or Chinese or whatever concept of fiction, but rather to promote pluralism and diversity of thought and of creativity in fiction and fiction theory, and to promote the recognition of the value of different literary traditions, regardless of whether they conform to Western, Chinese or any other norms, values and ideologies.

The Problem of the Nature of Fiction and Transcultural Theories and Concepts of Fiction

Finally, a third reason why I am skeptical of transcultural/universal theories and concepts of fiction is, as discussed in the first section of this paper, that new theories and concepts are not more "scientific" than the older ones. It is not like research within the natural sciences; we cannot discover the essence of fiction since there is no essence to be discovered. There are no laws of nature governing fiction. Fiction is a cluster of features that are in constant change and can be changed in any way at any given moment by those who are able to create or change the ideas about fiction in people's minds. We cannot establish an all-encompassing concept of fiction that applies to fiction in all forms, in all cultures, in all past times and in the future too. New theories, concepts or paradigms are still intellectual and social constructs based in contemporary human and cultural value judgments and prevailing ideologies. In Wendell Harris's interpretation of Thomas Kuhn's view of paradigms: "a scientist who believes that the paradigm he or she employs is an explanatory model that may well be replaced in the future knowingly utilizes a fiction." (Harris 1992, 103) And in that sense, any attempt to create a transcultural theory of fiction amounts to "creating a fiction about fiction." Our theories about fiction are inevitably replaceable "fictions" colored by our contemporary beliefs, values and motives – and so are my thoughts about transcultural fiction theory expressed in this paper.

Bibliography

Anonymous. "Mao shi xu" [Preface to the Mao Edition of Shijiing]. *Zhongguo lidai wenlun xuan* [A Collection of Chinese Literary Theories Through the Ages]. Vol 1. Ed. Guo Shaoyu. Shanghai: Shanghai guji chubanshe, [1979] 1999. 63–64.

Ban Gu. *Hanshu* [The History of the Former Han Dynasty]. Vol 5. Beijing: Zhonghua shuju, [1962] 1975.

Bergman, Pär. "Inledning" [Preface]. In Cao Xueqin. *Guldåldern*. Vol. 1 of *Drömmar om Röda Gemak (Hongloumeng)*. Trans. Pär Bergman. Stockholm: Atlantis, 2005. 16–57.

Callahan, William A. "Chinese Visions of World Order: Post-Hegemonic or a New Hegemony?" *International Studies Review* 10.4 (2008): 749–761.

Campany, Robert Ford. *Strange Writing: Anomaly Accounts in Early Medieval China*. SUNY series in Chinese Philosophy and Culture. New York: State University of New York Press, 1996.

Chang, Kang-i Sun and Stephen Owen, eds. *The Cambridge History of Chinese Literature*. 2 vols. Cambridge: Cambridge University Press, 2010.

Cuddon, J. A., ed. *A Dictionary of Literary Terms and Literary Theory*. Rev. C. E. Preston. 4th ed. Oxford: Blackwell Publishing, 1998.

Currie, Gregory. *The Nature of Fiction*. Cambridge: Cambridge University Press, 1990.

DeWoskin, Kenneth. J. "Gan Bao (fl. 315). In Search of Spirits: Twelve Tales." *Classical Chinese Literature: An Anthology of Translations. Vol. I: From Antiquity to the Tang Dynasty*. Eds. John Minford and Joseph S.M. Lau. New York: Columbia University Press; Hong Kong: The Chinese University Press, [1996] 2000. 651–665.

Eagleton, Terry. *Literary Theory: An Introduction*. 2nd ed. Cambridge, MA: Blackwell Publishing, [1996] 2003.

Fang Xuanling et al. *Jinshu* [History of the Jin Dynasty]. Beijing: Zhonghua shuju, 1974. 2149–2151.

Feng Guanglian, Liu Zengren and Xu Pengxu, eds. *Zhongguo jin bainian wenxue tishi libian shi* [A History of the Evolution of Literary Forms in China During the Past Century]. 2 vols. Beijing: Renmin wenxue chubanshe, 1999.

Gan Bao. "Soushen ji xu" [Preface to In Search of Spirits/ In Search of the Supernatural: The Written Record]. *Zhongguo lidai xiaoshuo lunzhu xuan* [A Collection of Chinese Treatises on Fiction Through the Ages]. 3rd ed., vol. 1 (*shang*). Eds. Huang Lin and Han Tongwen. Nanchang: Jiangxi renmin chubanshe, 2000. 20.

— *Soushen ji* [In Search of Spirits/In Search of the Supernatural: The Written Record]. Wanjuan chuban gongsi illustrated edition. Jiacang siku series. Shenyang: Wanjuan chuban gongsi, [2008] 2009.

Gu, Ming Dong. *Chinese theories of fiction: A Non-Western Narrative System*. SUNY series in Chinese Philosophy and Culture. Albany, NY: State University of New York Press, 2006.

Guo Honglei. *Zhongguo xiaoshuo xiuci moshi de shanbian – Cong Song Yuan huaben dao wushi xiaoshuo* [The Evolution of the Rhetorical Mode of the Chinese Novel – From Song and Yuan Dynasty Novellas to May Fourth Novels]. Qishan xinwen series. Shanghai: Shanghai sanlian shudian, 2008.

Guo Shaoyu, ed. *Zhongguo lidai wenlun xuan* [A Collection of Chinese Literary Theories Through the Ages]. 4 vols. Shanghai: Shanghai guji chubanshe, [1979] 1999.

Harris, Wendell V. *Dictionary of Concepts in Literary Criticism and Theory*. Reference Sources for the Social Sciences and Humanities, 12. New York, Westport and London: Greenwood Press, 1992.

Hsia, Chih-ts'ing [C. T Hsia]. *The Classic Chinese novel: A Critical Introduction*. New York and London: Columbia University Press, 1968.

Hu, Ying. "Records of Anomalies." *The Columbia History of Chinese Literature*. Ed. Victor H. Mair. New York: Columbia University Press, [2001] 2010. 542–554.

Hu, Zhengrong, Zhang Lei and Ji Deqiang. "Globalization, Social Reform and the Shifting Paradigms of Communication Studies in China." *Media, Culture & Society* 35.1 (2013): 147–155.

Huang Lin and Han Tongwen, eds. *Zhongguo lidai xiaoshuo lunzhu xuan* [A Collection of Chinese Treatises on Fiction Through the Ages]. 3rd ed., 2 vols. Nanchang: Jiangxi renmin chubanshe, 2000.

Idema, Wilt L. and Lloyd Haft. *A Guide to Chinese Literature*. Michigan Monographs in Chinese Studies, 74. Ann Arbor: Center for Chinese Studies, University of Michigan, 1997.

Legge, James, trans. *The Four Books: The Great Learning, The Doctrine of the Mean, Confucian Analects, and The Works of Mencius. Zhong ying duizhao sishu* [Chinese-English Bilingual Edition of the Four Books].Taibei: Wenhua Tushu Gongsi, n.d.

Li Guiqi and Jiang Qi. "Xiaoshuo tishi juan" [Chapter on the Forms of Novels]. *Zhongguo jin bainian wenxue tishi libian shi* [A History of the Evolution of Literary Forms in China During the Past Century]. Vol. 1 (*shang*). Eds. Feng Guanglian, Liu Zengren and Xu Pengxu. Beijing: Renmin wenxue chubanshe, 1999. 3–323.

Liang Qichao. "On the Relationship Between Fiction and the Government of the People." Trans. Gek Nai Cheng. *Modern Chinese Literary Thought: Writings on Literature 1893–1945*. Ed. Kirk A. Denton. Stanford, CA: Stanford University Press, 1996. 74–81.

— "Lun xiaoshuo yu qunzhi zhi guanxi" [On the Relationship Between Fiction and the Government of the People]. *Liang Qichao wenji* [The Collected Works by Liang Qichao]. Beijing: Beijing yanshan chubanshe, 1997. 282–287.

Lin, Shuen-fu. "The Formation of a Distinct Generic Identity for *Tz'u*." *Voices of the Song Lyric in China*. Ed. Pauline Yu. Studies on China, 18. Berkeley, Los Angeles and Oxford: University of California Press, 1994. 3–29.

Lindberg-Wada, Gunilla, ed. *Literary History: Towards a Global Perspective*. 4 vols. Berlin and New York: De Gruyter, 2006a.

— "Introduction: Genji Monogatari and the Intercultural Understanding of Literary Genres." *Literary History: Towards a Global Perspective. Vol. 2. Literary Genres: An Intercultural Approach*. Ed. Gunilla Lindberg-Wada. Berlin and New York: De Gruyter, 2006b. 1–16.

Liu, James J. Y. *The Art of Chinese Poetry*. Chicago and London: The University of Chicago Press, 1962.

— *Chinese Theories of Literature*. Chicago and London: The University of Chicago Press, 1975.

Lu Xun. *Zhongguo xiaoshuo shilüe* [A Brief History of Chinese Fiction]. Beida Daketang Edition. Beijing: Beijing daxue chubanshe, 2009.

Mair, Victor H., ed. *The Columbia History of Chinese Literature*. New York: Columbia University Press, [2001] 2010.

Minford, John and Joseph S. M. Lau, eds. *Classical Chinese Literature: An Anthology of Translations. Vol. I: From Antiquity to the Tang Dynasty*. New York: Columbia University Press; Hong Kong: The Chinese University Press, [1996] 2000.

Pettersson, Anders. "Conclusion: A Pragmatic Perspective on Genres and Theories of Genre." *Literary History: Towards a Global Perspective. Vol. 2. Literary Genres: An Intercultural Approach*. Ed. Gunilla Lindberg-Wada. Berlin and New York: De Gruyter, 2006. 279–305.

Qian Maiqun, Wu Fuhui, Wen Rumin and Wang Chaobing. *Zhongguo xiandai wenxue sanshinian* [Thirty Years of Modern Chinese Literature]. Shanghai: Shanghai wenyi chubanshe, 1987.
Rydholm, Lena. "The Theory of Ancient Chinese Genres." *Literary History: Towards a Global Perspective. Vol. 2. Literary Genres: An Intercultural Approach.* Ed. Gunilla Lindberg-Wada. Berlin and New York: De Gruyter, 2006. 52–110.
Sommardal, Göran. *The Empty Palace: An Archaeology of Ruts and Ruins from the Chinese Literary Mind*. Diss. Stockholm: Stockholm University, 1998.
Tian, Xiaofei. "From the Eastern Jin through the early Tang (317–649)." *The Cambridge History of Chinese Literature*. Vol I. Eds. Kang-i Sun Chang and Stephen Owen. Cambridge: Cambridge University Press, 2010. 199–285.
Tong Qingbing. *Wenti yu wenti de chuangzao* [Style and the Creation of Style]. Wentixue series. Kunming: Yunnan renmin chubanshe, [1994] 1999.
Waley, Arthur, trans. *The Analects of Confucius*. London: Unwin Hyman, [1938] 1988.
Walton, Kendall L. *Mimesis as Make-believe: On the Foundations of the Representational Arts*. Cambridge, MA and London: Harvard University Press, 1990.
Wang Jia. "*Shiyi ji (xuanlu)*" [Record of Uncollected Works (a Selection)]. *Zhongguo lidai xiaoshuo lunzhu xuan* [A Collection of Chinese Treatises on Fiction Through the Ages]. 3rd ed., vol. 1 (*shang*). Eds. Huang Lin and Han Tongwen. Nanchang: Jiangxi renmin chubanshe, 2000. 25.
Wang Meng. "Wentixue congshu xuyan" [Preface to the Series on Literary Stylistics]. In Tong Qingbing. *Wenti yu wenti de chuangzao* [Style and the Creation of Style]. Kunming: Yunnan renmin chubanshe, [1994] 1999. 1–3.
Wong, Siu-Kit. *Early Chinese Literary Criticism*. Hongkong: Joint Publishing Co., 1983.
Wong, Siu-Kit, Allan Chung-hang and Kwong-tai Lam, eds. *The Book of Literary Design*. Hong Kong: Hong Kong University Press, 1999.
Yu, Pauline, ed. *Voices of the Song Lyric in China*. Studies on China, 18. Berkeley, Los Angeles and Oxford: University of California Press, 1994.
Zhang Yi. *Wenxue wenti gailun* [An Introduction to Literary Style]. Beijing: Zhongguo renmin daxue chubanshe, [1993] 1996.

Torbjörn Lodén
Literature as a Vehicle for the Dao: Changing Perspectives of Fiction and Truth in Chinese Literature

When the famous Chinese writer Ba Jin (1904–2005) visited Stockholm in the 1980s, we asked him about literary theory, and he replied that he was too busy writing to think about literary theory. Ba Jin's words come to my mind as I sit down to write about fiction in China. When we think of Chinese literature since its very beginnings some three thousand years ago, we can throughout this period find innumerable examples of fiction in the basic sense of descriptions of imagined rather than real people and events. But often the literary writings seem far away from the theoretical discussions about literature, which have often expressed a disparaging attitude towards fiction in this sense. Literature itself and theories and doctrines about literature have lived separate lives, as it were, and writers, especially the most original and creative writers, have often followed principles quite different from those espoused by orthodox theory.

Literary theories and doctrines have been formulated and discussed in China and literary works have been created for more than two thousand years. That is to say, ever since the first millennium BCE there have been extant Chinese texts which fit our notion of literature. There is poetry, there are stories written in prose and there are dramas, sung dramas that we therefore often call "operas" in the West. But we will look in vain in the classical Chinese tradition for a word equivalent to the modern concept of "literature" or its modern Chinese equivalent *wenxue*.

In premodern China, there was *wen*, which often carried a meaning close to our word "text," and there was *shi*, which referred to rhymed texts or poetry. Then there were many different kinds of *wen* and *shi* with different labels. For example, there was *xiaoshuo*, "small talk," which gradually came to refer to short stories and novels but which, first referred to street talk or street gossip.

Fiction as a literary concept refers in its broadest sense to descriptions of imagined rather than real events and people in literary works, irrespective of genre, and in contemporary discussions "fictionality" is often used to capture "fiction" in this broad sense. In a narrower sense, fiction can, as we know, also refer to novels and short stories as a literary genre.[1]

---

[1] For penetrating discussions of the notion of "fiction," see Currie 1990 and Walton 1990. For an excellent analysis of views of fictionality in early European tradition, see chapter I, "In the

In Chinese tradition, we can find some discussions about fiction in the broad sense of fictionality, but there was no one established word for it. Different words and concepts were used at different times. (Gu 2006, 48) In modern times, *xugou*, which is made up of one character meaning "empty" and another meaning "to construct," has come to be used to refer to fiction in the broad sense of fictionality. Although *xugou* is an old word, it began to be used as a literary and artistic category only in the early twentieth century when it was borrowed in this sense from Japanese. As for fiction in the narrow sense, referring to the literary genre of novels and short stories, the modern concept is *xiaoshuo* "small talk." As we shall see, this is a word with a long history, which began to be used very early to refer to certain kinds of stories. But there have also been several other words referring to stories of more or less fictional character.[2]

In this paper, I will move back and forth between these two meanings of fiction – fiction as fictionality and as the genre of novels and short stories – and I will make use of "fictionality" to make clear when I use "fiction" in the broader sense.

Literature and Dao

When we look for pronouncements about literature in the Chinese tradition, we find that often these were made with reference to *wen*, texts, in general, rather than to a specific kind or genre of *wen*. Since the Song dynasty (960–1276), the most quoted literary precept or slogan has been to say that "texts are used to convey the Dao" (*wen yi zai Dao*), and Dao – the Way – referred to what is true and right. This slogan meant that literature should reflect the basic principles of our existence and of the universe and convey these principles as norms for readers to try to live up to. One of the founders of the neo-Confucian school of thought, Zhou Dunyi (1017–1073), wrote:

> Literature [*wen*] is that by which one carries the Way. If the wheels and shafts [of a carriage] are decorated but no one uses it, then the decorations are in vain. How much more so in the case of an empty carriage! Literature and rhetoric are skills; Dao and

---

World of Make-Believe," in Anders Cullhed's study of European Late Antique views of fictionality from the third to the seventh century (2015).

[2] For a discussion of these different categories, see Lu Hsun's [Lu Xun] famous work *A Brief History of Chinese Fiction* (*Zhongguo xiaoshuo shilüe*) (1959). The original Chinese version based on lectures in Beijing 1920–24 came out in 1925, to be revised by the author and republished in 1930.

virtue are realities. When someone devoted to these realities and skilled [in writing] writes down [Dao], if it is beautiful, then [people] will love it, and if they love it, then it will be passed on.³

The idea of seeing "literature as a vehicle for the Dao" (*wen yi zai Dao*) became a part of the ideological orthodoxy upheld by the imperial dynasties. In its use as an ideological tool, the meaning of Dao was defined outside the realm of literature and encompassed the truths considered important by those in power. The definition of these truths was in the final analysis the prerogative of the emperor, who not only had absolute power over social and political affairs but who also, in his capacity as Son of Heaven, had absolute authority over questions of right and wrong, true and false.

In modern times, as we shall see, the revolutionary iconoclast Mao Zedong took over this role of the emperor and defined the Dao to be propagated by writers, artists, scholars and the like. Of course, the content of Mao's Dao was different from that of the emperor's Dao, but in terms of power and authority and the subordination of writers and intellectuals to political power, Mao's regime in this respect resembled rather closely the imperial order.

Throughout the centuries there have been discussions about the interpretation of the doctrine that literature should be a vehicle for the Dao, and there are examples of writers who have opposed the idea that their role should be reduced to producing attractive packages for ideas already defined within the prevailing ideological orthodoxy. For example, Su Dongpo (1037–1101), one of the greatest poets in the Chinese tradition, proposed an alternative formulation to the one coined by Zhou Dunyi, saying that literature should "link up with the Dao" rather than just "carry" or "convey" it. (Lynn 1986, 337–354) By the change of just one word, he sought to protect the creative integrity and, if you will, the freedom of the writer to seek and discover his own truths.

The doctrine that literature is and should be a "vehicle for the Dao" was for centuries used as an ideological tool; as such it was an ideologized version of a fundamental and widespread idea in the history of Chinese thought, namely the notion that the universe or the natural world embodies a pattern or some basic principles, which human beings should strive to emulate. We may think of this as a religious or quasi-religious belief in a moral order inherent in "heaven" – Tian – a word often translated as "nature." While it is our duty to emulate the inherent order or basic principles of the natural world, these principles are also, according to the dominant current in ancient Chinese thought, in some way innate in all human beings as germs or potential quali-

---

3 James J. Y. Liu's translation with minor modifications, quoted from Liu 1975, 114.

ties. Therefore to emulate also means to realize one's innate potential, rather than acquiring qualities that were from the beginning external.

The notion of an inherent order in Tian that serves as a model to emulate was considered universally valid for all human action and thought, not as specific for writing or literature, but as far back as we can go, there is also the idea that texts should somehow emulate the order of heaven. An element in this is that the word *wen*, which means text, from the beginning also meant something like "pattern" or "configuration" and was used to refer to the pattern inherent in Tian. But *wen* could also mean "embellishment." These three meanings – text (mainly prose text as opposed to rhymed texts), pattern and embellishment – were often blended in premodern Chinese discussions on literature.

At least in embryonic form we can find the idea that written texts manifest, and should manifest, the Dao of Tian in very early Chinese texts. For example, we find it in the commentaries to the *Book of Changes*, texts that were probably written during the late Warring States period (403–221 BCE). We can also find it in the chapter on music in another classical text, the *Book of Rites*, as well as in so-called apocryphal texts dating back to the centuries before and after the beginning of our era.

Somewhat later, probably beginning in the third and fourth centuries of our era, we may find more clear and elaborated statements stating that literary texts manifest the principles of the natural world. For example Zhi Yu, who is supposed to have died around 312 CE, authored a text entitled *Records of and Discourses on the Ramifications of Literature*, which contains the following passage that I quote in James J. Y. Liu's translation:

> Literature [...] is that by which we manifest the signs above and below [i.e. in heaven and on earth], clarify the order of human relationships, exhaust principles, and fully understand human nature [...]. (Liu 1975, 20)[4]

A contemporary of Zhi Yu, Lu Ji (261–303) expresses the same idea in his poetic essay on literature *Wenfu*, where he describes literature as "the means by which all principles are known." (Liu 1975, 20–21)[5]

Around the year 500 CE, Liu Xie (died ca. 523) completed his *The Literary Mind and the Carving of Dragons*, the most comprehensive text on literature in

---

[4] Concerning Zhi Yu, see Guo Shaoyu, *Zhongguo wenxue piping shi* [A History of Chinese Literary Criticism], 2008, 64–67 and Luo Genze, *Zhongguo wenxue piping shi* [A History of Chinese Literary Criticism], 1984, 155–157.

[5] For an English translation of the whole text, see Sam Hamill. For an annotated edition of the Chinese original with an excellent translation, see Yang Mu, *Lu Ji Wenfu jiaoshi* [Wenfu Annotated and Explained] 1985.

premodern China, in which the discussion of *wen* and *dao* is a central theme.⁶ Indeed, the first chapter is entitled "Tracing the origin of literature to Dao." Here Liu Xie emphasizes how the *wen* of the human world – literature, culture and so on – should manifest the principles of the universe and by doing so exert great influence.

In an ideologized and, if you will, vulgarized form, we find Liu Xie's dual conception of literature as manifesting Dao in the slogan about "literature as a vehicle for the Dao." This precept was used both to remind writers that their main task was to give a palatable form to the basic truths defined within the ideological orthodoxy and to make sure that literature inculcated the established and correct values in the readers.

Dao, Imagination and Fiction

To what extent has fictionality been seen as a means or as a hindrance for conveying Dao? Among the Confucians, we find much scepticism with regard to imagination and fiction. Confucius himself saw it as his task to transmit the insights of ancient sages rather than create anything himself. In insisting that texts, including literary texts, should convey the Dao, Confucians seem generally to have believed that in order to fulfil this task, texts should describe real rather than imagined people and events. On the whole, they have emphasized the importance of truthfully recording historical events and therefore preferred historical records to fictional narrative.

However, the Confucian scepticism does not mean that imagination and creativity are absent as positive values within traditional Chinese high culture. Even Mencius, second in the Confucian tradition only to Confucius himself, distinguished between fictional and historical descriptions, allowing poetic hyperbole in reading a poem while dismissing a more literal reading.⁷ Many examples of exalting literary creativity could be cited from old Chinese texts. For example, in his *Wenfu* [On Literature], Lu Ji writes: "Tax non-being and acquire being, / Knock on silence and seek sound,"⁸ and in Liu Xie's *The Literary Mind and the Carving of Dragons* we find discussions of the role of imagination. Chapter 26 in this work is entitled "Spiritual thought," a concept which carries a meaning closely related to "imagination." The opening sen-

---

6 An English translation is available (Liu Xie 1983). For an excellent introduction to Liu Xie's conception of literature and the Dao, see Liu 1975, 21–27.
7 See Zhang Longxi 2005, 54.
8 Lu Ji, *Wenfu*, quoted by Yang Mu 1985, 36–40. Author's translation.

tence reads, in my English translation: "My body may be on a river or at sea, yet my mind is beneath the palace tower. This is what is meant by spiritual thought."⁹

As Professor Wang Yuanhua (1920–2008) pointed out in a brilliant lecture in Stockholm in 1987, this sentence was first used by a Prince to criticize the attitude of someone in the countryside who hankers after officialdom, but Liu Xie used it to refer to the human capacity for mental leaps – "the body is here but the mind is there" – so important for a writer. (Wang Yuanhua 1988, 7–25)

For Liu Xie, as for many other scholars in premodern China, imagination was important primarily as a way of letting one's thinking move beyond words and beyond what is here and now. One famous expression of this idea is found in the text *Classes of Poetry* by Zhong Rong (ca. 468–ca. 518): "When the words have already been exhausted, there is still meaning,"¹⁰ and a very similar idea can also be found in Chapter 26 of *The Literary Mind and the Carving of Dragons*: "Thought expresses subtle points; innuendos are achieved beyond the words, where the phrases should not pursue and the brush should know when to stop."¹¹

A closely related aspect of the function of imagination according to Liu Xie was his idea that "clumsy words may be pregnant with clever meanings; common things may grow into new ideas."¹² In Professor Wang Yuanhua's interpretation, Liu Xie meant:

> How can one make "clumsy words," which do not look pretty, be pregnant with significant meaning? How can one make "common things," with which everyone is familiar, grow into new ideas which were never known before? There is no need for the writer to turn clumsy words, which appear to be plain and uncouth, into flowery utterances. Neither is it necessary for him to turn common things, which are in everybody's experience, into strange and tall tales. The things the author writes are still clumsy words [...]. The writer still writes about "common things," which take place in everyday life. [...] He is simply using his imagination to uncover "the clever meanings" in them, which are ignored by other people, and reveal the "new ideas" in them, which are not noticed by other people. (Wang Yuanhua 1988, 16–17, in my slightly revised translation)

We can certainly agree with Professor Wang that Liu Xie was preoccupied with the role of imagination for literary creation. However, the function of imagination that he discussed did not explicitly reach the topic of creating

---

9 Liu Xie, *The Literary Mind and the Carving of Dragons* (*Wenxin diaolong*), quoted by Lu Kanru and Mou Shijin 1981, vol. 2, 85. Author's translation.
10 Zhong Rong *Classes of Poetry* (*Shipin*) quoted by Yang Ming 1999, 36. Author's translation.
11 Liu Xie, quoted by Lu Kanru and Mou Shijin 1981, vol. 2, 93. Author's translation.
12 Liu Xie, quoted by Lu Kanru and Mou Shijin 1981, vol. 2, 93. Author's translation.

imagined rather than real people and events. In other words, while obviously paying much attention to *imagination*, we can hardly say that the notion of *fiction* or *fictionality* was a central concern for him.

This distinction between imagination and fictionality is probably relevant for analyzing pronouncements made by a great many scholars in the classical tradition of Chinese high culture. While paying tribute to the role of imagination for thinking beyond what is explicitly stated, they were less interested in, and often sceptical of using their imagination to describe imagined rather than real people and events. Thus, the above discussion of Liu Xie may serve to remind us that creating fiction is not the only function of imagination in literature.

Small Talk and Fictional Narrative

In the Chinese tradition, there is an abundance of myths and legends and we may ask to what extent these should be regarded as fiction. Take, for example, the myth of Pangu, who some 18, 000 years ago woke up in a big egg, used a giant axe to separate heaven and earth and then stood between these two and pushed up heaven. Should we regard this legend as fiction or rather as an attempt to describe what really happened when human life was born? Was it perhaps a little of both? Were this and other myths attempts to use metaphorical language to capture some profound truth and facts that ordinary descriptive language cannot describe? Or were they conjectures that served to explain things that people knew that they did not or could not really know?[13]

It seems natural to consider legends and myths such as the one about Pangu as a kind of fiction, which uses imagined creatures and events to capture elusive truths. As we know, myths about an imagined golden age in the distant past play an important role in classical Chinese high culture. Legendary figures said to have lived during this golden age such as the Yellow Emperor and his scribe Cang Jie, who has been described as the inventor of the Chinese characters, the sage-kings Yao, Shun and Yu, among many others, were incorporated with the official Confucian narrative of the earliest history.

Such myths and figures have served as important means to convey essential aspects of the Dao in the Chinese tradition, be it in the narrow sense of an ideological orthodoxy or in the broad intellectual universe of imperial China with Confucianism, Daoism and Buddhism representing the three major currents of thought. Although one can say that these myths were presented as

---

[13] Concerning fiction, legends and myths, see Walton 1990, 95–98.

historical records, one can also say that their literal historical veracity was hardly discussed. Therefore it seems natural to assume that they were from the beginning not taken as literally accurate historical descriptions but rather as attempts to use fictionality to provide explanations of events that people felt were needed (as in the case of Pangu), or to capture some fundamental insights or truth, as in the case of the sage-kings Yao, Shun, and Yu.

Moreover, the earliest Chinese poetry, handed down to us in the collections the *Classic of Poetry* (*Shijing*) and the *Songs of Chu* (*Chuci*), abound with fictional descriptions, yet the former came to be an essential part of the Confucian canon.[14] Also in early Chinese philosophy – consider, for example, the Daoist Classic *Zhuangzi* – we find clear examples of fictionality.

Thus, there can hardly be any doubt that there is fiction, or fictionality, in the broad sense of descriptions of imagined people and events from the very beginning of Chinese civilization.[15]

The modern Chinese word for "fiction" in the narrow sense of short stories and novels *xiaoshuo* – literally "small talk" – is a category so old that it can be found in some texts that date back to the time before the beginning of our era, such as the *Zhuangzi* and the *Xunzi*, where it refers to insignificant comments on philosophical and political questions. In the Han dynasty, Ban Gu (32–92 CE) compiled *Hanshu* [The History of the Former Han Dynasty] with the important bibliography of all writings known at that time entitled *Yiwen zhi*, and he placed *xiaoshuo* among "The Philosophers'." Ban Gu explained this category by saying that the *xiaoshuo* writers of his day succeeded the *xiaoshuo* writers of the Zhou dynasty, whose task it had been to collect the gossip of the streets. He listed fifteen different categories of *xiaoshuo* – for example, texts on historical events, witchcraft, medicine, mathematics and so on. (Ban Gu 1963, 38–39) Unfortunately, none of the texts that he mentions has survived, so it is still an open and somewhat controversial question to what extent these early *xiaoshuo* texts were descriptive accounts of factual events and to what extent they were fictional.

Some later scholars, such as the historian Liu Zhiji (661–721) in the Tang dynasty, moved the "small talk" category from the philosophy to the history section in the traditional classification of texts into four categories: classics, history, philosophers and collections (sometimes rendered as "miscellaneous"

---

[14] Regarding the presence of fictionality in classical Chinese poetry, which surprisingly enough is quite a controversial question, see Zhang Longxi's brilliant discussion on "History and Fictionality," 2005, 45–61.
[15] As for the evolution of narrative fictional writing in China, see Gu 2006, passim. This work also contains an extensive bibliography of studies of fiction in pre-modern China.

or "belles-lettres"). However, later in the eighteenth century, the bibliography compiled for the monumental *Complete Library in Four Branches of Literature* (*Siku quanshu*) again followed Ban Gu and placed it among the philosophers.

There are diverging opinions as to the extent to which there was fictional writing during the Han dynasty, but there is no denying that there were numerous such writings in the period between the Han and the Tang Dynasties, 220–618 CE, many of which are still extant.

In the fourth century CE, the *Soushen ji* – a title that literally means "Records of searching for spirits," (variously translated as *In Search of Spirits* and *In Search of the Supernatural*), was published. In his introduction to this collection of stories, the compiler Gan Bao brings us back to the question of the relationship between fiction and Dao. Gan writes that his intention in compiling these stories was "to illuminate the truthfulness of divine Dao" (Gan Bao 2008, vol. 1, 19) which shows how important it was at the time to link literature with the Dao.

Gan Bao discusses the lack of historical veracity in the stories in the *Soushen ji* as a weakness. (Gan Bao 2008, vol. 1, 19) Maybe this was a concession to the ideological orthodoxy, which required that he should seek accurate historical descriptions and not encourage giving free rein to writers creating fiction. However, in saying that the stories of *Soushen ji* illuminate the Dao, it is also possible that he meant that these stories give the readers insights into the basic principles of the universe. Perhaps he felt that fictional stories, by virtue of being fictional, could provide such insights, although the intellectual climate of his time made it virtually impossible to state this explicitly.

Slightly later than Gan Bao, Tao Yuanming (365–427) entered the literary scene. Generally considered the greatest poet of the period between the Han and the Tang dynasties, Tao also wrote essays, and his most famous essay is *The Tale of Peach Blossom Spring*, a utopia set in the imagined land of Peach Blossom Spring. He included this tale in a collection of stories entitled *Soushen houji*, a sequel to the *Soushen ji*. It depicts how a fisherman sails into a river that flows through a forest of blossoming peach trees and ends up in Peach Blossom Spring. The people there explain to him that their ancestors had once taken their refuge in Peach Blossom Spring to escape the unrest of the Qin dynasty (which was ruled by the tyrant Qin Shihuang, "the First Emperor"). The fisherman finds how people here live in harmony with nature, happily unaware of the strife and problems of the outside world. There is no doubt that although Tao drew inspiration from visits to existing places in his native land of present-day Hunan province, this is a work of imagination; he made the story up to contrast an imagined, ideal way of life with the actual conditions prevailing at the time.

In the Tang dynasty (618–907), the art of narrative fiction developed further, not least as the result of the influence of the Buddhist stories known as *bianwen* – or "transformation texts" to use Victor Mair's English rendering (1988) – which played a very important role for the evolution of fictional narrative writing in China. It was during the Tang that the *chuanqi* – "tales of the strange" – genre developed and flourished.

From the Tang dynasty onwards, the evolution of fictional literature continued and culminated in the five great classical novels *Romance of the Three Kingdoms* (*Sanguo yanyi*), *Water Margin* (*Shuihu zhuan*), *Journey to the West* (*Xiyou ji*), and *Jin Ping Mei* (also known as *The Plum in the Golden Vase* or *The Golden Vase*), which all date back to the Ming Dynasty, and *Dream of the Red Chamber* (*Hongloumeng*), also known as *The Story of the Stone* or *Dream of Red Mansions*, written in the eighteenth century.

The Story of the Stone (*Hongloumeng*), which represents the high point of this development, has clearly taken the leap from history to fiction and uses fictionality to achieve such psychological depth and cultural and social criticism that it stands out as a masterpiece in world literature.

From this long period of Chinese history up until the late nineteenth century, when modernity started to become an issue, we can find many scholarly comments on fiction in the sense of short stories and novels. We may think of such names as Yu Ji (1272–1348), Hu Yinglin (1551–1602), Mao Zonggang (1632–1709?), Zhang Zhupu (1670–1698), Jin Shengtan (1610?–1661), Zhang Xuecheng (1738–1801) and others.[16]

Thus, there are many examples in Chinese tradition of insights into the importance of imagination for literary creation. But often these insights have to do with imagining what is not explicitly stated in a text rather than with the significance of describing imagined rather than real people and events. We can also find texts, especially from Ming and Qing times, which exalt fiction, but we cannot say that the exaltation of fiction represents a main current in traditional Chinese literary thought. The Confucian ideological orthodoxy has generally expressed a disparaging attitude towards fictional writings, and it seems to me that this has been rooted mainly in two circumstances.

Firstly, the Confucian upholders of the ideological orthodoxy have generally assumed that truthful descriptions of real people and events are better suited than fictional descriptions to conveying the Dao. There has been a predilection in Chinese tradition for historical accounts over fictionality, to the extent that fiction has often been dressed up as historical accounts.

---

[16] Gu's work (2006) is very valuable in summarizing and analysing the discussions about the evolution of Chinese fiction by Chinese scholars in premodern and modern times as well as by non-Chinese scholars.

Secondly, the ideological orthodoxy was very elitist. Its *raison d'être* was to represent and define a unified elite culture, which served to keep together the huge empire, the cohesion of which was always threatened by inherent centrifugal forces, which in turn drew nourishment from the multifarious popular culture(s), and the major part of fictional literature had its roots in popular culture.

Fiction and Modernity

The re-evaluation of traditional Chinese culture, which began in the wake of the Opium War, was a response to perceived threats to China's survival, so the attention was focused on defining the means to save China. The phrase "in search of wealth and power" is often used to characterize the thrust of discussions in different fields in this period. China's modernization began as a search for an answer to the question: What kind of changes and reforms in different areas should be undertaken in order to regenerate a viable new China?

The publication in 1918 of Lu Xun's (1881–1936) short story *A Madman's Diary* (*Kuangren riji*) is often taken to mark the beginning of modern Chinese literature. Written in *baihua*, the vernacular language, rather than in the literary language *wenyan*, and depicting the traditional society as "cannibalistic," which Lu Xun's story did, would a few decades earlier have been an impermissible blasphemy. There is no doubt that this story marked something radically new in Chinese literature. At about the same time, leaders of the New Culture Movement – Chen Duxiu (1879–1942) and Hu Shi (1891–1962) being the two most famous names – published articles proclaiming literary reform and even "a literary revolution."

However, one may also argue that the modern turn in Chinese literature predated Lu Xun's madman by a couple of decades. Socially critical novels published at the turn of the century 1900 anticipated the literary revolution. (Doleželová-Velingerová 1980) Most conspicuously, the earlier somewhat disparaged genre of *xiaoshuo*, fiction in the sense of short stories and novels, began to be seen as extremely important in modernizing Chinese culture and society. In 1902, the reform intellectual Liang Qichao (1873–1929) wrote:

> If one intends to renew the people of a nation, one must first renew its fiction. Therefore, to renew morality, one must renew fiction; to renew religion, one must renew fiction; to renew politics, one must renew fiction; to renew social customs, one must renew fiction; to renew learning and arts, one must renew fiction; and to renew even the human mind

and remould its character, one must renew fiction. Why is this so? This is because fiction has a profound power over the way of man.[17]

The emergence of modern fiction as the main literary genre is indeed a salient feature of modern Chinese literature. The modernizers felt that the old elitist literature had become ossified and could not appeal to large groups of people. The new novel should deal with contemporary topics which could engage many readers and be written in a language that was easily accessible.

In the 1920s, novels and short stories written in the new "national language," based on the *baihua* of the classical Chinese novels but with a great number of new words and concepts imported from Western countries, usually via Japan, already constituted the main stream of the emerging modern literature. At the same time, new poetry also emerged, as did the spoken drama. However, there is no doubt that fiction in the narrow sense of short stories and novels constituted the main stream.

During this time, the discussion about China's new literature was lively, not to say heated. Much of the discussion focused on the role of literature, especially fiction, for the regeneration of a new, respected China. Among those who wanted to see Chinese literature radically modernized there were different opinions, but the overwhelming majority saw literature in the broad context of a Chinese literary renaissance as a core aspect of China's modernization. For example, this was the case of those writers and theorists who in 1921 founded the Creation Society and promoted a literature based on the *l'art pour l'art* principle. The members of this society – which included the poet and historian Guo Moruo (1892–1978), the playwright Tian Han (1898–1968) and the writers of short stories Yu Dafu (1896–1945) – opposed the notion that writers in their works should argue for this or that non-literary objective, but they very much saw this literature, whose value was essentially literary in an exclusive sense, as a necessary part of a modern, advanced Chinese culture.

The same year, another group of writers and critics set up the Association for Literary Studies and launched the slogan that "literature should be for life," and by this they explicitly emphasized that the main task of literature was to contribute to social and political change. To this group belonged several novelists who would later become very prominent on the literary scene such as Mao Dun (1896–1981), Ye Shengtao (1894–1988), Lao She (1899–1966) and Zhou Zuoren (1885–1967).

The new fiction that these and many others wanted to promote consisted of realistic short stories and novels, which gave as truthful a picture as pos-

---

17 Liang Qichao in the essay "On the Relationship Between Fiction and the Government of the People" from 1902. Trans. Gek Nai Cheng (Liang 1996, 74). Translation slightly modified.

sible of life in China at the time and which focused on problems that had to be resolved. The people and the plots were to be fictional but should still be anchored in real life and serve the purpose of making the readers aware of the need for change; ideally, they should stimulate people to become more engaged and take an active part in reforming Chinese society and culture. For them, the function of literature was rather similar to sociological studies, the difference being that literature uses imagined persons and events to depict social or cultural issues, whereas sociology uses scholarly methods.

Typical examples of this kind of literature are Ba Jin's novel *Family* (1933), which is perhaps our most important source for understanding the problems of an extended family in the early twentieth century, and Mao Dun's *Midnight* (1933), which depicts the lives of new industrialists in Shanghai. Of course, these writers made a distinction between literature and social science. They did care about aesthetics and literary qualities, but their main focus was on the function of literature. In terms of literary quality, the works created in this literary climate varied greatly. Some of Lu Xun's early stories are true masterpieces, and Ba Jin's *Family* is really engaging, while for many of us Mao Dun's *Midnight* does not really stand out as very good literature, although it certainly contains interesting passages.

Influenced by Marxist ideas, many radicals soon felt that realistic descriptions of the present were not enough. The new fiction should also point out the way to a better future, thereby spurring the readers to exert themselves in the struggle for social and political change. Under the banner "from literary revolution to revolutionary literature," some revolutionaries towards the end of the 1920s began to deliver vitriolic attacks on the most well-known radical writers such as Lu Xun and Mao Dun for merely describing "China's sorrow," while not pointing out the road to a better future.[18] This was what the debate on proletarian literature in the late 1920s was about. (Lodén 1980)

This extremely politicized view of fiction met with much resistance, not least from leftist writers and intellectuals who refused to accept that literature and art should be totally reduced to being a vehicle for political messages defined by a political movement. There can be no doubt that the most interesting works of fiction produced during the first half of the twentieth century were produced by writers who guarded their independence and refused to become mouthpieces for political propaganda – writers like Lu Xun, Lao She, Shen Congwen (1902–1988), Qian Zhongshu (1910–1998) and others.

---

18 "Cong wenxue geming dao geming wenxue" [From Literary Revolution to Revolutionary Literature] was the title of an article by Cheng Fangwu (1897–1984) published in 1928. It is available in English translation (Cheng Fangwu 1996, 269–275).

However, as the communist movement in China gained force, so did the pressure on writers to conform to the Party's demands on literature. After the Long March, when the communists established their headquarters in Yan'an, Mao Zedong formulated in 1942 his views of literature in his "Talks at the Yan'an Conference on Literature and Art" and made it clear that it was the duty of writers to promote the revolution by propagating the Party's messages.[19]

After gaining power in 1949, Mao and his Party managed to implement the ideas of the Yan'an Talks efficiently and with disastrous results for literature. This harsh judgment does not mean that I deny that there were some talented writers who managed to write reasonably interesting works of fiction, while at the same time exerting themselves to conform to Mao's precepts. One example is Zhao Shuli (1906–1970), whose most important books dealing with peasant life in northern China were published during the Yan'an period. Another example is Hao Ran (1932–2008), the only writer of novels and short stories from the period of the Cultural Revolution 1966–1976 who is still remembered. One should not deny that the works of Zhao Shuli and Hao Ran's have their merits. Yet, in the works of both these talented writers, one can easily see the adverse effects of Mao's literary ideology: the characters tend to be stereotypes rather than people of flesh and blood.

According to the ideological orthodoxy in Mao's China, literary works should "combine revolutionary realism with revolutionary romanticism." This doctrine was used to emphasize that literature should not depict people and events as we meet them in ordinary everyday life, but describe ideals and heroes fighting for the realization of communism. This may seem to be encouraging imagination and fantasy, but in fact very little was left to the writers' own imagination: the ideals they should propagate and the heroic qualities they were supposed to portray were strictly defined within the ideological orthodoxy.

Literature in the People's Republic of China became a vehicle for the Party's Dao. Mao hated Confucianism and throughout his life wished to radically transform Chinese culture and society. But obsessed with this task and entangled by the traditional ideas and perspectives of imperial China, he was unable escape their influence. That is why Mao the revolutionary was also very traditional. His values were different from the Confucian values of traditional China, but his view of the ideological and spiritual rule of the Party still resembled the way the ideological orthodoxy in imperial China had operated.

---

19 For a detailed discussion about the differences between the first version of this text published in 1943 and the revised version to be found in Mao's Selected Works, see McDougall 1980.

Fiction in Post-Mao China: Liberation from Political Power?

The reforms in China after the death of Mao Zedong in 1976 opened the way for a rebirth of Chinese literature, and since then Chinese literature has become very much more diversified than it was during the preceding twenty-seven years; more diversified in different genres with works ranging from the most sophisticated to the simplest and most vulgar.

During the post-Mao era, writers have continued to operate under political restrictions. Some topics have remained forbidden, while the authorities have encouraged literature on other topics. On the whole, this period has seen much more space for creative freedom. At least, writers have no longer been under any absolute obligation to propagate an official Dao, defined and handed down from the Party to the writers through the Writers' Association. Looking back on serious literature in China during the past thirty-five years, we can see how getting away from official political ideology stands out as a major trend in serious literature from the poet Bei Dao (b. 1949) and the playwright and novelist Gao Xingjian (b. 1940), who both became well-known just a few years after Mao's death, to the novelist Yan Lianke (b. 1958), who gained fame only in the early years of the twenty-first century.

Bei Dao's line "I don't believe the sky is blue" was a rejection of officially proclaimed truths. Rather than just repeating what the Party preached, one should seek one's own truths.[20] Gao Xingjian has striven to free his literature from ideology, insisting that true literature does not preach. He sees Confucianism, and especially the insistence that literature should propagate Dao, as very harmful to literature. Significantly, one of his books bears the title *I have no Ism*. (Gao Xingjian 2000) Closely linked with his opposition to literature being reduced to a vehicle for a Dao defined by ideologists and politicians is his personal strategy to distance himself spiritually and physically from the centre of Chinese culture and politics. He finds living in France rather than in China not to be an artistic problem but rather to be positive for his creativity.

While opposing the idea that literature should be used to propagate the official truths proclaimed by the Party has been one salient feature of literary thought in post-Mao China, the idea that literature should transcend the really existing world and create people and events that are in some ways more true and authentic than the world we have around us here and now represents

---

[20] Quoted from Bei Dao's famous poem "The Answer" as translated by Bonnie S. McDougall (Bei Dao 1988, 33).

another trend. This exaltation of fictionality is closely linked to the efforts to create a literature independent of and free from politics. This is a perspective that we find among those who want to promote "pure literature." Interestingly, we also meet it in the early writings of Liu Xiaobo (b. 1955), the political dissident and democracy fighter (Liu Xiaobo 1987), who in 2010 was awarded the Nobel Peace Prize.

The exaltation of fiction and of pure literature and the tendency to divorce literature from politics might lead to an aestheticism which provides argument for staying away from sensitive subjects, and it may not be all wrong to see such a tendency in some contemporary Chinese literature. But we can also find examples of writers who see fictionality as a tool to formulate more important truths than those that are accessible through observation of the really existing world.

This attitude we find in Yan Lianke (b. 1958), a writer who is best known for his daring and revealing descriptions of the abuse of power and the corruption of power-holders in China. I asked him what kind of role he wants "fictionality" (*xugou*) to play in his own writing and he replied:

> In my view, the existence of fictionality in literature is not related to descriptions of actual events. It is not that only because there are descriptions of actual events can there be fictionality and imagination. For me "fictionality" represents truth in another mode of existence. In our lives, the truths that we may see with our own eyes are simple, superficial truths. The truths that we can see are by far not as complex and deep as the truths we can experience with our spirits, our feelings and our souls. Moreover the truths that we may experience with our souls are often truths that we cannot see with our eyes. Therefore, the role of fictionality is to show those truths that our soul can experience but our eyes cannot observe.[21]

Behind Yan Lianke's words, written in July 2012, we may see the image that Liu Xie invoked one and a half millennium earlier to describe the wonder of imagination: "My body may be on a river or at sea, yet my mind is beneath the palace tower," and we may think of Aristotle, who contrasted history and poetry, saying: "The true difference is that one [history] relates what has happened, the other [poetry] what may happen. Poetry, therefore, is a more philosophical and a higher thing than history: for poetry tends to express the universal, history the particular." (Aristotle 1898, 1.9: 1451b) For Yan Lianke, fictionality is not attractive as a means to escape the injustice and inhumanity of today's society; on the contrary, he sees it as a tool to attain deeper understanding of the human predicament. When I asked him how he looks upon the relationship between realistic writing and fictionality, he replied: "In my

---

21 Private email message from Yan Lianke, 13 July 2012. Author's translation.

view, [...] fictionality [...] elevates and takes realistic writing a step further, it fulfils a function of writing that realistic writing cannot fulfil."[22]

For Yan Lianke, fictionality is not a way to escape the painful truths of our actual existence, but a key to open the door to profound insights and truths that can help us deal with the reality around us. We meet here a dualistic tendency, not to say a religious orientation, which he shares with many others in post-Mao China and which reflects a deep disillusionment with the Marxist materialism.

Conclusion

When I started to write this paper, I thought of Ba Jin's remark that he was too busy writing to have time to think about literary theory. Having now reached the end of this rather cursory discussion of Dao and fiction in Chinese literature, Ba Jin's remark still seems relevant. As far back as we can go in Chinese tradition, we find traces of imagination and fictionality in Chinese writings. Behind the many stories that have been preserved from the past three millennia, we can surmise that delight of fantasizing and making up stories which is universally human.

At the same time, or at least since Confucianism began to serve as state philosophy, fantasy and fiction have often been regarded with suspicion. Imagining was set against recording, fiction against history; the task was to transmit, not to create. Literature should be a vehicle for the Dao, and in practice Dao referred to the ideological orthodoxy of the day. Thus, throughout much of China's history, writers who wanted to tell stories did not have the approval of the authorities. Yet they continued to tell their stories, and fiction continued to develop and even gave rise to masterpieces. In modern China, fiction in the sense of novels and short stories became *the* exalted literary genre, but writers of fiction continued to be burdened by the duty to convey Dao, now no longer a Confucian but a Maoist Dao.

Today there are still many truths not allowed to be publicized in China, but there is not much of an official Dao left to convey. In this situation, it is up to the writers to use the literary means they have to seek the truth for themselves, and fiction is certainly an important tool for seeking and expressing important truths. In the words of Yan Lianke, "the role of fictionality is to show those truths that our soul can experience but our eyes cannot observe."

---

[22] Private email message from Yan Lianke, 13 July 2012. Author's translation.

Bibliography

Aristotle, *Poetics*. Trans. S. H. Butcher. The Internet Classics Archive. http://classics.mit.edu/Aristotle/poetics.html (19 February 2013).
Ban Gu. *Hanshu Yiwen zhi* [Treatise on Literature in the History of The Former Han Dynasty]. Hong Kong: Xianggang taiping shuju, 1963.
Bei Dao. *The August Sleepwalker*. Trans. Bonnie S. McDougall. London: Anvil Press Poetry, 1988.
Cheng, Fangwu. "From literary revolution to revolutionary literature." *Modern Chinese Literary Thought: Writings on Literature 1893–1945*. Ed. Kirk A. Denton. Stanford, CA: Stanford University Press, 1996. 269–275.
Cullhed, Anders. *The Shadow of Creusa. Negotiating Fictionality in Late Antique Latin Literature*. Trans. Michael Knight. Beiträge zur Altertumskunde. Berlin: De Gruyter, 2015.
Currie, Gregory. *The Nature of Fiction*. Cambridge: Cambridge University Press, 1990.
Doleželová-Velingerová, Milena, ed. *The Chinese Novel at the Turn of the Century*. Toronto: University of Toronto Press, 1980.
Gan Bao. *Xinji Soushen ji*. [New Edition of In Search of Spirits]. 2 vols. Beijing: Zhonghua shuju, 2008.
Gao Xingjian. *Meiyou zhuyi* [I Have No Ism]. Taipei: Tiandi tushu youxian gongsi, 2000.
Gu, Ming Dong. *Chinese theories of fiction: A Non-Western Narrative System*. SUNY series in Chinese philosophy and culture. Albany: State University of New York Press, 2006.
Guo Shaoyu. *Zhongguo wenxue piping shi* [A History of Chinese Literary Criticism]. Tianjin: Baihua wenyi chubanshe, 2008.
Hamill, Sam. *Lu Chi's Wenfu: The Art of Writing*. 2nd revised ed. Minneapolis, MN: Milkweed editions, 1991.
Liang Qichao. "On the Relationship Between Fiction and the Government of the People." Trans. Gek Nai Cheng. *Modern Chinese Literary Thought: Writings on Literature 1893–1945*. Ed. Kirk A. Denton. Stanford, CA: Stanford University Press, 1996. 74–81.
Liu, James J.Y. *Chinese Theories of Literature*. Chicago and London: The University of Chicago Press, 1975.
Liu Xiaobo. *Shenmei yu ren de ziyou* [Aesthetics and Human Freedom]. Diss. Shanghai renmin chubanshe, 1987.
Liu Xie. *The Literary Mind and the Carving of Dragons: A Study of Thought and Pattern in Chinese Literature*. Trans. Vincent Yu-chung Shih. Hong Kong: The Chinese University Press, 1983.
Lodén, Torbjörn. *Debatten om proletär litteratur i Kina 1928–1929* [The Debate on Proletarian Literature in China 1928–1929]. Diss. Stockholm: Föreningen för orientaliska studier, 1980.
Lu Hsun [Lu Xun]. *A Brief History of Chinese Fiction*. Trans. Yang Hsien-yi and Gladys Yang. China Knowledge series, 7. Beijing: Guozi shudian, 1959.
Lu Ji. See Yang Mu.
Lu Kanru and Mou Shijin. *Wenxin diaolong yizhu*. 2 vols. Jinan: Qilu shushe, 1981.
Luo Genze. *Zhongguo wenxue piping shi* [A History of Chinese Literary Criticism]. Shanghai guji chubanshe, 1984.
Lynn, Richard. "Chu Hsi as Literary Theorist and Critic." *Chu Hsi and Neo-Confucianism*. Ed. Wing-tsit Chan. Honolulu, HI: University of Hawaii Press, 1986. 337–354.

McDougall, Bonnie S. *Mao Zedong's "Talks at the Yan'an Conference on Literature and Art": A Translation of the 1943 Text with Commentary.* Ann Arbor: Center for Chinese Studies, 1980.

Mair, Victor H. *T'ang Transformation Texts: A Study of the Buddhist Contribution to the Rise of Vernacular Fiction and Drama in China.* Cambridge, MA: Harvard University Press, 1988.

Walton, Kendall L. *Mimesis as Make-believe: On the Foundations of the Representational Arts.* Cambridge, MA and London: Harvard University Press, 1990.

Wang Yuanhua. "On Certain Categories in the Book *Wen Xin Diao Long*." *The Stockholm Journal of East Asian Studies* 1 (1988): 7–25.

Yang Ming. *Wenfu Shipin yizhu* [Annotated Translations of Wenfu and Classes of Poetry]. Shanghai: Shanghai guji chubanshe, 1999.

Yang Mu. *Lu Ji Wen fu jiaoshi* [Wenfu Annotated and Explained]. Taibei: Hongfan shudian youxian gongsi,1985.

Zhang, Longxi. *Allegoresis: Reading Canonical Literature East and West.* Ithaca, NY: Cornell University Press, 2005.

Zhong Rong. See Yang Ming.

Gunilla Lindberg-Wada
Murasaki Shikibu and *The Tale of Genji*: Fate and Fiction

In the "Hotaru" [Fireflies] chapter of *Genji monogatari* [The Tale of Genji], hereafter *Genji* from the beginning of the eleventh century CE, we find a discussion of the merits and demerits of fictional tales as compared to historical chronicles. In this often quoted meta-fictional text passage, the male protagonist Prince Genji finds his stepdaughter Tamakazura busy reading various fictional tales. At first he expresses a negative attitude to this kind of stories with "hardly a word of truth" in them, read by women, who are "obviously born to be duped without a murmur of protest." But he also acknowledges that they will make good entertainment and "among the lies" will still have some "plausibly touching scenes, convincingly told." When Tamakazura, however, retorts that it seems impossible to her that they should be anything other than simply true, Genji concludes that, after all, the historical chronicles "give only a part of the story. It is tales that contain the truly rewarding particulars!" (Murasaki 2002, 460–461)

Prince Genji's initial negative remarks on fictional tales above may be seen as typical of the time when the work was written. For centuries, Chinese Classics, Buddhist sutras and historical chronicles were placed at the top of the genre hierarchy in Japan, followed by poetry in Chinese (*kanshi*) and in Japanese (*waka*). Narrative works written in the Japanese syllabic script such as fictional tales of the *monogatari* genre were placed at the bottom. Evidently this was a thriving genre, but comparatively few works have remained to posterity. They were accorded little cultural value and regarded mainly as a pastime for women. In this context, *Genji* is exceptional. This work has occupied readers through the centuries and has been read and reread in various fashions; in our days even as a highly praised "modern" novel.

By tracing the reception of *Genji* through the ages, the aim of this paper is to investigate views of fiction in a Japanese context – the fate of the work as a world of fiction and as fictionalisation of the biographical fate of its author.

The Work

No original manuscript by the court lady Murasaki Shikibu remains, but it is generally believed that she completed *Genji* in the first decade of the eleventh century. The oldest extant picture scroll of *Genji*, *Genji monogatari emaki*, probably dates back to the middle of the twelfth century. It is assumed that it originally comprised scenes from the whole of *Genji*, but today only fragments of the text and twenty pictures depicting scenes from nineteen chapters remain. The oldest extant manuscripts of *Genji* date back to the first half of the thirteenth century.[1]

Genji consists of fifty-four *chō*, "leaves" or chapters. The story spans three generations and is in contemporary research usually divided into three parts in accordance with the development of events in the tale. Part one[2] can be generally described as the success story of the amorous Hikaru Genji [The Shining Prince Genji]. However, rather than forming the focus of the tale, I would argue that through his relationships with a number of women and some men, he mainly serves as a uniting factor for the stories told about them, not only here but also in Parts two and three; the title might as well be translated as *Tales of Genji*. By the end of Part one, the residence Rokujōin, built by Prince Genji at his height of glory, embodies the harmony, power and perfect beauty of his life, with his unofficial wife Lady Murasaki as the First Lady among the women installed there.

Part two[3] depicts the gradual inner decay of the flawless world of Rokujōin and ends with the death of Prince Genji, which is never described but only hinted at as an established fact in the succeeding chapter. The focus of the tale is transferred from Prince Genji to the generations following him; and notions of the changes of time and of the karma of human life dominate the tale.

In Part three,[4] the scene of large parts of the tale shifts from the capital to the mountain village of Uji, the name of which evokes images of the brooding melancholy of this ephemeral world, and where the roaring sound of the Uji River appears ominous. The complex character of Prince Genji in Parts one

---

1 The so-called *Aobyōshibon* [The Blue Cover Book], the edition of Fujiwara Teika, was completed in 1225, and *Kawachibon* [The Kawachi-book], the edition of the father and son Minamoto Mitsuyuki and Chikayuki was completed in 1255. In addition, there are various manuscripts, which are usually known under the collective term *Beppon* [Other Books]. Most modern editions of *Genji monogatari* are based on the *Aobyōshibon* manuscript. The oldest extant picture scroll, *Genji monogatari emaki*, is traditionally ascribed to the authorship of Fujiwara Takayoshi.
2 Chapters 1–33, from "Kiritsubo" [The Paulownia Pavilion] through "Fuji no Uraba" [New Wisteria Leaves]; ca. 48 % of the entire text volume. My calculations of the volume of the text are based on Yamagishi 1974–1975. Translation of the titles into English in accordance with Murasaki 2002.
3 Chapters 34–41, from "Wakana Jō" [Spring Shoots I] through "Maboroshi" [The Seer]; ca. 20 % of the entire text volume.
4 Chapters 42–54, from "Niou-no-miya" [The Perfumed Prince] through the last chapter "Yume no ukihashi" [The Floating Bridge of Dreams]; ca. 32 % of the entire text volume.

and two, torn as he is between his quest for amorous pursuits and political power on the one hand and longing for a withdrawn life in religious pursuits on the other, is in Part three split into two. The story here evolves around three women and two men – one of a religious bent, the other of an amorous nature. The psychological realism and stretches of inner monologue in the description of the intricate relationships between the two men and three women appear strikingly modern by our present standards.

The story is set in the introductory paragraph in some vaguely defined past, maybe a hundred years back or so. The life style, thought, language use and physical surroundings of the characters, however, all seem to reflect those of the author's time. The narrator is omniscient and mostly covert, obviously a woman well acquainted with life and human relations at court. Once in a while, she comments briefly on the thoughts and actions of the characters, often with an ironic touch when Prince Genji is in focus. Some comments are of a meta-narrative nature.

Genji is a text rich in allusions. A number of emperor-sponsored or otherwise well-known anthologies of poetry were available to the presumptive readers of the time, the poetry of which could be expected to come to the reader's mind when alluded to in the text. There are also numerous recitals and exchanges of poetry in the pieces of dialogue and letters quoted in the story, about eight hundred poems in all. The chain of events in the story is narrated in a fairly laconic type of prose, interchanging with scenic descriptions of a lyrical character and emotive highlights couched in poetry.[5]

The Author

The authorship of *Genji* is attributed to the Court Lady Murasaki Shikibu (ca. 970–ca. 1014) and it was probably written in the first decade of the eleventh century. The factual evidence of her life is scarce and beside *Genji*, fragments of a diary and a private poetry collection which might have been compiled after her death, no texts by her remain. Her father, Fujiwara no Tametoki, served as a provincial governor and was also a scholar of Chinese. In her diary Murasaki mentions that he deplored the fact that she was born a woman, since she was much better at learning the Chinese classics than her brother, his own student. (Fujioka *et al.* 1971, 244) Chinese was the language of governance and power, of the official life that excluded women. However, the rich allusions in

---

[5] For a detailed analysis of the functions of poetic allusion in *Genji monogatari*, see Lindberg-Wada 1983.

Genji to the Chinese classics and Buddhist sutras in Chinese translation attest to Murasaki's knowledge of the language. And although they received no formal education and seem to have been discouraged from displaying their knowledge, there were evidently educated women beside Murasaki at court who had a good command of Chinese.

Murasaki accompanied her father to the province of Echizen in 996, was married a couple of years later and gave birth to a daughter. She was widowed in 1001 and it is generally assumed that she started writing *Genji* around this time. Around 1006, Murasaki was called to serve Empress Shōshi. By this time, she seems to have been well known as the author of *Genji*, probably still a work in progress. She mentions in her diary reading texts in classical Chinese with the Empress, but she also indicates that she was very careful not to show off her academic learning since this would not make her very popular among her fellow court ladies. (Fujioka *et al.* 1971, 245, 240–242)

According to the legend, Murasaki Shikibu started writing *Genji* on the fifteenth night of the eighth month in a room facing Lake Biwa at the Buddhist temple in Ishiyama, of the Shingon sect. Even today you may have the story retold orally in the very room where it all supposedly happened. We are told that one of the princesses, being bored, asked Empress Shōshi if she had some unusual books to read. Since the princess was already well acquainted with old tales such as *Utsubo monogatari* [The Tale of the Hollow Tree] and *Taketori monogatari* [The Tale of the Bamboo Cutter], the Empress asked Murasaki Shikibu to make up a new one. Spending the night at the Ishiyama temple, Murasaki prayed for inspiration. While she was absorbed by the beauty of the moon shining on the waters of Lake Biwa, the idea for the tale rose up before her. In order not to forget it, she begged Kannon, the Bodhisattva of Compassion that the temple of Ishiyama is dedicated to, for the paper on the altar and immediately wrote down the "Suma" and "Akashi" chapters. The paper was meant for copying the Great Wisdom Sutra. The six hundred fascicles of this sutra that Murasaki later on personally copied and dedicated to the Kannon of Ishiyama in order to expiate her misdeed are said to be there still.[6]

The Alleged Fate of the Author

In the century following Murasaki Shikibu's death, a belief spread that she was sent to hell for the sin of writing lies and empty words. In *Genji ippon kyō*

---

[6] The part on how Murasaki was asked by the Empress to write a new tale appears in *Mumyō-zōshi* [Untitled Book] from between 1196 and 1202. (Higuchi and Kuboki 1999, 276–277) The full legend first appears in *Kakaishō* [Sea of Comments], a seminal commentary on *Genji* from 1367. For an English translation see Tyler 1994, 377–378.

[Genji One Volume Sutra] (ca. 1166), a brief essay in which Buddhist and Confucian writings are contrasted with other kinds of texts, the well-known preacher Chōken (1126–1203) of the Tendai sect argued that although *Genji* was superior to other fictional works, it doomed author and reader alike to hell by encouraging people in the ways of love. We are told that Murasaki revealed in someone's dream that she suffered deeply from her sins and asked for prayers on her behalf. The essay concludes with a description of a memorial service to save the souls of the author and readers of *Genji*. And according to *Hōbutsushū* [A Collection of Treasures], a collection of Buddhist tales from ca. 1179, Murasaki Shikibu appeared in the dreams of various people, telling them that she suffered deeply in hell and asking for *Genji* to be thrown away and sutras to be transcribed on her behalf. (Goff 1991, 54–55)

In the Noh play *Genji kuyō* [A Memorial Service for Prince Genji] attributed to Zeami (1363–1443) but with unclear authorship, the unhappy souls of Murasaki and The Shining Prince Genji finally gain salvation. The priest Agoi is on his way to the Buddhist temple of Ishiyama when a local woman stops him. She asks him to hold a memorial service for the salvation of the soul of Prince Genji, since she forgot to include this when she wrote *Genji* and is therefore unable to attain Buddhahood. The priest understands that this is the spirit of Murasaki Shikibu and holds the memorial service as asked. She then reappears and gives him a petition which is recited while she performs a dance of gratitude. In the text, twenty-eight of the chapter titles of *Genji* (the same number as the volumes of the *Lotus Sutra*) are interwoven with a sermon on the impermanence of this world of illusions. The priest realises that Murasaki was actually an incarnation of Kannon, the Bodhisattva of Compassion, who wrote *Genji* as a *hōben*, a didactic text meant for religious enlightenment. (Sanari 1931, 1025–1042)

The expression used for fictional writing in the play, "wild words and fancy phrases" (*kyōgen kigyo*), comes from a famous prayer by the Chinese poet Bai Juyi (772–846), who was highly esteemed in Heian-period Japan (794–1185): "May the worldly writings throughout my life, the excesses of wild words and fancy phrases, in later ages serve as a hymn in praise of Buddha's teachings, and help the Wheel of the Law to turn." (Goff 1991, 54)

The Fate of the Work

The historical tale *Imakagami* [The Mirror of the Present] (1170) ends with a brief chapter on the genre of the fictional tale (*tsukurimonogatari*). Mentioning the belief that Murasaki went to hell for the sin of writing fiction, the narrator then proceeds to making a distinction between good and bad fictional writing, arguing in the following way: There are righteous people both in China and Japan who write in a way that makes a deep impression on the readers and leads them on the way to a deeper understanding. In the case of those who just write stories of empty words and lies, pretending this is what really happened, they certainly deserve to be accused of committing a sin. However, the Chinese poet Bai Juyi, who in his writings used embellishments and metaphors to enlighten people, became regarded as an incarnation of the Bodhisattva of learning. Shakyamuni himself used metaphors and made up stories to reach the unenlightened when he expounded the Law. In this case, we do not speak of lies, falsehood or delusion. The fact that Murasaki, being merely a woman, was able to create a work such as *Genji* proves that she was not an ordinary human being. She wrote not just one or two but sixty chapters,[7] all on a high level of precious knowledge and without a flaw. Actually, it had happened before that a Bodhisattva expounded the law in female incarnation. The narrator concludes that Murasaki was no doubt the incarnation of a Bodhisattva whose work leads to enlightenment. (Kokumin 1926, 604–607)

Genji was thus distinguished from other fictional tales by being designated as a *hōben,* and the author was placed on a par with one of the most appreciated and highly regarded Chinese poets known in Heian Japan, in spite of being a woman; even her thorough knowledge of the Chinese classics and Buddhist sutras were thus excused and explained, we might say.

Sometime between 1196 and 1202, *Mumyōzōshi* [Untitled Book] appears, the earliest extant piece of literary critique of narrative literature in Japan. It is tentatively attributed to a member of one of the important families of court poets of the time, the daughter of Fujiwara Shunzei (ca. 1171–ca. 1250).[8] Within the fictive framework of a discussion one late evening among a small number of women, retold by an old, venerable nun who lies down to rest and listens to their voices, this work deals mainly with the *monogatari* genre in a critically evaluative way. *Genji* is seen as the epitome of the genre at its very best and occupies about one third of the comments on the genre. Within the fictive framework, the woman who leads the discussion is obviously well acquainted with *Genji*, while some of her young discussion partners seem to have scanter knowledge. For the implied reader, the book thus serves a dual purpose. Those

---

[7] The number of chapters here does not necessarily mean that six chapters are missing from the extant versions of *Genji*. It was probably chosen because of the good connotations of the number sixty.

[8] Actually, she was granddaughter of Fujiwara Shunzei (1114–1204), and Shunzei's son Fujiwara Teika (1162–1241) was her uncle on the maternal side.

with only scant knowledge of *Genji* get an informative introduction to various aspects of the work and quotations of a number of poems placed in context. Those who know the work well get critical comments of all kinds to react to and enter into dialogue on. (Higuchi and Kuboki 1999, 188–220)

After a brief introduction to the impressive traits of each of the chapters, the female characters of *Genji* are evaluated in accordance with a list of characteristics, as individuals or because of their situation: women who impress with their noble and composed character (*medetaki wonna*), women who impress with their strong integrity (*imijiki wonna*), likable women (*konomoshiki hito*), and pitiable women (*itōshiki hito*). In addition, the same woman may appear under more than one characterisation. The main male characters are then critically evaluated, basically focusing on their treatment of the female characters of the work. For instance, far from acting as the perfect lover, The Shining Prince Genji turns out to be both reckless and dishonest, while his brother-in-law is praised as a model of loyal friendship. (Higuchi and Kuboki 1999, 191–197, 198–200)

Somewhat more that half of the piece on *Genji* critically evaluates scenes. The bulk of this part deals with scenes and paragraphs that the discussants find touching, that leave a deep impression and linger in the mind of the reader, elegant, well-formed scenes and paragraphs. Most of the presentations of scenes are built up around the poems as emotive highlights. Death scenes dominate, closely followed by partings and loneliness. The remaining part brings up impressive scenes (*imijiki koto*), preferably with a woman cleverly managing an intricate situation, and some paragraphs present scenes of pitiable situations (*itōshiki koto*), upsetting scenes (*kokoroyamashiki koto*), and horrible things (*asamashiki koto*). (Higuchi and Kuboki 1999, 189–191, 203–212, 212–220)

Considering what makes a good *monogatari* in the opinion of the discussants, we find this expressed in condensed form in the introductory passage of the evaluation of *Hamamatsu chūnagon monogatari* [The Tale of the Hamamatsu Middle Counsellor] (ca. 1053). A good *monogatari* has freshness about it, with an interesting story and well-formed language; it is both deeply moving and impressive; the poems are good and the protagonist epitomises the ideal hero. (Higuchi and Kuboki 1999, 235)

The majority of the tales mentioned in *Mumyōzōshi* have been lost to posterity. The *monogatari* genre was not a prestigious one. Until the modern era, *Genji* was praised mainly on account of the poetry recited and alluded to in the tale and was first and foremost read as a handbook of poetry composition. The high esteem of *Genji* as a model of poetry is clearly expressed in Fujiwara

Shunzei's often quoted judgement in a poetry contest, "The poet who has not read *Genji* is deplorable."⁹

The research tradition on *Genji* goes back to *Genji monogatari shaku* [The Tale of Genji with Annotations] (also called *Koreyukishaku* or *Genjishaku*) by Fujiwara Koreyuki, and *Genji monogatari Okuiri* [Inside The Tale of Genji] by Fujiwara Teika from the 1230s. They set the norm for centuries to come and deal almost exclusively with the relations between *Genji* and the Japanese, Chinese and other literary sources of allusion that can be considered important for a proper understanding of the text. Beside frequent allusions in the text to Japanese poetry collections, Buddhist sutras and the Chinese classics are alluded to.

Genji played an important role as a handbook of poetry also throughout the fourteenth and fifteenth centuries, not only for classical *waka* poets but increasingly also for poets of *renga*, linked poetry. It is not clear when linked poetry became popular among commoners as well, but already by the first quarter of the thirteenth century there is evidence that this pastime had spread beyond the ranks of the court aristocracy. Composing linked poetry was a group activity and some knowledge of *Genji* was expected of anyone who wanted to participate successfully in the gatherings of *renga* poets. However, *Genji* was hardly accessible beyond an exclusive group of specialists. It was a large work in a remote language that was difficult to understand and only available in manuscript form. This gave rise to a genre of *Genji* handbooks, which provided lists of words for *renga* linking, plot summaries and digests. Some handbooks were aimed at poets of *waka* and linked poetry, others were of a more general character, providing the reader with an outline of the principal characters, episodes and poems in *Genji*, arranged by chapter. Most widely read of those digests was *Genji kokagami* [A Small Mirror of Genji], which focused on the most famous episodes and poems of the work. (Goff 1991, 18, 25–27)

Genji embodied for the poets the aesthetic quality of *yūgen*, which had come to denote "elegance and grace," a quality that was emphasised in the process of elevation of linked poetry from a pastime to an art form.¹⁰ *Genji* and the aesthetics of *yūgen* also had a deep impact on the Noh theatre and there are a number of plays based on famous scenes and stories from *Genji*. For Zeami, the concept of *yūgen* not only denoted the elegance and grace of the language but also included the lives of the aristocrats in the world of *Genji*, whose appearance and demeanour in his opinion embodied this quality. (Goff 1991, 21, 34)

---

9 Author's translation. In Japanese: "*Genji mizaru utayomi wa ikon no koto nari.*" Quoted in Kuboki Tetsuo, "Kaisetsu" [Commentary] (Higuchi and Kuboki 1999, 294).
10 Fujiwara Shunzei, who regarded *yūgen* in the sense of "mystery and profound depth," had referred to this aesthetic quality as *yūen* (Goff 1991, 21).

From the seventeenth century, Neo-Confucianism became the dominant ideology of government. *Genji* was widely condemned as immoral by the Confucians, who found its sexual permissiveness, the fictitious character of the work and its frivolity unacceptable. The influential Neo-Confucian scholar Hayashi Razan (1583–1657) used the work to argue the moral inferiority of pre-warrior society and as evidence of the "debauched conduct" of the Heian court society. (McMullen 1999, 58–59) However, Kumazawa Banzan (1619–1691), another important Neo-Confucian scholar, saw in *Genji* a repository of humanistic Confucian values and a historical semi-utopia that could be used as the basis for criticising certain aspects of his contemporary feudal society and values. (McMullen 1991, i) He claimed that *Genji* was not a fictional tale but for the most part recorded facts. Like many of the commentators of preceding centuries, he placed the events of *Genji* in the first half of the tenth century, a time that was traditionally seen as a period of direct imperial "good rule." He believed that the institutions depicted in *Genji* had been transmitted from the ancient Chinese Sages and were basically excellent. (McMullen 1999, 310, 333–334, 338)

Regardless of the views of the Neo-Confucian scholars, *Genji* was made accessible to an ever-widening general readership thanks to the commercial publishers. During the first seven decades of the seventeenth century alone, some eight printed editions were published, and more than a dozen editions of the above-mentioned *Genji kokagami* from the fourteenth–fifteenth century were published between 1651 and 1680, including illustrated wood-block editions. In the 1650s, Nonoguchi Ryūho (1595–1669) created the first digest aimed at a commercial audience, the illustrated *Jūjō Genji* [Ten-Book Genji], shortly followed by a simplified version for children, *Osana Genji* [The Juvenile Genji]. Both works were published in innumerable editions and reprints in the seventeenth century. (Kornicki 2005, 149)

Adaptations and parody versions of *Genji* also appeared, including numerous erotic versions, for example, *Genji on'iroasobi* [Erotic Play à la Genji] (1681) produced by the prominent illustrator Yoshida Hanbei (active ca. 1664–1690). From the 1670s, it became a common practice to assign nicknames derived from the chapters and characters of *Genji* to the courtesans in the licensed pleasure quarters for men, and in a guide to the writing of love letters published in 1698, probably for the benefit of courtesans, *Genji* is recommended for inspiration and reference in such letter writing. (Kornicki 2005, 173, 175) Between 1829 and 1842 *Nise Murasaki inaka Genji* [A Fraudulent Murasaki's Bumpkin Genji] was published in instalments. The author was Ryūtei Tanehiko (1783–1842), and the book became the most widely read popular adaptation and parody of *Genji*. It was illustrated by Utagawa Kunisada (Utagawa Toyokuni III, 1786–1864) in close cooperation with the author, in a fashion typical of the *gōkan* genre, characterised by its intermeshing of pictures and text. (Emmerich 2008, 211–213)

Returning to the scholars, in 1673 Kitamura Kigin (1624–1705) completed *Kogetsushō* [Lake Moon Commentary], one of the most widely circulated and influential commentaries on *Genji*. This provided the reader with a reproduction of the entire text of *Genji* with extensive annotation. The introductory section contained short entries on the authorship of the *Genji*, praise for the work and its author, a genealogy of characters and historical sources of characters and events that appear in the work. (Caddeau 2006, 22–23)

The most influential annotated version of *Genji* beside Kitamura Kigin's *Kogetsushō* was *Genji monogatari tama no ogushi* [A Little Jewelled Comb of The Tale of Genji] (1796) by Moto'ori Norinaga (1730–1801). He was one of the leading figures of *kokugaku*, "National Learning,"[11] who argued that rather than trying to establish Japanese counterparts of Chinese literature, Japanese works were inherently superior and did not need to be judged in terms of non-native ideologies, such as Confucianism or Buddhism. (Caddeau 2006, 25) Like his fellow scholars of National Learning, Norinaga studied *Genji* as a tool to reach the original pure Japanese mentality they believed had existed before Chinese writing and the Buddhist sutras entered in the fifth and sixth centuries. He saw *Genji* as the embodiment of *mono no aware*. He did not invent the concept of *mono no aware*, but he developed it as a notion of aesthetics. Literally, it may be translated as "the pathos (*aware*) of things (*mono*)." *Aware* stands for the deeply moving impact on the sensitive, refined beholder of an aesthetically and emotionally moving scene or phenomenon, and *mono* for the concrete phenomena of the outer world, which inherently possess the deeply moving quality of *aware* that in turn causes the emotion of *aware* inside the mind of the sensitive and refined beholder. Norinaga regarded literature as an autonomous entity, separate from religion or morals, and equated knowing *mono no aware* with knowing "the heart (*kokoro*) of existence (*mono*)." (Hisamatsu 1941, 119)[12]

Hagiwara Hiromichi (1815–1863) planned his commentary on *Genji* in a form that would make this work available also to the reader without a thorough education. In addition to headnotes with material from earlier commentaries, he planned to include Chinese characters and colloquial equivalents of his time alongside the text in the original language of the Heian period so that

---

11 None of the translations into English of the term *kokugaku* are very satisfactory. The translation "National Learning" falsely implies continuity between the *kokugaku* visions of Japan and modern Japanese nationalism. I use the term with this reservation. Cf. Burns 2003, 231–232, note 1.

12 In Japanese, Norinaga's definition reads "*Mono no kokoro wo shiru wa sunawachi mono no aware wo shiru nari.*" (Hisamatsu 1941, 21).

even an amateur would be able to read *Genji* without difficulties.¹³ He did not approach *Genji* from the viewpoint of a Confucian or a scholar of "National Learning," but as nothing other than a work of literature; and he emphasised elements that define *Genji* as a work of narrative fiction rather than as a didactic work or lyric prose. For Hiromichi, the defining characteristic of *Genji* was its deliberate and artful way of creating a work of prose fiction that allows the reader to experience and engage with a fictional world in a meaningful and satisfying way. He also noted that it was not only what was written that determined the sophistication of the text of *Genji* but also what was omitted from the story; and he regarded Murasaki Shikibu's mastery of the art of descriptive understatement as a sign of her creativity, reserve, and aesthetic sensibility. (Caddeau 2006, 46, 49, 78, 109)

Tsubouchi Shōyō's (1859–1935) seminal work *Shōsetsu shinzui* [The Essence of the Novel] (1885–1886) is widely regarded as the central theoretical text in the history of the development of the modern Japanese novel. The high prestige of the novel in the West led to a re-evaluation of narrative fiction in Japan, and Tsubouchi's work is in large part written as a handbook for budding authors of the "artistic realistic novel," which should depict human feelings and social relations and practices the way they actually are in real life, without shunning the unseemly sides of human nature, yet avoiding obscenities, since such were not suitable for the novel as a work of Art. (Tsubouchi 1977, 46–49)

Literary genres are described in *Shōsetsu shinzui* in evolutionary social Darwinist terms, crowned by the Victorian novel, as Tsubouchi would have it, with authors such as George Eliot, Sir Walter Scott and Sir Edward Bulwer-Lytton to emulate and possibly surpass. By two substantial quotations in parallel fashion, on the one hand of the British critic John Morley's praise of George Eliot, on the other hand from Moto'ori Norinaga's *Genji monogatari tama no ogushi* mentioned above, Tsubouchi implicitly places Murasaki Shikibu on a par with the authors of the realistic novel he argues for. Morley praises Eliot for her deep critical insight into society and the human mind and her mastery in making the readers critically realise aspects of society they were not previously aware of. Morinaga criticises those who judge *Genji* from a Confucian or Buddhist perspective, arguing that this is a work of fiction, not a book of morals; what is morally good or bad in the work depends on whether it is in accord with *aware* or not. Prince Genji is not all through a morally good hero, but this is balanced by the great insight into *mono no aware* that the reader gains, Norinaga argues, and likens this to the lotus flower that grows from the

---

13 Illness prevented Hiromichi from completing his work beyond a treatise on *Genji* as a whole and a detailed commentary covering the first eight chapters of the tale (Caddeau 2006, 50).

mud: when the author speaks of forbidden love, this is not in order to praise the mud but in order to make it possible for the flower of profound feelings and awareness, of *aware*, to blossom. (Tsubouchi 1977, 21–42, 49–53)

Also in more explicit terms Tsubouchi treats *Genji* as a forerunner of the realistic novel. Like others before him, he is critical of the "indecency" of some parts of *Genji* and the "effeminate and weak" nature of the language and the world depicted. However, he argues, such were the times and nothing to blame the author for. As writers of the realistic school, Tsubouchi argues, Murasaki depicted people's life and character as they actually were in her days and *Genji* constitutes a good source of the manners and customs of the time it was written, thereby also supplementing official history writing, one of the merits of the realistic novel listed by Tsubouchi. (Tsubouchi 1977, 64–65, 83, 150–151, 70)

Concluding Discussion

Fiction as a concept appears already in the introductory quotation from *Genji* above, and the term fictional tale, *tsukurimonogatari* [invented tale], goes back at least to the latter half of the twelfth century, when it appears in *Imakagami* [The Mirror of the Present]. This was a subgenre of the *monogatari* genre, which included fictional as well as non-fictional works. The latter were distinguished from the *tsukurimonogatari* by their connection to historical – or putatively historical – individuals.

The view of fiction as empty words devoid of truth-value, also expressed in the quotation from *Genji*, runs through the reception of this work as a backdrop. Interestingly enough, this has not resulted in the work being discarded as unworthy of attention, but has led to various strategies of overcoming, or reaching beyond, the fictional nature of *Genji* – at times de-fictionalising the work, as it were.

The earliest example appears in the reading of *Genji* as a *hōben*, found in *Imakagami* mentioned above and reappearing in the Noh play *Genji kuyō* [A Memorial Service for Prince Genji]. Implicitly, we find it also in the legend of Muraski Shikibu's initialising the work at the temple of Ishiyama. Moto'ori Norinaga and Tsubouchi Shōyō provide other examples of this strategy of providing the fictional work with a higher goal: fiction as a means of teaching, edifying and enhancing the minds of the readers – giving them new insights in a pleasant form. (Tsubouchi 1977, 52–53, 13–14) It is worth mentioning, however, that Tsubouchi is critical of didactic writing and anxious to point out that this is not the aim of literature as such, but a beneficial side effect.

Reading *Genji* as a handbook of poetry represents the most prevalent strategy of overcoming the fictional nature of *Genji* and the low status of the invented tale. The format of combining prose and poetry in the tale is not unique for *Genji*; it is a common trait in other works of the *monogatari* genre. The proportions and role of prose versus poetry varies, however. In *Taketori monogatari* [The Tale of the Bamboo Cutter], hereafter *Taketori*, for instance, which is mentioned in *Genji* as the originating work of the genre, the prose parts dominate, whereas the stories in two other *monogatari* from the first half of the tenth century, *Ise monogatari* [Tales of Ise], hereafter *Ise*, and *Yamato monogatari* [Tales of Yamato], hereafter *Yamato*, are basically built up around the poems, which play a dominant role in the tales.

Taketori has traditionally been classified as *tsukurimonogatari*, whereas *Ise* and *Yamato* have been classified as *utamonogatari* [poem-tales] and read as non-fictional works. In the case of *Yamato*, the majority of the stories and poems are connected to specific individuals and locations. In *Ise*, the stories as a rule start by "once there was a man" (*mukashi otoko arikeri*) or "once a man [...]" (*mukashi otoko ...*) but the poems are attributed to the famous poet Ariwara Narihira (825–880), who was then generally seen as the protagonist of the tales, although he evidently did not compose all of the poems.

Taketori and *Genji* alike are not connected to historical individuals, but the role of poems and poetry in *Genji* is far closer to that of *Ise* and *Yamato*. Reading *Genji* mainly on account of the poetry alluded to or recited in the work, or as a handbook of poetry, may thus be comparable to reading an *utamonogatari* [poem-tale], on the surface at least a non-fictional genre, where the narrative parts provide background to the poems. Reading *Genji* as a historical tale, as some of the Neo-Confucian scholars did, may be seen as yet another strategy for overcoming the fictional nature of the work.

By the middle of the nineteenth century, the modern Western concept of literature had been introduced into Japan. Literary history writing, canon formation, and new modes of poetry and prose became part of the race of catching up with the West in all areas of society, which was set in motion by the Meiji restoration in 1868. Literary production was nothing new in Japan, but the idea of incorporating a wide array of disparate genres into one overarching concept, such as poetry, or literature, was novel. The high prestige of fiction in the West at the time revolutionised the reading of *Genji*. Read as a novel, as demonstrated by Hagiwara Hiromichi (Caddeau 2006, 49) and Tsubouchi Shōyō (1977), this work proved to be an exquisite work of Art. Moreover, seen in this light, *Genji* showed that in Japan the modern novel could trace its roots further back in time than anywhere else in the world.

The examples presented here represent only a fraction of the rich repertoire of readings, re-readings and adaptations of *Genji*, a work that has in our days become a global event, created by the ever-expanding multimedia industry of *Genji monogatari / The Tale of Genji*.

Bibliography

Burns, Susan L. *Before the Nation: Kokugaku and the Imagining of Community in Early Modern Japan*. Durham and London: Duke University Press, 2003.

Caddeau, Patrick W. *Appraising Genji: Literary Criticism and Cultural Anxiety in the Age of the Last Samurai*. Albany, NY: State University of New York Press, 2006.

Emmerich, Michael. "The Splendor of Hybridity: Image and Text in Ryūtei Tanehiko's *Inaka Genji*." *Envisioning The Tale of Genji: Media, Gender, and Cultural Production*. Ed. Shirane, Haruo. New York: Columbia University Press, 2008. 211–239.

Fujioka Tadaharu et al., eds. *Izumi shikibu nikki, Murasaki shikibu nikki, Sarashina nikki, Sanuki no suke nikki* [The Izumi Shikibu Diary, The Murasaki Shikibu Diary, The Sarashina Diary, The Sanuki no Suke Diary]. Nihon koten bungaku zenshū, 18. Tokyo: Shōgakkan, 1971.

Goff, Janet. *Noh Drama and The Tale of Genji: The Art of Illusion in Fifteen Classical Plays*. Princeton: Princeton University Press, 1991.

Higuchi Yoshimaro and Kuboki Tetsuo, eds. *Matsura no miya monogatari, Mumyōzōshi* [The Tale of the Matsura Shrine, Untitled Book]. Shinpen nihon koten bungaku zenshū, 40. Tokyo: Shōgakkan, 1999.

Hisamatsu Sen'ichi. *Kokugaku: Sono seiritsu to kokubungaku to no kankei* [The Formation of National Learning and its Relation to National Literature in Japan]. Tokyo: Shibundō, 1941.

Kokumin Tosho Kabushiki Kaisha, ed. *Imakagami* [The Mirror of the Present]. Kōchū Nihon bungaku taikei, 12. Tokyo: Kokumin tosho, 1926.

Kornicki, Peter F. "Unsuitable Books for Women? *Genji Monogatari* and *Ise Monogatari* in Late Seventeenth-Century Japan." *Monumenta Nipponica* 60.2 (2005): 147–193.

Kuboki Tetsuo. "Kaisetsu" [Commentary]. *Matsura no miya monogatari, Mumyōzōshi* [The Tale of the Matsura Shrine, Untitled Book]. Eds. Higuchi Yoshimaro and Kuboki Tetsuo. Shinpen nihon koten bungaku zenshū, 40. Tokyo: Shōgakkan, 1999. 289–310.

Lindberg-Wada, Gunilla. *Poetic Allusion: Some Aspects of the Role Played by Kokin Wakashuu as a Source of Allusion in Genji Monogatari*. Diss. Stockholm: University of Stockholm, 1983.

McMullen, James. *Genji gaiden: The Origins of Kumazawa Banzan's Commentary on The Tale of Genji*. London: Ithaca Press for Oxford University, 1991.

— *Idealism, Protest and The Tale of Genji: The Confucianism of Kumazawa Banzan (1619–91)*. Oxford: Clarendon, 1999.

Murasaki Shikibu. *The Tale of Genji*. Trans. Royall Tyler. New York: Viking Penguin, 2002.

Sanari Kentarō. *Yōkyoku taikan* [Encyclopedia of Noh Recitations]. Vol. 2. Tokyo: Meiji shoin, 1931.

Tsubouchi Shōyō. *Shōsetsu Shinzui* [The Essence of the Novel]. Shōyō senshū bessatsu, 3. Tokyo: Daiichi shobō, [1885–1886] 1977.

Tyler, Royall. "The Nō Play *Matsukaze* as a Transformation of *Genji monogatari*." *Journal of Japanese Studies* 20.2 (1994): 377–422.

Yamagishi Tokuhei, ed. *Genji monogatari* [The Tale of Genji]. Nihon koten bungaku taikei, 14–18. Tokyo: Iwanami, [1958–1963] 1974–1975.

Fictional Spaces: Image, Language & Identity

Marcia Sá Cavalcante Schuback
The Fiction of the Image

The question of fiction in global contexts can be treated in very different ways. It can be a question of comparing different kinds and genres of fiction in different cultures in order to overcome the limits of national literatures and ground a comparative world literature. It can further be a question of how the notion of world literature changes the very concept of fiction, demanding a consideration of the development of its concept and a reconsideration of its value and actuality. Moreover, there is still the question of the uses and abuses of fiction, of the right and duties of fiction in a world that more than ever has to struggle to make heard the stories and the history of hunger and poverty, of wars and catastrophes, of migrations and exiles, that increase the faster new liberal forms of globalizing the local and localizing the global are installed. Since the tremendous events of World War II, a consciousness about the past, present and future atrocities of colonialism, contemporary genocides and the prospects of natural and technical catastrophes to come have showed how the question of the ways of telling the truth of historical reality and of the reality of history became one of the main questions in contemporary humanities. The debate between fiction and truth, fiction and reality is itself a testimony of the profound ethical, political and philosophical implications of this very question. The main concern at stake is, however, not merely whether fiction can or cannot represent and present reality without falsifying it, whether the contemporary mind should choose description rather than fiction, witness literature rather than literature grounded on the force of the *persona dramatica*.

The main question in these debates is rather how to represent and present what is un-representable, how to image what cannot be imagined insofar as it surpasses the representable and imaginable limits of human cruelty, atrocity, suffering and despair. It is the question of how to represent what oversteps the laws of presentation and representation, how to image what cannot be imagined by any imagination. This extreme question can be formulated in terms of how to fictionalize the un-fictionalizable. Considered in these terms, the question of fiction and fictionality does not merely involve a discussion about these concepts but also shows the urgent need to address the still quite unaddressed question of the meaning of reality on the basis of which different theoretical discussions about fiction and fictionality relies on. Affirming that the uses and abuses of fiction in modern and contemporary society and their theoretical implications touch on the difficult question of how to fictionalize the un-fictionalizable; we are claiming that in its overwhelming shaking force, reality is un-imaginable, un-representable, and hence un-fictionalizable insofar as it presents itself as the force of an appearing, of a coming to image. The aim of the present article is to present some reflections on the relation between fiction and reality which are based on this claim.

The question of how to fictionalize, represent or image the un-fictionalizable, the un-representable and the un-imaginable involves several intricate dimensions. Arnold Schönberg's opera *Moses and Aron* can be considered one of the most radical artistic elaborations of this question in its several intricate dimensions. In this opera, written at the beginning of the 1930s in Nazi Germany, the Jewish Austrian composer Arnold Schönberg chose the narrative of Exodus centered on the un-representability, un-imaginability and un-figurativity of the God of salvation. "You shall not make for yourself a carved image, or any likeness of anything that is in heaven above, or that is in the earth beneath, or that is in the water under the earth." (Exodus 20:4) This passage, considered by Kant to be the most "sublime" passage of the Old Testament,[1] can be perceived as an "opera of opera," as George Steiner formulated it (1998), insofar as it stages the struggle between music and word that defines opera as such. Whereas the realm of the word always deals with representation, images, fiction and hence with referentiality, the realm of music appears as the realm beyond representation, images and fictions. Schönberg's opera can be described as "opera of opera" because it stages the paradox of representing the realm of the word through non-representation (music), of imaging through what has no image (music), of fictionalizing through non-fiction (music).

However, it presents not only the un-mimetical nature of music in its attempt to mimetize but also the aporetical situation of a struggle to say the unsayable, to image the unimaginable, to fictionalize the unfictionalizable, a struggle that forms the core of the Exodus' passage chosen by Schönberg as the basis for the libretto. Figuring, representing, imaging or fictionalizing what

---

[1] "We have no need to fear that the feeling of the sublime will suffer from an abstract mode of presentation like this, which is altogether negative as to what it is sensuous. For though the imagination, no doubt, finds nothing beyond the sensible world to which it can lay hold, still this thrusting aside of the sensible barriers gives it a feeling of being unbounded; and that removal is thus a presentation of the Infinite. As such it can never be anything more than a negative presentation – but still it expands the soul. Perhaps there is no more sublime passage in the Jewish Law than the commandment: *Thou shalt not make to thyself any graven image, nor the likeness of anything which is in heaven or on the earth or under the earth*, etc. This commandment alone can explain the enthusiasm, which the Jewish people, in their moral period, felt for their religion when comparing themselves with others, or the pride inspired by Mohammedanism." (Kant 1973, 127).

cannot and shall not be imaged, represented or fictionalized – the Godhead – Schönberg's opera finds the sublime bond between music and reality. Indeed, writing an opera about this "most sublime passage of the Jewish Law" that defines the "destiny of the Jewish people," Schönberg advanced the tremendous "destiny of the Jew people" in the horror of the camps, a horror that has to be told although it surpasses all possibility of telling. Theodor Adorno insisted in his commentaries on this opera, considered by him to be Schönberg's *chef d'œuvre*, that it stages not only this struggle but also the necessity to transgress the law and to write what cannot be written, the need to present, image and fictionalize what is in itself un-presentable, un-imaginable and un-fictionalizable. (Adorno, 1998) For him, Schönberg's opera is a "sacral fragment" of the impossibility of the sacral, a cultic piece in a world where cult became impossible. (Adorno 1998) Adorno saw clearly that *Moses and Aron* brings to image, to figure, to fiction what has no images, no figures, fictions – that is, music itself in its unsolvable conflict with the word, and what is un-imaginable, un-figurable, un-representable, un-fictionalizable (God and History). In the inseparable connection between the question of how music can or cannot, should or should not try to figure, to image, to represent or to fictionalize words, the historical situation, that is, "reality" and the question of the very impossibility of bringing image itself to an image, figure to a figure, fiction to a fiction opened up opera itself to its extreme possibilities. But how can this discussion illuminate the question of fiction in global contexts?

The (Fictional) Image of Our Global World

Despite the numerous debates about the diffuse and multifarious meaning of "globalization," a certain image operates in this term. It is the image of the globe, an image that seems quite a convincing way to describe our world today. It is the image of a *globus terraqueus* that Immanuel Kant had long before selected as the image for the place inhabited by the peoples of the earth.[2] Indeed, "globalization" not only defines our world but it defines it by means of an image that seems to reproduce, apparently without fictions, not only the place inhabited by all peoples of the earth but also and maybe even more the way all peoples of the earth inhabit the earth. Globalization as a mode of inhabiting the earth can be described as the mode of inhabiting the earth through images. This image says about our world that it is a world

---

2 *Metaphysik der Sitten*, § 62: "Kugelgestalt ihres [der Völker der Erde] Aufenthalts als globus terraquaeus." (Kant 1956, 259).

grounded on images and that a world grounded on images seems to be the only possible image of the globalized world. In different approaches to "globalization," "global contexts" or "global world," the chiasmic relation between the image of the world and the world of images presents itself. Indeed, in this "global world," everything appears as image; nothing seems to be capable of existing without an image and nothing that is not image seems to have the right to exist. In this sense, it is legitimate to claim that we live in a world saturated with images that are themselves saturated by the world. Framing the meaning of the "global" in this way, the question of "fiction in globalized contexts" is given a certain direction. It is the question of fiction in a world of images, and it is therefore the question of fictions in and of images, of images in and of fiction, and last but not least of fiction and image. If our world, the global world, is a world of images of reality rather than of realities, what does fiction mean, and furthermore how should we define the fiction of an image rather than the fiction of a reality? What happens to the concept of fiction if the meaning of reality seems to be transformed in our global world into an image? The question of fiction in global contexts can hence be re-formulated as a question of the fiction of the image.

The term *fiction* comes, as is well known, from the Latin *fingo*, meaning to shape, to form, fashion or feign. The original signification was to knead or form out of clay, that is, to produce. From this root are derived both the words figure and fiction.[3] Thus fiction means firstly the production of figures and images; it was only later that figuration and imagination received the connotations of dissimulation, ruse and invention. Meaning the coming to figure and image, figuration and imagination, fiction is the name of the mimetic action as such and not necessarily its possible or impossible fidelity or adequacy towards a model.[4] Indeed, the huge problem of mimesis and representation – which since Plato's expulsion of mimetic representation from his philosophical State has known so many variations, including the post-modern deconstruction of representation – deals not only with the correspondence between image and reality but also with the very nature of images and figures, with the "invention" or more precisely the intervention within reality of what never existed before its own invention. The intervening invention – fiction (as figuration and imagination) is indeed an excess in relation to the process of reality. The magic mystery of fiction is the one that constitutes the figurativeness of figures, the imaginativeness of images, namely the way figures and images *appear* as figures and

---

[3] See the heading *fingo* in Ernout and Meillet 1951, 419–420.
[4] For an inspiring philosophical discussion about fiction as mimetic action, see Lacoue-Labarthe 1998.

images. Thus what bewitches so-called "primitive people" is not that they do not see the difference between the image of an ancestor and the ancestor himself but precisely the contrary, namely, that they do see how the image of the ancestor *is* the ancestor precisely by being his image and hence by *not* being the ancestor in body and flesh.[5] Indeed, the magic mystery of the image is that it shows itself as image showing something else than itself.

The magic mystery of the image is the impossibility of the image of image. What would be the image of image, the figure of figure or the fiction of fiction? These questions can perhaps only be answered through an antinomy. This antinomy can be formulated as follows: there is no image of the image, no figure of the figure, no fiction of fiction and every image is an image of imaging, every figure a figure of figuration and every fiction a fiction of fictionalization. It belongs to the enigma of image, of figure, of fiction that it is impossible to find an image, a figure, a fiction that is not an image, a figure, a fiction *of* something else. In this sense, we could say that Schönberg's *Moses and Aron* is the opera, that is, the bringing to image, to figure, to fiction the antinomy of the image, of the figure, of fiction: it stages that there is no image of image, no figure of figure, no fiction of fiction and that every image is an image of the imaging, every figure a figure of figuration, every fiction a fiction of fictionality. It stages this antinomy as antinomy, that is, as what can never be solved but only remain as an open tension. In other words, image as such, figure as such, fiction as such appears as something else, in the image of something, in the figure of something, in the fiction of something, even if this "something" is like the king in Hamlet, "a thing – Of nothing" (Scene 4.2), an "absolut" as in Malevich's black quadrat, a "non-object" or "non-figure" in abstractionist and concretist paintings, or even a "probject," recalling the term suggested by the Brazilian artist Hélio Oiticica to describe his *"parangolés."*

Malevich's black square, Rauschenberg's "white paintings," the exhibition of a white canvas without any artistic incision are still images *of* a black square, *of* a white painting, *of* a white canvas. They are *images-of*, appearing as images while with-drawing in images-*of*. An image that would be pure image and not an image of (something else even if this something were nothing), could only be an image without image or even a non-image, a figure without figure or a non-figure, a fiction without fiction or a non-fictional fiction. To be an image, a figure, a fiction *of* something or *of* nothing, to be an image (or figure, or fiction) *of*, even if an image of image (a figure of figure, a fiction of fiction) is still a *reference to* something else than itself. Critique of representation, in the core of its gesture, is still representation; critique of

---

5 For some thoughts on this paradoxical statement, see Warburg 1988.

Fig. 1: Narcissus.

mimesis is still mimetical, something that Platonic dialogues have shown in their own structure and form. Even if this image could be described as image of itself, as presented in the image of Narcissus looking at himself in the pond (see the image above),[6] it is still an image *of* the antinomy of image as much as Schönberg's *Moses and Aron*, showing as well that there is no image of image (no figure of figure, no fiction of fiction) and that every image is an image of image, the figure of figure, the fiction of fiction.

---

[6] This is a public domain image of Narcissus, copied from http://karenswhimsy.com/roman-mythology.shtm (12 August 2013).

It shows how image shows itself as image appearing *as* the imaged, *as* something else that is nevertheless itself. The drama of Narcissus, the drama of the image, is not that he could only see himself but rather that he could never see himself, he could never see the seeing, but only the seen, the imaged.

To show the image as the imaged, to show the seeing as what is seen, means to show something as something else. To show something as something else defines both *representation* and a *fake*, in Latin, a *fictus*, that is, a fiction, in the sense of inventing, constructing, and producing something else in relation to given nature and reality. From *fingere* comes also the Portuguese verb *fingir*, to fake, that defines for the Portuguese poet Fernando Pessoa poetry itself. Saying that: "The poet is a faker, / Who's so good at his act / He even fakes the pain / Of pain he feels in fact,"[7] Pessoa is not affirming poetry as "image" or "representation" of the real but rather showing *the fictional reality of image*. Indeed, more than affirming that fiction is creation of images, at stake here is how images are fictional. Images are fictional not merely because they may disguise or cover up reality, not because they "trompe l' (d)'œil," they cheat the eyes, so to speak, but because there is no image of image and every image of something is an image of imaging. This means that fiction defines the way images *appear* and reveal themselves as image and not the way images may or not correspond to a given reality. *Fiction has to do here with the truth of an appearing and not with a definition of truth as correspondence.* The fictional reality of the image appears when we observe the way an image shows itself as image, never showing itself as itself but always as something else, the one that is already two, the one in itself differentiated. Image is fictional in the sense that, in the image, the one is always two, the one is always broken, as Narcissus and his wreath reflected in the water.

If our global world can be defined as a world saturated with images saturated by the world, then it is the world where everything appears as two, where every hegemony appears as broken. Global world is the world of the hegemony of broken hegemonies, broken hegemony of the subject, of tradition, of history, of hope, of religion, of the human, of reality, of illusion, of rationality, of representation, and so on. Defining image as the one appearing as broken in two, as the unity of something appearing as something else, defining image as fiction (or, what would be the same, defining fiction as fracture of the real), it is possible to understand why a world saturated with images saturated by the world, why a world of images, is a world of "broken hegemonies" (or vice-versa). It is

---

7 From the poem "Autopsicografia": "O poeta é um fingidor. / Finge tão completamente / Que chega a fingir que é dor / A dor que deveras sente." (Pessoa 1986, 98) Trans. Richard Zenith. (Pessoa 1998, 247).

the world where everything appears as something else – the good as bad, the bad as good, the beautiful as ugly, the ugly as beautiful, and so on.[8] It is a world of ambiguities. It is a world to such an extent saturated by the world that it is experienced as a world without world. However, even if this world, this global world, is the stage where the disgrace of ambiguity is performed, the world of "total insecurity" as Foucault expressed it, it still exposes a certain grace, the grace of showing everywhere that there is no image of image and that the image of everything is an image of imaging. Our global world, the world of "total insecurity," the world of "broken hegemonies," the world where every one appears as broken in two or in many, where everything appears as something else, is perhaps nothing but the image of imaging itself, the figure or figuration, the fiction of fictionalizing.[9]

In a conversation with Michel Foucault in the 60s, Claude Bonnefoy asked him who or what work of art could replace Velázquez's *Las Meninas*, in the attempt to find an image of our world, the world of "total insecurity" and of "broken hegemonies," that is, of our world of images. Foucault did not hesitate to answer:

> It seems to me that Klee's painting is the one that best represents our century, compared to what Velázquez was to his. Insofar as Klee brings to visibility all the gestures, actions, graphics, signs, features, surfaces that constitute painting, he makes the act of painting wide and brilliant knowledge about painting itself. His painting cannot be defined as art brut but as a painting that re-captures the knowledge of its most fundamental elements. And these, apparently the simplest and most spontaneous, even those that did not appear and that seemed would never appear, are what Klee spreads over the surface of the canvas. *Las Meninas* represented all elements of representation, the painter, the models, the brush, the canvas, the image in the mirror, decomposing painting itself into the elements that made it a Representation. Klee's painting, in contrast, composes and breaks down the painting in its simplest elements that are sustained, haunted, and inhabited by the knowledge of painting. (Foucault 2001, 671)

Foucault considered Paul Klee's paintings the image or icon of our century, for him the century of the disappearing of man and the century where every existence appears as its own *epistheme*. Klee's painting is for him the painting of the knowledge of painting, as every existence in this century seems to be the knowledge of existence. I would like to rephrase this suggestion of Foucault's and assume Klee's painting as the image of the fictional way an image appears as image, in the antinomy of never appearing as pure image, appearing always as image of something even if this something is nothing or no-thing at all.

---

8 See Karl Marx's readings of Shakespeare's *Timon of Athens* in *Economic and Philosophical Manuscripts of 1844* (Kottman 2009, 125–130).
9 Concerning the philosophical meaning of the concept of hegemony, see Schürmann 2003.

Sketching a Meaning of Fiction with Paul Klee

The well-known phrase by Klee that "art does not reproduce the visible; it makes visible" defines indeed his work.[10] Klee's painting makes visible the making visible of images, the way images appear as images, being therefore a lesson not about "images" the way images appear as images, a lesson from and only then about the movement of an appearing that we call "image." The appearing of an image, the movement of a coming-to-image has itself no image, is un-imaginable, but appears withdrawing itself in what appears, in the image. This withdrawing movement of the appearing as such can be called the fictional nature of the imaging. It is fictional not because it dissimulates or hides the "real" but because it exposes reality on its coming-to-image, as the movement of an appearing. I have proposed elsewhere to define the sketch as the movement of a coming-to-image that becomes visible, withdrawing itself in the image, rather than a provisory, ephemeral or fulminant image (Sá Cavalcante Schuback 2011, 2012). In this sense, we could say that fiction or the fictional character of the appearing or coming-to-image is sketch-like. Klee's painting can be described as painting of drawings and sketches, as a *poetics of the sketch*, and he a painter of the coming-to-image. In this sense, Klee is a painter of the fictional nature of image. Looking carefully at Klee's painting of drawings and sketches, trying to understand how his "images" are images of the coming-to-image, it may be possible to accomplish what could be considered a need of our times, namely the need for unlearning the images in order to learn how to see in images the coming-to-image, in forms the coming-to-form, the sources or birth of images and forms. Here it becomes possible to learn visions of a coming-to, and thereby another meaning of otherness, a new meaning of the new, no longer as new or other worlds but as in-between worlds. Klee's poetics of the sketch exhibits a new meaning of fiction as lucidity of the in-betweens. This can be considered Klee's poetics of fiction.[11]

How does this painting of drawings and sketches, this painting of fiction, the paintings of Paul Klee make visible in images the appearing of an image? They do so, making visible the moving of a movement and not merely moving things. This making-visible demands first of all a kind of *"deformation,"* to use Klee's own expression, of a world of things based upon an understanding of the thing as that which is accomplished, formed and shaped, individualized

---

[10] "Kunst gibt nicht das Sichtbare wieder, sondern macht sichtbar." (Klee 1956, 76).
[11] Paul Klee does not use the term fiction. He prefers the term fable in some titles of drawings and furthermore the concept of simile, *Gleichnis*, in his theoretical work (Klee 1956, 78–80).

and autonomous – that is, as object.[12] Deformation is to be understood here as dis-formation, as moving the eyes away from pre-formed forms, from forms carried through to an end – "*Form-enden*" – in order to discover within the formed the forming forces, "*Formenden,*" continuing to use Klee's own vocabulary. (1956) The demand is neither to leave behind the realm of forms, nor to vandalize or abuse the forms, but rather to learn to un-learn the formed, the images, in order to rediscover the power of seeing within the formed the coming-to-a-form, in images the coming-to-image, in being the coming-to-be. Dis-formation could be considered a kind of translation from substantives to verbs that enables to see what slides away from any vision, namely the moving meanwhile of a movement. Besides, dis-formation, the making-visible of the making-visible also demands "*abstraction,*" defined by Klee as "a drawing out of pure plastic relations." (1956) This drawing out of pure relations is realized by Klee in his "pedagogical sketches," in his "pedagogy of the line." This pedagogy of learning, to unlearn images in order to see in the images the coming to images, their birth and source, is realized in a painting that draws the drawing of lines. To make visible the making-visible, the way the coming-to-image appears, withdrawing itself in images, Klee investigated another meaning of tautology, quite different than the one criticized by Didi-Huberman in his discussions about minimalist art. (1992) He investigated the tautology of drawing the drawing, of making visible the making-visible, of bringing to image the coming-to-image, keeping without any attempt to solve the antinomy of image: there is no image of image and every image is an image of the image.

This tautological investigation of the hand drawing the drawing of lines is an exercise of holding oneself in the tension between the unformed and the unformable, between the imageless and the unimaginable. The transformative force of Klee's works lies in the transformation of the meaning of art unfolded in this vision of the image as the place in which the appearing as such appears as withdrawing itself in what appears. That is why Klee's works are not "images," as Heidegger remarked, but "situations," the movement in which human being is brought to the experience of nothingness becoming space.[13]

---

[12] "Ich möchte nun die Dimension des gegenständlichen in einem neuen Sinne für sich betrachten und dabei zu zeigen versuchen, wieso der Künstler oft zu einer solchen scheinbar willkürlichen 'Deformation' der natürlichen Erscheinungsform kommt" [I want to observe the dimension of objects in a new sense trying to show how the artist arrives at this apparently arbitrary 'deformation' of the natural forms of appearances] (Klee 1956, 92).

[13] Heidegger had plans to critically review his essay on the *Origin of the Work of Art* (1935–36) after the impact that Klee's works made on him. He also planed to write a book on Klee. In connection to these plans he wrote some notes on Klee, published for the first time by Günter Seubold, under the title "Heideggers nachgelassene Klee-Notizen" (1993, 5–12). For some comments on Heidegger and Klee, see Pöggeler 2002 and Petzet 1983.

Fig. 2: Paul Klee's *Seiltänzer* (1923).

Klee's paintings of drawings and sketches can be called a sojourn in the in-between, in the midst of the formless and the un-formable, in the meanwhile of a becoming. His painting is therefore more than a lesson in painting the knowledge of painting as Foucault proposed; it is rather a lesson in another meaning of transformation, beyond teleological and aleatoric views. Klee is neither trying to overcome the image in order to reach a state of pure imagelessness nor trying to accomplish the most accomplished image that would be the image of image itself. To draw the drawing of lines appears as a holding on to the tightrope that separates and unites the unformed and the un-formable, as a hovering at the co-incidence of what is both no longer and not yet image.

In Klee's *Tighttrope Walker* (*Seiltänzer*, 1923, see image above),[14] we see how straight lines rather than "breadthless length" are drawn lines, tensioned and concentrated movements and counter-movements. The walker on a tightrope makes visible the multidimensional simultaneity of movements involved within and evolving from out of a drawn line. Horizontally and vertically are given dimensions through scales of the walker's weight. They appear as paths that cross, oscillating between abysses, where walking is a being-drawn by the drawing in such a way that almost falling to the ground is already heaven not being yet heaven and the other way around.

In Klee's poetics of the sketch, space is in-betweeness and time meanwhileness. What defines the sketch is this spatio-temporality experienced as the meanwhile of an in-between, a profound experience of life as hovering and oscillation. The "Poetics of the Sketch," presented in Klee, is as much a poetics of hovering (*Schweben*).[15] But how should we grasp the hovering, the meanwhile in-betweeness that in Klee's works allows for a meaning of the sketch as appearing in its own withdrawal, as becoming while in dissolution?

In the *souvenirs* of the Journal *Sturm* and of the Bauhaus, the artist Lothar Schreyer, who taught performing arts at the Bauhaus, narrates a testimony of Klee's that concerns this matter, part of a conversation that took place in his studio. Klee said there:

> I overstep neither the image's nor the composition's limits. But I do stretch its content by introducing into the image new subject matter – or rather, not so much new as barely

---

14 This image of Klee's painting is reproduced with the kind permission of Zentrum Paul Klee, Bern.

15 In a book not often referred to, that bears the title *Metaphysik des Schwebens. Untersuchung zur Geschichte der Ästhetik*, Walter Schulz, an important Schelling scholar, presents the problem of hovering (*Schweben*) as a metaphysical, logical and aesthetical problem insufficiently investigated in the tradition and as something that has a fundamental importance for contemporary philosophy in its struggles with the question of the dissolution of subjectivity and categorial confusion (Schulz 1985).

> glimpsed subject matter. Obviously this subject matter, like any other, maintains its ties to the natural world. By natural world I am not referring to nature's appearance (as naturalism would) but to the sphere of its possibilities: this content produces images of nature's potentiality ... I often say ... that worlds have come into being and continuously unfold before our eyes – worlds which despite their connection to nature are not visible to everybody, but may in fact only be so to children, the mad and the primitives. I have in mind the realm of the unborn and the already dead which one day might fulfill its promise, but which then again might not – an intermediate world, an interworld. To my eyes, at least, an interworld; I name it so because I detect its existence between those exterior worlds to which our senses are attuned, while at the same time I can introject it enough to be able to project it outside of myself as symbol. It is by following this course that children, the mad, and the primitive peoples have remained faithful to – have discovered again – the power of seeing.[16]

Klee stresses here that what we call things, words, and images are worlds coming into being and unfolding continuously before our eyes. Children, the mad and the primitives "remained faithful" – which for Klee means "discovered again" – the "power of seeing" insofar as they discovered once more the coming into being of the world as "Interworld" (*Zwischenwelt*). The coming-to, the becoming is a world in-between worlds, between the exterior, perceived world and the interior, sensed world. It is a world in-between the already dead and the unborn, the realm that might or might not, one day, fulfill its promise. It is the realm of the making possible of the possible rather then the making possible of real actualities. The significance of the notion of "Inter-world" (*Zwischenwelt*), of a world between the already dead and the unborn, is so decisive to Klee that the words chosen for his epitaph were: "I cannot be understood at all on this earth. For I live as much with the dead as with the unborn. Somewhat closer to the heart of creation than usual. But still not nearly close enough."[17]

In-between the dead and the unborn is the hovering place of an is-being, the event of existence. In-between the unformed and the un-formable, the imageless and the un-imaginable, the wordless and the unsayable, is the hovering place of a coming-to-be. Indeed, coming-to-be is nothing but the is-being, the eventfulness of a meanwhile, the (tautological) drawing of the drawing of lines. This, for Klee, is the wisdom of the line as in his *Träger für ein Schild* (1934) (see image below).[18]

---

[16] *Erinnerungen an Sturm und Bauhaus. Was ist des Menschen Bild?* (1956), quoted in Felix Klee 1962, 183–184.
[17] "Diesseitig bin ich gar nicht fassbar, denn ich wohne grad so gut bei den Toten wie bei den Ungeborenen, etwas näher dem Herzen der Schöpfung als üblich und noch lange nicht nahe genug." (Klee 1957, 427) Quoted in Franciscono 1991, 5.
[18] This image of Klee's painting is reproduced with the kind permission of Zentrum Paul Klee, Bern.

Fig. 3: Paul Klee's *Träger für ein Schild* (1934).

The line is the trace of the being-drawn, that is, of the drawing. A trace is what shows the presence of an absence. A drawing exposes the withdrawing way in which the line drawing appears. In the outlines of the after-while appearing of the erstwhile, the drawing makes visible the sketching structure of the appearing as such, namely, that the appearing as such appears withdrawing itself in what appears. Appearing as such, the image of image can only appear in something else, in what appears.

If Klee's paintings of drawings and sketches can be seen as the image of our world saturated with images saturated by the world is because they make visible the in-between the imageless and the unimaginable, the unformed and the un-formable, the figureless and the unfigurable, the fictionless and unfictionalizable, a possible existence in the tensional hovering and oscillation of an in-between. Showing this tensional in-between, Klee points toward another meaning of fiction, enabling us to understand fiction as the movement of an appearing, of the coming-to-image and to form that withdraws itself in the imaged and formed. Our global world is a world in which ended forms and meanings do not end to end and where other forms and meanings are still unborn. The world of saturation is the world that is neither here nor there, both here and there, neither before nor after, but the con-fusion and co-incidence of before and after. This world of ambiguity, our world of images, where everything appears as something else, where the one appears as broken in two and, even more, makes visible the unapparent tensional realm of in-betweens, that neither a critical theory of representation nor a critique of representation seems able to account for. When the any-longer touches the not-yet, when ends confound with beginnings, it becomes possible to see the traces of an "in-between," the traces of the fictional, in its sketching way of appearing. In the poetics of fiction sketched by Klee, *fiction* means the absenting way the in-between the dead and the un-born, the formless and the un-formable, the imageless and the un-imaginable comes to presence.

Bibliography

Adorno, Theodor. "Schönberg's Moses and Aron." *Quasi una fantasia: Essays on Modern Music*. Trans. Rodney Livingstone. [German original version 1963]. Verso Classics, 17. London and New York: Verso, 1998. 225–248.

Didi-Huberman, Georges. *Ce que nous voyons, ce qui nous regarde*. Collection "Critique." Paris: Éditions de Minuit, 1992.

Ernout, Alfred and Antoine Meillet. *Dictionnaire étymologique de la langue latine*. Paris: Klincksieck, 1951.

Foucault, Michel. *Dits et écrits. 1: 1954–1969*. Paris: Gallimard, 2001.

Franciscono, Marcel. *Paul Klee: His Work and Thought*. Chicago, IL: University of Chicago Press, 1991.

Heidegger, Martin. "Heideggers nachgelassene Klee-Notizen." Ed. Günter Seubold. *Heidegger Studies* 9 (1993): 5–12.

Kant, Immanuel. *Immanuel Kant's Werke. Band IV. Schriften zur Ethik und Religionsphilosophie*. Wiesbaden: Insel, 1956.

— *Critique of Judgment*. Trans. J. Creed Meredith. Oxford: Clarendon, 1973.

Klee, Felix. *Paul Klee: His Life and Work in Documents*. Trans. Richard and Clara Winston. New York: G. Braziller, 1962.

Klee, Paul. *Das bildnerische Denken. Schriften zur Form- und Gestaltungslehre*. Ed. Jürg Spiller. Basel: B. Schwabe, 1956.

— *Tagebücher 1898–1918*. Ed. Felix Klee. DuMont Dokumente. Köln: M DuMont Schauberg, 1957.

Kottman, Paul A., ed. *Philosophers on Shakespeare*. Stanford, CA: Stanford University Press, 2009.

Lacoue-Labarthe, Philippe. *Typography: Mimesis, Philosophy, Politics*. Ed. Christopher Fynsk. Meridian. Stanford, CA: Stanford University Press, 1998.

Pessoa, Fernando. *Obra poética em um volume*. Ed. Maria Aliete Galhoz. Biblioteca luso-brasileira, série portuguesa. Rio de Janeiro: Nova Aguilar, 1986.

— *Fernando Pessoa & Co.: Selected Poems*. Trans. Richard Zenith. New York: Grove Press, 1998.

Petzet, Heinrich Wiegand. *Auf einen Stern zugehen: Begegnungen und Gespräche mit Martin Heidegger, 1929 bis 1976*. Frankfurt am Main: Societäts-Verlag, 1983.

Pöggeler, Otto. *Bild und Technik: Heidegger, Klee und die moderne Kunst*. München: Fink, 2002.
Sá Cavalcante Schuback, Marcia. *Att tänka i skisser*. Göteborg: Glänta, 2011.
— "The Poetics of the Sketch." *Paul Klee: Philosophical Vision, from Nature to Art*. Ed. John Sallis. Chestnut Hill, MA: McMullen Museum of Art, Boston College, 2012. 149–156.
Schulz, Walter. *Metaphysik des Schwebens. Untersuchungen zur Geschichte der Ästhetik*. Pfullingen: Neske, 1985.
Schürmann, Reiner. *Broken Hegemonies*. Trans. Reginald Lilly. [French original version 1996]. Studies in Continental Thought. Bloomington, IN: Indiana University Press, 2003.
Steiner, George. *Language and Silence: Essays on Language, Literature and the Inhuman*. New Haven: Yale University Press, 1998.
Warburg, Aby. *Schlangenritual. Ein Reisebericht*. Kleine kulturwissenschaftliche Bibliothek, 7. Berlin: Wagenbach, 1988.

Anders Pettersson
Linguistic and Psychological Mechanisms Behind Literary Fiction

Introduction

In the present paper I will be looking at fictional literary discourse against the background of literary discourse in general. Literary discourse, in its turn, will be viewed against the even larger background of human psychology and human communication. Ever since the emergence of Russian Formalism in the early twentieth century, and with it the beginnings of modern literary theory, there has been a tendency, at times a prevailing tendency, to think of literature as a phenomenon *sui generis* and to perceive profound differences between literature and other types of discourse. My own theoretical instincts point in a different direction. If you are to gain an adequate perspective on literature and literary fiction, you should be attentive to the continuity between literary discourse and other forms of linguistic communication and consider how literature can be fitted into an overarching pattern of human needs and human occupations.

What I will offer is a bird's eye view of literature and literary fiction. I will start from one psychological mechanism, namely analogical thinking, and one linguistic mechanism, namely relevance to the addressee, explain how those two mechanisms apply to literature, and then describe fictionality as a device which enables literary discourse to achieve its objectives.

My view of literature and literary fiction is by no means uncontroversial. For example, my standpoints are not really compatible with the aesthetic approach to literature – that is, with the idea that the reader primarily adopts an aesthetic attitude towards the text in a narrow sense of "aesthetic" – or with the assumption that the reader primarily enters into the world of the literary work psychologically. It would be counterproductive to embark on a discussion of different current approaches to literature in this short paper,[1] so I suggest that you take my essay as outlining a perspective on literature and literary fiction that I myself find convincing, a perspective also meant to be enlightening, or at least thought-provoking, to my readers.

---

[1] For a comprehensive discussion of such approaches, see Pettersson 2012a.

Analogical Thinking and Relevance to the Addressee

Analogical thinking has been analyzed in considerable depth by Keith J. Holyoak and Paul Thagard in their book *Mental Leaps: Analogy in Creative Thought* (1995, see also Gentner et al. 2001). When thinking in analogies, you compare two objects or two situations, using one of them as a model of the other one. For example, faced with a situation that is in some respect new to you, you can search your experience for similar situations and seek guidance from them.

Holyoak and Thagard describe how the American President Harry Truman, when deciding how to react to the North Korean attack on South Korea in 1950, considered some of the events leading up to the Second World War – the Japanese invasion of Manchuria, the Italian attack on Ethiopia, and the German annexation of Austria – and on that basis found it necessary to counter the attack forcefully. Viewing the North Korean attack on South Korea in the light of the German annexation of Austria (et cetera), Truman found that it may have dire consequences to leave massive aggression unchecked, even when it is directed against countries that seem unimportant from a strategic point of view. Truman's reasoning illustrates analogical thinking at work. In analogical thinking you map a source analog – which is the model that you use to think with; here: the German annexation of Austria (et cetera) – on to a target analog – which is the situation you want to understand; here: the North Korean attack on South Korea – and you evaluate the similarities and dissimilarities that you can find between the two situations.

As Holyoak and Thagard point out, comparing things and considering their similarities and differences is at the very root of our processing of the world around us. Analogical thinking is grounded in absolutely basal human capacities and is ubiquitous in human thought. As the two authors write in *Mental Leaps*: "Comparing novel situations to familiar ones and finding correspondences between them, and then using these correspondences to generate inferences about the new cases, is integral to human thinking." (Holyoak and Thagard 1995, 262) It follows from this that your experiences have a significance for you that transcends their immediate practical importance. The things you experience will also form part of your store of experiences, your store of possible source analogs, which you will be able to draw upon in your attempts to come to grips with new situations in life. To put it differently: the things you experience will be of interest to you both as those things themselves and as models of things that may happen in the world. (cf. Holyoak and Thagard 1995, 84)

This means that when you are confronted with an utterance or a text, that encounter too will possess the dual character of the experiencing of an individual event and the acquisition of a potential source analog. For instance, when you read a news story about a car accident in a newspaper, the text will supply you with factual information about an actual incident but also with a potential example, which you will be free to interpret and use – perhaps you will take it as an example of what may happen to you on the road in a given kind of traffic situation. Indeed, not only the factual content of the text, but also the explicit or implicit attitudes behind it – the tone, the point of view – will form part of your reading experience and have the capacity to serve as a model to be accepted or rejected: the attitudes may be ones you will be ready to adopt or ones from which you will want to distance yourself. The duality to which I have been drawing attention is a constant feature of our experiences.[2] You can find it in connection with experiences of utterances or texts, just as you can find it in connection with other kinds of experience, and it makes no difference whether the utterance or text is literary or non-literary, fictional or non-fictional.

Understanding analogical thinking plays an important role for understanding what literature is and how literature functions, but since analogical thinking permeates all our experience, including all our experience of linguistic discourse, something more is needed for the explanation of literature specifically. On this point, I would like to bring in the concept of relevance to the addressee. Relevance to the addressee is a basic requirement concerning acts of communication. When you speak or write, you should have something to say, something that can possibly interest the person or persons that you address. That is a simple, almost self-evident principle, but certainly a principle of fundamental importance for the communication between people. It is the Swedish philosopher Mats Furberg who has spoken, in this connection, of relevance to the addressee. "The fact that someone says something to somebody," writes Furberg, "entitles us to infer that the speaker thinks that the things said are relevant to the addressee." (Furberg 1971, 94)

Relevance to the addressee can assume two basic forms. You can impart information by the things you say or write, or you can issue directives: there are statements and there are imperatives.[3] It should be kept in mind, though,

---

2 In our experiences we are of course much more focused on the things experienced as apprehended in their own right than on the things experienced taken as possible models of other objects or situations. My point is that our experiences nevertheless function in both ways: as experiences of something in the world and as an acquisition of possible models of other circumstances in the world.

3 Consider, e.g., John Searle's distinction between two basic directions of fit between language and the world (Searle 1979). Perhaps the expressive aspect of language should be said to be the most elementary one, but note that statements are expressive of psychological states in the sense that they express beliefs and that imperatives are expressive of psychological states in the sense that they express wishes.

that utterances and texts can also form the starting-point of analogical thinking. It is normally an unintended feature of a piece of discourse that it has the capacity to form the starting-point of analogical thinking: news stories, summonses to meetings, et cetera, are not normally written in order to invite analogical thinking but in order to inform you or control your behaviour. Yet it is entirely possible to compose a piece of discourse meant, primarily, to invite analogical thinking. Your addressee will, justifiably, look for relevance to himself or herself in what you say or write. If your utterance or text does not possess any value worth mentioning as factual information or concrete direction, but can give food for thought in other ways, your addressee will, predictably, consider whether your utterance or text can be of interest as a source analog, an opportunity for analogical thinking. That is precisely what happens in connection with literature. Literary discourse could be described, coarsely and preliminarily, as discourse specially designed to invite analogical thinking in the addressee: to invite implicit or explicit reflection on the wider applicability of the states of affairs that are being described or the attitudes that are being expressed. Analogical thinking and the search for relevance to the addressee are two of the most fundamental mechanisms behind the emergence of literature and its continued existence.

I do not want to overstate that point. Certainly, innumerable psychological, linguistic, and social mechanisms are involved in literary transactions. I have pointed to analogical thinking and relevance to the addressee as being, taken together, of crucial importance, but a comprehensive understanding of what goes on when literature is created, transmitted, and understood requires the consideration of very many more processes.

Presentational Discourse

I just described literature as discourse composed specifically for inviting analogical thinking. When writing a literary work, an author does not assert or issue directives but introduces descriptions of actual or imagined realities, descriptions intended to form the starting-point of analogical thinking.[4] I refer to that special characteristic of literature as its "presentationality."

If presentational discourse does not, at least not primarily, convey information or directives, one may ask wherein its relevance to the addressee can

---

4 I do not mean that literary authors would self-consciously describe their texts as composed for inviting analogical thinking (a concept with which they may not be familiar), but that that description is nevertheless correct (as formulated from an outside perspective) as a characterization of what their texts are implicitly expected to achieve.

consist. I remarked in passing that such discourse can give food for thought. It can also provide affordances of many other kinds, like emotional values or formal delight. As Nicholas Wolterstorff has formulated it, speaking of what is, in practice, what I call presentational discourse, the author of a work of this kind presents its descriptions of actual or imagined realities to us "for us to reflect on, to ponder over, to explore the implications of, to conduct strand-wise extrapolation on. And he does this for our edification, for our delight, for our illumination, for our cathartic cleansing, and more besides." (Wolterstorff 1980, 233) Presentational literary discourse can afford cognitive, emotional, and aesthetic values of many kinds – but in this context I will not attempt to be more specific than that.

Before proceeding from presentationality to fictionality, I would like to introduce two caveats. First, I do not conceive of presentationality as an all-or-nothing affair. I have said that analogical thinking is possible in connection with all utterances and texts, indeed, in connection with all experience. The analogical potential of a text can be more or less activated by the reader or listener, and more or less pushed into the foreground by the writer or speaker. Think, for instance, of Sappho's famous poem on her beloved conversing with a man, a poem which begins, in Willis Barnstone's English translation (Barnstone 2009, 57):

> To me he seems equal to gods,
> that man who sits facing you
> and hears you near as you speak
> softly and laugh.

When originally sung by Sappho, her poem may well have referred to an actual situation and actual characters, and have been understood by her audience as being, among other things, a description of specific actual realities. Even so, its presentationality will have constituted an important aspect of its relevance, but not to the exclusion of an element of assertion. Readers or listeners today, however, will no doubt concentrate on the aspects of Sappho's poem that have wider applicability, like the attitude of the speaker and the experience that she interprets in words, and they will take less interest in the factual circumstances behind the situation described in the poem. Conversely, we know that even completely fictional presentational discourse can be written and read as something coming close to a seriously meant statement. That is what happens in the *roman à thèse*, emblematically represented by such novels as Harriet Beecher Stowe's *Uncle Tom's Cabin; or, Life Among the Lowly* (1852). Linguistic and literary transactions are often complex affairs, where many tendencies, and several kinds of relevance to the addressee, are active at the same time.

As a second caveat, I would like to emphasize that reference to presentational discourse is not sufficient if you want to explain or analyze the concept of literature. That concept is the complex product of a number of historical and cultural circumstances. I do believe, though, that what I have called presentationality captures very well a key defining property of what we call literature when we use that term in its predominant modern sense. (cf. Pettersson 2006) If we understand how presentational discourse operates, and how it can benefit an audience, we have a good preliminary grasp of what distinguishes literature from other types of verbal composition.

The Raison d'Être of Literary Fiction

The time has now come to address literary fiction directly. I will be quite brief, but nevertheless refer to a concrete example: J. M. Coetzee's novel *Disgrace* (1999). Let me begin by quoting the novel's slightly provocative opening paragraph.

> For a man of his age, fifty-two, divorced, he has, to his mind, solved the problem of sex rather well. On Thursday afternoons he drives to Green Point. Punctually at two p.m. he presses the buzzer at the entrance to Windsor Mansions, speaks his name, and enters. Waiting for him at the door of No. 113 is Soraya. He goes straight through to the bedroom, which is pleasant-smelling and softly lit, and undresses. Soraya emerges from the bathroom, drops her robe, slides into bed beside him. 'Have you missed me?' she asks. 'I miss you all the time,' he replies. He strokes her honey-brown body, unmarked by the sun; he stretches her out, kisses her breasts; they make love.

In the novel, we follow the male protagonist, David Lurie, as he successively loses the escort girl Soraya, his university position – he is fired because of a sexual relationship with a female student –, his money, his social life, and his hopes of composing a chamber opera, as he is being swallowed up by a poor and violent South African outback in the Eastern Cape. What he may have won instead, at the end of the novel, is a deeper insight into life and a larger capacity for compassion. However, there is little in the novel that is simply and straightforwardly good or bad. Even the opening passage just quoted should not, I believe, be read as being univocally ironic. The need of love, including physical love, is something David Lurie is not ready to renounce, or ask forgiveness for, even at high costs, and even if Coetzee does not endorse David Lurie's persistence in defending his integrity, such as it is, the author should not, I believe, be considered to distance himself from that aspect of his protagonist either.

As I said, *Disgrace* figures in my paper simply as an example of fictional discourse,[5] and what I want to state about fictional discourse can be said in very few words. My principal contention about fictional discourse is that literary fictional discourse is a variety of literary presentational discourse. Presentationality is a more fundamental characteristic of literature, also of literary fiction, than fictionality. The point of a novel like *Disgrace* has to do with its presentationality, with the fact that it invites, indeed is created to invite, analogical thinking. We can have no real interest in David Lurie per se, or in the woman who calls herself Soraya, already because they do not in fact exist. They are, literally, fictions, illusions. Yet the descriptions of these imagined characters, and of the events in which they are supposed to be engaged, can make us think and feel about many things. That is the whole point of the discourse to which David and Soraya belong. Indeed, the fiction is there to aid the presentationality; fictionality in literature is at the service of literature's presentationality. If, as an author, you are not restricted by what is or was actually the case, if you can transcend the factual and have recourse to fictionality, you can create stories which, when read as invitations to analogical thinking, have a larger potential for emotional, cognitive, and formal-aesthetic impact on your audience than if you had had to restrict yourself to narrating things that actually transpired. And that is the whole point of using fictionality in literature. In principle, as I have repeatedly underlined, real life and true accounts of events can function very well as releasers of analogical thinking. But fictional discourse offers us extra promising tools if we wish to tell stories not for their truth but for their analogical productiveness.

The Importance of Literary Fiction as a Subject of Research

The explanation of literary fictional discourse just offered can be seen as a deflationary account. I am saying that there is nothing very mysterious about literary fiction – the things recounted in literary fiction are invented, and expected to be understood as having been invented, and that is all there is to it – and I am saying that fictionality, while being a significant and potent feature, is by no means a fundamental characteristic of literature. I often get

---

5 Someone may want to point out that not everything in *Disgrace* is fictional: for example, the novel is clearly set in South Africa, partly in Cape Town, partly in the province of Eastern Cape. I do not deny that, but the fact has no real importance for my argument: I am speaking about the fictional aspects of the novel and their role.

the impression that both philosophers and students of literature invest the fictional in literature with more depth and enigma than that. As examples I could point to important thinkers about literature, like Wolfgang Iser, who tend to make the fictional into a key to the literary,[6] but also to frequently held convictions or frequently asked questions concerning fiction.

For instance, it is commonly assumed that a piece of fiction creates a fictional world. Philosophers have been prone to argue that fictional worlds contain not only elements explicitly or implicitly described in the work itself but also many other facts – it is not said in *Disgrace*, for example, that David Lurie has never travelled to the moon; nevertheless, many philosophers would argue, it is a fact in the fictional world of *Disgrace* that David Lurie never undertook such space travel. The philosophers will also make it sound as if the existence of such "extra" elements in a work were a feature particular to fictional discourse.[7] I do not believe, however, that there is anything in the world of such a work as *Disgrace* that is specific for fictional discourse, except the content's being invented, and being expected to be understood as having been invented. In a trivial sense, it is true that a novel like *Disgrace* contains a fictional world: a number of imagined states of affairs are introduced, like the imagined circumstance that David and Soraya have for some time been making love on Thursday afternoons in a flat in Windsor Mansions, and it could be said, metaphorically, that those imagined states of affairs, taken together, make up a fictional world. But in that trivial sense all texts that contain descriptions create textual worlds, the world of the states of affairs which are explicitly or implicitly described in the text: a newspaper notice about a car accident will also introduce ideas about certain states of affairs, and these could be said to make up the world of the text. It is an entirely unfounded belief that more could be contained in the world of a text, fictional or non-fictional, than the states of affairs that have been explicitly or implicitly introduced by the writer. Where would such extra content come from?[8]

Likewise, there is a much-discussed problem sometimes called the problem of fiction and emotion. That problem is often presented as the question of how we can have real feelings for made-up characters: how can we fear or pity persons who do not exist?[9] Let us suppose, for example, that some readers

---

[6] I am thinking, particularly, of Iser's attempt to explain the literary by reference to an interplay between the real, the fictive, and the imaginary. See, e.g., Iser 1991, 18–19.
[7] This discussion was initiated by David Lewis' article "Truth in Fiction." (Lewis [1978] 1983) The debate is still ongoing; see, e.g., Lamarque 2009, 197–202.
[8] I have analyzed the conception of a fictional world in more depth in Pettersson 2012b.
[9] This discussion, now very extensive, was sparked off by Colin Radford's paper "How Can We Be Moved by the Fate of Anna Karenina?" (Radford 1975). See also notes 10 and 11 below.

allege that they feel contempt towards Soraya for her prostituting herself or contempt towards David Lurie for his buying sex – is it really possible to harbour such real-world feelings towards non-existing characters, and if so, how can such feelings be explained? This may appear to be a deep problem in connection with fictional discourse, and a problem specifically associated with fictionality. I would say, however, that the problem of fiction and emotion has two aspects and that neither of them concerns fictionality in particular.

One aspect of the problem is the question of why feelings arise even in connection with representations of states of affairs that cannot have any direct consequences for us. A narrative involving invented characters is admittedly one example of such representations, but other obvious examples are narratives about real persons from bygone eras, or narratives about real persons that we are not likely ever to meet.[10] In all these cases, I would say that the narratives invite analogical thinking, and that the scenarios produced in our analogical thinking actualize risks and possibilities in our lives. The actualization of such risks and possibilities gives rise to feelings in us. *The thought* of the fictional characters does *occasion* our feelings, but I do not think we can therefore automatically say that *the fictional characters in themselves* are what our feelings are *directed at*.

That has to do with the second aspect of the problem of fiction and emotion, an aspect which concerns the very concept of an emotion. What do we want to mean by an "emotion"? Do we want to construe the concept in such a way that only *real* entities can be the objects of an emotion? And what do we require in order to call something the *object* of an emotion? If we construe the concept of an emotion liberally in these two respects, Soraya and David Lurie can no doubt be the objects of such emotions as fear or pity or contempt, but not if we construe the concept of the emotion restrictively.[11] How we should best define an emotion, and why we should construe the definition precisely in that manner, are questions about the concept of an emotion (and about our reasons for employing the concept), not about the nature of fictionality.

There is, thus, a belief, among many philosophers and students of literature, in the deep peculiarity of the fictional and in the literary-theoretical importance of that assumed peculiarity, and I think we should cease to subscribe to such beliefs. My real objective with this paper is not, however, to deflate the idea of fiction but to put literary fiction into perspective: to place literary fiction against a broader linguistic and psychological background and

---

10 That is an observation also made by Blakey Vermeule: see esp. Vermeule 2010, xiii. Vermeule's explanation of the feelings we have in such cases differs considerably from mine.
11 On this point, cf. also Pettersson 2000, 225–228.

try to make it clear how fictionality contributes towards the realization of the goals that lie behind literary discourse. There is no doubt in my mind that fictionality is a very important literary device, even if an understanding of what it is to be a fiction should not be taken as being at all central to an understanding of what it is to be literary. Nor do I doubt that there are genuine and interesting research questions with respect to fictionality, whether we approach the subject from a philosophical or a literary angle.

From a philosophical point of view, I suppose, ontological questions must be the ones most natural in connection with fictions. If you construct an ontological system, you will most probably want your system to cover all entities whatsoever, and then it becomes imperative to also raise the question of how fictional entities, including literary characters, should best be characterized in ontological terms. Moreover, the ontological question carries with it questions related to the concept of reference. How are we to interpret statements about fictional characters like David Lurie or Soraya? Do such statements refer, and if so, what do they refer to?[12]

If, on the other hand, you are a student of literature, another set of questions about literary fiction is likely to attract your interest, particularly if you occupy yourself with the history of literature. How has fictionality in texts been understood and evaluated in various societies over the centuries and millennia? And how have the functional possibilities that fictional devices can open up been successively discovered and put to use through the ages?[13] Both questions clearly concern matters that are of much direct and indirect importance in literary history.

Bibliography

Barnstone, Willis, ed. and trans. *Ancient Greek Lyrics*. 4th ed. Bloomington, IN: Indiana University Press, 2009.
Coetzee, J. M. *Disgrace*. London: Secker and Warburg, 1999.
Davies, David. "Fiction." *The Routledge Companion to Aesthetics*. Eds. Berys Gaut and Dominic McIver Lopes. London and New York: Routledge, 2001. 263–273.
Furberg, Mats. *Saying and Meaning: A Main Theme in J. L. Austin's Philosophy*. Oxford: Basil Blackwell, 1971.
Gallagher, Catherine. "The Rise of Fictionality." *The Novel*. Vol. 1. Ed. Franco Moretti. Princeton, NJ: Princeton University Press, 2006. 336–363.

---

[12] Concerning philosophical questions about fiction see, e.g., Davies 2001.
[13] Cf., e.g., Gallagher 2006.

Gentner, Dedre, Keith J. Holyoak and Boicho N. Kokinov, eds. *The Analogical Mind: Perspectives from Cognitive Science*. Cambridge, MA, and London (A Bradford Book): MIT Press, 2001.
Holyoak, Keith J. and Paul Thagard. *Mental Leaps: Analogy in Creative Thought*. Cambridge, MA, and London: MIT Press, 1995.
Iser, Wolfgang. *Das Fiktive und das Imaginäre: Perspektiven literarischer Anthropologie*. Frankfurt am Main: Suhrkamp, 1991.
Lamarque, Peter. *The Philosophy of Literature*. Malden, MA: Blackwell Publishing, 2009.
Lewis, David. "Truth in Fiction." [1978] Lewis' *Philosophical Papers*. Vol. 1. New York and Oxford: Oxford University Press, 1983. 261–275.
Pettersson, Anders. *Verbal Art: A Philosophy of Literature and Literary Experience*. Montreal: McGill-Queen's University Press, 2000.
— "Introduction: Concepts of Literature and Transcultural Literary History." *Literary History: Towards a Global Perspective. Vol. 1. Notions of Literature across Times and Cultures*. Ed. Anders Pettersson. Berlin and New York: Walter de Gruyter, 2006. 1–35.
— *The Concept of Literary Application: Readers' Analogies from Text to Life*. Basingstoke and New York: Palgrave Macmillan, 2012a.
— "The Idea of Fictional Worlds." *Mimesis: Metaphysics, Cognition, Pragmatics*. Eds. Gregory Currie, Petr Kot'átko and Martin Pokorný. London: College Publications, 2012b. 193–218.
Radford, Colin. "How Can We Be Moved by the Fate of Anna Karenina?" *Proceedings of the Aristotelian Society*, suppl. vol. 49 (1975): 67–80.
Searle, John R. "A Taxonomy of Illocutionary Acts." *Expression and Meaning: Studies in the Theory of Speech Acts*. Cambridge: Cambridge University Press, 1979. 1–29.
Vermeule, Blakey. *Why Do We Care about Literary Characters?* Baltimore: John Hopkins University Press, 2010.
Wolterstorff, Nicholas. *Works and Worlds of Art*. Oxford: Clarendon, 1980.

Lars-Erik Berg
Photons of the Human Mind: The Fiction of Personal Identity

A satirical cartoon on psychotherapy:
Therapist: You must go deep inside of yourself, Liza, behold your Ego and find the character of the feelings that worry you. You must find your Self!
Liza: I did try. I found nobody there.
(Author's translation from Swedish)

As long as you feel that your Self and your face are not fixed to each other totally, as long as they are only slightly loose from each other, then your face will never get rigid.
(Swedish radio entertainer, summer 2012)

Introduction: The Concept of Personal Identity

In any modern general encyclopedia we can learn that *photon* is a concept referring to light. Photons have *no rest mass*. This allows for *interactions* at *distances*. A photon may be refracted by *reflexion in a lens* or exhibit wave *interference with itself*. Still it can give *definite results* of its existence when its *position is measured*. I will allegorically use these physical observations to illustrate a position concerning the *fictional character* of *human personal identities*.

Personal identity and *fiction* have for thousands of years occupied just as weighty a place in the various art forms as they have for the last century in behavioral and cultural science. I will point out two positions in this development: ancient Greece and the heterogeneous picture of modern behavioral science and cultural analysis. The history of the concepts of personal and identity is multi-varied and puzzling.

The term *person* comes from Latin *per sonare,* which means "to sound through." Actors wore masks in the ancient drama and they talked through them. Thus *person* has much to do with the visible face, the mask. The term "identity" also comes from Latin *idem entitas*, meaning "the same essence/character."[1] Yes, the ancient Greek drama has a specific trait with high rele-

---

[1] Neither of the two terms were used in classic Latin and do not appear in my Latin dictionary, but they came to use during the Middle Ages (according to the *Concise Oxford Dictionary* 1993). To make things more mixed, the *Concise Oxford Dictionary* turns the two into synonyms (under both terms in the dictionary). On top of this the concept of *Individuality* is presented to make the two more precise. In the Greek drama individuality was opposite to both personality and identity; the latter both were presented on the screen as typical examples of general human fates, common to all men, far from specific individual traits. The two concepts are not easy

vance for identity. I take the Oedipus drama as an example. It is based on a religious belief in "fate." Fate directs the story and logic of Oedipus. The logic of his life and career is determined, *fatally* determined. This is the point. Translated into psychological terms, this means at least two important things. First, Oedipus' identity is presented as extrinsic to his own will, power and even consciousness; he does not know his own identity until too late. The story is composed as if Oedipus' psychic identity is predetermined, to be cheated or stolen from him, as an object. He has no more influence over his own destiny than to apply his whole life to an aimless struggle against himself. Second, although the determining forces for Oedipus' fate are *external, he still experiences* his identity as his own. This division gives the play its tragic character.

The exact counterpart of this external and fate-determined identity perspective is that of the postmodern world, both in the arts and in science. The list of examples is endless. In my opinion, in social psychology Anthony Giddens' *Modernity and Identity* (1991) gives a comprehensively brilliant exposé of the historical development of the theory of identity.[2] In philosophical terms, the Oedipus story is an illustrative example of fatalism: man is subjected to fate. Fate has control not only over important acts he commits but also over his total identity. Oedipus makes enormous efforts to escape the prediction of the oracle, but he still incarnates the identity of a man committing both parricide and maternal incest. Once this is done, the rest of his life is determined by this destiny. His social identity is contaminated by the fulfillment of his fate. And his self-induced stigma of blindness is like a symbol of his original blindness to his fate and identity.

Much later in history, another philosophical line of reasoning called *determinism* appears. In behavioral science the best-known examples of this are Locke's empiricism in philosophy and its modern counterpart, behaviorism in psychology, which is found in social psychology in versions of role theory from its classic days (Brown 1965, Newcomb, Turner and Converse 1965), up until now (Cook, Fine and House 1995; Aronson, Wilson and Akert 2005; Manstead and Hewstone 1996).[3]

---

to present in a clear cut way. This is reflected in behavioral science where the urge for unambiguous precision is hard.

[2] He also presents a tendency to a history of fatalism → determinism → voluntarism (1991, ch. 4), which I think could be developed to a conceptual/cultural history of the constellation "persona and identity."

[3] Manstead and Hewstone take up a long article on "personality" but none on "identity" although the latter appears with concepts like "gender" and "Self." The article on "personality" also presents several themes that are often found under the concept "identity." (1996) This might indicate intricate connections between "identity" and "personality."

This is paralleled on a middle-range level in structural functionalism in sociology. Here we have (semi-)causal reasoning: carrying a role *causes* the personality that the person has. It is not a question of choosing or of living in accord with one's innate biological tendencies; role playing *results* in a personality. This is also valid for both role theory and behaviorism although the two use different vocabularies. Talking of causes in these ways is to adopt determinism.

For two decades now there has been a growing third version: biology/neurology. The determinism is just as strong here. Today, it seems that, for example, the possibility to modify personality traits, even where psycho-social problems are evident, is mostly conceived as being a matter of medication.[4]

In psychotherapy, long treatment is used in different forms. Here we have *voluntarism* involved, as an alternative to fatalism and determinism. Anthony Giddens distinguishes these three in his historical exposé, assuring us that voluntarism is predominant in Western-oriented countries today. (Giddens 1991, ch. 4) The act of choosing is stressed. Voluntarism, as applied in our modern, individualistic society, implies that there is a real personal will that can be expressed and enacted by the individual, and/or by others that s/he influences. In today's research and philosophy on identity, will is linked to identity: we want to behave in a way that is consistent with our own identity. Identity seems to be of the utmost importance to people in our society. This is also verified by the growing number of books and other treatises on the subject, and the increasing occurrence of identity relevant factors in courts, in journalism, in discussions on ethnic and religious problems, and in therapeutic connections where identity problems are mentioned as a growing reason for therapeutic treatment.

Giddens and others refer these tendencies to increasing mobility and reflexivity, both institutionally and individually. This trait is the main theme of Giddens' theory of identity, with its stress on increasing flexibility. (1991, ch. 3, 4, 7)

Thus we have an increasing concentration on identity problems in the world influenced by Western ways of life and of modernization at large. If identity is a set of factors that are intrinsic to the individual and his/her biological and psychic setting, it is difficult to explain the historically increasing concentration on and questioning of identity; it is today conceived as something quite different from only 50 years ago. Not only problems concerning people's experience of (or the *phenomenon* of) identity, but even the theoretical

---

[4] This can be seen as illogical; psycho-social problems should be solved by psycho-social help, not medical.

concept of identity itself are subject to rapid changes and developments. (Beck and Beck-Gernsheim 1991, Bauman 2001)

This development raises a problem: what is the *basis* of identity? Is there a "substance" that is bound to the individual as such? And, given that there is, how is it that cultural and structural developments seem to have such a great influence on people's identity and their experience of it? Is there a greater concern for identity problems today than formerly, as many researchers maintain?[5]

Identity and Personality as Sets of Meanings

I am male, 67 years, married and a father. These conditions are basic to my identity, and at the same time and to the same extent are essential meanings about myself. Identity is made up of a system of meanings linked to each other in a fashion that is, at best, more or less coherent and patterned. The study of identity and its development can be done by investigating these systems; identity is constructed from meanings that have bearing on myself as a visible actor. When I look at myself and see an identifiable object, I see my identity.

There is, however, an illuminating distinction to make between identity and personality. The author carried out a pilot interview study with some friends. One result was relatively consistent: identity is regarded as more external. My identity is what "society" defines me to be. I am looked upon by most people as male, in his 60s, a professional behavioral scientist and so on. These are socially recognized traits; this is my identity.

Personality is more internal: it is my individual way of being a male in his 60s, a professional behavioral scientist and so on. However, even personality is seen as composed of a set of meanings. Therefore both identity, as externally determined, and personality, as internally determined, derive their components from one and the same set of phenomena: meanings linked to human beings and their psychic and social characteristics.[6]

It might introduce a difficulty to draw a sharp distinction between the two, as they spring from the same source. This difficulty is recognized in the literature. To make things worse, researchers distinguish the two aspects, social identity and personal identity, from each other (Augoustinos *et al.* 2006), thus

---

[5] There is an almost endless list of contributors to the social psychological identity literature. I mention only Mead, Christopher Lasch, Erving Goffman (almost any one of his books), Anthony Giddens and Ulrich Beck.

[6] These opinions from my respondents are also on the whole in accord with definitions of the two terms found in current textbooks and with the writings of the founder of modern identity theory, Erik Erikson.

mixing them with each other and at the same time separating social and personal aspects.

A Pragmatist View of Identity as Meaning

Pragmatist philosophy and related social psychology, developed by Charles Cooley, George Herbert Mead and John Dewey, can substantially help us to bring order into the matter. My inspiration is primarily Mead (1969).

An object's meaning is not primarily a question of intrinsic traits in the object or of innate capacities of a person relating to the object. It is primarily a phenomenon derived from the responses that "Other" gives to gestures made by "Self" to the object. So, if Self (one-year-old Anne) makes gestures, either physical or vocal or both, to the object "lamp," the meaning of the object is found in the response that Other gives to Anne's gestures. In the end, the vocal gesture "lamp" comes to mean the lamp and its light. This indicates the path from the dog's or cat's existence within conditioned associations but without conscious meaning, to an existence with meaningful words and conscious experiences of relations between human subjects and all the objects in the world that they inhabit.

The cat or dog has a twofold relation to the object, while the human being has, depending on the presence of Other, a threefold relation, from which consciousness of meaning with the object emerges from Other's reaction to Self's gestures toward the object. Meaningless vocal gestures are transformed into "significant symbols," to use Mead's term. (1969) In the same process it also gives to the user of vocal gestures in relation to other such users a characteristic that is the basis for both personality and identity: a possibility to discover, observe and thereby *objectify* Self.[7] Both personality and identity are thus results of vocal gestures becoming significant symbols, making not only the material object in question, for example "chair," meaningful, but also Self and Other as objects for Self's perception/action. Thus meanings, emerging in social processes, are the basis for the process of Homo sapiens becoming human. Language in its incipient stages creates human beings rather than the other way around. Homo sapiens, by becoming a member of the language community, can observe, and hence objectify, Self and Other, and thereby become fully human.[8]

---

[7] I do not here have possibility to go into the theory. I can just refer to Mead's representation of it (Mead 1969, ch. 9–11). I have also given my own extensive interpretations in Berg 1976, 1992.
[8] Some of the recent paleontology indicates that Homo sapiens' best advantage over Homo neanderthalensis was the anatomical possibilities to develop a differentiated language.

Thus: spontaneous vocal gestures in social interaction → meanings → significant symbols → meaningful objects in the world → e.g. Self-identity and Other.

Now let us return to the distinction between identity and personality, and the possibility for conscious thought to observe them. Personality, taken in the above sense of the experience of a conscious "inner" psychic world, has an objective basis. This goes for sex (but not for *experienced* sex, i.e. gender), age and several more subtle traits, for example the psychologically important character of temperament in so far as it is influenced by the individually specific biochemistry. Without biochemistry, you would have no temperament at all. But the *meaning* of your temperament for yourself is not at all identical with the biochemical basis for it.

In the case of purely external reality, there is much evidence of objective sorts of meaning systems occurring: stones are hard and heavy in comparison with grass or water. This is true for anybody and much easier to agree about than Self's or Other's degree of aggressiveness or kindness. The latter are more exposed to subjective evaluations and reactions. What for Abel is a high degree of aggression in Caesar's behavior is not so for Bertha. Caesar's personality is not so easy to have fixed opinions about. The characteristics of a stone are easier.

Whether we regard it as (internal) personality or (external) identity, the degree of subjectivity is high concerning a great number of human traits in psyche and behavior. This depends on the subjective flow of meaning.

In pragmatic social psychology, it is impossible to understand either Self's personality or identity without also understanding Other's evaluations of this Self. Both should by definition be understood as something relating to the individual *and* his/her social environment. But if we take only identity, this is more evident than for personality, given that identity is more ascribed from "outside."

Now, what is the substance of the ascription that Other makes to Self's identity and personality? Is it objectively true? And is it made (by Other) and received (by Self) in a pure form as Other's response to Self's gestures? Does Self receive objective truth from Other about Self's identity?

No! There are many subjective interpretations, misunderstandings and errors in Other's reactions to Self. If Self is to get correct information about his/her identity, this is only possible if there is a third, objective, source of knowledge. But there is no such source. What is given is only Other's reactions to Self's gestures. This is the only material available to Self to create a meaning of his/her Self. Self cannot observe his/her own gestures at the moment of giving them. (This thesis may be easiest to accept concerning small infants who have not yet stabilized a conception of the world.)

There is, however, one more external resource for Self's experience of identity with more objective information than Other's opinion. This is societal, cultural, opinion. Mead called this "the Generalized Other." (1969, part 4) It is the ensemble of all Others that Self has a connection with. Look at this actor's solidity for a second, using the example of HBT identity.

At present, homosexuality is accepted in many Western countries. Only 30 years ago, it was not. The situation for HBT people is still very vague. A transsexual person is often seen as odd, showing patterns of life that are difficult to accept in society. This equals saying that the Generalized Other has not been able to make up his mind concerning these people. The fact that they feel problems concerning their sexual profile and preferences confirms this. To be HBT is problematic. The identity that other people ascribe to HBT people is ambiguous and problematic. This is true in spite of the fact that medical science today recognizes that there are not only two sexual physical standards. Sex is not a dichotomy any longer, it is a continuum. Thus it should not be such a problem as it seems to be. Science has got rid of the problem in an objective way, but people in society subjectively have not. This is still so hard to accept that many people prefer not to "come out."

This example concerns both personality and identity. Take another example, with far fewer physical aspects, that is extreme on the other side: Woody Allen made a film in which he played the character Zelig, which is also the title of the film (1983). Zelig takes on several, widely different identities, which are associated with different professional capacities, for example the physician working in a hospital. Allen's story is built on a real model, and there are many stories about similar cases.[9]

My point is that Allen's figure concerns both identity and personality, and that Zelig easily lets the two merge. When he is seen by Other as a special person, he readily adopts that picture as his own. Without difficulty, he reports that he can feel within himself tendencies to go into this or that role; Zelig does not distinguish between identity and personality. These are for him aspects of the same phenomenon.

This concerns traits that are not objectively as clearly distinguishable as biological sex or age. It concerns purely psychic and social phenomena; Zelig's behavior is very much a reaction to what Other thinks he is.

Now let us go back to the Meadian theory of meaning: an object's meaning for Self is the response that Other gives to Self's gestures. (1969) If Other tells Self that he is a doctor, Self might be able to perform a doctor's activities, so

---

[9] The classic would be Robert Louis Stevenson's Dr. Jekyll and Mr. Hyde-story (1886), which has had great influence on literature as well as psychiatry.

long as they are at all known to him/her. This is known in social psychology as a version of "the self-fulfilling prophecy," resting on what is called "labeling theory" and related sources in literature. (C. H. Cooley, H. Becker, E. Lemert, R. Laing, E. Goffman, T. J. Scheff) Very briefly, labeling theory says: treat a person as a criminal/teacher/alcoholic/intelligent person/stupid person/schizophrenic, or whatever, and he will become one, as long as enough important and established Others confirm the ascription for a long enough period.

This is a type of general identity theory, applied to deviant behavior especially, that grew rapidly from the 60s for about two to three decades. Then it was shown to be not that simple to apply. Today there are many psychological and biological theories that take up the theme of deviance in its diverse forms. Labeling theory has no strong position today. But it is evidently of high relevance for identity theory.

How, then, is its relation to Meadian theory of meaning? It is strong. Mead maintains that the sort of meaning system (about Self) that we call identity is derived from Other's response to Self's acts. If I choose to work with behavioral science, this should be referred to historical facts about Other's comments about me in my early life. It does not say anything about my "real" inclinations. It says that I do not build up my identity from facts about myself, but from Other's responses to acts that I do. (1969)

To draw the conclusion: Most objects in my reality are such that I can have some objective basis for my knowledge about them, even my personality, although it is much more esoteric than stones, wood, chairs and my own mother. There is one object of which I can have no first-hand knowledge: my own identity. I can see it only indirectly through the reflections that Other gives to me, revealing Other's reactions to my acts.

There is a basis for my identity that relates to me and my Self, namely my own acts, but I cannot see them in the process of doing them, only after they have been done, and the meaning that I can then ascribe to them is derived not from myself or my actions but from Other's responses to and evaluation of them.

To summarize: (1) Meaning is created in interaction between at least two subjects and an object. Then the only way I have access to my identity as a meaningful object is (2) to receive Other's reactions to my own actions. If Other says I am a good boy, giving my candy to Caesar, then I establish the meaning of "good boy" through this giving my candy to Caesar. This is a social evaluation. (3) Meaning capacity is created in both the *cognitive* sense of being able to establish, grasp and keep a meaning with an object, *and* in the *emotional* sense, the evaluation of it.

Consequences for the phenomenon of identity creation: without Other reacting to me, I will not be able to develop a consciousness of myself as a human person at all. I will remain on an intelligence level more like the other primates, given mostly to the kind of intelligence that is dominated by behavior conditioning/reinforcement and innate instincts.[10]

Other gives me the specific intelligence of being conscious of Self, to know my own person as an active human being with choices to make for my activities. Both the *existence*, and the *specific character* of identity emerge for Self through Other's responses.

Personal identity's specific character has two main aspects which can be called Gestalt and Narrative. Both are necessary for developing a persistent will and choice of life career. (Berg 2008)

There is one special concept that makes this theory more accessible: *distance*. This concept literally means: standing in two positions.[11] To have a consciousness of an object necessarily implies to have a certain distance to it. If you are too close to the object, you cannot see it clearly, nor be aware of its characteristics.

Think of your own perspective on your own eyes. That perspective is evidently impossible in pure form. You need a mirror to see your eyes. This reflective process – in its psychical version – is what Mead means by the necessity of having an Other to discover yourself. Charles Cooley developed a special concept for this aspect of identity formation: the Looking Glass Self. ([1902] 1967) But Mead goes far beyond this concept, while still recognizing it.

Identity as Imitation and Discrimination

Imitation is a necessary aspect of identity development. This behavior probably depends neurologically on the "mirror neurons." (Ward 2012, ch. 3) The basic function is that when Self sees Other (or Other sees Self) performing some behavior, there is an automatic neurological tendency to perform the same behavior. This is also true concerning emotions and feelings. For example, when Self sees Other's hand getting hurt, Self can feel the pain in his own hand. The functions of these mirror neurons have been known practically for millenia, and they have always been used as tools by good pedagogues in child rearing and education. Without them, Homo sapiens would not be the human being that we know.[12]

---

10 Today we gain more knowledge of presumed Self-consciousness among certain animals. I would say that this occurs in coherence with their related language capacity.
11 Photons, we remember, have the capacity to exist at two points at the same time.
12 The mirror neurons are also known in many other "higher" mammals, as primates and apes. However, their functions are not merely to get individuals to imitate each other. Imita-

In the case of Mead's theory, the imitative mechanism has a special importance: vocal gestures are heard by the user in the same way as by the receiver. The same response is called forth in both sender and receiver, and depending on the receiver's action, both start to exchange "roles" with each other, being both sender and receiver sequentially. When it comes to vocal gestures, this evolutionally is the beginning of human speech. One actor calls forth similar reactions in himself as in Other. (Mead 1969, ch. 8–10, Berg 1976, ch. 2) This makes him well equipped to respond to Other's response to him; the response is already directed neurologically.

But when the gestures indicate the individuals themselves and their acts, for example a cry of physical pain, rather than external objects, the process ends up in "taking the attitude" of the Other to one's Self, and the result will be consciousness of this Self. Other's cry calls forth my own pain reaction. I cry myself, and a rebounding process starts between us. So, this is the beginning of identity formation: I see myself at a distance, by seeing my acts (and body) in Other's reactions to them, where the direct reference or indication of my identity is found. I take it back only indirectly. My identity is fiction, because it is *not me* that I see, but *Other's reactions to me*.

A very easy example of identity and physical pain: Anne hurts her knee when falling. Mother confirms the pain by voice and mimicry. Anne's cry intensifies. She feels the pain more strongly after mother's confirmation.

Identity seems much like a paradox. I am nearest to myself of everything in the world, but I cannot see me. But this is not paradoxical, as soon as we realize that I am too close to myself to be able to see me.

But still, there is something genuine with myself, in spite of all this. The paradox remains a paradox, but turned upside down. How come? It is understandable as soon as we realize that Other, pointing out who, and where, I am for myself, also gives me a capacity to build up a story of myself. Other has told me that I exist as an *actor*. When act adds to act in a long chain, a history of my life is built up. In it I can walk to and fro. I can construct a picture (Gestalt) of myself and my history (Narrative). I can find consistency in this scenery, because my first views of myself are pictures of something coherent. The Gestalt in its Narrative is not chaotic, if I am lucky enough to have coherent Others to reflect my acts. I try, therefore, to keep a coherent picture of myself.[13]

---

tion does not always occur, and the mirror neurons also have other functions, making up a rather complicated picture to analyze.

13 In fact, almost all social psychologists discussing this matter define the concept of identity in terms of coherence (James, Cooley, Mead, Berger, Goffman, Lasch, Giddens, Beck and many others).

Thus: when I meet a person that reflects and defines me in a manner that is totally strange in relation to all my earlier definitions, then I can set up a defense, if I disagree with the new person. In this way I get the capacity to resist reflections that are "wrong" or that do not harmonize with my actual Self-image.

So, the new paradox is this one: my only way to know myself derives from Other's definitions of me. They cannot possibly reflect a "reality." Therefore I am exposed to fictitious and virtual pictures of myself. But in this way, I develop a capacity to keep a definition of myself that I am content with and that does not violate the definitions that I have built up until now.

The Paradoxical Game of Identity Fiction: An Example

I will end this exposition with an example. In July 2011, Anders Bering Breivik killed about 70 young people on the island of Utöya near Oslo in Norway, after having detonated a large bomb in the government center of the city. An intensive debate about the personality and identity of Breivik started. It was still going on in court and in the mass media during autumn 2012.

Google makes available a huge mass of information about Breivik. I will point out one single identity/personality dilemma that Breivik himself, the agents in the court, and, not least, all the people who mourn their children, siblings and friends, have to face. Is Breivik mentally ill? Or is he not? He himself tries to prove that he is totally sane and responsible for his acts, which he maintains have been right. He is said to have practically no relation to his father, who does not figure much in the process. However, his mother does, although not as a witness. Breivik as a child and youth was close to her and seems to have a deep and complicated relation to her.

These glimpses of a family story invite confusion – for Breivik and his observers.

Many reflections can be made around the scenario as an application of my main theme: identity and personality. The concepts refer to three different areas:
1. the *inner (psychic) life* of an individual (sane or insane, rational or blocked in racism?);
2. the *external social structure* (murder, court, experts, juridical positions etc.);
3. the *concrete social/cultural life* (the court process, media, parents/relatives/friends, political agents, scientific statements etc.) that he is involved in.

Early in the juridical process, a radical contradiction occurred. Two psychiatric experts maintained together in court that Breivik is mentally ill with a paranoid schizophrenic disturbance. Soon after this, two other experts maintained that he is not mentally ill. And after this, the two pairs of experts carried on a public discussion in court about their different opinions.[14] A female senior journalist problematizes the question of Breivik's possible mental illness. She points to his total emotional "frigidity" for the catastrophe he has created, and that he weeps quietly and happily when he sees pictures of the ruined buildings caused by his bomb in central Oslo. This reaction was also shown in TV during the process.

Breivik explains that his "frigidity" is a result of extended rational training that he conducted before realizing his mission to save Norway from Islamic infiltration. He feels sad *and* good about this. He also takes an active part in the discussion of him as ill or sane, convinced that he is sane and therefore responsible for his acts. The journalist decides his status as being mentally sane but unstable. To me, Breivik gives the impression of having a stable personality, although also blocked up. All this refers to area (1) above.

I also get the impression, however, that a major part of the story does not concern Breivik's psychic status but more the court's necessary compliance with many people who need to see conviction and penalty exercised, and with juridical and psychiatric rationality. This refers to a combination of areas (2) and (3).

The point of departure for our judgment is that a *person* (area (1)) is either mentally sound or ill. The court here should be able to make the right decision (area (2)). But if you feel it is impossible, as a professional psychiatrist or judge/jury, to deem Breivik as either sane or insane, then you risk being regarded as incapable of delivering reliable knowledge. To understand the case, it might be a better choice to concentrate on the perspective that persons are not racist without living in a culture of racism (area (3)).

Photons both exist and do not exist, and they can exist in two places at the same time. Traditional logic and understanding has difficulties with this pattern of quantum physics. Likewise, to decide whether Breivik is sane or not is difficult, and not productive. He both is and is not, just as cultures can be racist in spite of the scientific fact that there is only one human species with only superficial racial differences and in spite of government authorities' asser-

---

14 My reported material on Breivik, among them authoritative statements from different psychiatrists/ psychologists, that Breivik both is and is not insane, can be found in the confusing and rich documentation on address Google.com: anders behring breivik psychiatric evaluation.

tion of non-racism. The scenario of racism and of sanity/insanity in relation to this is built on fiction about human identities, and hence does not exist. However, the problem of racism exists and has consequences. This case is similar to the photon.

Many reflections can be made around the scenario as applied to the theme of identity and personality and their reference to all the three above-mentioned areas. Understanding is impossible as long as we keep these areas distinct from each other.

One year and a half after the catastrophe Breivik is receiving admiration and love letters from people, mostly young women.

The nationally well-known Swedish TV literature presenter Daniel Sjölin said in his Summer program on Swedish Radio in 2012: "The Self is not a place for the truth about ourselves; it is a place for lifelong Self-deception." (author's translation) This can be applied to Breivik's Self-image and with the same right also to the intensive social and cultural scenario that took place. This tragic fact illustrates both the fictive and the real consequences of identity fiction and identity's position in different places and persons.

Bibliography

Allen, Woody. *Zelig*. [Film drama]. 1983.
Aronson, Elliot. Timothy D. Wilson and Robin M. Akert. *Social Psychology*. Boston. MA: Pearson Education International, 2005.
Augoustinos, Martha, Iain Walker and Ngaire Donaghue. *Social Cognition: An Integrated Approach*. London: Sage, 2006.
Bauman, Zygmunt. *The Individualized Society*. Cambridge: Polity, 2001.
Beck, Ulrich and Elisabeth Beck-Gernsheim. *Individualization: Institutionalized Individualism and Its Social and Political Consequences*. Theory, Culture & Society series. London [u.a.]: Sage, 2002.
Berg, Lars-Erik. *Människans födelse – en socialpsykologisk diskussion kring G. H. Mead och J. Piaget* [The birth of the human being]. Diss. Göteborg: Korpen, 1976.
— *Den lekande människan. En socialpsykologisk analys av lekandets dynamik* [Man playing]. Lund: Studentlitteratur, 1992.
— "Aspects of Identification in Computer Gaming." *HumanIT* 9.3 (2008): 37–61.
Brown, Roger. *Social Psychology*. New York: Free Press, 1965.
Concise Oxford Dictionary. 7th reprint. Oxford: Oxford University Press, 1993.
Cook, Karen S., Gary Alan Fine and James S. House, eds. *Sociological Perspectives on Social Psychology*. Boston, MA: Allyn and Bacon, 1995.
Cooley, Charles Horton. *Human Nature and the Social Order*. New York: Scribners, [1902] 1967.
Giddens, Anthony. *Modernity and Self-Identity*. Cambridge: Polity, 1991.
— *The Transformations of Intimacy: Sexuality, Love, and Eroticism in Modern Societies*. Cambridge: Polity, 1992.

Lasch, Christopher. *Haven in a Heartless World. The Family Besieged*. New York: Basic Books, 1977.
— *The Culture of Narcissism*. New York: Warner Books, 1979.
Manstead, Anthony S. R. and Miles Hewstone, eds. *The Blackwell Dictionary of Social Psychology*. Oxford: Blackwell, 1996.
Mead, George H. *Mind, Self and Society: From the Standpoint of a Social Behaviorist*. Ed. Charles W. Morris. Phoenix Books. Chicago, IL: University of Chicago Press, [1934] 1969.
Newcomb Theodore M., Ralph H. Turner and Philip E. Converse. *Social Psychology: The Study of Human Interaction*. New York: Holt, 1965.
Stevenson, Robert Louis. *The Strange Case of Dr Jekyll and Mr Hyde*. London: Longman, 1886.
Ward, Jamie. *The Student's Guide to Social Neuroscience*. New York: Psychology Press, 2012.

Live Fiction: Play & Performances

Ayling Wang
Interaction Between the Reader, the Critic and the Author: The Qing Dramatist Hong Sheng's Historical Play *Changshengdian* and Wu Yiyi's Commentary

The Performance and Publication of *Changshengdian* and the Emergence of Wu Yiyi's Commentary on the Play

In the year 1688, a poet in Beijing composed a remarkable play. One year later, the play premiered in the Imperial Palace. It won immediate popularity and created a sensation in the literary and theatrical worlds; and before long a grand gathering was held in the capital. All the official and academic celebrities were invited, and they were anxious to see for themselves this stirring masterpiece – Hong Sheng's (1645–1704) *Changshengdian* [The Palace of Eternal Youth].[1] Indeed, the play's success was so striking that it resulted in a political incident. Since it had been performed in a period of national mourning (1689), a censor, Huang Liuhong, reported the event to Emperor Kangxi (r. 1662–1722) as an offense to the court. The Emperor then read the play himself and was infuriated by what he considered Hong Sheng's deliberate use of historical events to provoke Chinese nationalistic sentiments. The Emperor decided to punish the author and the audience severely. Consequently, Hong Sheng's close friend Zhao Zhishen (1662–1744), who was responsible for the gala performance, was dismissed from office. Hong Sheng was expelled from the Imperial Academy, and nearly fifty other scholars were struck off the official list. This was the famous

---

[1] The English version of *Changshengdian* used in this paper is Hong Sheng 1955b, hereafter cited as *TPEY*. While this translation is somewhat prosaic, it is, on the whole, accurate and lucid. I therefore generally follow it, though I occasionally propose revised or alternate translations of certain passages. The Chinese text used is Hong Sheng 1955a, which includes Wu Shufu's comments, hereafter cited as *CSD*. I have also consulted the edition annotated by Tseng Yong-i 1985, who not only offers detailed footnotes for the play, but also discusses the arrangement of music in terms of the development of the dramatic plot, see also Hong Sheng 1988.

case referred to in the couplet: "Alas! For a one-night performance of the play, *Changshengdian*, he forfeited official rank for life."[2]

Contrary to general expectation, however, after Hong Sheng returned to his hometown Hangzhou, *Changshengdian* was published by his disciple Wang Zeng with the help of his close friend Wu Yiyi (dates are unknown, alive in 1692) and Chu Seng in 1704, and was further endorsed by many famous scholars such as You Tong, Mao Qiling (1623–1716), Zhu Yizun (1629–1709), Wang Tingmo and Zhu Xiang, who wrote prefaces or inscriptions for the play.[3] In the meantime, the play was performed in Suzhou, Hangzhou, and Songjiang: and finally Emperor Kangxi's favorite minister Cao Yin (1658–1712), the Textile Commissioner of Jiangning, presided over a three-day grand performance in honor of Hong Sheng in Nanking [Nanjing] (1704). From then on, this play again became a favorite during feasts and other special occasions, and its text has also been widely read and cherished.

Changshengdian is a *chuanqi* play which takes as its theme the love story of Emperor Ming Huang (r. 713–756) (r. title, Emperor Xuanzong) of the Tang Dynasty and his favorite consort Lady Yang Yuhuan (i.e. Yang Guifei, 719–756).[4] Among the masterpieces of Chinese drama, Hong Sheng's *Changshengdian* is one of the most famous romances in Chinese literary history.[5] For a thousand years, this love story has frequently been a subject of literary works. By the end of the Ming dynasty, there were already twenty-one plays dealing with this popular love story.[6] The popularity of *Changshengdian* and its great

---

[2] See Chang Weiping, ed. *Guochao shiren zhenglüe chubian* [The First Collection of the Biographical References of the Qing Poets] (N.p. 1842), *juan* 11, quoted by Chen Wannai 1970, 131. For a further discussion of this political incident of *Changshengdian*'s performance, see Zhang Peiheng 1979, 371–404 and Chen Wannai 1970, 119–134.

[3] Among the various editions of *Changshengdian*, the Baxi caotang editon published in the Kangxi period is the earliest, which, however, has only one preface by Hong Sheng's disciple Wang Zeng, and one postscript by Chu Seng (pseudonym). As Chu Seng points out, "When the play was first performed, it resulted in a political incident in Kangxi's reign. The first edition of *Changshengdian*, compared with other plays, is therefore very precious and matchless; this is why we are anxious to publish it." (Hong Sheng 1954, "Preface").

[4] *Chuanqi* originally referred to the "tales of the strange" of the Tang dynasty (618–906). Literally meaning "the transmission of the marvelous," *chuanqi* became generally accepted as a form of southern drama in Ming (1368–1644), and as the antithetical designation to *zaju* [variety play] during the early Qing dynasty (1644–1911) after the earlier form had already passed its zenith.

[5] *Changshengdian* is acclaimed as one of the China's "Four Great Classical Dramas," along with *The Peony Pavilion, The Peach Blossom Fan* and *The Story of the Western Wing*.

[6] But except for the plays *Wutongyu* [Rain on the Phoenix Tree] by Bai Pu, *Jinghong ji* [The Frightened Swan] by Wu Shimei, *Caihao ji* [The Colored Writing Brush] by Tu Long, some songs of *Kuxiangnang* [Crying for the Scented Bag] by Guan Hanqing, Wang Bocheng's *Tianbao yishi zhugongdiao* [Medley of the Splendor of the Tianbao Period], and Sun Yu's *Tianbao qushi*

influence on the period's drama are due to the fact that in his play Hong Sheng surpassed all previous works on the same theme, both in his artistic treatment of the subject and in his poetic technique. In fact, as a culmination of a number of earlier treatments of the tale in poetry and music drama, the dramatic achievement of *Changshengdian* has won praise from all connoisseurs of Chinese drama. The famous Qing drama critic Liang Tingnan (1796–1861), for example, praised *Changshengdian* as "one of the greatest masterpieces in the history of Chinese drama." He further noted that, "the language and musical composition are beautiful and the theatrical arrangement of its plot is perfect." (Liang Tingnan 1982, 267) Again, *Changshengdian* is a play which the famous Qing critic Jiao Xun (1763–1820) "values above all the others." (1982, 154)

While *Changshengdian*'s spectacular reception results from its text and its performance, interestingly, the transmission of Hong's artistry owes much to his friend Wu Yiyi. Right after Hong finished his text, Wu contributed an annotated, scene-by-scene commentary on the play, which Hong warmly welcomed and for which he was especially grateful. Nevertheless, since *Changshengdian* is a long play with fifty scenes, some theatrical troupes have arbitrarily shortened the play for commercial purpose. Wu Yiyi was really angry with this action, and he emulated Feng Menglong's method of theatrical adaptation to abridge the *Changshengdian* to twenty-eight scenes. While Hong Sheng was also displeased with the arbitrary adaptation of his play, in the "Introduction" to *Changshengdian*, he not only praised Wu Yiyi's adapted version as "proper and irreplaceable," but also reminded the theatrical troupes, "Be sure to find my friend Wu Yiyi's adapted version for rehearsal if you need an abridged version of the *Changshengdian* for public performance." (1988, 1) Hong Sheng also gave his affirmation to Wu Yiyi's commentary, commending its comprehensive elaboration of the thematic construction and artistic thinking of his play. Hong Sheng's instantaneous and welcoming feedback to Wu Yiyi's commentary is significant evidence of "the reader's response." The arbitrary revisions were caused by the differences in reading influenced by different visions from diverse readers. While Hong Sheng's dissatisfaction with those arbitrary revisions of his play was based on his expectations as a writer and his appreciation of Wu Yiyi's reception and commentary, he was content with Wu Yiyi's abridged version since he was able to take the stand of a new reader and a new audience of his own play. Hong Sheng's positive response clearly discloses the fact that he regarded Wu Yiyi as his confidant and Wu Yiyi was gifted with unusual insight and good taste.

[A History in Song of the Tianbao Period], those plays were already scattered and lost before Hong Sheng's time.

As a matter of fact, Hong Sheng's appreciation and endorsement of Wu Yiyi's commentary also demonstrate a fusion of respective aesthetic views of the reader, the critic and the author. The discernible interactions between Hong and Wu in the commentated text suggest the possibility of a two-way interpretation. The convergences and divergences of artistic understanding between the author's aesthetic experience and the critic's comprehension of the author's artistry through his own aesthetic experience are worthy of close examination. Wu's commentary examines poetry and narrative literature, bringing Chinese dramatic theory to a new height. Especially noteworthy are his elaboration on the "*qing* [love] cult" and his employment of narratology in analyzing the text of a *chuanqi* play.

On the Thematic Design of the Text: The Interpretation of the Idea of Love (*qing*) in *Changshengdian*

In his "Introduction" to *Changshengdian*, Hong Sheng has given a clear account of the process of his writing this play (1988, 1), which shows his positive response to his friends' comment on his manuscript. Over more than a decade, Hong Sheng revised the play three times, each time changing its thematic focus. At last, this play, in which Hong voices his ideal of love by focusing on the "unswerving love pledge with the golden hairpin and jewel box" between Emperor Ming Huang and Lady Yang, was entitled *Changshengdian*. In *Changshengdian*, Hong Sheng concentrates his attention on the love theme, and further, has greatly improved and perfected his theatrical design. In 1688, Hong Sheng completed his masterpiece, *Changshengdian*. Hong composed twelve plays in all, yet in his mind, *Changshengdian* was the fruit of a lifetime's painstaking labor.

It should be noted that behind Hong's dramatic writing is a literary concept inherited from the Chinese poetic tradition. In his preface to *Changshengdian*, Hong Sheng mentions that, "to compose the play, I have borrowed and quoted from the historical context of the former splendor of the Tianbao period." The expression used in this quote in Chinese, *duan zhang qu yi*, literally means "to take a passage from its context and make a deliberated interpretation according to its literal meaning," reveals that, indeed, Hong Sheng intends to formulate his own view of the material and express something far beyond the narrative interest of the Lady Yang story itself.

Though the love story of Emperor Ming Huang and Lady Yang was depicted frequently before Hong Sheng's time, it was usually presented as a collection of historical anecdotes. For the popular Chinese audience, the main attraction of those earlier works was the reenactment of historical events whose proximity to reality they are willing to accept from the start. However, due to his discontent with most previous historical and dramatic works on the same story, Hong Sheng deleted much of the historians' "indecorous accounts" of sexual misbehavior on the part of his protagonists.[7] While drawing information for plotting from other sources, Hong Sheng relied largely on Bai Juyi's "Song of Everlasting Sorrow" ("Changhenge") as his emotional source. In the *Changshengdian*, by changing the title from Bai Juyi's (772–846) "everlasting sorrow" (*changhen*) to "eternal life" (*changsheng*), Hong Sheng implies an unprecedented interpretation of the love between Emperor Ming Huang and Lady Yang. In the "Preface" Hong Sheng clearly explains his motive for composing the play:

> After reading Bai Letian's [Bai Juyi] "*Changhenge*" and Bai Pu's *Wutongyu* [Rain on the Phoneix Tree], I felt sick for several days. The Southern play *Jinghong ji* [The Frightened Swan] also cannot avoid depicting lewdness. A dramatist will not excel others if he does not describe *qing* [love] in his works. But recently most dramatists have composed unreasonably fictitious love dramas. Thus, quoting the historical context to make a new interpretation, and following the former splendor of the Tianbao period, I composed the play. Besides, I have deleted some historians' indecorous records, not for the purpose of concealing defects but for maintaining the honesty and integrity of a poet. (*CSD*, vol. 1, 1a)

What makes Hong Sheng disappointed with most of the previous plays on the romance of Emperor Ming Huang and Lady Yang is their contradictory treatment of the royal couple's love, a treatment which was basically influenced by inconsistencies in the historical record. Earlier dramatists who worked on

---

7 The so-called "indecorous records" refer to the dramatic treatment in the Yuan Dynasty play *Wutongyu* [Rain on the Phoneix Tree] by Bai Pu (1226–1306). Though Bai Pu has deleted some of the disreputable aspects of Lady Yang depicted in earlier works, Bai Pu still makes Lady Yang reveal her love affair with An Lushan in the first act of the play. This revelation calls into question the sincerity of Lady Yang's affection for the Emperor. In addition, we are told that An Lushan's rebellion is primarily motivated by his ambition to "seize Lady Yang only, rather than the beautiful land of Tang." Lady Yang is thus shown to be the cause of the nation's ruin. This kind of treatment significantly diminishes the reader's compassion for the love between the Emperor and Lady Yang. It is ironic that, since in this play the royal couple's secret vow is made immediately after the scene disclosing Lady Yang's craving for An Lushan, she seems not to deserve the Emperor's deep longing for her after her death. The blindness and confusion of the Emperor not only reflects his deep infatuation for Lady Yang but also arouse our sympathy for him. Thus it is the Emperor's inner world rather than the couple's interaction that Bai Pu took as the theme of the *Wutongyu*. Hong Sheng felt that Bai Pu's unsympathetic treatment of Lady Yang was a defect of the play *Wutongyu*. Nevertheless, Hong Sheng was moved by the tragic atmosphere created in Bai Pu's *Wutongyu*. Cf. Bai Pu 1968, 79–113.

the same theme tended to either limit the plot to Lady Yang's death and the Emperor's sorrowful memories of her, or to emphasize Lady Yang's licentiousness. (Bai Pu 1968, 79–113; Wang Bocheng 1940) Regarding Lady Yang as a *femme fatale*, these earlier dramatists also exaggerated the illicit relationship between Lady Yangh and An Lushan, or that between the Emperor and another imperial consort, Lady Plum Blossom. For their emphasis on sensuality Hong Sheng charges them with vulgarity.

In the preface to *Changshengdian*, Hong Sheng clearly states that, "since there are many indecorous records regarding Lady Yang in the historical documents, in composing this play, I have decided to follow only Bai Juyi's "Changhenge" [Song of Everlasting Sorrow] and Chen Hong's *Changhenge zhuan* [Story of the Song of Everlasting Sorrow]." (*CSD*, vol. 1, 1a) Among the literary works dealing with the love story of Emperor Ming Huang and Lady Yang, the "Song of Everlasting Sorrow" written by the famous Tang poet Bai Juyi in 806, is the earliest. In his "Song," Bai Juyi is concerned more with the intensification of the love theme than the sequential narration of a momentous historical event. What is shown in the "Song" is the poet's conscientious choices of what he deems the most significant theme to be drawn from the rebellion. By stressing the value of the spiritual contrast of the lovers, Bai beautifies the royal couple, depicting them as eternal lovers who resemble "two birds flying on one pair of wings in heaven" and "two branches of one tree growing together on earth." (Bai Juyi 1979, 238) Following it line by line, Chen Hong also wrote a "story" in "historical biography" (*shizhuan*) style – the *Changhenge zhuan*. (*CSD*, vol. 1, 1a) Being an oft-quoted and widely admired poem, the "Song" became the inspiration for many literary works in subsequent ages.

Unlike earlier version of the same story, *Changshengdian* is especially concerned with the quality of *qing* [love]. In the prologue of *Changshengdian*, Hong Sheng asserts his ideal of "true love" and his intention to "offer a new play in praise of love":

> Since ancient time how few lovers
> Have really remained constant to the end;
> But those who were true have come together at last,
> Even though thousands of miles apart,
> Even though torn from each other by death. And all
> Who curse their unhappy fate are simply those,
> Lacking in love. *True love* moves heaven and earth,
> Metal and stone, shines like the sun and lights.
> The pages of old histories: loyal subjects
> And filial sons are all of them *true lovers*;
> Even Confucius did not delete the love poems
> When he compiled the Songs; so we shall now

> Take music and the tale of Lady Yang
> To offer a new play in praise of *love*!
> (*TPEY*, v)

In order to affirm the purity, sincerity and eternal quality of human affection, Hong Sheng concentrates all his artistic energy on the portrayal of an ideal love, going so far as to conceal many historical facts which would detract from the image of true lovers. Love, perhaps literature's most common theme, is reexamined under a new and different light by Hong Sheng. This is because, unlike earlier authors, he cherishes it more than any other human characteristic. For Hong Sheng, *qing* is a form of energy which combines love, passion, sympathy and affection. It enables an individual to transcend his or her circumstances as defined by time and space, by the boundary between life and death, and by the difference between being and non-being. It is by virtue of this power that lovers are brought together across thousands of miles, dream and reality become one, the inanimate is brought to life, the dead are resurrected, and the living immortalized. In contrast to the Ming writers' elaboration of the lovers' worldly passion and desire, Hong Sheng is concerned not only with prerequisite of "true love," but also with its affirmation. Hong Sheng's shift of allegiance at this time from worldly love to "true love" evidences his extreme sensitivity to the changing spirit of his age. While the idea of *qing* in the Late Ming era inspired him, Hong Sheng breathed the fresher air of a new ideal struggling to find expression, and gave it an elevated, even immortal form.

To Hong Sheng's strategy of "deleting the indecorous historical record" and "mainly depicting the authenticity of *qing*," Wu Yiyi gives his affirmation in his "Preface to *Changshengdian*" and points out:

> Hong Sheng's lyrics are extremely refined and rhythmically matched. Those who love literature are fond of his lyrics and those who understand music appreciate his melody. The play has thus been more widely circulated. Those who own a family theatrical troupe were eager to transcribe the play, enthusiastically teaching and learning the lyrics from each other. The actors and actresses who could sing and perform the play well will multiply their prestige immediately. While some friends of mine who visited the West River have seen the play performed many times, it can thus be imagined how well this play has been received in the south and the north. Though this play mainly presents romantic love, it is based on graciousness and compassion without overlooking the moralizing purpose of admonishment. Recently, some readers and audiences who could not perceive the profound meaning implied in the play suspected that the romantic plot might provoke licentiousness. To prevent such reckless comments, I therefore took the opportunity to write a commentary on the play and wrote a preface to it. (Wu Yiyi 1989, 1582)

Wu Yiyi claims that, although Hong Sheng's play won immediate popularity after its premier, the enthusiastic response of the majority of audiences does not guarantee their proper understanding of the profound meaning implied in the play. However, not only an "implied reader" but also an "informed reader" who is an expert in Chinese theater himself, Wu Yiyi, understands completely the profound meaning contained in the romantic plot of Hong Sheng's play as well as its moralizing purpose. To avoid the ambiguity in reading the play which might provoke misapprehension, Wu Yiyi decides to employ the strategy of commentary, through which he could "realize" and "concretize" the implied meaning hidden in the context of the play on the basis of his experience and proficiency as an "informed" reader and audience of Chinese theater.

Changshendian is a play that touches precisely upon the distinction between lust and love. Hong Sheng's comprehensive and deep reflection on the theme of "true love" is revealed in his "Preface," in which he maintains:

> The Imperial Consort Lady Yang Yuhuan shook the empire and was finally sacrificed. Had she had consciousness after her death, how endlessly regretful she would have been! If her remorse and grief were not so deep, there would be no immortal resurrection for her. Is this why Confucius edited the *Classic of Documents* (*Shujing*), yet reserved the chapter of "Qinshi" [The Qin Pledge] to laud the Lord Wu of Qin for his repentance after he was defeated in the war of Yao? However, since it is hard to end a play harmoniously, I have borrowed the Moon Palace as the lovers' meeting place to finish this play. The Mid-Autumn night when the lovers listened to the music in the Guanghan Palace is the same night they ascended to the highest heaven. However, although they could live together permanently in heaven due to the Twin Stars' assistance, *love conditioned by external reality is, after all, illusory and transient*. When hearing the chimes of bells at midnight, we, too, may be startled awake from our delusive dreams. (*CSD,* vol. 1, 1b)

The reason why the affection conditioned by external reality is illusory and transient is because this kind of love is "worldly love" which will fade away when the conditions disappear. It is in this sense that Hong Sheng asserts love should not be judged or assessed from the angle of external conditions or social value, and that true love itself may move human hearts powerfully and endure eternally. While the affection conditioned by outer reality is ephemeral and illusive, love which is nurtured with innermost sincerity is real and beyond the limit of time and space. Therefore, while most of the earlier love dramas in the Chinese tradition concentrate on the process of the lovers' courtship and their struggles against an unsympathetic environment, Hong Sheng's emphasis is placed upon the married couple's spiritual progression in love as they elevate their affection from desire to total devotion through purification.

It is noticeable that, while Hong Sheng focuses on the "unswerving love pledge" between Emperor Ming Huang and Lady Yang in the play, he also emphasizes that "love conditioned by external reality is illusory and transient." Wu Yiyi pays tribute to Hong's statement and comments:

> The most regrettable thing in the arena of love is that there are countless lovers who are not fated to be conjugally tied. However, if we combine love and death to elaborate the romance, we then could explain how the lovers are predestined to be conjugally tied.[8]

In Wu's view, "true love" could transcend the limit of space and time, life and death. Being different from "infatuation," "true love" should be pure and deep. It would be illusory if we assume that only infatuation could compensate the regrets of love. As Wu Yiyi emphasizes frequently in his commentary,

> When coming to the moment for repentance, we always feel that we are worthless. That is why Confucius teaches us to live by way of "repentance" so that we know how to pursue good fortune and avoid disaster.[9]

The only way to purify our worldly passion, elevating it to a higher level, is "repentance," for repentance could lead us to awakening from the illusion of infatuation. Wu Yiyi thus comments on the last scene of the play:

> While those who are emotionally detached desire to be in love, those who are committed to love aspire to be emotionally detached. The basic nature of love (*qing*) is reason (*li*), which is indispensible to life; the love beyond reason is simply a kind of desire, which is unpermitted for life. This song inspires us by elevating us to the heaven. Those who are still infatuated with love should severely repent.[10]

Wu Yiyi maintains that if only we could awaken from the delusion, we could be committed to love without being indulged in love, and finally achieve the state of "emotional detachment" (*wang qing*), which could fulfill the wish of those who are committed to love and let those who transcend love be carefree.

Orchestration of Theme and Plot – Discussion on the Art of Dramatic Composition

Hong Sheng's revision of the Lady Yang story is designed to express his personal reflection on one of life's most crucial issues: love. In his "introduction" ("Liyan") to *Changshengdian*, Hong Sheng clearly explicates his motive for composing the play:

---

8 See Hong Sheng, *CSD*, vol. 1, 1b, Wu Yiyi's commentary on "Scene I."
9 See Hong Sheng *CSD*, vol. 2, 17a, Wu Yiyi's commentary on "Scene XXX."
10 See Hong Sheng *CSD*, vol. 2, 100 a–b, Wu Yiyi's commentary on "Scene L."

> Later, I thought that true love is rarely seen in an Emperor; The Mawei event had made Emperor Ming Huang betray his vow. According to the popular Tang legend, Lady Yang returned to the immortal Penglai court after her death, and Emperor Ming Huang once visited the Moon Palace. Therefore, exploiting these legends, I depicted specifically the "unswerving love bond of the hairpin and jewel box" between Emperor Ming Huang and Lady Yang and entitled it *Changshengdian*. (*CSD*, vol. 1, 2a)

Changshengdian is based on the affirmation of an ideal. The leitmotif of Hong's play is the eternal love between the Emperor and Lady Yang which transcends the boundary of life and death. Hong's idealism is most powerfully expressed by his invention of a fictitious symbolic reunion of the hero and the heroine, and his use of mythical figures like the Weaving Maid and the Cowherd as a counterpart to Lady Yang's story.

In order to elaborate upon the ideal of "true love" – a kind of pure and devoted love (*jingcheng zhi ai*),[11] which should not contain any element of desire – Hong Sheng purifies the historical Emperor Ming Huang and Lady Yang, making them into pilgrims of true love. In other words, Hong's ambitions are on an epic scale, in terms of both the lovers' outer lives and their inner spiritual progress. The couple change, if and when they change at all in the course of the play, by the process of development; inner potentialities for purification are gradually brought into view as the play proceeds. The development of the drama is determined by the progress of the couple's love, which, as the couple endeavor to achieve the fulfillment of their pledge, manifests many varieties of love itself. This process of love's purification is also reflected in the plot of *Changshengdian*, where it becomes an essential condition for the embodiment of the theme of true love.

To present the process of purification whereby the two banished angels, the Emperor and Lady Yang, gradually extirpate their earthly sins through self-sacrifice and candid repentance, earning their redemption and achieving the fulfillment of true love, Hong Sheng traces the couple's love through four distinct stages: desire, repentance, redemption, and fulfillment. Through these stages, the royal couple reaches their full potential. In other words, the main plot of *Changshengdian* is built on Hong Sheng's design of four stages of love. In the thematic sense, the play places its emphasis on the relationship of the lovers, which develops in a condition of obstruction – caused both by their

---

[11] In the "Prologue," Hong Sheng says: "Since ancient times how few lovers have really remained constant to the end; those who were true and devoted have come together at last, even though thousands of miles apart." (*CSD*, vol. 1, 1a) In Hong's opinion, only when the lovers are "true and devoted" (*CSD*, vol. 1, 1a) to each other can their love transcend their separation in time and space, and last forever.

inner weakness and by outer reality, that is, the An Lushan rebellion which precipitates national turmoil. The whole impetus of such a historical romance is toward the deaths of the lovers, deaths which prove redemptive not only for the lovers themselves but also for the empire whose destiny is closely associated with the lovers' fate. In order to efficiently manipulate the play's action and steer its main ideas resolutely home, Hong Sheng takes these ideas along planned course, a line of intention. Real coherence becomes possible because, through the four-stage purification of the couple's love, the play synthesizes the different levels of love: something that binds one love-level to another, that provides a temporary center for interest while showing us a direction in which to look.

Hong Sheng's design of the four stages of love, in the dramatic sense, reminds us of the crucial component parts of a play in Li Yu's theory. Li Yu's four-part theory is probably inspired by and certainly corresponds to the four doctrinal principles in the writing of Chinese prose: "rise" (*qi*), "continuation" (*cheng*), "turn" (*zhuan*), "closure" (*he*). These principles are dramatically translated into the "prologue" (*jiamen*), the "first scene" (*chongchang*), the "small closure" (*xiaoshousha*), and the "big closure" (*dashousha*).[12] Through a brief poem, the prologue should show the overall structure of the play. Immediately after the prologue comes the "*chongchang*" scene, which Li Yu feels is vital to the success or failure of a play, the purpose of which is to introduce the main characters.

In *Changshengdian*, like the *chongchang* scene, the first scene introduces the protagonists and their pledge of love – the major theme of the play. While Lady Yang's "Death at the Post Station" (Scene XXIV), the "small closure" of the first half of the play, is the beginning of the lovers' enforced separation in two different worlds, the final scene "The Lovers' Reunion" (Scene IVIX), is a "big closure" which brings the protagonists together in heaven. From the first scene to the conclusion of *Changshengdian*'s first half, the lovers revel in the earthly passion and gaiety of love's first stage, which is rooted in obsessive desire. The scene "The Secret Vow" (Scene XXII) brings the lovers to the climactic moment in their love. In order to pledge their mutual sincerity, the couple makes a secret vow under the witness of the twin stars – the Weaving Maid and the Cowherd. However, immediately after this climax of worldly

---

[12] See Li Yu 1985, 54–58. The German critic Gustav Freytag introduced what is known as a "Freytag Pyramid." He characterized the typical plot of a five-act play as a pyramid shape, consisting of a rising action, climax, and falling action. We may equate Li Yu's prologue with Freytag's introduction; the first scene with the rise; the small closure with the climax and return; and the big closure with the catastrophe, see Freytag 1974, 807.

love, their felicitous time is unfortunately ended by Lady Yang's death during the An Lushan rebellion. This, appropriately, is the prelude of the second stage of love: repentance for the lovers. The lovers are compelled to fall from the peak of their bliss to the abyss of endless affliction. This is the part of the "small closure" where the suspense continues, and the audience's anticipation increases. Then, the "returning" period during which Lady Yang's spirit and the Emperor are separated in two different worlds corresponds to love's second stage, which is the lovers' self-repentance. While Lady Yang's earnestness finally moves heaven to redeem her with resurrection, the Emperor also atones for his sin and is allowed to return to Heaven after his death. Following this third stage of "redemption" comes the *denouement*, the final stage of "fulfillment." This fourth stage is enacted in the final reunion scene of the Moon Palace, in which the lovers' wish to be husband and wife is eventually fulfilled forever. It is at this point that the couple of banished angels are brought back to Heaven after all their earthly ordeals.

For Hong Sheng's condensed and tight structure, Wu Yiyi employs a kind of "art of composition" which takes narrative as its model and utilizes concepts such as "thick," "tidy orderly" and "ingenious" to discuss the premise of "unity" for the dramatic structure. The first principle Wu Yiyi proposes is to hold a critical point as the "dramatic nucleus" (*xihe*) of the play to connect the plot from the beginning to the end and thus construct a whole context for the dramatic performance. *Changshengdian* revises the flaws of complexity, inconsistency and looseness in the play *The Frightened Swan* by Wu Shimei. Wu Yiyi maintains that the "tightness" of *Changshengdian*'s dramatic structure lies in the main thread of "the unswerving love of the hairpin and jewel box." The royal couple's "pledge" with the hairpin and jewel box as love tokens and the "secret vow" made at the *Palace of Eternal Youth* thus become the two major cruxes.

Wu Yiyi's critique is so penetrating that it goes straight to the heart of the matter. In the major scenes which bring a sequence of actions to culmination, Hong Sheng usually avoids any blurring of impact or dissipation of energy by eliminating marginal matters. He creates a sweeping crescendo of tension focused on one particular dramatic issue. Many such scenes often achieve even greater clarity by organizing themselves around a physical object. The major scenes of *Changshengdian* are centered on the hairpin and jewel box. These two objects, established as the royal couple's love tokens during their first meeting in the Palace of Eternal Youth, are expedients for Hong Sheng; he uses them to connect the couple's emotions and inner struggle for their love. The tapestry of "the unswerving love of the hairpin and jewel box" is woven by means of frequent recurrences of the couple's love symbols. In addition to the theme of four stages of love whose main function is to integrate scenes, the play, like an opera, contains music leitmotifs – short flexible fragments recurring with great frequency, associated with the poetic image of the love pledge. Throughout the entire play, the tokens serve as a message which always appears in time to reaffirm and sustain the couple's love bond. As Wu Yiyi has pointed out, the play is quite saturated with such recurring images, which gather force as the play proceeds: after the first pledge scene, Lady Yang returns the love tokens to the Emperor in the Emerald Chamber in a scene of reconciliation. At later points in the play, she asks for them to be buried with her body to record her resentment in the Mawei Station; she strokes them at the tomb in expression of her regrets; she brings them to the immortal land to hold her love; and she displays them in the Xuan Palace to the priest to confirm her love. The priest then sends the tokens as a message to convince the Emperor that his mission has been successful.

Finally, like the lovers, these two divided keepsakes are reunited in the Moon Palace as a symbol of everlasting love. At the first mention and presence of the love tokens, their effect may be limited, but with each successive repetition the audience half-consciously recalls all the others, so that rich associations and inter-associations are set up in the imagination. Add to the image of the love tokens all the related images – the phoenixes on the pin which fly together, the love-knot on the box which represent two hearts as one, the twin branches on one tree, and so on and so on – and you can see that they are painstakingly integrated into the play by the author to evoke a pervasive sense of the lovers' sincerity and earnestness even in difficult tests of their love. While separated, the couple, with steadfast confidence, repeatedly confirm their love through their love tokens. We are granted flashes of insight into the real stability of their souls, so we learn a dramatic lesson about the pure heart. This is developed and emphasized in the succeeding scenes by the oscillation of regrets and devotion in the afflicted minds of the Emperor and Lady Yang. The love which was first expressed by a pledge is re-kindled by the love tokens. The love tokens initiate and help fulfill the lovers' wish for eternal love. One of the Emperor's first proposals, issued in the first scene, "And may we two become/ Like the phoenixes on the pin, always flying together; / Like the love-knot on the box – two hearts as one" (*TPEY*, Scene I, 6), is echoed in the final reunion scene, "Now the box is complete again, / the divided hairpin is whole." (*TPEY*, Scene XLIX, 268)

The second principle Wu Yiyi asserts is "tightening the needle and thread in composition." He praises the structure in *Changshendian* for being rigid and condensed, in which the plot and scenes are not only coordinated consistently but also connected effortlessly as a whole. Wu's principle reminds us of Li

Yu's theory. The famous Qing critic Li Yu (1610–1680), in his advice to dramatists, suggests the principle of "tight texture" (*mizhenxian*) for plot construction. In Li Yu's view, a dramatic composition is similar to fine needlework: "The entire cloth is first cut into pieces and sewn in a pattern. The art of integration lies in the tightness of the texture of the needlework, since one careless stitch will render the whole piece imperfect." (Li Yu 1985, 10) Therefore, in composing a scene, a playwright must consider what went before and what will follow: "The previous scenes serve to point to and foretell the present one, while the subsequent scenes serve to echo, to recall, and to suggest." (Li Yu 1985, 10) Furthermore, he must have the overall structure of the play constantly in mind, including all the characters to be presented and all the related incidents. In other words, the action must correspond to the demands of the intellect and the heart. Whatever does not serve this purpose, the playwright is in duty bound to throw away. The end result should be a well-constructed play with no signs of disjointedness. "Like the blood vessels of an organism," the play should flow smoothly from beginning to end with all parts contributing to the ultimate unity of the plot. (Li Yu 1985, 3) Wu Yiyi's and Li Yu's emphasis on "the tightness of texture" shows that the integral structure is a prerequisite of a well-constructed play.

Before analyzing the art of integration of a dramatic composition which is like a fine piece of needlework, we must have a good command of the pattern from which it is seen as a whole. The aspect of plot arrangement and construction strategy Wu Yiyi is concerned with is also relevant to the meaning of "texture," which refers to "the arrangement of the particular or constituent parts of any material, as wood, metal and the like, as it affects the appearance or feel of the surface: structure, composition, grain, and so on." (*CSD*, vol. 2, 55a) Hong Sheng developed a great variety of strategies to ensure coherence and organic unity in his play. Hong Sheng's skill therefore lies not simply in his ingenuity and economy in solving problems which his predecessors had failed to solve. The very texture of Hong Sheng's work emerges as he develops consistent strategies to deal with dramatic problems and incorporates them in a coherent structural design for the whole play. It is his flexible and protean application of basic devices which has engaged our attention. He tries to maintain variety by working from the small-scale to the full-scale deployment of structural strategies, dealing at times with a pair of scenes or one relationship and at other time with a whole play or a complete network of interactions. A great dramatist very frequently uses his craft to conceal the ways he is achieving his effect upon us. There is a texture in Hong Sheng's work, but it is not an abstract technique which we can codify in a specification in a play-writing manual. Texture, used in a sense of veins and fibers which reveal structural organization, helps to differentiate the quality of the material where it appears. We can understand the texture in Hong Sheng's work only by responding to the variety of the material in which we find it.

The Purification of Mortal Love as the Core of Characterization: the "Transformation" of Romantic Idealization

The elevation of worldly passion to immortal love illuminates love's essential equality. Through the four stage development of love, the transformation of romantic idealization in Hong's play encourages the proliferation of dramatic patterning. Hong's new romantic pattern enables the mode of love drama to articulate more perfectly the variety of spiritual attitudes within the changing sensibility of the age, and the broader historical shift in idealization from worldly love to eternal "true love."

If romantic love is a "passionate spiritual-emotional sexual attachment between two people that reflects a high regard for the values of each other's person" (Branden 1988, 220), the lovers' mutual earnestness should be the major premise of the portraiture of their love relationship. In the *Changshengdian*, what the lovers seek is emotional commitment from the beloved, which is "a kind of merging, a 'oneness,' the ecstatic bliss of mutual reciprocation." (Brehm 1988, 242) By the depiction of the lovers' union, separation and reunion, Hong Sheng demonstrates that reciprocated love (union with the other) is associated with fulfillment and ecstasy, and unrequited love (separation) with emptiness, anxiety, or despair. In fact, the reinforcement of the lovers' mutual commitment enhances their perpetually rejuvenating passion in that Hong Sheng attempts to actualize a higher vision of conjugal love. The four stages of love (self-indulgent desire, repentance, redemption, and the fulfillment of love's eternity) are a tangible process of emotional cultivation. If love is the most fragile seed that can be planted in the field of the human heart, its initial cultivation needs unabated, cautious care, otherwise it will immediately wither and decline. Once withdrawn, love can never again be revived with its initial generosity but only with a resistance equal to its early heedlessness, a resistance that contorts its natural spontaneity into a wary distrust. It is therefore crucial for Hong Sheng to present the episodes of emotional crisis in the first stage, where the lovers are challenged and prompted to engage in the assiduous cultivation of their love. In the earlier stage of love, the obstruction to true love is the internal barrier to full commitment posed by an initial complacency. Redemption from such sensual love is accomplished only through a tragic initiation, that is, Lady Yang's death, which develops the lovers' capacity for the faith they have sworn. It is also based on this conviction that Hong Sheng provides a lesson in the art of love. The significance of love between man and woman is thus unprecedentedly featured for love's own sake in Chinese literature; love can achieve its consummation through the power of two hearts' reciprocal sincerity and total dedication.

In order to highlight the theme of ideal love, Hong Sheng demonstrates the purification of love in the characters, who change inwardly, gradually supplementing their human passion with spiritual commitment. While true love is conceived of as a rare quality that is embodied only in a chosen few, lust, obsessive desire, and passion in human beings are regarded as commonplace. In this play, Hong Sheng depicts the Emperor and Lady Yang as banished angels – the God Kongsheng and Fairy Penglai – who have been sent down to the mortal world as a punishment for their mistakes. Only after the lovers pass through various tests of love do they come to see that, instead of passion and obsession, total devotion is the only way to elevate their earthly love to one of eternity. In the combination of human passion and total devotion lies the unique intensity and purity of true love. By portraying the inward change of the hero and heroine, characterization becomes a crucial vehicle for Hong Sheng to substantiate his ideal of love. This theme, the primary focus of the play, must be expressed through the characters, who reciprocally derive their significance largely from their subordination to the theme. As the plot develops, the intensity of love gradually increases. This is illustrated through the protagonists' purging of earthly desire, in which Emperor Ming Huang and Lady Yang, the two angels fallen from heaven, must undergo four different stages of love – the stages of desire, repentance, redemption, and fulfillment – before their final reunion in the highest heaven.

To Hong Sheng's adoption of the purification of mortal love as the core of characterization, Wu Yiyi perceptively proposes the concept of "transformation" (*bian*)[13] to interpret Lady Yang's change in the course of love, which not only dexterously responds to the popular religious concepts of *xian* [immortal], *fan* [mortal] and *hun* [spirit] but also highlights Lady Yang's female driving force in the progression of love's purification and elevation.

After the An Lushan rebellion, the Emperor flees from the capital with Lady Yang and her family. But when they reach Mawei Post Station, the mutinous guards kill Yang Guozhong and Lady Yang's sister, since they hold them responsible for the country's decline. Finally, under pressure from Commander

---

13 See Hong Sheng *CSD*, vol. 2, 22a, Wu Yiyi's commentary on "Scene XXXII."

Chen Xuanli and the army, the Emperor is forced to let Lady Yang take her own life. From the scene "Death at the Post Station" (Scene XXVI) onwards, Lady Yang frequently reappears as a spirit, and after her resurrection, as a fairy. By depicting Lady Yang's spirit, the author gives free rein to his imagination and demonstrates how the lovers transcend the secular love of the first stage of desire and sublimate their love to a higher level of spirituality. As Wu Yiyi suggest, this progression of love is illustrated through Lady Yang's "three transformations": before the Event at Mawei Post Station she is a human being (whose former life was Fairy Penglai), but from "The Spirit Follows" (Scene XXVI) onwards, she becomes a spirit, who then turns into a fairy after the "Resurrection" (Scene XXXVI).[14] The three periods of Lady Yang's life actually correlate with her progression in her first three stages of love – her transformation into a spirit and then into a fairy corresponds with her progression from the first to the second and the third stage of love.

In the play, the spirit of Lady Yang, although she has left the human world, is not permitted to return to heaven immediately. She remains suspended and struggling in an intermediate stage between earthly desire and immortal love. The sharp contrast between her worldly life as an imperial consort and her ethereal life as a spirit also intensifies the sense of tragedy underlying Lady Yang's death. Her corpse – all that is left of her past earthly life – is buried in the earth, while her spirit – her enduring love – hovers above, still aspiring to meet the Emperor. Nevertheless, the wandering spirit of Lady Yang is so fragile and helpless that even a gust of wind can make her shrink back and lose her direction. Trembling with fear, she beholds the spirits of her cousin Yang Guozhong, and her sister the Duchess of Guo, both dripping with blood and being dragged to hell. The thought that her entire family is ruined because of her fills her with immense anguish and regret.

When Lady Yang's spirit finds her own corpse, she brims over with redoubled sadness. A feeble spirit as she is, she is again struck by the lonely appearance of her dead body. But even so, the spirit is still confident that her love will remain steadfast in death. Though her body is dead, her love, like her spirit, lives on. Earnestly, Lady Yang's spirit confesses all her past sins and prays to Heaven for forgiveness. Even though she admits her guilt, however, she does not regret her love: "Only my love I can never repent, for I am still drowning in a sea of love; and even if I cannot be reborn, I will go on loving the emperor in hell." (*TPEY*, Scene XXIV, 156) Opening her heart to the stars and the moon, Lady Yang confesses her sins with tears and sighs, begging to

---

14 See Hong Sheng, *CSD*, vol. 2, 22a, Wu Yiyi's commentary on "Scene XXXII."

make amends. Moved by her piety and sincerity, Heaven finally pardons her faults and grants her resurrection.

The resurrection of Lady Yang occurs only after her spirit has gone through the most pious remorse during her long wandering. At the crucial moment of resurrection, the Tutelary God reminds Lady Yang: "You were once an immortal, but when you went to the palace, you were *led astray by love*; now you have tasted pleasure and pain, and though you have left the world of men, you are not permitted yet to return to heaven." (*TPEY*, Scene XXIX, 157) While Lady Yang still possesses an original, immortal, true nature, she has been "led astray by love." But why is love misleading? The Tutelary God's words suggest that mortal love brings both pleasure and pain. In the immortal realm, by contrast, there is no such emotional fluctuation. But since Lady Yang has not given up her secular passion, she is not permitted yet to return to heaven.

The Tutelary God's severe warning in the "Resurrection" scene reveals the significance of the purification of mortal love. In the original Chinese text, the author uses the term *chimo* [delusion, obsessiveness or infatuation] to describe Lady Yang's "earthly desire" which "increases immediately" (*dunzeng*) after Lady Yang is banished to the earthly palace. According to Chinese Buddhism, *chi* (*Moha* [Buddhism], delusion) is one of the three major "Unwholesome roots" (*Mula* [Buddhism]) of human nature.[15] *Chi* is exceedingly harmful because obsessive desires such as greed, jealousy, hatred and intolerance can transform human nature from its original carefree state into a state of insatiability. The author also employs the Taoist idea of *Shangqing*,[16] the second stratum of the Taoist heaven, to describe the essence of the immortals – pure, clean, and without secular desires and disquiet. With so many sins, and having been "sent down to the earthly palace" (*TPEY*, Scene XXIX, 157), Lady Yang loses her true nature and is entangled in the emotional ensnarement of the mortals. Because immortals should be free of worry and anxiety, they regard love, which almost always evokes emotional instability, as undesirable. Since Lady Yang's sinfulness is rooted in her emotional ensnarement, her salvation from it may be sought only in the extirpation of all her obsessive desire, that is, by freeing the spirit from its obsession with earthly love and leading

---

15 *Moha* [delusion] is one of the three unwholesome roots (*Mula*): Greed, Hate, Delusion, see "Miszheng" *pin* 31 and "Daming" *pin* 32 in Kumarajiva 1924. *Mula* [roots] are those conditions which through their presence determine the actual moral quality of a volitional factor. There are six such roots, three karmically unwholesome and three wholesome roots: Greed, Hate, Delusion (*lobha, dosa, moha*) and Greedlessness, Hatelessness, Undeludedness (*aloha, adosa, amoha*).
16 According to Taoism, there are three "pure strata" in heaven: *Yuqing* [Jade Purity], *Shangqing* [Supreme Purity] and *Taiqing* [Greatest Purity].

it back to its spiritual source. It is for this reason that Lady Yang is not allowed to return to heaven immediately; before earning her redemption and regain her true nature, she must first forsake her old ways.

In Hong Sheng's view, true love is manifest in unconditional devotion, free from all the suspense and disquiet provoked by secular desires. As a kind of pure and total devotion, "true love" can be regarded as the true nature of human beings. In this play, through the lives of the protagonists, we repeatedly note Hong Sheng's efforts to portray and to affirm the permanent nature and unlimited strength of *qing*. Like the Ming dramatist Tang Xianzu, Hong attaches supreme importance to *qing* precisely because *qing* appears to him to be the distinguishing feature of human existence. As Tang maintains in the preface to his *Mudanting* [The Peony Pavilion], "We do not know where *qing* comes from. However, once *qing* has arisen and taken deep roots in one's heart, it can bring death to the living and life to the dead."[17] Likewise, Hong also asserts that "love transcends life and death, / And lovers will meet at last." (TPEY, Scene XLIX, 272)

In the same "Resurrection," scene, when Lady Yang's spirit is startled and confused by her own revived body, the Tutelary God claps his hands and shouts:

> Don't hesitate! You and she are one.
> (He points at the corpse.)
> This is your body! (He points at her.)
> And you are her spirit!
> *Now let true nature reassert itself,*
> And the spirit clothes itself in flesh again!
> (*TPEY*, Scene XXXVI, 193, author's italics)

Later, when Lady Yang's spirit and body are reunited, the Tutelary God shouts, "Now I see the spirit entering the body, like a child re-entering its mother's womb, or like two rings that join in one." (*TPEY*, Scene XXXVI, 194) In Lady Yang's pursuit of true love during her mortal life, her "true nature" (*zhenxing*) *can never be entirely detached from her body, or the "illusory human skeleton"* (*jiakulou*). Before her resurrection, Lady Yang's true nature is temporarily contaminated by the sinfulness associated with emotional ensnarement. However, due to her earnest repentance, Lady Yang's purged spirit is reincarnated and her "true nature reasserts itself." That is why, as soon as Lady Yang is revived, she sings: "I have woken from a deep sleep, after losing myself so long; but

---

[17] See Tang Xianzu, "Preface," *Mudanting* [The Peony Pavilion], collated and annotated by Xu Shuofang and Yang Xiaomei 1987, 1. Trans. Birch 1980, ix.

now my body and spirit are one again. I wonder in a daze. Where is the spirit that flew like a butterfly?" (*TPEY*, Scene XXXVI, 194) Like a traveler who is lost and finally returns, the true nature of Lady Yang now "returns to her body" (*yuanshen rugou*). Here Hong Sheng uses the tangible images of child, mother's womb, rings (Lady Yang's name, *Yuhuan*), butterfly, traveler, and home in unusual ways as Lady Yang goes about "reasserting her true nature" and the author's own ideal of "true love." In the Tutelary God's words, the comparison of the union of Lady Yang's spirit and body – discarding one's old self and beginning a new life with the affirmation of true-self – with a child's birth by re-entering its mother's womb, effectively sums up the play's theme of purification. The birth of a baby is a symbol for Lady Yang's removal from the mud of worldly delusion which engulfed her in her former life. The images of butterfly and traveler, referring to the butterfly dream of Zhuangzi, constitute an apt allusion to the Taoist concept that there is no distinction between dream and reality. This allusion expresses Lady Yang's awakening from the dream of earthly delusion to become the true-self, which is finally blessed by Heaven. The concrete image of a traveler returning to his original home, which, here, refers to Lady Yang finding her "original true-self," is also a reflection of her state of mind. These images are used to reveal spiritual experiences that could not have been as richly expressed in the language of abstract statements. The use of such metaphorical language not only enriches the texture of the lyrics but also expands the scope of the play, thus adding to its thematic significance.

The "Resurrection" episode gives a revealing glimpse of the significance of Lady Yang's "transformation." It is Lady Yang's undying love that removes the line between life and death, the difference between the worldly and the unworldly. Thus the "transformation" of Lady Yang virtually becomes an embodiment of the truth inherent in the play: that true love can redeem the human spirit from sins and enable spiritual immortality. It is in this sense that Lady Yang, after her resurrection, regains her original identity as Fairy Penglai – a true lover with purified spirit.

Lady Yang's resurrection is the triumph of infinite love over the detestable facts of death, a triumph accomplished only through the earnest repentance of her past sins. It is the full acceptance and earnest confession of their guilt that elevate the love between the Emperor and Lady Yang to a more pure and lofty level. With wholehearted repentance and mutual forgiveness, they drive out all the impure elements of love. Through sincere repentance and efforts to make amends for each other, their love transcends the first two stages, and is uplifted to the third stage, redemption. Since the author cannot elevate his hero and heroine by changing all the historical facts, he eagerly explores the quintessential part of their characters and presents them in a purged and idealized form. There are two conflicting sides in the characters of the hero and heroine: one is their "true nature," which persists despite their fall into the human world; the other is the degenerated and earthly characteristics of their mortal life, which can only be extirpated through repentance. In their mortal life, "true nature" and "earthly desire" coexist but conflict with each other. It is only after they have undergone a complete purgation to reach the highest level of awakening that their "true nature" can reassert itself. Hong Sheng's play does not transcendentally pursue a kind of religious infinite value. The division of two worlds in *Changshengdian* does not mean that Hong Sheng intends to create a transcendent value which is beyond this world.

For Hong Sheng, there is no real existence of the other world, whose signification in the play merely lies in its symbolic implication of the purified, immortal "true love." The dichotomy of the two worlds is an actualization of two abstract concepts of love – ideal "true love" and worldly love. True love is not a kind of abstract, transcendent other-worldly value; rather, it is motivated and accumulated by the affection generated from the lovers' concrete actions in the play. Every action, even the episode of the triangular relationship, which happens in the process of the lovers' contacts, has its spiritual value through which the meaning of true love is gradually crystallized. The abstract concept of true value and the value derived from action are combined as a unity in reality, but in the play, they are divided to create a special dramatic effect. Nevertheless, even if Hong Sheng were personally indifferent to Taoism and Buddhism, Taoist and Buddhist ideas would have crept into his plays as a matter of course, in view of their wide currency in the popular literature of the Yuan-Ming period. Likewise, even if Hong Sheng were not philosophically concerned with such concepts as *sheng* [life] and *qing* [love] of late-Ming thought, he would still have affirmed life and love in conformity with the *chuanqi* tradition of Ming drama.[18] Actually, Hong Sheng employs and dramatizes popular concepts after the Six Dynasties (220–589) such as

---

18 Hong Sheng's salute to human affection is in fact derived from the ideological system of Late-Ming culture. *Qing* is a central concept in Late-Ming philosophy, and is one of the most important themes of Late-Ming literature. Among the more important philosophers who have contributed to bringing the term *qing* into prominence are Luo Rufang and Li Zhi. It is Luo Rufang whose thinking influenced the Late-Ming literati's understanding of *qing* [love] by his substitution of the term *sheng* [life] for the term *xin* [mind] as the generating and animating force of the universe, and through his further equation of *sheng* with the term *ren* [humanity, benevolence, love]. Luo Rufang was a teacher of the greatest Late-Ming playwright Tang Xianzu, who advocated the supremacy of *qing*. For a brief survey of Luo Rufang's influence on Tang Xianzu, see Hsia 1970, 249–290.

"immortal" (*xian*), "mortal" (*fan*) and "spirit" (*hun*). These concepts are employed to express the need for spiritual, emotional fulfillment in the depths of the human heart. Hong Sheng's four stages of love crystallize in the growth from the hallucination, conflict and struggle to the full awakening of the human mind. It is also through the four stages of love: desire, repentance, redemption, and fulfillment, that the hero and heroine are gradually purified and able to reach their full potential.

Epilogue

Commentary, primarily a reader's or the author's notes, or clues written between the lines, has gradually developed into a special form of literary criticism in traditional Chinese fiction and drama. While most Chinese read fiction in editions with an extensive commentary printed on the same page as the fiction itself, the reader or audience "reads" a play with a commentary not only to facilitate textual understanding but also to consult evaluative remarks which might be helpful for the appreciation of the dramatic performance as well. It is interesting that, in the face of the commentary trend prevalent in the Ming-Qing period, the authors tended to leave space in their texts for readers to compose their own commentaries, and sometimes even wrote their own commentary to promote or transmit their own works.

In the case of *Changshengdian*, as Hong Sheng's close friend, Wu Yiyi's commentary is unique in the history of Ming-Qing commentary for winning the author's immediate affirmation and friendly feedback. Hong Sheng is also particularly fortunate to have had a confidant's companionship during his long period of playwriting and to have acquired a scene-by-scene commentary for the whole play. A connoisseur of *Kunqu* [*Kun* opera], Wu Yiyi, with his "Preface" and commentary, actually reflects not only his understanding and interpretation of Hong Sheng's play but also his important viewpoints on drama theory and performance.

To evaluate the artistic achievement of *Changshengdian*, we have to consider the following two questions: What is the play's thematic presentation as a whole and how does Hong Sheng's intention manifest itself? As we know, we judge a play by its effectiveness as a whole, because the playwright expects to be judged by his total effect. The final step towards understanding the meaning of a play as a whole is to sense where its weight and balance are felt. Hong Sheng's primary contribution to Chinese drama is that, rather than being confined by the preceding dramatic conventions, he views the play *as a whole*; by combining the dramatic and poetic characteristics of Chinese drama, he conveys a consistent, spiritual value – that is, true love.

Compared with the traditional commentators on Chinese drama, Wu Yiyi has made a breakthrough by treating the commentated play as a whole and taking into account the "dramaturgy" organically rather than focusing merely on the sporadic or casual appreciation of the poetry, lyrics and music of the play. In fact, Wu Yiyi has commentated extensively on the subject matter, the author's intentions, the theme, the dramatic structure, the characterization, the narrative skills, the composition, the dramatic language, and even the aesthetics of performing the play. When Wu Yiyi comments on and interprets the artistry of Hong's play, he not only takes the stand of a "virtual author" conceiving the necessary and practical strategies for playwriting, but also takes the stand of a critic, reader and audience who endeavor to evaluate thoroughly the practical effect of the play's dramatic design and performance. While the interpretation of *qing*, the "principle of unity" in narrative structure and the techniques of description that Wu Yiyi has proposed are partly inherited from the Late Ming and Early Qing dramatists and theorists like Tang Xianzu, Mao Zonggang, Jin Shengtan and Li Yu, his commentary has shed new light on Chinese dramatic theory. At this point, Wu Yiyi's background and experience as an "informed reader" is extremely close to that of Hong Sheng.

We assume that as an informed reader, Wu Yiyi does not simply reflect passively like a "mirror" when facing the "structures-of-appeal" of the *Changshengdian*; rather, he accepts the text with his own original aesthetic expectations. His commentary shows his effort to combine the multiple roles of reader, audience, critic, author, narrator and character; he has engaged the imagination, filled the blanks between the lines, constructed the significance of the text, and evaluated Hong Sheng's artistry and the aesthetic effect of the play. Being praised as "understanding words" by the author, Wu's commentary successfully creates a dialogue between the reader/ the critic and the author. The discernible interactions between Hong Sheng and Wu Yiyi in the commentated text suggest the possibility of a two-way interpretation. The convergences and divergences of artistic understanding between the author's aesthetic principle and the critic's comprehension of the author's artistry through his own aesthetic experience are worthy of close examination. When the author's and the reader's aesthetic taste and vision gradually get closer and closer, the author unconsciously accepts the commentary as part of his own play. Thus the author interestingly enough turns into a reader of the commentated play himself.

Bibliography

Baker, George Pierce. *Dramatic Technique*. Reprint. Boston: Da Capo Press, 1989.
Bai Juyi. *Bai Juyi ji* [Bai Juiyi Collection]. Ed. Gu Xuejie. Beijing: Zhonghua shuju, 1979.
Bai Pu. *Wutongyu* [Rain on the Phoenix Tree]. *Yuanren zaju zhu* [An Annotated Collection of the Yuan Zaju Drama]. Ed. Yang Jialuo. Taipei: Shijie shuju, 1968.
Birch, Cyril. *The Peony Pavilion: Mudan Ting*. Bloomington: Indiana University Press, 1980.
Branden, Nathaniel. "A Vision of Romantic Love." *The Psychology of Love*. Ed. Robert J. Sternberg and Michael L. Barnes. New Haven, CT: Yale University Press, 1988. 218–231.
Brehm, Sharon H., "Passionate Love." *The Psychology of Love*. Ed. Robert J. Sternberg and Michael L. Barnes. New Haven, CT: Yale University Press, 1988. 232–263.
Chen Wannai. *Hong Sheng yanjiu* [A Study of Hong Sheng]. Taipei: Xuesheng shuju, 1970.
Freytag, Gustav. "Technique of the Drama." *Dramatic theory and criticism: Greeks to Grotowski*. Ed. Bernard F. Dukore. New York: Holt, Rinehart and Winston, 1974. 804–820.
Hong Sheng. *Changshengdian* [The Palace of Eternal Youth]. Ed. Baixi caotang. Reprint. Shanghai: Wenxue guji kanxingshe, 1954.
— *Changshengdian* [The Palace of Eternal Youth]. Beijing: Wenxue guji kanxingshe, 1955a.
— *The Palace of Eternal Youth*. Trans. Yang Xiangyi and Gladys Yang. Beijing: Foreign Language Press, 1955b.
— *Changshengdian* [The Palace of Eternal Youth]. Ed. Xu Shuofang. Beijing: Remin wenxue chuanshe, 1988.
Hsia, Chih-tsing [C.T. Hsia]. "Time and the Human Condition in the Plays of Tang Hsien-tsu." *Self and Society in Ming Thought*. Ed. William Theodore De Bary. Studies in Oriental culture, 4. New York: Columbia University Press, 1970. 249–290.
Jiao Xun. *Jushuo* [On Drama]. *Zhongguo gudian xiqu lunzhu jicheng* [The General Collection of the Critical Theories of Traditional Chinese Drama]. Vol. 8. Beijing: Zhongguo xiju chubanshe, 1982. 73–220.
Kumarajiva, trans. "Treatise on the Great Prajnaparamita" [Sutra]. *The Tripitaka in Chinese*. Vol. 8. Eds. Junjiro Takakusu and Kaigyoku Watanabe. Tokyo: Society of the Publication of the Taisho edition of the Tripitaka, 1924. 847.
Li Yu. *Xianqing ouji* [Sketches of Idle Pleasure]. Ed. Shan Jinheng. Hangzhou: Zhejiang guji chubanshe, 1985.
Liang Tingnan. *Quhua* [Criticism of Qu]. *Zhongguo gudian xiqu lunzhu jicheng* [The General Collection of Critical Theories of the Traditional Chinese Drama]. Vol. 8. Beijing: Zhongguo xiju chubanshe, 1982.
Tseng Yong-i. *Changshengdian yanjiu* [A Study of Changshengdian]. Taipei: Shangwu yinshuguan, 1980.
— *Zhongguo gudian xiju xuanzhu* [An Annotated Collection of Classical Chinese Drama]. Taipei: Guojia Publishing Co., 1985.
Wang Ayling. *Ming Qing xiqu mingzuozhong renwu kehua zhi yishuxing* [The Artistry of Chraracterization of the Masterpieces of Ming-Qing Drama]. Taipei: Zhongshan xueshu wenhua jijinhui, 1998.
— *Wanming Qingchu xiqu zhi shenmei gousi yu qi yishu chengxian* [The Aesthetic Construction and Dramatic Presentation of the Drama from Late Ming to Early Qing]. Taipei: Institute of Chinese Literature and Philosophy, Academia Sinica, 2005.
Wang Bocheng. *Tianbao yishi zhugongdiao* [Medley of the Splendor of the Tianbao Period]. *Xueshu* 3. Ed. Zhao Jingshen. Reprint. Beijing: Xueshu chubanshe, 1940.

Wu Yiyi. "Preface to *Changshengdian*." *Zhongguo gudian xiqu xuba huibian* [Collection of Prefaces and Postscripts to Chinese Classical Drama]. Vol. 3. Ed. Cai Yi. Jinan: Qilu shushe, 1989. 1582.

Xu Shuofang and Yang Xiaomei, eds. Beijing: Renmin wexue chubanshe, 1987.

Zhang Peiheng, *Hong Sheng nianpu* [Chronological Biography of Hong Sheng]. Shanghai: Shanghai gujichu banshe, 1979.

Christina Nygren
Performing Life and Live Theatre: Fiction in Popular Performances

By way of introduction, I would like to share what an actor in a Japanese travelling theatre group once said to me, "We do not *play* theatre, we *live* theatre." This statement radically challenges the accepted concept of theatre as something that is not "real," but also gives an apt account of the role that a travelling actor has, or believes he or she has in society. I regard popular theatre, as performed by travelling theatre groups, as being inseparable from the society and the social, human or divine context in which it is being performed. Therefore it should not be seen as an isolated work of art but in context with a wide social and human perspective. Further, my focus is on the communicative encounter between performer and spectator, "the theatrical event," consisting of the presentation of a performance and the attention of an audience. (Sauter 2000)

In my paper, I will give examples of the role and importance of fiction in social contexts investigated through studies of and field work among travelling theatre groups, who are deeply appreciated, especially in the countryside and often in relation to folk festival traditions.[1] I will investigate popular performances in their contexts – from the hot-spring poolside in Japan and freezing cold coal mines in northern China to melodramatic stories performed in soaking hot tents throughout the night in Bangladesh and a crowd of people watching a performance at a crossroads in Indian West Bengal. Theatre life in very different countries in Asia where I have been working intensively for more than twenty-five years exhibits a great variety of examples of the significance of theatre and dance for the public at large, in everyday life as well as in religious or secular festivals and holidays. A wide range of events keeps the tradition of popular theatre and dance alive and the many different kinds of performances are of undeniable importance to the general public. Consequently, I primarily analyse here the context, letting the stage art take a subsidiary role in order to find common aspects of the function of fictionality in popular performances.

---

[1] This paper is based on more than twenty years of research into theatre, dance, popular performances and festival culture, including extensive field studies in the region. The situations in China and Japan are further described and analysed in Nygren 2000. My research on India and Bangladesh was published in Swedish (2006a). In addition to these monographs written in Swedish, the bibliography appended to this article registers some further titles on the subject published by the author in English.

Let me first sum up the basic definitions I use in my research:

Popular theatre refers to performances that are created to be performed for a wide audience, often in cities and particularly in major cities or for extensive touring. It includes comic or sentimental performances in the entertainment districts of cities or at venues that offer various forms of entertainment. I cannot, however, identify any obvious delineation between the theatrical structure of popular theatre/lowbrow theatre and elite theatre/highbrow theatre. There are often links between popular theatre, lowbrow films, and popular music and songs. Audience members are observers and do not physically participate in the event.

I use the term *folk theatre* to indicate theatre and dance that is provincial and linked to traditions, customs and patterns of behaviour in defined geographical locations. This form of theatre is particularly useful for teaching people about religion, history and moral values, and has long been an integral part of the lives of people in the provinces. In recent years, it has had stiff competition from television. Performances are often linked to a broad festival tradition. Audiences tend to participate in the event, either directly by dancing, speaking or singing, or by merely being present, feeling like participants in sacrificial rites, thanksgiving ceremonies or purification rituals.

In this paper, the main attention is on the popular theatre, according to the definitions above. Popular theatre is often used as a contrast to "serious" or "artistic" theatre in the media, in newspapers and in research. In theatre science, however, popular "light entertainment theatre" has been given low priority compared to so-called "serious/artistic theatre" (which, according to this terminology, would supposedly lack entertainment value!), and discussions have often been based on strictly subject-specific issues. Further, I consider the serious/elite theatre as most of the time not being provinsional, and so it is left aside in my paper.

Now, please let me share with you a few situations from the countries where I have been working for quite a few years. The "situations" or "events" I will talk about are chosen from hundreds of such experiences during field work, and I have intentionally selected very different contexts in order to represent a broad perspective. Let us look at some diary notes from a performance at a hot-spring resort in Japan. The *tabi shibai* [travelling theatre], is well known by the general public. At present, more than a hundred organised companies perform once or twice a day all the year round. In addition to this, at a rough estimate there are some two hundred unorganised touring troupes of varying sizes. An average performing rate of 45 shows per month for every troupe makes some 55,000 performances annually, rarely mentioned or included in outlines of Japanese theatre.

We are at a huge hot-spring resort in Kyūshū in southern Japan. It is early in the afternoon and the estimated 250 men and women in the audience had already arrived in the morning to this palace of joy and delight, alone or in small groups. The entrance fee is low enough to let in even the less privileged citizens and includes not only unlimited bathing in numerous pools with a selection of rejuvenating waters, but also admittance to afternoon and evening performances of theatre, song and dance – all with fictive content and form, far from the everyday life of the audience.

The first of two daily performances has just started. The stage is dark, a popular *enka*-song is blaring from the loudspeakers, setting the atmosphere for the first scene of the play *Tokujirō shigure* [Drizzling Rain over Tokujirō], a story about a married woman who is secretly having an affair with a gangster and becomes pregnant by him. The well-known *enka*-song is not a part of the play but conveys in sentimental words and easily accessible music the emotions of the upcoming performance. The music becomes more subdued, the stage brightens and a man who is quite obviously looking for someone appears. He talks with the audience, chatting and joking with them to build up an intimate rapport.

One by one the audience has been entering the auditorium, taking their seats on the cushions placed on the floor. They are all dressed in cotton bath-

Fig. 1: Theatre in the health resort *Bāpasu* [Bypass] in Kyūshū with the audience sitting on the floor, dressed alike in robes provided by the resort. Photo: Christina Nygren.

robes patterned with sea waves provided by the resort. Many are nibbling from small lunchboxes filled with a variety of foods. Most of them fill their cups with tea from big thermos bottles, while a few sip beer or sake. As a billowing blue and white sea, the spectators, newly emerged from the baths, refreshed and fragrant with soap and dressed alike, find transient affinity in the expectant atmosphere.

On stage, the introductory chat has ended and the play has moved on. The acting is fragmented, improvised and unpretentious but strongly melodramatic. The simple stage set does not change, and with only the lines of the actors to guide them, the audience is enticed to imagine time and space. The play proceeds with an air of despair and abject misery; eventually the husband finds out his wife's well-kept secret concerning the boy whom he always regarded as his own son. His inner feelings are again conveyed to the audience through a well known *enka*-song, loudly accompanying his changing of clothes on stage – an outer manifestation of his inner change, while the pre-recorded singing fills the air.

With strongly exaggerated gestures, first hesitating and then resolute, with distanced but expressive inner acting, he forces himself out the door, accompanied by the song:

... playing games of life and death ... tearful ... I am leaving, I am leaving ...[2]

He turns his head to look back at the closed door to the home he is leaving, then, lifting his eyes to an imaginary sky, performs a powerful and carefully choreographed pattern of movements with a final frozen pose. He then continues his bitter walk on the narrow bridge extending the stage to the left. The audience grasps for breath, applauds and cries out its admiration for both the hero of the play, Tokujirō, and the actor Momotarō.

Everybody has had their share of sentimental grief; the painful atmosphere is soon broken by a lovely woman dressed in a white silk-kimono with her head covered by a silken veil who slowly moves through the audience. The masculine hero from the play has been transformed into an *onnagata* – a male impersonator of women. Graceful and with well-balanced gestures, she dances with a traditional touch to another pre-recorded, well known *enka*-song. It is erotically enticing, suggestive of passion but still pleasantly beautiful, attainable yet unattainable at the same time. The experiences of the spectators are comprised in three layers of fictional reality: the actor, the hero of the play and the feminine *onnagata*.

---

2 A line from the popular song *Jinsei* [Life].

Fig. 2: The *onnagata* Ichikawa Eiji is appreciated by the audience who tucks money inside his costume after the dance. Photo: Christina Nygren.

Fig. 3: Dramatic final scene in the play *Zenka mono* [A Criminal Person] by the theatre group *Momotarō Ichiza*. Photo: Christina Nygren.

He is admired and has a close, almost familiar contact with the audience, sometimes shocking them with unconventional and unexpected moves for an elegant woman, such as jumping with both feet together from the stage and running into the audience with a masculine shout "*Irasshai!*" [Welcome!] At the end of his *onnagata* dance performance, he sometimes first thanks the audience in a soft feminine manner – then hoists his skirt, trotting off the stage with masculine steps. An illusion so perfected that he boldly dares to puncture it!

Let's move to China and an example of fieldwork I did there some years ago. Leaving the dull theatre environment of Beijing, where even the famous theatre form *jingju* did not seem to be alive any longer; even the more local theatre forms in the Beijing area are rarely performed for commoners in the capital, but regularly in specially arranged programs for foreign tourists or on TV. All this made me interested to know more about the situation of local theatre in the countryside. During study and research in China, I was told by the authorities that private travelling troupes no longer exist. But by scratching at the surface, I met several and heard about hundreds of other troupes.

Now I am in a village in the dry and cold area of northern Shanxi province. It is already eight in the evening, 14 degrees below zero (Celsius) and thou-

Fig. 4: Stage set, props, music instruments and costumes arrive by truck in the morning to the empty village stage. It will take some six-seven hours to put everything in order for the evening performance. Photo: Christina Nygren.

sands of stars are visible in the clear, dark sky. The audience has waited for hours in front of the outdoor stage, dressed in padded clothes and woollen or fur caps. Many of them are holding small children, wrapped in padded sacks and woollen blankets. A wooden *bangzi*-clapper precedes the beginning of the performance, together with a drum with a metallic sound, giving a hint to the villagers that the play will start very soon. As the actors or the audience breathe, it seems they are exhaling smoke, due to the freezing temperatures.

The play starts with song, music and dialogue, dance and acrobatics, colourful costumes and heavy, mask-like make up. As in all other kinds of traditional Chinese theatre, these components jointly give the performance its character and attraction. The music of this local theatre form, *shangdang bangzi* is intensive and led by a rhythmic wooden clapper, reinforced by percussion instruments to underline special activities in the storyline. The piercing song style supports the drama and conveys a tense atmosphere of excitement and beauty in the sad, sometimes bitter-sweet story. Tonight's play is a sequence of the long drama *Yangmen nüjiang* [The Women Generals of the Yang Family] based on a novel from the Ming Dynasty (1368–1644) set in the much earlier Song Dynasty (960–1279).

Fig. 5: The actress who will perform the main female role makes herself ready in the narrow green room behind the stage. Photo: Christina Nygren.

Fig. 6: The theatre manager, who performs the main male role puts on his make up in an empty classroom in the school close to the open air stage. Photo: Christina Nygren.

The spectators follow the play attentively; people are standing in front of the stage with their hands stuffed inside the arms of their coats. Sometimes one or two people leave, shivering, sadly shaking their head because of the severe cold weather, but many still remain. When a part of the stage set falls to the floor, a murmur of disappointment goes through the audience, but as nobody expects realism on the stage, the incident is forgotten as soon as the piece is put back in its original place.

Just before midnight, the performance ends abruptly, without conclusion or applause. The spectators rush home in the dark, quickly and without uttering a word. The actors run around each other. Withdrawn and shivering, they wait for a free washbowl and hot water from thermos bottles to wash off their oily make up. Everybody is in a hurry to find the place they have been shown to rest and sleep during their stay in the village, such as a villager's kitchen, a small space in an entrance hall nearby or the tiny school gatekeeper's room. Some actors have found an empty classroom in the village school with some desks to put together as a bed, while youngsters have spread their tarpaulin-clad sleeping bags side by side on the earth floor in another empty classroom, where a coal heater gives off lots of smoke and a minimum of warmth. I am taken, walking between dark and already silent houses, to a peasant family on the outskirts of the village. They have given me the use of a small room with a coal heater and I share the space with a motorbike, two bicycles and a pigeon.

Let's now move to Bangladesh and attend a performance of the Bengali local theatre form *yatra* staged by a travelling troupe in a small village. Since the division of the former province of Bengal in 1947 into Indian West Bengal and East Pakistan, the latter in 1971 becoming the independent state of Bangladesh, *yatra* has been politically and religiously controversial. It has still managed to survive through the dedication of the travelling theatre groups and their audiences. The number of these groups however, has been constantly diminishing over the past few years for political and religious reasons.

The village is situated in the south of Bangladesh, not far from the Sundarban mangrove forest. On a riverbank, a *pendel*, a temporary performance space, has been constructed of bamboo poles covered by a huge tent. It is late evening and the performance will continue through the night. The spectators, who started to arrive hours ago, take their seats on the ground close to each other, surrounding the square, raised stage platform placed in the middle of the tent. A piece of cloth barely hides the rough wooden stage enclosed by a fence. Though it is rather hot and humid, the spectators are all wrapped in shawls as protection from the heavy dew that they know will fall far into the night.

The play is preceded by young girls singing a patriotic song, followed by scantily clad women showing their bellies and long, loose hair, while dancing to the latest popular songs from Mumbai or Bengali films.

The young men of the audience shout with joy, standing up dancing with jerky movements while the very small group of female spectators keep close together, hiding their faces behind their shawls. After a few dances, the performance continues with a traditional play, *Kamalar banabas* [Kamala's Exile in the Forest]. The dramatic and sad story, full of both unfaithful intrigues and heroic behaviour, is presented through dialogue, intensive music and singing, and melodramatic acting. The acting style follows an expressive tradition of well-known movement patterns, aiming to reach all spectators on the four sides of the stage. During the night, the play is interrupted twice for short interludes of dance and popular songs with no relevance to the content of the play.

Suddenly, dawn comes and *azan*, the Muslim call for morning prayer, is heard at a distance and the performance comes to an end in the middle of the story. Within a minute we are deprived of the illusion, the dream world where deep love and honesty overcome any evil conspiracy, and where the inhabitants show their strong emotions of life and death in full coloured beauty and awkwardness. Now, the rough wooden stage, the actor's worn and somewhat soiled costumes and heavy make-up bring us back to reality, from the bewitchment of the dim, damp light – the spell is broken. Everybody feels sleepy in the raw morning cold and in haste the *yatra* artists are served one of their two free daily meals on the grounds behind the combined green room and sleeping tent. In a matter of minutes, they eat their rice and exhausted withdraw in silence to their mosquito net covered mattresses spread out on the ground.

The teacher of the village school, who has been sitting among the audience, speaks up, as if he would like to make an excuse to the foreigner to smooth over the feeling of vulgarity, triteness and poverty. "Madam ... *yatra* is a health resort for the Bangladeshis ... we don't have any night clubs or dance palaces ..."

Some young men are standing around us, nodding and wanting me to understand their appreciation of *yatra*, which has been the most popular theatrical entertainment since their childhood. Nowadays, however, this theatre form is often deprived of its full appreciation, not only by religious fundamentalists but also by intellectuals, the highly educated and representatives of highbrow performing arts.

Now, let's look at some of my diary notes from another *yatra* performance in Indian West Bengal some years ago which made clear to me the strength of a theatre that is not ensconced in an elite situation, as is often the case with performances in the theatre halls of the big cities.

Performing Life and Live Theatre: Fiction in Popular Performances — 147

Fig. 7: During the night the theatre performance is interrupted by popular dances by scantily clad women, much appreciated by the male audience. Photo: Christina Nygren.

Fig. 8: A boatscene from *Beder Meye Jyotsna* [The Snake Charmer's Daughter Jyotsna] by *Shitala Opera* performing on a temporary stage in a tent in West Bengal. Photo: Christina Nygren.

It is also a good example of how a theatre audience can move between fiction and reality within a moment.

> We are driving north of Kolkata on gravel roads in the darkness, the velvety black pierced by stars and the glow of a full moon. Two roads intersect in the city of Satgarchia and it is just there that the temporary stage has been built. Thousands of spectators are crouching there, sitting on the road and around the square platform. The heat is smooth and humid and I make my way through the masses of men, women and children who are silently watching a play entitled *Ganga tumi moila keno?* [Ganga, Why Are You So Dirty?]. This drama puts an ambiguous question directed both at the mighty river Ganga and an exploited and humiliated woman in the story. The play goes on with dialogue and music, alternating between being passionate and pleasantly melodious. The tempo is high and beads of perspiration are visible on the actors' heavily made-up faces. But, suddenly, an unrestfulness is felt, first only as a vague misgiving and then with a recognisable sound that creates an impalpable frenzy.
>
> – Watch out for the ambulance!
>
> The already dense mass of people leap to their feet, crowd even closer together, serious and silent, trying to create some open space. The siren is ear-splitting. Cautious but intractable, it cuts through the open swath of the crowd, skirting around the stage, then driving to the south. This immediate encounter between reality and fiction emphasizes

the disparity between real life and a dreamlike feeling. The sound of the sirens slowly fades away. The spectators sink back into their places, moving from the reality of life back to the fiction of theatre. The play continues. The theatre gave life a chance – the encounter is unforgettable.

(Diary notes from Satgarchia, West Bengal, 17 November 1999)

*

In my experience, the integration of popular theatre in society and in people's everyday lives is not merely an aesthetic experience and a form of entertainment. The fictional performances also often have an important function in creating a sense of community and are a unifying force in groups within the social structure. Traditions are passed down through families or through the knowledge and wisdom of masters or elders, and are proudly kept alive by the general public.

The theatre situations we have been talking about do not reflect the modern reality in which the audience lives. Historical and mythological figures and roles are portrayed in theatre and dance, bringing fictional beings to life by inspiring and awakening the spectators' emotions and imaginations, hopes and desires. The "agreement" between spectators and performance creates possibilities to move between reality and non-reality and to experience and enjoy the nature of fiction.

The performing arts do in fact create a platform linking reality and fantasy, where it is possible to confront things that are otherwise unattainable or frightening in the same manner as our own dreams. Everyday life has no real place in performances of the travelling groups or in the dramatic art of popular theatre. Rather, these performances provide an entertaining breathing space where anything can happen.

Bibliography

Nygren, Christina. *Gastar, generaler och gäckande gudinnor. Resande teatersällskap, religiösa festivaler och populära nöjen i dagens Japan och Kina.* [Ghosts, Generals and Georgeous Goddesses. Travelling Theatres, Religious Festivals and Popular Amusements in Contemporary Japan and China]. Stockholm: Carlssons, 2000.
— "Tabi shibai: Popular Theatre in context." *Japanese Theatre & the International stage.* Eds. Stanca Scholz-Cionca and Samuel L. Leiter. Leiden: Brill, 2000. 231–240, ill. Nr. 8–15, 470–475.
— "A breathing space where anything can happen … Travelling theatre in Japan, China, India and Bangladesh in a contextual perspective." *Ethnicity and Identity, Global performance.* Eds. Ravi Chaturvedi and Brian Singleton. New Delhi: Rawat Publications, 2005. 401–416.

- *Brokiga Bengalen. Resande teatersällskap, religiösa festivaler och populära nutida nöjen i indiska Västbengalen och Bangladesh.* [Boundless Bengal. Travelling Theatres, Religious Festivals and Popular Contemporary Amusements in Indian West Bengal and Bangladesh]. Stockholm: Carlssons, 2006a.
- "Appropriations of European Theatre in Japan, China and India." *Literary History: Towards a Global Perspective. Vol. 4. Literary Interactions in the Modern World, 2.* Ed. Stefan Helgesson. Berlin and New York: De Gruyter, 2006b. 199–240.
- "Festivals in Religious or Spiritual Contexts: Examples from Japan, China, India and Bangladesh." *Festivalising! Theatrical Events, Politics and Culture.* Eds. Temple Hauptfleisch, Shulamith Lev-Aladgem, Jacqueline Martin, Willmar Sauter and Henri Schoenmakers. Amsterdam and New York: Rodopi, 2007. 261–280.
- "Impressions From a Visit to the Takarazuka Revue: Theatre in the Parlours of Popular Culture." *Drama, Culture, and Event: Essays on the Theatre of the East and the West.* Ed. Yoshitake Kobayashi. Tokyo: Seijo University Graduate School of Literature, 2008. 133–142.
- "Yatra – Popular Theatre Moving with the Wind." *Folklore in Context. Essays in Honor of Shamsuzzman Khan.* Eds. Firoz Mahmud and Sharani Zaman. Dhaka: University Press, 2010. 227–241.

Sauter, Willmar. *The Theatrical Event: Dynamics of Performance and Perception.* Iowa City, IA: University of Iowa Press, 2000.

Fiction Past and Present: Historical Perspectives

Margalit Finkelberg
Diagnosing Fiction: From Plato to Borges

By any standard, Aristotle's *Poetics* is the foundational text for both the theory and the practice of fiction in Western cultural tradition. From ca. 1500, the *Poetics* became a seminal document that dominated European thought on art and literature in the subsequent three centuries; from ca. 1800, its authority started being questioned, and it was alternately attacked or endorsed for another two hundred years; today, it is still envisaged as an integral part not only of literary theory but also of the theory of drama, cinema, and art in general. (cf. Jauss 1974; Doležel 1988, 1998; Eco 1990) This does not mean, however, that the *Poetics* should a priori be regarded as relevant to any text created in any cultural tradition or indeed to any text that we would regard as literary today. The reason is simple: rather than being a context-free document, the *Poetics* firmly belongs to the time and place of its composition, namely, Athens of the fourth century BCE Furthermore, it cannot be taken separately from the literary theory that preceded it, above all that of Plato. In what follows, I will try to examine whether the idea of fiction as crystallized in ancient Greek literary theory, first and foremost, in Plato and Aristotle, may be considered universally valid. I will also try to descry certain common misapprehensions concerning this idea.

The Invention of Mimesis

The ontological status of artistic representation. The Ancient Greek theory of fiction was founded by Plato. It is indeed Plato who was the first to introduce a category which has once and for all isolated fiction as a special sphere of human production which cannot be measured by the "true/false" criterion. I mean the category of artistic representation, or mimesis. Since Plato's contribution is not as well-known as that of Aristotle, it deserves our special attention here.

In everything concerning Plato's theory of mimesis, Book 10 of the *Republic* is essential. (cf. Finkelberg 1998, 181–191) Here, Plato sets out to prove that any artistic representation is at a third remove from reality. The work of fine arts should be placed first after the idea of the artefact and second after the work of the craftsman who produces the artefact; by the same token, the work of poetry should be placed first after the idea of justice and second after the activity of the king. But did Plato really mean that, as is often supposed, the picture of a couch is an exact copy of the real couch made by the craftsman? In fact, his argument concerning the relation between the work of mimetic art and reality is not as straightforward as many are ready to believe.

Plato's argument in *Republic* 10 falls into two parts. It begins with a description of the mimetic artist who aims at creating a likeness of reality; yet, judging by what Plato says in *Republic* 10, he does not think it possible that mimesis is capable of producing exact replicas of its models. This is true not only of the painter who reproduces the couch made by the craftsman but also of the kind of mimesis in which the craftsman himself, reproducing the one and only idea of the couch, is involved: the work of both is only "a dim adumbration (*amudron ti*) in comparison with truth." (597b) The premise from which Plato proceeds in this and similar contexts is that *any* mimetic representation would involve distortion of the model, thus turning every form of reproduction into no more than "dim adumbration." This would be true even of the kind of reproduction supplied by the object's reflection in a mirror because, according to the view expressed by Plato more than once, in virtue of the fact that it exchanges left for right and vice versa the reflection in the mirror is actually a standard example of distortion of reality. (*Theaet.* 193c; *Tim.* 46a, 71b; *Soph.* 239d)

The second part of Plato's argument concerns only mimetic art and deals with the artist who has no intention to reproduce the exact likeness of his model. Plato's argument runs as follows. Whereas a real couch is always the same, although it appears different "according as you view it from the side or the front or in any other way," what the picture of a couch reproduces is only this very appearance without the sameness of the actual couch. Accordingly, such a picture is nothing more than a phantom:

> Then the mimetic art is far removed from truth, and this, it seems, is the reason why it can create everything, because it touches or lays hold of only a small part of the object and that a phantom (*eidôlon*), as, for example, a painter, we say, will paint us a cobbler, a carpenter, and other craftsmen, though he himself has no expertness in any of these arts, but nevertheless if he were a good painter, by exhibiting at a distance his picture of a carpenter he would deceive children and foolish men, and make them believe it to be a real carpenter.[1]

Obviously, neither the mirror-like imitation nor, moreover, the imitation which deliberately misrepresents its model can be regarded as an exact reproduction of the object it imitates. No such thing as the exact copy or replica of a real thing is therefore possible.

Both arguments are recapitulated and taken further in the *Sophist*. In this dialogue, which continues the discussion of the ontological status of the repre-

---

[1] *Resp.* 598b, c, trans. Paul Shorey, with slight changes; cf. also 598a.

sentational arts begun in *Republic* 10, Plato goes to great trouble in trying to eliminate the claim of the mimetic artist, adduced already in the *Republic*, that he is able "to create everything" by his art. Yet, he cannot avoid the conclusion that, in so far as the objects of art cannot be envisaged as replicas of already existing things, their presence produces an ontological problem. This is especially true of those sculptors or painters whose works are of colossal size:

> If they were to reproduce the true proportions of a well-made figure, as you know, the upper parts would look too small, and the lower too large, because we see the one at a distance, the other close at hand. [...] So artists, leaving the truth to take care of itself, do in fact put into the images they make, not the real proportions, but those that will appear beautiful. (*Soph.* 235e–236a, trans. Francis M. Cornford)

Further on in the same dialogue, Plato admits, again in full accordance with *Republic* 10, that even the images created by mirror-like imitation, that is, those that do not deliberately distort the proportions of their model, cannot be regarded as this model's truthful representations. The conclusion, again, is that there is no way in which the creation of the exact likeness of a given natural object can be possible.

There is thus no reality of which the "imitation" can be considered to be a copy. This fact turns the existence of the work of mimetic art into a real ontological puzzle:

> The truth is, my friend, that we are faced with an extremely difficult question. The "appearing" or "seeming" without really "being", and the saying of something which yet is not true – all these expressions have always been and still are deeply involved in perplexity (*aporia*). It is extremely hard, Theaetetus, to find correct terms in which one may say or think that falsehoods (*pseudê*) have a real existence, without being caught in a contradiction by the mere utterance of such words. (236e–237a)

That is to say, in so far as "falsehoods" cannot be regarded as, to put it in Plato's own words, "another truth" (*heteron ... alêthinon* 240a), they should inevitably be credited with some sort of real existence. This in fact is the conclusion Plato eventually arrives at in the *Sophist*. His reasoning is quite simple. In so far as the images of art cannot be regarded as copies of really existing things (and we saw that Plato envisages no condition on which this can be possible), these images cannot be regarded as reflections of reality any more than lies can be regarded as a reflection of truth. Or, to put it in Plato's words again,

> [...] anyone who talks of false statements or false judgements as being images (*eidôla*) or likenesses (*eikones*) or copies (*mimêmata*) or semblances (*phantasmata*), or of any of the arts concerned with such things, can hardly escape becoming a laughing stock by being forced to contradict himself. (241e)

Accordingly, the images of art should be credited with some sort of independent existence of their own: not being a reflection of reality, they can only be treated as a reality of a different order.

The response of the audience. At the same time, there is little room for doubt that not only ontological problems were in Plato's mind when he was formulating his conclusions as regards the status of poetry. This can already be seen from the apparent lack of coherence with which he treats the issue of mimesis in Book 3 of the *Republic*. Indeed, it is only through the use of a mixed criterion combining the relation of poetry to reality and its effect on the human soul that he eventually manages to banish almost any form of poetry from his ideal state. (cf. Finkelberg 1998, 4–5) The reception of poetry by the audience was thus no less important to him than its status in respect of reality. This strongly suggests that Plato's concept of mimesis cannot be properly understood unless it is placed within the historical context to which it belonged.

It would not be enough to state simply that according to Plato the effect of poetry is pleasure: we should define what exactly this pleasure meant in Plato's eyes. The first and more obvious answer is found, again, in *Republic* 10: Homer and tragedy act upon the inferior, that is, the irrational, part of the soul, in that they present characters who openly express the emotions which we are expected to suppress in real life, thus destroying the superior, that is, the rational, part of it:

> I think you know that the very best of us, when we hear Homer or some other of the makers of tragedy representing one of the heroes who is in grief, and is delivering a long tirade in his lamentations or chanting and beating his breast, are delighted, and abandon ourselves and follow the action, suffering together with the characters, and eagerly praise as an excellent poet the one who most strongly affects us in this way. (605d)

And further on:

> [...] the part of the soul which in the former case, in our own misfortunes, was forcibly restrained, and which has always hungered for tears and a good cry and satisfaction, because it is its nature to desire these things, is the very element in us that the poets satisfy and delight, while the best element in our nature, since it has never been properly educated by reason or even by habit, now relaxes its guard over the plaintive part, inasmuch as it is being engaged in contemplating the sufferings of others and it is no shame to itself to praise and pity another who, claiming to be a good man, abandons himself to excess in his grief – on the contrary, it thinks that this vicarious pleasure is so much clear gain, and would not consent to forfeit it by disdaining the poem altogether. (606a, b)

It can be seen from these passages that, although the eagerness of the soul to indulge in emotions is seen by Plato as a natural instinct, the process by which the emotions of the characters in Homer and tragedy take hold of the spectators' souls is represented by him as a sort of contamination: "our own emotions inevitably get advantage from those of the others." It can also be seen that in Plato's eyes the effect caused by poetry is not simply to arouse the emotions of fear and pity but to cause the audience actually to identify itself with the characters who experience such emotions: this is where the pleasure caused by poetry finally comes from. "We are delighted, and abandon ourselves and follow the action, suffering together with the characters" – this description in *Republic* 10 gives the clearest idea of the degree of emotional involvement experienced by the Athenian audience when Homer and tragedy were being performed.

This is where the illusion of reality created by mimetic art meets pleasure as its essential effect. Just as a good painter, by exhibiting at a distance his picture of a carpenter, "would deceive children and foolish men, and make them believe it to be a real carpenter," so also a good poet, by exposing his audiences to an illusionary reality created by his art, would make them lose their identities and be transported into a reality which has no direct correspondence to their real lives. In other words, it is only in virtue of its ability to cause the audience to sympathize with fictitious events as if they were real that poetry is presented as a full-scale competitor to real life. This was exactly where Plato saw the greatest danger of all.

There can be no doubt that Plato's theory of mimetic poetry acted as the groundwork for Aristotle's *Poetics*. But there equally can be no doubt that Aristotle uses Plato's theory of mimesis to build a hierarchy of preferences directly opposed to Plato's. (Else 1957, 97–100; Janko 1987, x–xiv; Finkelberg 1998, 10–11, 189–190) Like Plato before him, Aristotle recognized that the work of poetry had come to possess an ontological status of its own, but while in Plato this amounted to the emergence of a threatening rival to reality, for Aristotle the representation of "what might have happened" was more philosophical and therefore potentially more cognitively valuable than the actual events. Again like Plato, Aristotle saw that, in virtue of its ability to cause the audience to identify themselves with the characters, mimetic poetry exerts a profound emotional influence on the soul, but while Plato interpreted this influence as contamination of the soul by the emotions of fear and pity causing the spectators to lose their identities, Aristotle saw that if the action represented in poetry is of the right, "philosophical," kind, these very emotions can purge the soul and thus allow an ordinary man, by sharing for a while the edifying experience of the characters, to arrive at the kind of pleasure which comes as close as possible to the pure cognitive pleasure experienced by the philosopher.

Fiction as Cultural Artefact

Mimetic and non-mimetic poetry. Let us now try to outline the boundaries of literary fiction as drawn by Plato and Aristotle. It may come as a surprise that, its title notwithstanding, the subject of the *Poetics* is not poetry as such nor any kind of poetry. For historical reasons, of which the main one was the late appearance of prose on the Greek literary scene, poetry in Greece embraced both fictional and non-fictional genres, such as history, philosophy and science. When discussing "poetry" Aristotle, just as Plato before him, actually meant the mimetic, that is, representational, poetry, and first and foremost tragedy and Homer. Accordingly, it is only this kind of poetry that would correspond to what we call "fiction" today. Both Plato and Aristotle identified it as the art of mimesis, or representation (by no means imitation), of reality, whose final product is a plausible illusion, a reality *sui generis*, as it were, which cannot be judged by the "true/false" criterion. As Aristotle himself admits, there was no appropriate term to designate this phenomenon. The following passage from the first chapter of the *Poetics* is especially illuminating in this respect:

> There is another art which represents by means of language alone, and that either in prose or verse [...] but this has hitherto been without a name. For there is no common term we could apply to the mimes of Sophron and Xenarchus and the Socratic dialogues on the one hand; and, on the other, to poetic representations in iambic, elegiac, or any similar metre. People do, indeed, add the word "poet" to the name of the metre, and speak of elegiac poets, or epic poets, as if it were not the representation (*mimêsis*) that makes the poet, but the verse that entitles them all indiscriminately to the name. Even when a treatise on medicine or natural science is brought out in verse, the name of poet is by custom given to the author; and yet Homer and Empedocles have nothing in common but the metre, so that it would be right to call the one poet, the other natural philosopher rather than poet. (1447a28–b20, trans. Samuel H. Butcher)

For Aristotle, non-representational poetry is a form of philosophical or scientific discourse and thus indistinguishable from the philosophical or scientific discourse cast in prose. Plato too, was well aware of the fact that not all poetry is necessarily mimetic or, to put it differently, that poetry serves not only as the medium of fiction. In *Phaedrus*, for example, the mimetic poet is opposed to the one who composes "with a knowledge of the truth"; the kind of poetry represented by the latter is treated by Plato as a subdivision of philosophy. (278b–e; cf. also 245a, 248d–e) Thus, proceeding from the above-mentioned function of poetry as the vehicle of both fiction and non-fiction, Plato redefines non-fictional poetry as not being poetry at all.

Aristotle, however, goes much further than that. As the passage quoted above demonstrates, he subsumes such prose genres as the mime and the

Socratic dialogue, the only two forms of prose fiction which existed in his time, under the category of "poetry." To outline with greater precision the limits of poetry as envisaged in Greek literary theory, it would be sufficient to point out that consistent application of Aristotle's criteria would mean admitting into the realm of poetry the novels of, say, Tolstoy, but excluding from it the poems of, say, Hölderlin. It is not surprising, therefore, that lyric poetry, the only genre which, in virtue of being non-mimetic, was partly admitted by Plato into his ideal state, finds no classificatory niche of its own in Aristotle's *Poetics*.

Nevertheless, it is a common misapprehension that, since Aristotle's treatise ostensibly relates to poetry, any piece of poetry, or at least any piece of poetry produced within Western cultural tradition, is amenable to treatment in Aristotelian categories, especially that of the imitation of nature. This is how, for example, Stephen Owen, the author of a book on traditional Chinese poetry and poetics, distinguishes between Western and Chinese lyric poetry (1985, 34):

> In the Chinese literary tradition, a poem is usually presumed to be nonfictional: its statements are taken as strictly true. Meaning is not discovered by a metaphorical operation in which the words of the text point to Something Else. Instead, the empirical world signifies for the poet, and the poem makes that event manifest.

To bring his point home, Owen (1985, 14–15) compares two lyric poems, one by Wordsworth and the other by the eighth-century Chinese poet Du Fu, his main claim being that while the former is an authentic representative of Western fictionality (the imitation of nature etc.), the latter displays what he defines as Chinese factuality. In a similar vein, in his attempt to show that Chinese poetry does not fall short of its Western counterpart, the Chinese scholar Zhang Longxi (1996, 15–35) simply claims that it does possess the Aristotelian virtue of the imitation of nature after all. Both scholars seem to be unaware that in Aristotle's eyes any piece of first-person, or lyric, poetry, no matter whether ancient Greek, modern European or Chinese, would be equally non-mimetic and therefore non-fictional.

I would add in passing that one of the reasons for this terminological confusion seems to be that "fiction," the only contemporary term that does justice to Aristotle's idea of representational literature, is often seen as synonymous to such all-inclusive terms as "belles lettres" or "fine literature," which also embrace such non-representational genres as lyric poetry, biography, history, and the like. The two latter especially, some recent claims notwithstanding, should be kept separate from fiction for the simple reason that, as distinct from fiction, they are meant to be judged by the "true/false" criterion. Lubomír Doležel's (1998, 790) penetrating analysis saves me many words here:

> It is one thing to write in a certain style, but it is a completely different thing to make truth claims. Literariness and truth-functionality are two distinct qualities of writing: the former is a property of texture, the latter is a matter of the communicative aims and speech-act characteristics of textual activity. History, journalism, legal and political discourse, and so forth, all falling into the domain of cognitive communication, can be conducted in styles of various degrees of poeticity. But no flights of poetry or rhetoric can liberate them from truth-valuation. On the other hand, the most "pedestrian" styles have no effect on the lack of truth-valuation of fictional texts.

The lack of truth-valuation is indeed the most salient characteristic of the idea of fiction as crystallized in ancient Greek and, later, Western literary theory.

Fiction in context. This is not to say that the theory of fiction as developed in classical Greece should be regarded as universally applicable. Note indeed that both Plato and Aristotle approach literary fiction in distinctly illusionist terms (Finkelberg 2006). Thus, according to Aristotle, the elements of the tragic plot should form an indissoluble chain in which the arrangement of events would lead to the creation of a plausible illusion of real-life experience and, as a result, to the audience's emotional identification with the characters – the same identification whose danger was so vigorously emphasized by Plato (above). Everything that disrupts the tight cause-and-effect sequence of events would break the dramatic illusion and prevent the spectator's or the reader's identification with the characters. In other words, any interference with the artistic illusion would amount to what is today termed "emotional distancing," thus leading to the practice and theory of fiction essentially different from those introduced by the Greeks.

It is only rarely taken into account that artistic illusion is not a given but, rather, a cultural convention which, like any other convention, is ineffective unless socially interiorized. Niall Slater's caveat seems to be relevant here:

> A sustained, illusionistic representation of character and situation is a creation of a particular, historical moment. It is a convention, an agreement or contract (usually implicit but sometimes explicitly negotiated) between performers and audience on certain expectations about character and action.[2]

Note indeed that until quite recently it was the non-illusionist representation that was the norm in the non-Western traditions of fiction. It is not for nothing that Bertolt Brecht found in the Chinese theatre, with its tradition of performance in which the actor, rather than identifying with the character, "limits himself from the start to simply quoting the character played" (Willett 1964,

---

2 Slater 2002, 3. Cf. Bourdieu 1993, 35: "The work of art is an object which exists as such only by virtue of the (collective) belief which knows and acknowledges it as a work of art."

94), a welcome antidote to the illusionist performance traditions of the West. The distancing practices of both actors and audience in the Japanese traditional theatre and the highly elaborate metapoetic principles characteristic of the literary traditions of India point in the same direction. It appears, therefore, that, when taken in a broader historical perspective, it is the non-illusionist representation that proves to be the general practice, whereas the principles on which Plato's and Aristotle's theory of fiction is based are idiosyncratic. This brings us back to the specific historical context in which these principles were formulated.

As I have argued elsewhere, Athens of the fifth century BCE was where for the first time literary fiction was consolidated as an independent sphere, irreducible to any other sphere of human activity. (Finkelberg 1998, 172–181) The recognition of the fact that fiction created a new cultural space that needed its own nomenclature was signalled, among other things, by the famous definition of tragedy given by Gorgias:

> Tragedy is a deception (*apatê*) in which the deceiver is more just than one who did not deceive and the deceived is more wise than one who was not deceived.[3]

As Gorgias' words indicate, the Athenian festivals in the course of which Homer and tragedy were performed created an audience sophisticated enough to demand from what was presented on the tragic stage a degree of artistic illusion allowing for the spectators' emotional identification with the characters. Characteristically, Gorgias' definition of tragic *apatê* is adduced by Plutarch (*Mor.* 15 C–D) in the context of an argument that only a cultivated audience is susceptible to an effect of this kind:

> For the deception (*to apatêlon*) of poetry does not affect utterly foolish and witless persons. This is the reason why, when asked "Why are the Thessalians the only ones whom you fail to deceive?", Simonides answered: "For they are too ignorant to be deceived by me"; and Gorgias called tragedy a deception etc.

A passage from Plato's *Ion* describes how both Ion, an illustrious performer of Homeric poetry, and his audience react to Ion's recitation of Homer. Ion acknowledges that he weeps whenever he recites a pitiful episode and his hair

---

[3] *Gorgias* 82 B 23 DK. My translation. Cf. Bierl 1990, 367–368, commenting on the tragic *apatê*: "The precondition of the function of theatre is an agreement between poet and audience on the process of communication. The poet must have the ability to exert 'deception' on the public; but the public must be willing to be 'deceived', that is to become involved in the illusion the poet produces."

stands on end with fear whenever an episode of terror is told; he also admits that the same effect is produced in his audiences as well:

> As I look down at them from the stage above, I see them, every time, weeping, casting terrible glances, stricken with amazement at the deeds recounted. In fact, I have to give them very close attention, for if I set them weeping, I myself shall laugh when I get my money, but if they laugh, it is I who have to weep at losing it. (535b, e, trans. L. Cooper)

Causing emotional turmoil in the listeners is therefore the very thing the performer is paid for. To quote Gorgias again:

> There comes over the audience of poetry a fearful horror and tearful pity and doleful yearning. By means of the discourse their spirit feels a personal emotion on account of the good and bad fortune of others. (82 B 11.9 DK. Trans. Oliver Taplin)

It was above all this audience whose demands prescribed much of what was happening on the Attic stage. As far as our evidence goes, these demands can be epitomized in two words – "illusion" (*apatê*) and "pleasure" (*hêdonê*).[4]

Gorgias addressed the illusionist tendencies that started to develop in the performance of Homer and tragedy in Athens in the second half of the fifth century BCE In the fourth century these tendencies became predominant. The Old Attic Comedy, with its face-to-face contact with the audience, gave place to the Middle and New Comedy. To quote Slater (2002, 7) again:

> From Greek New Comedy descends a long and rich tradition in western comedy, whose variations still play themselves out on stage and screen. [...] Most of these plays rely on a sentimental identification of audience with the play's participants and avoid any disruption of that identification with a stage illusion.

The illusionistic trends in fourth-century Greek painting and sculpture should also be mentioned in this connection.[5] Plato's criticism of mimetic poetry and painting in *Republic* 10 and of mimetic sculpture in the *Sophist* as adduced above emerged as a direct reaction to these developments, and it was these developments again that Aristotle's theory of mimesis addressed.

Thus, when placed within its historical context, the *Poetics*, with its privileging of the illusionist representation, proves to be strongly rooted in the time and place of its composition. It was, however, the historical circumstances of

---

[4] Commenting on the power of the ancient theatre to influence mass audiences, P. E. Easterling (1997, 214) brings forward a quotation from the pseudo-Platonic *Minos* (321), where tragedy is described as the branch of poetry "most delightful to the mass of the people (*dêmoterpestaton*) and most powerful in its appeal to the emotions (*psuchagôgikôtaton*)."

[5] On painting, see e.g. Richter 1959, 277–278; on sculpture, see Pollitt 1972, 157–159, 174–178.

its reception in early modern Europe and the ensuing worldwide dominance of Western cultural tradition that determined the all-pervasive influence of the *Poetics* not only on Western but eventually also on non-Western literary theory and practice, thus bestowing on its rather idiosyncratic idea of fiction an aura of universality.

Afterword: "Averroes's Search"

Let me conclude with a story. The main thesis of this paper can be found in encapsulated form in "Averroes's Search," a short story by Jorge Luis Borges. (1970, 180–188; trans. J. E. Irby) Its plot outline is as follows. When working on his commentary on Aristotle's *Poetics*, Averroes is halted by two mysterious words which appear at the very beginning of the treatise. "He had encountered them years before in the third book of the *Rhetoric*; no one in the whole world of Islam could conjecture what they meant." The words whose meaning escapes Averroes are "tragedy" and "comedy." "Averroes put down his pen. He told himself (without excessive faith) that what we seek is often nearby ..."

This was a routine day in the life of the great Andalusian scholar, a day on the evening of which he was supposed to dine with the Koran scholar Farach and his guests, among them the poet Abdalmalik and the traveller Abulcasim Al-Ashari, who claimed to have reached the dominions of the empire of Sin (China). When still at home, Averroes watches through the balcony a group of playing children who impersonate a muezzin, the minaret, and the worshippers. Later on, during the dinner at Farach's, Abulcasim gives the learned company a detailed account of one of his Chinese experiences, namely, his visit to the theatre (Borges 1970, 184):

> They suffered prison, but no one could see the jail; they travelled on horseback, but no one could see the horse; they fought, but the swords were of reed; they died and then stood up again.

Abulcasim's audience perceives the theatrical performance he described as "the acts of madmen." "These were no madmen," Abulcasim tries to explain. "They were representing a story, a merchant told me." "No one understood, no one seemed to want to understand." (Borges 1970, 184)

The conversation switches to a discussion of Arabic poetry, in the course of which Abdalmalik claims that the pastoral images and Bedouin vocabulary of the great pre-Islamic poet Zuhair (Zuhayr), such as for example his comparison of destiny to a blind camel, are not appropriate for the poets of contemporary Damascus or Cordova. Averroes disagrees, presenting a highly sophisticated argument concerning the suggestive nature of a poetic metaphor. (Borges 1970, 186) When back home, he suddenly feels that something has revealed for him the meaning of the two obscure words (Borges 1970, 187):

> With firm and careful calligraphy he added these lines to the manuscript: "Aristu (Aristotle) gives the name of tragedy to panegyrics and that of comedy to satires and anathemas. Admirable tragedies and comedies abound in the pages of the Koran and in the *mohalacas* of the sanctuary."

It is not difficult to discern that both the children's play and the account of the Chinese theatre act as stray hints, as it were, which the Muslim sage fails to understand. The former represents the universal basis of the phenomenon of which the Greek theatre and the Chinese theatre are two particular realizations. "What we seek is often nearby..." is said immediately before the description of the children's play; "no one understood, no one seemed to want to understand" is the author's comment on the audience's reaction to the description of the Chinese theatre. But, if I read Borges correctly, the exquisite metaphors of Arabic poetry are meant to represent a cultural option – a "strategic possibility," as Michel Foucault would have put it[6] – that a cultural tradition no less sophisticated than Greek or Chinese but alien to the idea of fiction chose to develop.[7] And there is nothing to it to be worried about.[8]

Bibliography

Bierl, Anton. "Dionysus, Wine and Tragic Poetry: A Metatheatrical Reading of *P. Köln* VI 242A = *TrGF* II F646A." *Greek, Roman and Byzantine Studies* 31 (1990): 353–391.
Borges, Jorge Luis. *Labyrinths*. Eds. Donald A. Yates and James E. Irby. Penguin Modern Classics. Harmondsworth: Penguin, 1970.
Bourdieu, Pierre. *The Field of Cultural Production. Essays on Art and Literature*. Ed. Randal Johnson. New York: Columbia University Press, 1993.
Doležel, Lubomir. "Mimesis and Possible Worlds." *Poetics Today* 9.3 (1988): 475–496.
— "Possible Worlds of Fiction and History." *New Literary History* 29.4 (1998): 785–809.

---

[6] Cf. Foucault 1977, 37: "Rather than seeking the permanence of themes, images, and opinions through time, rather than retracing the dialectic of their conflicts in order to individualize groups of statements, could one not rather mark out the dispersion of the points of choice, and define prior to any option, to any thematic preference, a field of strategic possibilities?"
[7] On this subject see e.g. Heinrichs 1969, esp. 37–46. The same appears to be true of the other Near Eastern traditions as well, the Babylonian and the Hebrew ones being the most notable examples.
[8] An earlier version of this paper was read at the conference Fiction Across Cultures held at the Institute for Advanced Studies, Jerusalem, in December 2007.

Easterling, Patricia E. "From Repertoire to Canon." *The Cambridge Companion to Greek Tragedy*. Ed. Patricia E. Easterling. Cambridge: Cambridge University Press, 1997. 211–227.

Eco, Umberto. "Thoughts on Aristotle's *Poetics*." *Fiction Updated: Theories of Fictionality, Narratology, and Poetics*. Eds. Calin-Andrei Mihailescu and Walid Hamarneh. Toronto: University of Toronto Press, 1990. 229–243.

Else, Gerard F. *Aristotle's Poetics: The Argument*. Leiden: Brill, 1957.

Finkelberg, Margalit. *The Birth of Literary Fiction in Ancient Greece*. Oxford: Clarendon, 1998.

— "Aristotle and Episodic Tragedy." *Greece and Rome* 53 (2006): 60–72.

Foucault, Michel. *The Archaeology of Knowledge*. Trans. Alan M. Sheridan Smith. London: Tavistock, 1977.

Heinrichs, Wolfhart. *Arabische Dichtung und griechische Poetik*. Wiesbaden: Steiner, 1969.

Janko, Richard. *Aristotle. Poetics*. Indianapolis, IN: Hackett, 1987.

Jauss, Hans Robert. "Levels of Identification of Hero and Audience." *New Literary History* 5.2 (1974): 283–317.

Owen, Stephen. *Traditional Chinese Poetry and Poetics: Omen of the World*. Madison, WI: University of Wisconsin Press, 1985.

Pollitt, Jerome Jordan. *Art and Experience in Classical Greece*. Cambridge: Cambridge University Press, 1972.

Richter, Gisela M. A. *A Handbook of Greek Art. A Survey of the Visual Arts of Ancient Greece*. Oxford: Phaidon Press, 1959.

Slater, Niall W. *Spectator Politics: Metatheatre and Performance in Aristophanes*. Philadelphia, PA: University of Pennsylvania Press, 2002.

Willett, John, ed. *Brecht on Theatre: The Development of an Aesthetic*. New York: Hill and Wang, 1964.

Zhang Longxi. "What is 'wen' and why is it made so terribly strange?" *College Literature* 23 (1996): 15–35.

Bo Utas
Classical Persian Literature:
Fiction, Didactics or Intuitive Truth?

The concept of "fiction" is problematic when applied to Classical Persian literature, that is, texts of a literary character composed in the New Persian language from around 1000–1500 CE – written as well as oral. There is not even in Modern Persian an indigenous term for "fiction," so we may conclude that the concept as such did not exist in the period we are discussing either. A number of circumstances led to an integrated mixture of fact and fantasy in the literary experience of the Iranians, which means that it is generally quite difficult to sort out fictional and imaginary elements in their texts. For a discussion of Classical Persian fiction, a simple way out would be to equate fiction with narration. That is what we find in the solid entry on "Fiction" contributed by J. T. P. de Bruijn (1999, 572–579) to the *Encyclopædia Iranica*. There he begins by stating that the general Persian word for narrative is *dāstān* and that "the concept of 'fictionality', in the sense of narrative not based on reality, was not much discussed in traditional criticism." (1999, 572) (He means, I think, that generally it was not considered at all). Then de Bruijn goes on to treat all kinds of narratives, be they in prose or verse, in popular language or high literary style, oral or written.

There is a wealth of narrative texts in Classical Persian, but what we know about how those texts were produced and received makes it likely that there was little consideration of how they related to factual events. Like most peoples, Iranians have been fond of stories since time immemorial, but before the Classical period (1000–1500), storytelling was almost completely oral and thus not accessible to us today. By chance, we can glean something of it from later records, like the Persian elements occurring in the *Arabian Nights*, earlier recorded in a Middle Persian collection called *Hazār afsānag* [Thousand Tales]. Later on, a number of cycles of stories were taken down in writing, but such popular texts were never considered to be part of what we now would call "fine literature." (known at the time as *adab*; Utas 2006, 203). Moreover, the wide array of such texts that have been passed on to modern times, in oral as well as in written form, were hardly thought of as being fictive stories but rather as tales of adventures and events that really had taken place somewhere and sometime. This would also include stories featuring demons, djinns, witches, magicians, fairies and angels. Many of those stories would have a strong didactic bent while others were more clearly meant for entertainment – often both at the same time.

Traditional Persian stories generally describe the adventures of heroes, warriors, kings, princes and loving couples, often belonging to national legendary history integrated in what was considered true and factual history. Those legendary heroes and kings partly originated in pre-Islamic religious traditions and partly in secular traditions and myths. This amalgamated historical tradition was collected in written form already before the advent of Islam (in the seventh century) in a compilation entitled *Khvadāy-nāmag* [Book of Lords], which unfortunately is lost. At the dawn of the Classical Persian period, it was displayed anew in the glorious national verse epic *Shāh-nāme* [Book of Kings] by Ferdousi (d. around 1025). Here, we meet completely legendary kings, belonging to the religious tradition found also in the Zoroastrian canon *Avesta* gradually passing over to historical rulers like Darius the Great and Alexander the Greek. Moreover, *Shāh-nāme* features a wealth of marvellous heroes of war, some of whom possibly depended on a distant factual historical background, as well as romantic stories of love, some of which may be traced more than a millennium back. In the *Shāh-nāme*, the major stories are regularly called *dāstān* [narrative], and they became the model for numerous later epic poems, both short works developing one story and comprehensive works that feature series of stories within a historical or romantic frame.[1]

Naturally, this national lore cannot be expected to differentiate between legendary and real history, and this seems to be a pattern that is repeated all through the extremely rich repository of traditional stories from which tales, exempla, parables and allegories were drawn in popular as well as literary compositions in various genres during the whole Classical period. Imported stories also became part of the Iranian narrative world. Thus we meet stories from India, like the fables known under their Arabic title as *Kalila and Dimna* (two jackals that figure in the frame story),[2] as well as Aramaic, Hebrew and Arabic traditions, not least Biblical and Koranic stories, and from the integrated Greek-Near Eastern culture that is called "Hellenism." To this, of course, new stories, about both historical persons and freely invented events, were continually added. Generally, this narrative repertoire was anonymous, but the various works that culled their illustrations from it were written by authors known by name.

---

[1] For general information on Persian works and authors that appear here and in the following, see the index in Rypka 1968.

[2] This extremely influential collection of fables is known in the West as *Fables of Bidpai* or *Tales of Pilpay*, see e.g. Aravamudan 2011, 129–150. The fictionality of fables is, of course, beyond questioning. However, they belong to the complex of traditional wisdom literature which is focused on didactics rather than fiction.

Persian prose generally had a strong didactic orientation, either as strictly moral exhortation or as general wisdom of life, often slanting towards outright Machiavellian advice. The latter type is especially found in the popular genre *specula principum* [mirrors for princes]. One of the earliest and most readable examples of this is the *Nasīhat-nāme* [Book of Counsels], which is better known as *Qābūs-nāme* [Book of Qabus] after the name of the grandfather of the Ziyarid ruler who wrote it for his son at the end of the eleventh century. There we find a wealth of anecdotes illustrating good courtly behaviour and statesmanship. This is an eminently readable book that shows that the Sasanian art of storytelling had survived in the new Muslim era. It treats all aspects of social life and culture and discusses literary topics with much insight. However, questions of fact or fantasy are never touched upon. (Kai Kā'ūs 1951)

Later centuries saw the composition of a number of collections of useful anecdotes and tales. The largest of them was compiled in 1228 by Mohammad 'Oufi, who was also the author of one of the first substantial histories of Persian poetry, *Lobāb ol-albāb* [Quintessence of Hearts]. Such collections of stories were very useful not only for literati but also for all kinds of preachers. A good story was, as often as not, regarded as the best proof of a point – historicity left aside. The apex of this didactical tradition is the famous collection of narratives composed in elaborate prose in 1258 by Sheikh Sa'di under the title *Golestān* [Rose Garden]. There he tells a great number of stories, some allegedly autobiographical, in which the moral – and at times not so moral – points are underlined by small, cunning poems. This is possibly the most successful of all Persian literary works in prose, and it is still widely read and continually quoted in support of all kinds of ideas and persuasions.

Although such texts as the *Golestān* were considered *adab* – the closest we can get to our modern concept of literature, it was generally poetry that counted as fine literature in the Classical tradition. Poetry was not only composed in bound form, in a restricted number of carefully regulated quantitative metres and using obligatory final rhymes, but it was also characterized by the use of elevated and adorned language and a set of rhetorical figures and metaphors. Even prose works, like the *Golestān*, emulated poetry by using the same kind of language, as well as rhyming sequences and inserted verses (in both Persian and Arabic). The predilection of the Iranians for storytelling invaded their poetry, too. As I mentioned in the beginning, the national epic, *Shāh-nāme*, already excelled in telling stories and became the paragon of countless later works, but there was also an independent tradition of romantic verse epics. The seemingly oldest of these is *Vis and Ramin*, the names of two lovers who are embroiled in illicit love in a story that bears great resemblance to that of *Tristan and Isolde*. The first Persian version was written by Fakhr od-din Gorgani at the end of the eleventh century, but it is clearly based on a pre-Islamic narrative. The heroine, Vis, is married to the old king of Marv, Mubad Manikan, but she falls in love with the king's younger brother, Ramin, together with whom she was brought up. This long and erotically outspoken poem was obviously regarded as being so frivolous that it was repressed in the later, more Islamic tradition and then forgotten for centuries. Since there are no historical traces of the main characters, this could be regarded as a real piece of fiction, although it was probably still read as a report from the past. (Fakhr ud-Dīn Gurgānī 1972)

Another early romance that must be seen as fiction in a more precise sense is a poem with the title *Vamiq and 'Azra*, two telling names that mean "Ardent lover" and "Virgin." The earliest known Persian version was written at the beginning of the eleventh century by 'Onsori, a court poet in the East-Iranian capital Ghazna. It is a Persian adaptation in verse of a Greek prose novel known as *Metiokhos and Parthenope*. The Greek original is about a thousand years older than the Persian poem, and the ways in which the story reached Eastern Iran are obscure. Unfortunately, both the Greek original and the Persian poem are incomplete. Only fragments of the first part of the story are preserved, and it is impossible to follow the plot to the end. (Hägg and Utas 2003) It is of special interest to note that the original story belongs to the type of Greek romances that were written by authors like Khariton and Xenophon of Ephesos in the first centuries CE, since those prose texts have been considered precursors of the modern novel. However, this is not the only type of Greek narrative material that turns up in Persian literature. We also meet it in Persian versions of the so-called Alexander Romance and in a number of connected pseudo-historical narratives that appear in popular stories associated with Alexander's alleged Iranian half-brother Darab, that is, Darius.

Another type of romance was borrowed from the Arabs, namely the 'Udhri love story that features a couple of young nomad lovers, often cousins, who are separated through tribal customs or vicissitudes of life and who mourn to death. This is the theme that was celebrated by Heinrich Heine in his poem "Der Asra": "Jene Asra, welche sterben, wenn sie lieben." (*Romanzero*, 1851) The earliest known Persian example is a recently re-found poem by an otherwise unknown eleventh century poet, 'Ayyuqi, entitled *Varqe and Golshah*, names of the two lovers, meaning Leaf and Flower-King, reminiscent of the Medieval European romance *Floire et Blancheflor*, but the classical Persian version of this story was composed by the poet Nezami of Ganja (d. 1209), who transformed fragmentary legends and anecdotes into a complex but coherent romantic epic which gained a great reputation in the whole Muslim world under the title *Leili and Majnun* – again the names of the two unfortunate lovers. Two hundred years later, 'Abd or-Rahman Jami of Herat turned this romantic story into an allegory of mystic love, and this love story has remained a stock motif in Sufi writing. (Khairallah 1980)

Nezami's collection of five long poems, known as his *Khamse* [The Five], is generally regarded as the peak of Persian romantic epics. Apart from *Leili and Majnun*, we find among these five poems a version of the Alexander legend, *Eskandar-nāme* [Book of Alexander], and two pseudo-historical romances on the love stories of the Sasanian kings Khosrou Parviz and Bahram Gur. Nezami is a masterly poet, who uses all possible rhetorical figures as well as complex, interwoven images. He was obviously quite aware that his epics were his own invention and that he was creating a fictive world that had a life of its own. On the other hand, he knew that he had inserted his creation into a strong narrative and poetic tradition from which he took motifs, topoi and much of his plots. He both embellished the old stories and created them anew.

These verse narratives put my thesis of the generally non-fictive character of Persian literary experience to the test. They are all detailed, vivid, imaginative and fantastic, constructing worlds outside of normal reality, and must have been experienced in that way by most readers at the time of their composition as well as in the following centuries. Although we cannot enter into the minds of those readers, it is still my impression that no real distinction between fictive and factual narratives was made. As an illustrative, although much later, example, I can adduce the case of the first Persian translations (at the end of the 19th century) of *Le Comte de Monte-Cristo* and *Les Trois Mousquetaires* by Dumas Père that were obviously read as factual political social history and *La Dame aux Camélias* by Dumas Fils as a social report. (Rypka 1968, 391, 679)

However, the first of Nezami's great poems does not belong to the tradition of romantic epics. It is an ethico-philosophical work called *Makhzan ol-asrār* [Treasury of Mysteries] that rather belongs to the homiletic tradition founded by the Ismaili propagandist Naser-e Khosrou (d. c. 1075) and the court poet Hakim Sana'i (d. c. 1135). The latter's magnum opus, the *Hadīqat ol-haqīqe* [Walled Garden of Truth], is regarded as the inception of an exceedingly rich production of Sufi (mystical) didactic epics. Sana'i uses a wide array of anecdotes and exemplary stories to demonstrate ethical, philosophical and mystical truths, while Nezami's epic poem *Treasury of Mysteries* consists of twenty discourses, each presenting an exemplary story on religious and ethical topics that also allow of mystical interpretations.

The Sufi use of Persian literature became increasingly important from the eleventh century onwards, and towards the end of the Classical period it had become almost predominant. The works of the leading theologian and Sufi sheikh 'Abd or-Rahman Jami, who died in 1492, may be seen as a summary and conclusion of Classical Persian literature. His *Leili and Majnun* has already been mentioned, but he also used other traditional love stories, especially *Yusof and Zoleikha* (i.e. the story of Joseph and Potiphar's wife in the Bible) and *Salaman and Absal* (a "philosophic" story of Greek origin), in order to express the mystical quest. By then, Sufism had achieved a dominating position in Persian literature. This is particularly evident in poetry, both lyric and epic. With Sufism, an allegorical or metaphorical reading of almost any kind of poetry became possible. Profane songs of love and wine were taken metaphorically to refer to Divine love and mystical ecstasy. The long forms of poetry, known as *masnavī* (i.e. half-verses rhyming in pairs), came to be used as instruments of instruction of the adepts as well as presentations of hidden truths. Both the traditional repertoire of anecdotes and tales and the stories of romantic love were put to new uses.

As already mentioned, Hakim Sana'i, in his *Hadīqat ol-haqīqe*, made prolific use of anecdotes as parables in his homiletic discourse. After him Farid od-din 'Attar (d. c. 1220) used the same technique in his *Asrār-nāme* [Book of Secrets], but in his later epic poems he introduced long narratives as detailed allegories. His *Masnavī Manteq ot-teir* [Language of the Birds] has become especially famous (often called "Conference of the Birds" in the West). It tells the story of how thirty birds go through all sorts of vicissitudes to cross seven regions in search of their King, the Simurgh. Finally they reach his throne hall and find themselves standing in front of a huge mirror. Simurgh is not only the name of a mythical bird but also means – thirty birds!

By far the most important and influential of the Persian mystics who were also poets is Jalal od-din Rumi, also known as Moulana or Moulavi (Turkish Mevlevi). He was born in Balkh in northern present-day Afghanistan and lived through the greater part of the thirteenth century. Already in his youth, he moved to Konya in central Turkey, where he died in 1273. He is a master of the use of Sufi parables, and his great didactic poem, known as *Masnavī*, tells hundreds of them, often one within the other, in extremely fluent and lively verses. One of the most well-known begins like this:

Pīl'andar khāne-ye tārīk būd 'arse-rā āvorde būdand-ash honūd
Az barāy-e dīdan-ash mardom basī andar ān zolmat shod har kasī
Dīdan-ash bā chashm chūn momken na-būd andar ān tārīkiy-ash kaf mī-besūd
Ān yakī-rā kaf be-khortūm ūftād goft hamchūn nāvedān-ast īn nehād
(Rūmī 1925–1940, vol. 3, verses 1259–1262)

These are the first four distichs in a transcription of the original Persian text. The full parable runs as follows in the careful but more explanatory than poetic translation of Reynold Nicholson:

> The elephant was in a dark house; some Hindús had brought it for exhibition.
> In order to see it, many people were going, every one, into that darkness.
> As seeing it with the eye was impossible, (each one) was feeling it in the dark with the
> [palm of his hand.
> The hand of one fell on its trunk: he said, "This creature is like a water-pipe."
> The hand of another touched its ear: to him it appeared to be like a fan.
> Since another handled its leg, he said, "I found the elephant's shape to be like a pillar."
> Another laid his hand on its back: he said, "Truly, this elephant was like a throne."
> Similarly, whenever anyone heard (a description of the elephant), he understood (it only
> [in respect of) the part that he had touched.
> On account of the (diverse) place (object) of view, their statements differed: one man
> [entitled it "*dál*", another "*alif*."
> If there had been a candle in each one's hand, the difference would have gone out
> [of their words.
>
> (Rūmī 1925–1940, vol. 4, 71–72)

Obviously, this is originally an Indian tale. It is found in a *Jātaka* in the second part, *Suttapitaka*, of the Buddhist Pali Canon *Tipitaka* from around 400 BCE.[3] Unexpectedly, a modern Iranian commentator does not refer to the Indian origin but to a quite different source, namely Plato as quoted in an Arabic tradition. The same commentator also quotes earlier Persian versions of this parable, one by the famous theologian Abu Hamed al-Ghazali (d. 1111; known in Europe as Algasel), where the episode takes place in a village inhabited by blind people, and one found in an anonymous *'Ajā'eb-nāme* [Book of Wonders], in which a swarm of mosquitoes try to describe the enormous animal they have found. (Forūzānfar 1347, 96–98) Rumi's precursor, Hakim Sana'i, also told this story in elegant verse. His version starts:

> *Būd shahr-ī bozorg dar hadd-e Ghūr*   *v-andar-ān shahr mardomān hame kūr*
>
> There was a big city in the region of Ghur, and in that city all the people were blind.

Thus Sana'i chose the more original version of the story, but his conclusion is the same:

> Each of them felt one limb of the limbs; all of them drew a mistaken conclusion.
> (Sanā'ī [1329] 1950, 69, trans. Bo Utas)

That this parable on a general plane demonstrates the inability of our five human senses to grasp the true nature of the elephant is obvious, but what does this elephant represent? This depends on the context. Rumi was a Sufi, that is, a Muslim mystic, and for a Sufi it is clear that human beings need "a

---

3 *Udāna* 6,4; I owe this reference to my colleague Gunilla Gren-Eklund.

candle in the hand," as Rumi writes, or that light of the eye that the blind men lack. This light comes from our "heart's eye," that is, our intuition. With the help of that light we can see the true, or Divine, reality behind the phenomenal world that we perceive with our normal senses. The multiplicity of the elephant is only a deception. Furthermore, Rumi tells this story in a specific context, which becomes apparent from the verses that precede it:

> If you keep your gaze on the light, you will be delivered from dualism and the plurality
> [of your finite body.
> O you kernel of the existence, it is the view-point that creates the difference between the
> [Believer and the Zoroastrian and the Jew.
> (Rūmī, 1925–1940, vol. 3, verses 1257–1258, trans. Bo Utas)

Thus he wants to demonstrate that the difference between Islam, Zoroastrism and Judaism is only an illusion. It is probably just a coincidence that Christianity does not appear here. There is no room for it in the meter.

What kind of text, then, is Rumi's elephant parable? Can it in any sense be seen as a piece of fiction? Can it be regarded as an example of what we now call "literature"? Is it a didactic exercise or is it rather a reference to an esoteric truth? Using Rumi's own words, the reply obviously depends on the view-point (Persian *nazar-gāh*). As we have seen, this text stands in a long tradition, both of writing and reading, and this tradition does not end with Rumi. Even today thousands or even millions of readers relate to it. But if we confine ourselves to the intention of the poet, we must consider what kind of Sufi he was, and for that we need to know into what esoteric tradition he was initiated. This is a long and complicated story, and there is no room to tell it here. I will just conclude that Rumi, in spite of being a professor at the leading theological school of Konya, was not a systematic thinker and deliberate teacher when it came to his Sufi message. He was rather an intuitive and ecstatic nature. His verses were hardly meant as examples of verbal art but as something like effluences of the soul. This might sound like a cliché from the epoch of romanticism, but here it is deadly serious. Rumi's poetry was motivated by love of the Divine origin of the universe, the only truly existing reality, and inspired by the mirrored image of the Divine in the terrestrial – by the beauty of a human being, by the fragrance of the spice shops, by the rhythm of the hammers in the bazaar of the silversmiths, and so on.

In one of his short poems, a *ghazal*, Rumi writes:

> *chu dar rah be-bīnī borīde sar-ī*　　　*ke ghaltān ravad sūy-e meidān-e mā*
> *az-ū pors az-ū pors asrār-e mā*　　　*k-az-ū beshnavī serr-e penhān-e mā*

> When on the road you see a severed head, which is rolling toward our field,
> Ask of it, ask of it, the secrets of our heart: for of it you will learn our hidden mystery.
> (Rūmī 1898, 8, trans. Bo Utas)

These verses have a striking, melodious form, and they are aesthetically and emotionally attractive. However, we can be rather sure that the message intended by Rumi was not aesthetic. Poets often use the topos of the insufficiency of language, but in Rumi's case it definitely has a mystical meaning, as he writes later on in the same *ghazal*:

> What shall I say, what think? For this tale is beyond our limits and possibilities.
> How shall I remain silent, when every moment our confusion grows more confused?
> (Rūmī 1898, 8, trans. Bo Utas)

This is underlined by a statement by an earlier Sheikh in Rumi's esoteric tradition, namely Ahmad Ghazali (d. 1126; a brother of the theologian Abu Hamed), when he writes:

> The captivity of lovers is one thing and the talk of poets is another. They don't reach
> [beyond metre and rhyme.
> (Ghazālī [1359] 1980, 5, trans. Bo Utas)

The *Masnavī* of Jalal od-din Rumi has been living reading for countless Sufis all over the Muslim world for more than 700 years. It is still continually recited in Sufi gatherings from Indonesia to Bosnia, and not only among the Mevlevis, the Sufi order that started with Rumi but was established as a brotherhood by his son, Soltan Valad. His poetry is also read among Sufis of many other orders – in its original Persian as well as in Arabic, Turkish and many other languages. In this way, a specific Sufi hermeneutic tradition developed, in which parables like that of the elephant are expounded both in written commentaries and in direct communication between master and adept. The exceptional position of Rumi's *Masnavī* is shown by the fact that by later generations it is often called "the Koran in Persian." Still, the reception of this Sufi poetry changed through the centuries. Lately, Rumi's poetry has even become popular in the extremely free English versions ("re-translations") produced by the American poet Coleman Barks, who presents it as a kind of New Age Sufism.

Meanwhile, great changes took place in Iran proper, when a new dynasty, the Safavids, came to power in the 16th century and introduced Twelve-Imam Shi'ism as the state religion. This change had serious cultural consequences. Among other things, it led to the persecution of the Sunni Sufi orders. The new rulers as well as the new Shi'i clergy endeavoured to take over the wide and deep influence that the Sufi orders had among broad layers of people. Apart from wide-reaching religious consequences, this also changed the understanding of Sufi texts and especially Sufi poetry. During the previous centuries, most genres of Persian poetry had been penetrated by Sufi messages to such a degree that the differences between the various poetic forms and genres had diminished. With the weakening of traditional Sufism that set in as a consequence of Safavid rule, the Sufi reading of texts was aestheticised, and poetry like that of Rumi came to be read and enjoyed as art more than spiritual experience and Sufi instruction. At the same time, interest moved from longer forms of poetry to shorter, ingeniously constructed pieces. The classical system of genres lost its dynamics, as if the dominating Sufi reading of all sorts of poetry had eroded it. When serious Sufi reading became rarer, the forms were left empty, and aesthetically inclined readers looked for more refined combinations of emotion and form. This led to a specific Iranian view not only of poetry but also of language. According to this view, Classical Persian poetry is a perfect creation, as is the language in which it is composed. Perfection has no history and is consequently not available for analysis. Rumi's parables could be enjoyed like a glass of exquisite wine. (Utas 1998)

*

My conclusion of this odyssey through many centuries of Persian literature is, to make it very short, that "fiction" is a rather irrelevant concept when it comes to the understanding of its Classical texts. Even if writers and poets are known by name, they wrote their works within very strong, collective traditions and were not expected to produce individual works of narration or art. I do not think that they consciously intended to invent imaginary worlds. They rather took over traditional forms, genres, motifs, stories and metaphors, striving to embellish them, develop them and drive them towards perfection. Furthermore, those works were conceived and received in a culture that was steeped in a world-view of a Neo-Platonic type, according to which the world that we perceive with our senses only mirrors the truly existing world of ideas. This philosophical stance was re-enforced and made broadly popular by the Sufi view that this world, which we would like to see as factual, is nothing but a metaphor for the celestial world, as illustrated in this traditional verse:

> 'eshq haqīqī-st majāzī ma-gīr   'eshq dom-e shīr-ast be-bāzī ma-gīr
>
> Love is truth, don't see it as metaphoric! Love is the lion's tale, don't grab it in play! (Trans. Bo Utas)

What, then, would be the difference between an imagined and a metaphoric world?

Bibliography

Aravamudan, Srinivas. *Enlightenment Orientalism. Resisting the Rise of the Novel*. Chicago and London: University of Chicago Press, 2011.
Bruijn, Johannes T. P. de. "Fiction: Traditional forms." *Encyclopædia Iranica*. New York: Bibliotheca Persica, 1999. 572–579.
Fakhr ud-Dīn Gurgānī. *Vis and Ramin*. Trans. George Morrison. New York: Columbia University Press, 1972.
Forūzānfar, Badī' oz-zamān. *Ma'ākhedh-i qesas va tamsīlāt-i Masnavī* [Sources, Stories and Parables of the Masnavi]. 2nd ed. Tehran: Amir Kabir, [1347] 1968.
Ghazālī, Ahmad. *Savāneh* [Inspirations]. Ed. Nasrollāh Pūrjavādī. Tehran: Bonyad-e Farhang-e Iran, [1359] 1980.
Hägg, Tomas and Bo Utas. *The Virgin and her Lover: Fragments of an Ancient Greek Novel and a Persian Epic Poem*. Brill Studies in Middle Eastern Literatures, 30. Leiden: Brill, 2003.
Heine, Heinrich. *Romanzero*. Hamburg: Verlag Hoffmann und Campe, 1851.
Kai Kā'ūs ibn, Iskandar. *A Mirror for Princes*: the *Qābūs nāma* [Book of Qabus]. Trans. Reuben Levy. London: Cresset, 1951.
Khairallah, As'ad E. *Love, Madness, and Poetry: An Interpretation of the Magnūn Legend*. Beiruter Texte und Studien, 25. Beirut: Franz Steiner, 1980.
Rūmī, Jalāl od-din. *Selected Poems from the Dīvāni Shamsi Tabrīz*. Ed. and trans. Reynold A. Nicholson. Cambridge: Cambridge University Press, 1898.
— *The Mathnawí of Jalálu'ddín Rúmí*. 8 vols. Ed. and trans. Reynold A. Nicholson. London and Cambridge: E. J. W. Gibb Memorial series, 1925–1940.
Rypka, Jan. *History of Iranian Literature*. Dordrecht: Reidel, 1968.
Sanā'ī. *Hadīqat ol-haqīqe* [Walled Garden of Truth]. Ed. Modarres Razavī. Tehran: Sepehr, [1329] 1950.
Utas, Bo. "The Aesthetic Use of New Persian." *Edebiyât* [Literature] 9 (1998): 1–16.
— "'Genres' in Persian Literature 900–1900." *Literary History: Towards a Global Perspective. Vol. 2. Literary Genres: An Intercultural Approach*. Ed. Gunilla Lindberg-Wada. Berlin and New York: De Gruyter, 2006. 199–241.

Fritz Peter Knapp
Historicity and Fictionality in Medieval Narrative

When you tell a story, at least part of it is made up.[1] Even when the intention is merely to relate facts, human consciousness and language bring about a narrative transformation which goes beyond the mere facts, and this transformation cannot do without fiction. This occurs just as readily in everyday life as it does in scholarly and literary historical treatment. Indeed, fiction must here quite consciously fill out the series of facts to create a meaningful continuum for narration. All the same, fiction has only a complementary function here, however difficult it may be to define its limits. As for the rest, however, literature today is made up of a relatively autonomous system "in which speech is defined from the outset as 'speaking as if' and everything said is subject to the stipulations of a fiction contract."[2] This fictionality, which is thus no longer merely suppletive and functional, but autonomous, pure and substitutive,[3] can be made palpably visible in the text, but it need not be, since it is taken for granted, as it is. Just when a "fiction contract" of this kind was first concluded cannot be easily said. At any rate, Laurence Sterne[4] and Denis Diderot[5] 'lay bare' their fictionality intentions in the 18th century in such a way that, if they do not assume such a fictionality pact to be a given, they at least must necessarily provoke one.

For the Middle Ages a pact of this kind cannot be shown to have existed, for lack of unequivocal evidence in regard to reception. What we do have comprises poetological rules and metapoetic statements by poets about their

---

[1] It goes without saying that my paper refers only to narrative works in a narrow sense. I am not concerned with philosophical, mystic, autobiographic, didactic texts or lyrics. What is more, if an author expressly communicating in his work with his public demonstrates his self-confidence or his consciousness of literary freedom, this may, but need not prepare fictionality (as defined in my paper) and never suffices alone to create it, not even in narrative. The literature of the twelfth century shows an enormous increase of individuality, subjectivity and self-exposure of the authors, but very seldom unequivocal signals of fictionality.
[2] Müller 2004a, 285: "in dem Sprechen von vornherein als 'Sprechen als ob' bestimmt ist und jede Aussage den Bedingungen eines Fiktionskontraktes unterliegt."
[3] Consequently, fictionality means a fundamental attitude, a principle, a value of narration, not a natural practice of story-telling.
[4] Laurence Sterne, *Life and Opinions of Tristram Shandy Gentleman*, was published in nine volumes 1759–1767.
[5] Denis Diderot, *Jacques le fataliste et son maître*, written 1773–1775, was first published in 1796.

own and others' works, statements, to be sure, which may in turn be suspected of fictionality. All the same, Walter Haug postulated in 1985 the 'discovery of fictionality' by Chrétien de Troyes in the latter half of the 12th century. (Haug 1992, 105) In 2002, Dennis H. Green not only deemed, like Haug, most of the classical courtly romances to be purely fictional, but also concluded from certain older Latin works, such as 'Ruodlieb,' that a "contract between author and audience [...] in a game of make-believe" had existed. (Green 2002, 13; cf. 25) This unleashed a scholarly furor and in some places even triggered a veritable medievalistic 'pan-fictionalism.'[6] But at the same time, the ranks of the dissenters were formed, that is, those who viewed fictionality as a thoroughly modern phenomenon which was a priori not attributable to the Middle Ages.[7]

And indeed, the theoretical rules of medieval poetics handed down to us leave very little room for pure fictionality, for they are based on a strictly Christian (in particular, Augustinian) world view. According to these rules, God, the epitome of Being, the True, the Good and the Beautiful (in Latin: *esse, verum, bonum, pulchrum*), created the earth, but did not leave it to its own devices, but will go on preserving it the way it is until its demise. In keeping with the essence of its Creator, all entities (from Latin *ens*), ranked hierarchically by the Creator in decreasing orders of being, are true, good and beautiful;[8] consequentially, evil would be merely a deficiency of being. Man does not have this creative power, not even before the Fall, and certainly not afterwards; he can only shape anew what has already been created, in the crafts, for example. In the Christian-Aristotelian sense, there is only *one* reality. Man can neither reproduce it or supplant it. Whatever he produces in speech and writing, that is, the seemingly creative, is a non-entity. (Cf. Blumenberg 1957, especially 273 sq.)

Only with this backdrop is the cardinal passage from the *Etymologies* of the Visigoth Bishop Isidore of Seville (d. 636) really comprehensible. This monumental work showed the Middle Ages the way, for the *Etymologies* were one

---

[6] See some of the papers in Mertens and Wolfzettel 1993. For an extreme position, see Ernst 1999.

[7] See especially Müller 2004a, 311. Cf. Müller 2004b.

[8] Cf. Augustinus 1983, 18.35: *quoniam et per summam sapientiam ea fecit et summa benignitate conservat. Cur ea fecit? Ut essent; ipsum enim quantocumque esse bonum est, quia summum bonum est summum esse. Unde fecit? Ex nihilo, quoniam quidquid est, quantulacumque specie sit necesse est; ita etsi minimum bonum, tamen bonum erit et ex deo erit. Nam quoniam summa species summum bonum est, minima species minimum bonum est.* And, further on, 36.66: *vera in tantum vera sunt in quantum sunt*, 23.44: *Et est pulchritudo universae creaturae [...] inculpabilis*. Thomas Aquinas 1951 (*Summa theologica*), I q. 5 a. 3: *omne ens, inquantum est ens, est bonum*, II–II q. 109 a. 2, ad 1: *omne verum est bonum, et omne bonum est verum*, I q. 5 a. 4, ad 1: *pulchrum et bonum in subiecto sunt idem*.

of the main pillars of Bible exegesis and medieval instruction in general and thus could scarcely escape the attention of any schoolboy. Isidore compiles only ancient rhetorical, poetological and philosophical statements, but often with a view to their theological interpretation. This results in an extreme preference for *historia*, the telling of historical facts, and in the acceptance of only such free invention that symbolises reality, like fable or allegory, and thus produces nothing real, nothing extant, but *fabula*, just talk, however indirectly connected to reality. The world-view prerequisite for this is the equating of truth and reality, which, moreover, far removed from any modern epistemology, is regarded as fundamentally evident. Worldly reality consists of nature and history, both of which are viewed as emanating from God. If that assumption is accepted, history takes on the same dignity as nature in its mere existence, not just in its essence in accordance with some sort of rational principles of reality. These were what Aristotle was concerned with. That is why, in his *Poetics*, he regards poetry to be more philosophical than historiography. The poetic power of persuasion proceeds in his opinion a priori from "what is possible according to the rules of probability or necessity" (Chapter 9 [1459a]), not from the incidental factuality of real events. In the Christian view, however, any contingency is precluded by Divine Will and thus only seems to exist. Thus probability is trumped by facticity in medieval literary theory, too, until Aristotle's *Poetics* is rediscovered (in its original form) in the Renaissance. To be sure, even before that, probability (in Latin rhetoric *argumentum verisimile*) is needed for narrative, too, to fill in the gaps in the handed-down or assumed facts. It thus functions as a stopgap rather than as the guiding principle it became from the Renaissance onwards. (Knapp 2006) It was not until the modern era that it could dispense with the truth entirely, but this is not true, as some scholars have falsely assumed, for the Middle Ages – with the exception of the Biblical and other parables, which supplanted the *argumentum* in the genre theory of short epic poetry in the 13th century.[9]

Generally, the public expects from narrative – to put it plainly – the facts, nothing but the facts. This spared most medieval historiographers any express justification of what they did, as it was already provided by their subject matter. Any deviation from the facts, which could amount to going against the *historia*, could be blamed on the inadequacies of their sources.[10] To be sure,

---

9 On the genre theory of short epic poetry, see Knapp 2009.
10 See e.g. Beda 1997, 20: *Lectorem suppliciter obsecro, ut, siqua in his, quae scripsimus, aliter quam se ueritas habet, posita reppererit, non nobis inputet, qui, quod uera lex historiae est, simpliciter ea, quae fama uulgante collegimus, ad instructionem posteritatis litteris mandare studuimus.*

facticity was not measured with our yardstick. Here medieval chroniclers were probably guided by the principles of the ancients.[11] The literal truth was only required of the historical essence. Above these *fundamenta*, a substantive and verbal superstructure (*exaedificatio*) is erected by the rhetorically schooled historiographer, says Cicero.[12] These additions need only follow the principle of probability.[13] Fabular additions were to be strictly distinguished from the former and best labelled as such and set aside from them.[14]

The licence to deviate here and there from the facts was already blatantly exercised at times by the ancients, without impinging on the plausibility of such tales as, for example, the oriental adventures of Alexander the Great, in the Middle Ages. The authors' claim of relating facts was taken just as seriously in the case, say, of *Apollonius of Tyrus*, which we consider to be totally fabricated. There can hardly be any doubt that Geoffrey of Monmouth also wanted his *Historia regum Britanniae*, which was in large part obviously fictional, to be no less considered a relation of facts than William of Newburgh, say, did for his *Historia rerum Anglicarum*, although the latter is far more credible. If the latter historiographer harshly criticised the former, he did so because he considered him to be a member of the same 'trade', not a writer of romances, who is not bound to facts. Quite similarly voiced criticism was levelled at German heroic epics. They, too, were at least in principle taken to be historiography, but their credibility was to be sure by no means left unscathed. (Knapp 2005, 39–43)

Scarcely any French author of heroic epic tales forgoes the assurance of their historical accuracy. For example, to prove that he is not fabricating falsehoods, the author of the *Conquest of Orange* (*Prise d'Orange*, late 12th century) points to the weapons of Guillaume, his hero, which any pilgrim

---

11 For the following see Wehrli 1972 and Woodman 1988, 70–116 and passim.
12 M. Tullius Cicero 1902 (*De oratore*), 2.15.62–63.: *Nam quis nescit primam esse historiae legem, ne quid falsi dicere audeat? Deinde ne quid veri non audeat? Ne quae suspicio gratiae sit in scribendo? Ne quae simultatis? Haec scilicet fundamenta nota sint omnibus, ipsa autem exaedificatio posita est in rebus et verbis: rerum ratio ordinem temporum desiderat, regionum descriptionem; vult etiam, quoniam [...] in rebus gestis declarari non solum quid actum aut dictum sit, sed etiam quo modo, et cum de eventu dicatur, ut causae explicentur omnes vel casus vel sapientiae vel temeritatis hominumque ipsorum non solum res gestae, sed etiam, qui fama ac nomine excellant, de cuiusque vita atque natura.*
13 Cicero 1949 (*De inventione*, on the *narratio* in the *oratio*), 1.21.29: *Probabilis erit narratio, si in ea videbuntur inesse ea que solent apparere in veritate.* Cf. Nüßlein 1994 (*Rhetorica ad Herennium*), 1.9.16.
14 See e. g. Livius 2003, 6: *Quae ante conditam condendamue urbem poeticae magis decora fabulis quam incorruptis rerum gestarum monumentis traduntur, ea nec adfirmare nec refellere in animo est.*

could see for himself in Brioude, in the Auvergne (v. 7–9). In the same vein, Wolfram of Eschenbach places great value in his claim that what he relates in *Willehalm* (the adaptation of a French *chanson de geste*) will withstand the test of historic veracity. If we shake our heads at the gullibility of their contemporaries, we must remember that at that time innumerable miracles were part of what was thought of as reality, as long as they were sufficiently authenticated, that is, could be explained as phenomena of the macro- and microcosm which contradict the laws of nature, be it seemingly, because they are not entirely known to man, or be it in fact, because they are violated by divine or demonic powers.

In Antiquity and the Middle Ages, the licence to deviate at times from the facts was, of course, more readily granted to the poetic treatment of history than to historiography. In heathen Antiquity, indeed, the pure presentation of historical facts, although clothed in poetic raiments, was considered to be less than 'genuine' poetry if it made too little use of this licence. Thus, Lucanus' *Bellum civile* was not included among *poemata*.[15] However, after the Church Fathers Lactantius and Isidore, this reproach was turned into praise, which was repeated throughout the Middle Ages, and Lucanus was now *poeta et historiographus*. (von Moos 1976) In order to preserve Virgil's supremacy, he now had to be given the higher rank of *poeta et historiographus et philosophus*.

A claim to higher learning could just as readily dispense with strict adherence to the facts as less demanding works, as evidenced in vernacular poetry, in particular in oral heroic poetry. But here, too, the claim is usually expressly made that nothing but the truth is being related, which was, however, wrongly interpreted by scholarship, which either considered this to be irony or took the claim not to be about factual, but deeper, symbolic truth. But the example of the old French *Chanson de Saisnes* (*Lay of the Saxons*), a heroic epic by Jean Bodel (end of the 12th century), suffices in itself to prove the complete acceptance of Isidore's poetics. He distinguishes the tales from France, Britain and Rome. Those from Rome, he says, are "wise and impart wisdom," those from Britain "vain and amusing," those from France "at all times unambiguously

---

15 Servius 1881–1884 (*Commentarii in Vergilii carmina*), ad Aen. 1.235: *sciendum est, inter fabulam et argumentum, hoc est historiam, hoc interesse, quod fabula est dicta res contra naturam, sive facta sive non facta, ut de Pasiphae, historia est quicquid secundum naturam dicitur, sive factum sive non factum, ut de Phaedra.* – 1.382: *hoc loco per transitum tangit historiam, quam per legem artis poeticae aperte non potest ponere [...] Quod autem diximus eum poetica arte prohiberi, ne aperte ponat historiam, certum est. Lucanus namque ideo in numero poetarum esse non meruit, quia videtur historiam composuisse, non poema.*

true."[16] *Fabula* and *historia* are immediately discernible as models.[17] The author claims all rights to the latter and assigns the former to Arthurian romance with its *matière de Bretagne*. Finally, the value of the *roman d'antiquité* is said to lie above all in the imparting of knowledge.

When Jean Bodel calls the tales from Britain *vain* ("vapid, empty, vain"), he is, of course, only referring to that *fabula* which, according to Isidore, was merely written for diversion, without intending to arrive at a parabolical truth, as was the case with the animal fable and allegory. Here, Isidore had the comedies of antiquity as well as stories made up by folklore in mind.[18] The rival genre that the poet of the *Lay of the Saxons* would like to repel, and thus disparages, is the courtly romance, which does not come across as a symbolic tale and therefore arouses the suspicion of wishing to feign reality – a charge which only modern eyes could find absurd. It is thus no wonder that many, indeed most courtly romances take refuge in the insistence that they are preserving ancient historical tradition. Even Chrétien de Troyes does so in the prologue of *Cligès*, but not in *Lancelot ou le Chevalier de la charrette*, in *Yvain ou le Chevalier au lion* or in *Erec et Enide*. In a particularly authoritative manner, the prologue of the first romance, *Erec et Enide* (about 1170), leaves any claim to veracity unsaid (v. 1–26). In place of the customary historiographic attitude, there is only the declaration of intent "to tell well and teach well" (*A bien dire et a bien aprandre*), to compose a very beautifully arranged tale (*une mout bele conjointure*) from a sloppily told *conte d'avanture*. But Chrétien also in no way points to a concealed, deeper moral or philosophical truth, to a second, allegorical plane, but simply to the aesthetic treatment of the material. The learned *integumentum* theory is thus held at bay here, too. Neither here nor elsewhere does it make any inroads into the vernacular sphere. (Knapp 1997, 65–74)

On the whole, it must be said that genre-poetological efforts in vernacular texts are quite deficient. This is also true for *dicta* in the German didactic poem

---

16 Bodel 1989, v. 1–3, 6–11: *Qui d'oyr et d'entendre a loisir et talant, / Face pais, si escout bonne chançon vaillant / Dont li livre d'estoire sont testoing et garant! (...) N'en sont que trois materes a nul home entendant: / De France et de Bretaigne et de Rome le grant; / Ne de ces trois materes n'i a nule samblant. / Li conte de Bretaigne s'il sont vain et plaisant / Et cil de Romme sage et de sens aprandant, / Cil de France sont voir chascun jour aparant.*
17 Cf. the opposition of *chanson (de geste)* and *fable* in *Bataille Loquifer*. (See Knapp 2005, 165).
18 Isidore 1911, 1.40.3: *Delectandi causa fictas [fabulas], ut eas, quas vulgo dicunt, vel quales Plautus et Terentius conposuerunt.* This meaning comes near the German term *Trivialliteratur*. But the original opposition to *historia* never must be forgotten. Therefore an assertion as the following is highly misleading: "The word 'fable' is used by almost all writers to denote what might be called *Trivialliteratur*." (Brownlee et al. 2005, 443).

Der welsche Gast by Thomasin of Zerkläre (1214/15), which likewise contain clear references to Isidore's genre theory. They are limited to the claim that the invented tales (*âventiure*) of courtly romance are morally useful falsehoods because they can be implements of upbringing. But advanced readers were no longer supposed to need romances. Thus, unless their authors want to sell their books as children's books or indeed old wives' tales, they can hardly forgo the assurance of the facticity of their tales.

Chrétien de Troyes, with whom the Arthurian romance originated in the 12th century, nevertheless dared to do so, unless I am mistaken. Here, Walter Haug was probably right. For Chrétien did not tell stories after or taken from real history (*historia*), nor did he relate unnatural, unreal images from real nature or real human life, that is, theoretically legitimatised *fabulae*. As a clerically educated man, Chrétien had to be familiar with all the theoretical guidelines. These he simply ignores. He banks on the truth of the human word to create a non-existent reality. However, to declare fiction independent required unequivocal signals of indifference in regard to truth, its unfettering from the truth of real being. And in the romance these signals are most clearly given – thus my thesis, for which I cannot provide further evidence here – by the wondrous realm of the fairy-tale. It is inexplicable, it is not explained, because no explanation is needed. As it is, given in fine measure, unobtrusively, it of course does not reduce the romance to the "simple form" ("Einfache Form") of the magical fairy-tale. But it gives the whole of the tale, even its most banal aspects, a sheen taken from the magic of the unreal, producing in interdependence with the symbolic structure the fascinating impression of free suspension of disbelief, of intellectual play. (For romances and fairy-tales, cf. Knapp 2005, 191–224)

This 'metaphysical unseriousness' was never met with broad appreciation, then or now. All the same, Erich Auerbach ascertained the fairy-tale quality of Chrétien's romances in 1946 (1964, 126). Georg Lukács seems to have had an inkling of it as early as 1916 (1965, 102). In the Middle Ages, Chrétien de Troyes, with his vast oeuvre, is by far the most important source for the genre of the Arthurian romance. But only very few of his successors were willing or able to carry out his fundamental intention even in part, not to mention in radical fashion, if indeed they even comprehended it. This fictionality thus remains a very rare special case within romance production, which was otherwise dominated by pseudo-history. It thus fails as the beginning of a solid tradition of this kind in the Middle Ages.

The modern period can therefore not be traced back to it, either. It must grope its own way towards finding pure fiction. Ariosto (1474–1533) and Cervantes (1547–1616) clear the first broad swaths, but in their day they have no chance against Aristotelian mimesis theory with its probability postulate. Not until the 18th century will this theory be lastingly shaken in its universal acceptance. But this is not my topic.

Translated by Philip Mattson

Bibliography

Aristoteles. *Ars poetica/Poetik.* Ed. Manfred Fuhrmann. Stuttgart: Reclam, 1986.
Auerbach, Erich. *Mimesis. Dargestellte Wirklichkeit in der abendländischen Literatur.* 3. Aufl. Bern: Francke, [1946] 1964.
Augustinus. *De doctrina christiana.* Ed. Joseph Martin. CCSL, 32. Turnhout: Brepols, 1962.
— *De vera religione.* Ed. W. M. Green. Trans. Wilhelm Thimme. Stuttgart: Reclam, 1983.
Beda der Ehrwürdige [Venerabilis]. *Kirchengeschichte des englischen Volkes / Historia ecclesiastica gentis Anglorum.* Eds. Bertram Colgrave and Roger A.B. Mynors, trans. Günter Spitzbart. Texte zur Forschung, 34. Darmstadt: Wissenschaftliche Buchgesellschaft, [1982] 1997.
Blumenberg, Hans. "'Nachahmung der Natur.' Zur Vorgeschichte der Idee des schöpferischen Menschen." *Studium generale* 10 (1957): 266–283.
Bodel, Jean. *La Chanson des Saisnes.* 2 vols. Ed. Annette Brasseur. Textes littéraires français, 369. Genève: Droz, 1989.
Brackert, Helmut. *Rudolf von Ems. Dichtung und Geschichte.* Germanische Bibliothek. Dritte Reihe, Untersuchungen und Einzeldarstellungen. Heidelberg: Winter, 1968.
Brownlee, Kevin, Tony Hunt, Ian Johnson, Alastair Minnis and Nigel F. Palmer. "Vernacular Literary Consciousness *c.* 1100–*c.* 1500: French, German and English Evidence." *The Cambridge History of Literary Criticism, Vol. 2: The Middle Ages.* Eds. Alastair Minnis and Ian Johnson. Cambridge: Cambridge University Press, 2005. 422–471.
Chrétien de Troyes. *Erec und* Enide. Ed. Wendelin Foerster. Christian von Troyes sämtliche Werke, 3. Halle: Niemeyer, 1890.
Cicero. *Rhetorica, 1. De oratore.* Ed. Augustus J. Wilkins. Oxford Classical Texts. Oxford University Press, 1902.
— *De inventione. De optimo genere oratorum. Topica.* Trans. Harry M. Hubell. Loeb Classical Library, 386. London: Heinemann, 1949.
Ernst, Ulrich. "Formen analytischen Erzählens im *Parzival* Wolframs von Eschenbach. Marginalien zu einem narrativen System des Hohen Mittelalters." *Erzählstrukturen der Artusliteratur. Forschungsgeschichte und neue Ansätze.* Eds. Friedrich Wolfzettel and Peter Ihring. Tübingen: Niemeyer, 1999. 165–198.
Green, Dennis H. *The Beginnings of Medieval Romance. Fact and Fiction, 1150–1220.* Cambridge Studies in Medieval Literature, 47. Cambridge: Cambridge University Press, 2002.
Haug, Walter. *Literaturtheorie im deutschen Mittelalter von den Anfängen bis zum Ende des 13. Jahrhunderts.* 2nd ed. Darmstadt, [1985] 1992.
— "Die Entdeckung der Fiktionalität." *Die Wahrheit der Fiktion – Studien zur weltlichen und geistlichen Literatur des Mittelalters und der frühen Neuzeit.* Tübingen 2003, 128–144.
Isidore [Isidorus Hispalensis]. *Etymologiae.* Ed. Wallace M. Lindsay. Scriptorum classicorum bibliotheca Oxoniensis. Oxford: Clarendon, 1911.

Knapp, Fritz Peter. *Historie und Fiktion in der mittelalterlichen Gattungspoetik. Sieben Studien und ein Nachwort.* Beiträge zur älteren Literaturgeschichte. Heidelberg: Winter, 1997.
— *Historie und Fiktion in der mittelalterlichen Gattungspoetik (II). Zehn neue Studien und ein Vorwort.* Schriften der Philosophisch-Historischen Klasse der Heidelberger Akademie der Wissenschaften, 35. Heidelberg: Winter, 2005.
— "Der Dichter – ein ‚Affe der Natur' oder ein ‚zweiter Gott'? Historie und Fiktion am Übergang zur Neuzeit." *Anzeiger der philosophisch-historischen Klasse* 141.2 (2006): 17–42.
— "Fabulae – parabolae – historiae. Die mittelalterliche Gattungstheorie und die Kleinepik von Jean Bodel bis Boccaccio." *Mittellateinisches Jahrbuch* 44 (2009): 97–117.
Lactantius. *Divinae institutiones.* Eds. Samuel Brandt and Georg Laubmann. Opera omnia, 1; CSEL, 19. Vienna: Tempsky, 1890.
Livius. *Ab urbe condita, Liber 1.* Ed. and trans. Robert Feger. Stuttgart: Reclam, [1991] 2003.
Lukács, Georg. *Die Theorie des Romans.* 3rd ed. Neuwied and Berlin: Luchterhand, 1965.
Lucanus. *Bellum civile.* 3rd ed. Ed. Carl Hosius. Bibliotheca scriptorum Graecorum et Romanorum Teubneriana. Leipzig: Teubner, 1913.
Mertens, Volker and Friedrich Wolfzettel, eds. *Fiktionalität im Artusroman.* Tübingen: Niemeyer, 1993.
Moos, Peter von. "*Poeta* und *Historicus* im Mittelalter. Zum Mimesis-Problem am Beispiel einiger Urteile über Lucan." *Beiträge zur Geschichte der deutschen Sprache und Literatur* 98 (1976): 93–130.
Müller, Jan-Dirk. "Literarische und andere Spiele. Zum Fiktionalitätsproblem in vormoderner Literatur." *Poetica* 36 (2004a): 281–311.
— "Fiktion höfischer liebe und die Fiktionalität des Minnesangs." *Text und Handeln. Zum kommunikativen Ort von Minnesang und antiker Lyrik.* Ed. Albrecht Hausmann. Beihefte zum Euphorion, 46. Heidelberg: Winter, 2004b. 47–64.
Nüßlein, Theodor, ed. and trans. *Rhetorica ad Herennium.* Tusculum. Zürich: Artemis & Winkler, 1994.
Regnier, Claude, ed. "La Prise d'Orange." *Wilhelmsepen.* Trans. Bodo Hesse. Klassische Texte des romanischen Mittelalters in zweisprachigen Ausgaben, 22. München: Fink, 1993.
Servius. *Commentarii in Vergilii carmina.* Eds. Georg Thilo and Herman Hagen. Leipzig: Teubner, 1881–1884.
Thomas Aquinas. *Summa theologiae,* cura fratrum ejusdem Ordinis. Madrid: Biblioteca de autores cristianos, 1951.
Thomasin von Zerkläre. *Der wälsche Gast des Thomasin von Zirclaria.* Ed. Heinrich Rückert. Deutsche Neudrucke, Texte des Mittelalters. Berlin: De Gruyter, [1852] 1965.
Wehrli, Fritz. "Die Geschichtsschreibung im Lichte der antiken Theorie." (1947) *Theoria und Humanitas. Gesammelte Schriften zur antiken Gedankenwelt.* Eds. Heinz Haffter und Thomas Szlezák. Zürich and Munich: Artemis, 1972. 132–144.
Wolfram von Eschenbach. *Willehalm. Nach der Handschrift 857 der Stiftsbibliothek St. Gallen. Mhd. Text, Übersetzung, Kommentar.* Ed. Joachim Heinzle. Bibliothek des Mittelalters, 9 = Bibliothek deutscher Klassiker, 69. Frankfurt am Main: Deutscher Klassiker Verlag, 1991.
Woodman, Anthony J. *Rhetoric in Classical Historiography. Four Studies.* London: Croom Helm, 1988.

Wim Verbaal
How the West was Won by Fiction: The Appearance of Fictional Narrative and Leisurely Reading in Western Literature (11th and 12th century)

Introduction

When treating modern topics or applying modern denominations in a historical context, the scholar always ought to account for the validity of his endeavour. Too easily he is trapped by a kind of historical colonialism, which takes it for self-evident that all humanity of all periods has always been occupied by the same ideas and by the same premises as modern Western man. Too often, the result is an anachronistic interpretation of the past, seen in opposition to contemporary thought. Just as easily, however, scholars in modern literature reject any link to historical phenomena as if humanity since the Enlightenment had entirely shaken off its former shape to appear as the New Man, the *homo novus*, as he was evoked in Alain of Lille's allegorical epic, the *Anticlaudianus*. This surely results in an all too simple view on the past, as if it was some primitive state of modernity.[1]

But man's history is no snakeskin left behind without leaving any traces. Neither does it present any uniform, monolithic block, offering us an image of man as he is, as he was and as he always will be. Thus, the scholar of historical literature is obliged to keep to the difficult middle road of not wanting to treat historical texts as if they were modern, but not presenting them either as belonging to some other world, inaccessible to the modern mind.[2]

In this contribution, I must account for my application of modern terms like 'fiction' to phenomena appearing around 1100. This is less self-evident than it might seem to the scholar thinking in modern terms. Fiction nowadays – even when it is considered in an ever-enlarging sense – has been associated with genres and forms of expression that were entirely unknown

---

[1] As far as I know a thorough and critical study of scholarly approaches of the past has not yet been undertaken. It would involve indeed an enormous work but the results might be astonishing.

[2] Indeed, this makes the past in a certain sense the truly Other: too acquainted for being completely alien, yet too different for not causing any estrangement.

to pre- and early modern culture, one of the more important ones in literature being the novel. This specific application to this typical genre raises a problem of its own, for in many languages, modern novels and medieval romances have been denounced with the same name, that of the *roman*. So one might be tempted to consider both kind of texts as expressions of a similar or related fictionality. But I suppose every reader of a romance of Chrétien de Troyes or, even better, one of the *Romans d'Antiquité* will immediately sense the difference between both genres and even between the ideas of fiction that might lie behind them.

Is it not even more hazardous, then, to expand the idea of fiction to texts and genres that correspond even less to the modern interpretation of the term? Or to drop some of the seemingly obvious elements linked to our concept of fiction, such as the narrative? For this reason, as for others inherent to the subject of this contribution, it seems more fitting not to treat 11th- or 12th-century 'fiction' in its modern sense as opposed to 'fact'. Rather, I want to focus on some aspects in the literature of this period that helped true fiction come into being.

Antique Fiction?

For it is anything but evident that 'fiction' (from now on taken in one of its most customary senses as opposed to 'fact') exists always and everywhere. In many literary cultures, fiction does not have any right of existence, one of these being of the highest importance for the theme that will be treated here: Latin literature. Indeed, the Latin literature of Antiquity and of the Early Middle Ages does not concede a place to fiction, as fiction was already considered in Antiquity to be *mendacium* or a *fabula*, a liar's tale opposed to *historia*.

The very rare exceptions only confirm the general rule. Incidentally, this negative attitude toward fictionality as 'lying tales' does not mean that Latin literature and the Romans did not accept fiction as literature or that the concept of fictionality as opposed to factuality was entirely foreign to the ancients. On the contrary, at the same time as classical Latin literature was flowering during the late Republic and the early Empire, a genre in Greek literature now known as the classic novel (again a misleading name) was expanding. Describing young lovers separated and going through all kind of adventures before being reunited, it did not make any claim to historicity at all.

The Romans were acquainted with these texts. They were quite popular, as we can deduce from references, notably the parody on the genre by Petronius Arbiter in his *Satyricon*. What remains of this masterpiece of scabrous literature seems constructed according to the frame of a Greek novel.[3] The parody is achieved by the transplantation of the theme to Nero's time, thus making a contemporary and realistic novel out of it, breaking down the exotic and the fancy atmosphere of the models. Retaining all their characteristics, the writer rewrote it as a truly Roman equivalent, historicizing all the fabulous elements, thus turning *mendacium* into *veritas*, rewriting the *fabula* as a *historia*![4]

So not granting 'fiction' a place worthy of the name literature does not imply that writers could not play with the tension between 'fact' and 'fiction', between *mendacium* and *veritas*. This is clearly stated by a writer like Curtius Rufus in his history of Alexander, in which he declares that he does not believe everything he writes.[5] This tension lies beneath the entire structure of Apuleius' *Golden Ass*, presented as a fictitious story, as an autobiography and as an initiation account. Actually, all classical Roman writers knew about this tension and how to make literary use of it, but perhaps none did it in the same subtle way as Ovid. And he will be of the greatest importance for understanding what happened around 1100.

Emergence of the Schools

Thus Christianity only reinforced a tendency already clearly present in Latin thought and literary culture. Writing ought to occupy itself with the truth and give no place to *mendacia* or *fabulae*.[6] This attitude became even more prevalent during the Early Middle Ages. It cannot be the objective of this contribution to give an accurate account of the historical development of Latin literature from Late Antiquity to the period which concerns our subject, but Latin literature from around 1000 must be characterized briefly in order to give the right perspective on what happened afterward.

---

[3] This view can be traced back to Heinze 1899, repr. in 1960, 417–439. See the excellent evaluation of Heinze's still valid approach in Barchiesi 1999.
[4] One could wonder if the third term *argumentum* could have been considered applicable to Petronius' ludicrous writing. For a thorough discussion on the use of these categories from classical rhetorical thinking in medieval literature, see Mehtonen 1996.
[5] Quintus Curtius 1946 (9.1.34): *Equidem plura transcribo quam credo: nam nec adfirmare sustineo, de quibus dubito, nec subducere, quae suscepi.* ('As for myself, I report more things than I believe; for I cannot bring myself to vouch for that about which I am in doubt, nor to suppress what I have heard').
[6] Compare Augustine's famous defamation of the *Aeneid* in his *Confessiones* (2007, 1.13.20), but also Juvencus' Praefatio to his *Historia Evangeliarum* (1891), giving birth to the entire tradition of Christian poets opposing themselves against their pagan ancestors (and models).

Until around 1050, Latin literature was dominated by what could be called the monastic perspective. Learning Latin was still greatly restricted to the monastic schools, in which grammar and rhetoric constituted the basic courses. Latin was taught by way of the classical poets, notably Virgil, thus leading to a strongly classicist literature. Besides, as the language of schools and of religion, the aura of truthfulness was intact and even confirmed. Latin literature around 1000 was largely a didactic literature in the broadest sense of the word: it wanted to inform and instruct. The writer presented himself as a reliable witness or authority, whose words earned him the credibility of the reader. There was no place for *fabulae* in a literature of this kind, except where they served didactic purposes.

Now, from the late tenth century on, this monastic perspective in Latin literature was for several historical reasons slowly broken down by the writers educated at the emerging cathedral schools. The didactic programme here was more directed at the chancelleries and administrative functions, thus putting a stronger emphasis on dialectics, without neglecting for that matter grammar or rhetoric. Dialectics was first and foremost meant to be training in reasoning and ordering, implying questioning. Finally, to put it in a nutshell, questioning leads to doubts and doubting brings about new questioning and looking for rational answers.[7]

In the end, this created at the cathedral schools a more open atmosphere, less constrained by respect for the written or teaching authorities. (Verbaal 2010) Students were not expected to remain inside the community of their school, as was the case in the monastic schools. Their education was directed toward the world outside the school. Also, the educational programme was less uniform, depending more on the personality of each individual teacher. The canon of model writers was not questioned as such, but it was enlarged. Other classical writers entered the programme, one of the most important being none other than Ovid – not only the poet of the *Metamorphoses* but the love poet.[8]

Emergence of Love

Love poetry is, understandably, almost absent in Medieval Latin literature before 1000, the period in which the monastic perspective dominated. After

---

[7] To paraphrase Abelard's famous statement in the prologue to his *Sic et Non*: *Dubitando quippe ad inquisitionem venimus; inquirendo veritatem percipimus* (Boyer and McKeon 1976–1977, 103–104).

[8] On the *aetas ovidiana* much work has been done. For our purpose, I prefer referring to the treatment by Green (2002, 2012).

1050, it suddenly appeared and developed into a massive literary phenomenon, invading not only Latin literature itself but also becoming the core theme of the emerging vernacular literature in French. Finally, it reached its literary culmination in the love themes of courtly romances. (Moser Jr. 2004)

This might give us pause for thought. The works of Chrétien de Troyes offer both the love theme and the first fully developed fictionality in Western literature since the classic Greek novel. In his *The Beginnings of Medieval Romance. Fact and Fiction, 1150–1220*, Dennis Howard Green has given a stimulating view on this phenomenon, showing notably that a writer like Chrétien created his fictional romances out of the 'gaps' left in the historians writing on Arthur before him. Geoffrey of Monmouth still wrote a *historia* of Arthur, be it with a strong tongue-in-cheek tonality. He tells of all the military actions that made Arthur equal or even superior to the Roman emperors. At the same time, he mentions two periods of peace, on which he does not elaborate further. Chrétien does: the adventures of his Round Table knights take place in these peaceful periods, thus setting the *fabula* in the middle of *historia*. (Green 2002, 178–187, and 2012, 59)

Green also tries to delimit fictionality in twelfth-century Arthurian romance as opposed to the somewhat older *Romans d'Antiquité*: "The antique romance remains externally referential (its events were regarded as historically true), whilst the narrative plot of the Arthurian romance is self-referential."[9] He offers here a very good starting point for the definition of fictionality in general: fiction being auto-referential, that is, having no other reference frame than the world created and evoked in and by the medium, or, in our case, the text. This does not exclude fictional texts from alluding to factual events, but, as Green rightly argues, they are not alluded to as external *to* but rather as part *of* the textual world.

This leads to a crucial point in the thesis this contribution wants to present. Green takes this self-referential aspect of Chrétien's romances as a starting point and almost as self-evident. In my opinion, it is not self-evident, which is immediately clear when comparing the literature around 1000 with the literature around 1200. The earlier literature, especially that characterized by the monastic perspective, is always externally referential, which is simply implied by its dominating didactic tenor. These texts are not meant to be texts on their own and for their own sake. They always have an external reference point, ultimately the reader, whose instruction they aim at. Around 1200, literature, with the romances as the most notable example, can be considered to be sheer leisure reading, merely wanting to please the reader. *Delectatio* as

---

[9] Green 2002, 200. His working definition of fiction (4) is less workable and convincing.

opposed to *instructio*: both belong to the requirements of classical rhetoric, but the difference is that the romance wants to carry the reader away into its own fictional world, while the instructive texts want to allot the reader his proper place in his actual and factual world.

The first clear signs of texts taking over the factual reality of a reader appear exactly around 1100. In his short poem *De molesta recreatione* (On troubled recreation), Marbod of Rennes describes the effects a song about love and dying has on him. (See Bond 1995, 72–73, Jaeger 1994, 162–163) A knight is wounded to death and the song evokes the lament of his beloved. Melody and verses evoke in the listening poet the sadness and pains of the lady as they are sung. 'I believed I suffered myself whatever the harpist played.' 'Reality it seemed, no song.' Here, for the first time in Western literature as far as I know, we have the explicit expression of the power a fictional text has over the mind and feelings of a listener.

Almost contemporaneous is the other testimony. Guibert of Nogent writes in his autobiography how the reading of love poetry, notably by Ovid, started 'to titillate his flesh,' pushing him to write 'obscene words' himself. His master, finding out what he was writing, warned him that it was not his own hand that was writing these poems but that he was possessed by a force from outside.[10] While Guibert and his master still belonged to a monastic context, this anecdote shows how the power of fictional literature was experienced as an external force, taking over factual reality by absorbing the mind with its 'vanities'.

It seems clear that around 1100 fictional texts start to become a reality for contemporaneous readers, and even a problem in its conflict with the traditional didactics that literature is presumed to offer.

The Voices of Love

These observations raise the question of the origins and development of this auto-referentiality of the fictional text. It implies a textual autonomy that its monastic or didactic predecessors lacked. The text becomes a world of its own, no longer necessarily connected to its historical, contextual reality. Many elements could be adduced to illustrate this growing autonomy of the textual world. This article will limit itself to the changing relation between the writer and his text. The growing autonomy of the textual world, resulting in its expanding auto-referentiality, indeed implies a changed relation of the text to

---

[10] Guibert of Nogent 1981, 134–137. Cf. the remarks in Saenger 1997a, 249–250, and in 1997b, especially 153.

its creator. No longer can the text be considered a kind of prolongation of the author, as it must be from a didactic perspective. The autonomy of the text has become absolute when it starts to act independently of the writer, when the voice in the text can no longer be considered the voice of the writer.

Such a disjunction of voices is something new in literature after 1050. Of course, the voice of the text never did coincide with that of the writer, and writers were conscious of this difference. Yet, rarely or even never did the writer play a part opposed to his actual situation. He never presented himself in or as a 'lie'. This would not have corresponded to the truthfulness the didactic perspective of literature required. The writer appeared in the text with the voice of the master or with that of the reliable instructor.

This situation changed toward the end of the eleventh century. One of the most illustrative – and immediately one of the most extreme – examples is offered by the already mentioned Marbod of Rennes, who died in 1123 in the monastery of Saint Aubin at Angers. Before his election to the bishopric of Rennes in 1096, he had for almost thirty years been in charge of the cathedral school at Angers. In addition, he was one of the leading figures in the so-called School of the Loire, which actually was not a real "school," containing a master-poet and his followers, but rather a movement of closely related and friendly rivalling poets.[11]

It seems indeed that, in the Latin West, the origins of the autonomy of the textual world lie hidden in lyric poetry. This is partly due to the importance of poetry in Latin education, but even more important was perhaps the recovery of Ovid in the 12th-century school programme, notably by Marbod. He seems to have been the first to have an eye for Ovid's ironic play with fiction and reality, and he was surely the first to write new Ovidian love poetry. (Green 2002, 3, 20–21, and 2012, 50–51) Two cycles of his were published in the *editio princeps* of 1524, but they were largely censured by the successive editors of his work. (Bulst 1950)

The first cycle starts with a poem on spring that softens the sentiments of the poet. Then follow several poems on the subject of love and notably pederasty, in which are heard the voices of the poet, reproaching both a pederast and a boy that shows himself too willing, and of the pederast himself, complaining about the absence of his beloved or about his age that does not allow

---

[11] It is only recently that Marbod has started to gain some scholarly interest, notwithstanding the importance that has to be accorded to his didactic and poetical work. See Bond 1995 and Moser 2004, both of whom, however, are not entirely reliable in their historical accounts of Marbod's life and work. For information on this point, cf. Leotta's introduction to Marbod(e) 1998 and the studies of Walther Bulst, notably his article 1950.

him any love affairs anymore. The cycle concludes with the poem "On troubled recreation," almost as a warning to the readers against getting absorbed by the poetical world evoked.

Even more suggestive in this context is another cycle, consisting of short poetic letters in elegiac couplets after the model of Ovid. They are all from a young man to his beloved. In contrast to the other cycle, they contain a small 'narrative' following the evolution of the relation between the two lovers, from their mutual declaration of love through an attack of jealousy on the part of the girl to their reconciliation. All is seen from the perspective of the boy, but every letter of his, including the first one, is presented as the answer to a letter from the girl.

Now, it will be obvious that in neither of these cycles is the voice of Marbod the teacher heard. Yet it is also obvious that the voice heard in these poems does not even want to be understood as linked to the person of the poet. The disjunction is complete: the poet assumes the part of his depraved or honest lovers. As the title of two of the pederast poems states, they have been written *sub assumpta persona*, that is, 'in the guise of.' This expression was traditionally used for a secretary writing in the name of someone else, usually his patron, thus meaning 'in his name.' Here, however, it explicitly points to the poet disguised as the person to whom he gives voice. The poet plays a role in a small fictive story that is evoked by and limited to the texts.

It is tempting to see in this revival of Ovid's techniques a clear and pure literary consciousness.[12] Tempting but dangerous! Marbod's poetics can hardly be disconnected from his responsibility as a teacher and head of an important school. Probably we have to consider them partly as (strikingly original) didactic means, and partly as the independent fruits of his attempts to teach his students how to cope with Ovidian poetics.

Disjointed Voices

Marbod's poems met with vast recognition and success. An anonymous poem addressed to Marbod was inserted as authentic into the first edition (1524), probably based on the available manuscripts at Angers. It gives voice to a girl reproaching her lover that he promises her all the presents of the world, but that she does not get anything to see. This short poem shows all the characteristics of Marbod's own poems but with the difference of taking a female voice. The poem was undoubtedly a man's writing, thus we have a

---

[12] It is interpreted as such by both Bond (1995) and Moser (2004).

clear and logical continuation of the poetical techniques launched by Marbod. (Bulst 1975, 175)

Perhaps the most famous of Marbod's immediate followers was Baudri, Abbot of Bourgueil, the future Bishop of Dol. He is often supposed to have been a student of Marbod's before entering the monastery. He does not hide his adoration or his friendship for Marbod and was clearly acquainted with his poems. Baudri's poetry is in a formal sense much more classical than Marbod's, putting almost entirely aside the internal leonine rhyme. Yet he takes up in a very original way the disjunction of voices as part of a literary roleplay. The first medieval *Heroides*, composed in imitation of Ovid's poetical love letters between mythological partners, are probably of his authorship. Baudri wrote an exchange between Paris and Helen, taking the voice of both the seducer and the seduced. At the same time, he does not refrain from breaking the textual illusion by introducing some overtly contemporaneous references to his own monastery and to Henry II, King of England.[13]

Such a strategy of breaking down the fictionality of the text is well known to modern readers but is, in fact, another unique feature of the poetry in the period we are discussing. It testifies even more to the consciousness of these writers that they are creating a non-real, fictional world in their texts. The textual world becomes autonomous, but this opens up new, mostly parodist, tactics of playing with both facts and fiction!

Along the lines of his mythological letter exchange, Baudri also wrote a correspondence between Ovid and his friend Florus, and between himself and Constance, an educated nun in Britain. There seems to be no doubt about her real existence, nor that the poem formerly ascribed to her was actually written by Baudri, *pace* Peter Dronke (1968, 217). The autonomy of the textual world has gone so far that the writers have become conscious of being able to reshape factual reality by their fictional creations.

Another indication of the emancipation of the poetical/textual world, and of its disjunctive character in relation to the voice of the poet, can be seen in the growing complexity of the voices evoked. The anonymous poem *Pergama flere volo*, known as *Carmen Buranum* 101, offers a clear example. The poem starts as an unattributed lament on the fall of Troy, thus evoking the voice of a

---

13 In spite of his not being the most influential of the poets of the Loire, Baudri remains the most studied and best known of them all, thanks to the edition of his poems by Jean-Yves Tilliette (Baudry of Bourgueil 1998, 2002). See notably the attention he gets in Bond 1986. Hitherto, his *Heroides* have attracted most scholars' interest (Ratkowitsch 1991). No attention, however, has been given to the contemporaneous allusions in his work.

surviving Trojan. Then it focuses on Hecuba and gives voice to her lament. In the end, the reader is left bewildered by whose voice he is finally listening to.[14]

This bewilderment became a conscious satiric means in the hands of Hugh Primas, a Latin lyric poet and scholar from Orléans. He also wrote a lament on Troy (Carmen 10), probably parodying the Trojan wave of the early twelfth century. His poem contains all the traditional elements of the literary laments over Troy, and the reader is thus invited to hear a Trojan voice. Yet, at the very end of the poem, the speaker suddenly expresses his fatigue after such a long, hard day and retires to bed. The voice appears to be that of a Greek conqueror! (Adcock 1994)

*

All these examples are meant to illustrate the fast evolution of the autonomy of the textual world and the writer's consciousness in manipulating it. They are all poetical, because it was here – in lyric poetry – that the distinguishing features appeared first and most clearly. In the end, of course, it was not without consequences for other literary genres and for the general attitude toward textual creativity.

A very complicated disjunction of voices is achieved by Abelard in his *Historia calamitatum*, his famous autobiography. Actually, Abelard does not give a factual account of his life, as I tried to suggest in a recent article. He rather uses the autonomy of the text to reshape his own life, using the independent voice of the text to account for the life he lived as he ought to have lived it. By employing his own voice as the voice of the text, Abelard manages to achieve a very subtle manipulation of the reader, who cannot but lose sight of the autonomy of the textual world as a fiction on Abelard's own life. (Verbaal 2013)

Having arrived at Abelard, I should like to conclude with a hot topic in medieval studies during the last ten years. In the 1970s, Ewald Könsgen edited the correspondence between an anonymous man and woman. He did not try to identify either of the correspondents but only hypothetically pointed to the parallels with the love story of Abelard and Heloise as known from the *Historia calamitatum*. (Könsgen 1974) In 1999, this hint was taken up and elaborated by the eminent Abelard specialist Constant Mews. It exploded a bomb in the small world of medievalists. Vehement attempts were made to defend or to refute Mews' thesis everywhere in the world. For several years, the domain of Abelardian studies was dominated by this authenticity debate: a rather useless

---

14 On *Pergama flere volo*, see Boutemy 1946.

and, in my opinion, futile debate that only shows the difficulty modern scholars have in distinguishing between fact and fiction![15]

What do we have? A collection of very short letters, copied by a monk in the fifteenth century. Initially, he seemed only interested in the salutation formula and left out all the rest, but apparently his interest grew while copying and he started to copy more and more of the actual letters. Their style belongs undeniably to the twelfth century, but at the same time they succeed in evoking true lovers' sentiments without giving much actual information. Just as lovers' letters commonly do!

Now, a "true" or "authentic" correspondence would, for very practical reasons, never have survived. That it *did* survive shows it to have served a specific function. After all we have seen, it should not be very difficult to understand what function this might have been. It must have been the didactic purpose of teaching students how to write letters in a playful way. Actually, it combines the genre of Marbod's love poems with the style of the fictive letter exchange we saw in Baudri. It takes up Marbod's idea of evoking a sentimental narrative by way of two voices, a male and a female – only it does so in prose, in letters, no longer in poetry. And it seems clearly inspired by the famous factual story of Abelard and Heloise. Such was the story, then, of how truth became fiction, and this fiction, thanks to modern scholars, became fact again!

Bibliography

Adcock, Fleur. *Hugh Primas and the Archpoet*. Cambridge: Cambridge University Press, 1994.
Augustine. *Confessions*. I–II. Trans. William Watts. Loeb Classical Library, 26–27. Cambridge, MA: Harvard University Press, 1997–1999.
Barchiesi, Alessandro. "Traces of Greek Narrative and the Roman Novel; A Survey." *Oxford Readings in The Roman Novel*. Ed. S. J. Harrison. Oxford: Oxford University Press, 1999. 124–141.
Baudry of Bourgueil. *Baldricus Burgulianus. Carmina*. 2 vols. Ed. Jean-Yves Tilliette. Paris: Belles Lettres, 1998–2002.
Bond, Gerald A. "locus amoris: The Poetry of Baudry of Bourgueil and the Formation of the Ovidian Subculture." *Traditio* 42 (1986): 143–193.
— *The Loving Subject: Desire, Eloquence, and Power in Romanesque France*. Philadelphia, PA: University of Pennsylvania Press, 1995.
Boutemy, André. "Le poème *Pergama flere volo* et ses imitateurs du XIIe siècle." *Latomus* 5 (1946): 233–244.

---

[15] For a detailed bibliography and an elaboration of my opinion, see my forthcoming article at Brill (Verbaal 2013), footnote 4.

Boyer, Blanche and Richard McKeon. *Petrus Abaelardus. Sic et Non.* 2 vols. Chicago, IL: University of Chicago Press, 1976–1977.

Bulst, Walther. "Liebesbriefgedichte Marbods." *Liber Floridus. Studien Paul Lehmann gewidmet.* Ed. Bernhard Bischoff. St. Ottilien: Eos Verlag der Erzabtei, 1950. 287–301.

— ed. *Carmina Leodiensia.* Sitzungsberichte der Heidelberger Akademie der Wissenschaften. Philosophisch-historische Klasse. Heidelberg: Winter, 1975.

Dronke, Peter. *Medieval Latin and the Rise of European Love-Lyric.* Oxford: Clarendon, 1968.

Green, Dennis H. *The Beginnings of Medieval Romance. Fact and Fiction, 1150–1220.* Cambridge: Cambridge University Press, 2002.

— "The Rise of Medieval Fiction in the Twelfth Century." *Medieval Narratives between History and Fiction.* Eds. Panagiotis A. Agapitos & Lars Boje Mortensen. Copenhagen: Museum Tusculanum Press, 2012. 49–61.

Guibert de Nogent. *Autobiographie.* Ed. Edmond-René Labande. Les classiques de l'histoire de France au Moyen Âge. Paris: Belles Lettres, 1981.

Heinze, Richard. "Petron und der griechische Roman." *Hermes* 84 (1899): 494–519, repr. in *Vom Geist des Römertums.* Ed. Erich Burck. Stuttgart: Teubner, 1960. 417–439.

Iuvencus. *Evangeliorum libri quattuor.* Ed. Johann Huemer. Corpus scriptorium ecclesiasticoricum latinorum. The Prague, Vienna and Leipzig: Tempsky and Freytag, 1891.

Jaeger, C. Stephen. *The Envy of Angels.* Philadelphia, PA: University of Pennsylvania Press, 1994.

Könsgen, Ewald. *Epistolae duorum amantium: Briefe Abelards und Heloises?* Diss. Mittellateinische Studien und Texte, 8. Leiden: Brill, 1974.

Marbode of Rennes. *Incipit liber Marbodi [...]. Editio princeps.* Ed. Yves Mayeuc. Rennes, 1524 [Now Paris B.N. Rés. p.Yc. 1533].

— *De ornamentis verborum. Liber decem capitulorum: retorica, mitologia e moralità di un vescovo poeta (secc. XI–XII).* Ed. Rosario Leotta. Per verba, 10. Florence: SISMEL, 1998.

Mehtonen, Päivi. *Old Concepts and New Poetics: "Historia," "Argumentum," and "Fabula" in the Twelfth- and Early Thirteenth-Century Latin Poetics of Fiction.* Diss. Helsinki: Societas Scientiarum Fennica, 1996.

Moser Jr., Thomas C. *A Cosmos of Desire: The Medieval Latin Erotic Lyric in English Manuscripts.* Ann Arbor: University of Michigan Press, 2004.

Quintus Curtius. *History of Alexander, vol. II. Books 6–10.* Trans. John C. Rolfe. Loeb Classical Library, 369. Cambridge, MA: Harvard University Press, 1946.

Ratkowitsch, Christine. "Die keusche Helena: Ovids Heroides 16/17 in der mittelalterlichen Neudichtung des Baudri von Bourgueil." *Wiener Studien* 104 (1991): 209–236.

Saenger, Paul. *Space between Words. The Origins of Silent Reading.* Stanford, CA: Stanford University Press, 1997a.

— "Lire aux derniers siècles du Moyen Âge." *Histoire de la lecture dans le monde occidental.* Eds. Guglielmo Cavallo and Rogier Chartier. Paris: Seuil, 1997b. 147–174.

Verbaal, Wim. "Teste Quintiliano: Jean de Salisbury et Quintilien – un exemple de la crise des autorités au xiie siècle." *Quintilien ancient et modern.* Eds. Perinne Galand-Hallyn et al. Latinitates, 3. Turnhout: Brepols, 2010. 155–170.

— "Trapping the Future. Abelard's Multi-Layered Image-Building." *Abelardiana: A Collection of Critical Essays.* Ed. B. Hellemans (forthcoming). Brill Studies in Intellectual History. Leiden: Brill, 2013.

Telling Tales: Narratology & Fictionality

Ming Dong Gu
Toward a Transcultural Poetics of Fiction: The Fusion of Narrative Visions in Chinese and Western Fiction Studies

Significant changes have taken place in the studies of fiction, Chinese and Western. With the irresistible tide of globalization, there has appeared an ongoing fusion of horizons in Chinese and Western fiction studies. The fusion came about not just because of globalization. It was very much due to the fact that fiction as a literary form is conducive to comparative studies across cultural traditions and disciplines. Andrew Plaks, an eminent scholar of Chinese fiction, once pointed out, "the rise of the novel in both Europe and China as a major form of literary expression provides very fertile ground for comparative speculations." (Plaks 1987, 14) Since the 1970s, Chinese fiction has no longer been a subject of inquiry confined to scholars in China alone; it has aroused the interest of fiction scholars from Europe, North America, and Oceania, who have turned out remarkable studies of this literary genre from a comparative perspective. Franco Moretti, the internationally renowned authority on fiction theory, has gained new grounds in fiction theory through his comparative study of the Chinese and European novel. (Moretti 2008) His fresh and fascinating insights have broadened and enriched our understanding of the historical, conceptual, and aesthetical conditions of extended prose fiction across cultural traditions. In the global context, fiction study has become an interdisciplinary subject of narrative study which involves diverse disciplines such as history, sociology, linguistics, anthropology, psychology, philosophy, religion and others disciplines. As one historian of narrative theories notes, "Once freed of the notion that they should study only stories that are untrue and highly respected (the domain of traditional literature), critics realize that the anthropologist, folklorist, historian, and even the psychoanalyst and theologian are all concerned with narrative in one way or another." (Martin 1988, 23) A symposium on narrative, held at the University of Chicago in 1979 and attended by renowned scholars from diverse disciplines, examined narrative theories from multiple perspectives including the historical, philosophical, ideological, linguistic, semiotic, psychological, and cultural. The theoretical explorations at the symposium have proved beyond doubt that narrative or fiction has become a subject of study which is interdisciplinary and transcultural.[1]

---

[1] The presentations, discussions, and critical responses at the symposium were published in a special issue of *Critical Inquiry* in 1980, and later collected into a book, see Mitchell 1980.

As a result of the international interest and interdisciplinary concern, studies of Chinese fiction have made significant advances in historical research, theoretical inquiry, and critical practice both in and outside China. In the historical examination of the *xiaoshuo* (Chinese term for fiction) genre, there are quite a number of studies by both Chinese and Western scholars that have broadened our understanding of its evolution and development beyond Lu Xun's seminal study in the 1920s.[2] In theoretical inquiries into this genre, there have been a few brilliant studies that have deepened our understanding of its nature, function, aesthetic principles, and techniques from a cross-cultural perspective.[3] Critical studies of individual *xiaoshuo* writers and *xiaoshuo* works have sprung up like mushrooms. What is notable in these practical critical studies is that scholars have gone beyond the traditional approaches to initiate a series of tacit shifts in emphasis in the studies of Chinese *xiaoshuo* in response to a comparative interest in fiction study and to the advance of fiction theory. In this article, I intend to examine a series of changes and shifts in the study of Chinese fiction in relation to international narrative study, explore their implications and challenges in the context of fiction theory, and speculate on their significance for a better understanding of fiction as a transcultural genre, and for the construction of a transcultural poetics of fiction studies.

Changes and Challenges in Fiction Study

The first noticeable shift in Chinese fiction study is one from a view of fiction as social documents like history (unofficial and defective history or biography) that reflects or refracts social reality to a view of fiction as an art produced in particular social settings. This shift started in the 1970s and was initiated by the eminent historian Ying-shih Yu. After reviewing the then existent scholarly works on the *Hongloumeng* (variously translated as *Dream of the Red Chamber*, *Dream of Red Mansions,* and *The Story of the Stone*),[4] China's greatest classical novel, Yu lamented the fact that the novel had been studied more as a historical

---

[2] See Lu Xun 1973; *Zhongguo xiaoshuo shilüe* [A Brief History of Chinese Fiction], 1978; Hou Zhongyi 1990; Shi Changyu 1994; Wang Rumei and Zhang Yu 2001; Meng Zhaolian and Ning Zongyi 1998; Chen Meilin and Feng Baoshan 1998; Li Xiusheng and Zhao Yishan 2001.
[3] See Hanan 1967, 1973, 1981; Plaks 1977; Ye Long 1982; Wu Gongzheng 1985; Rolston 1990; Meng Zhaolian and Ning Zongyi 1998; Wang Rumei and Zhang Yu 2001.
[4] There are two complete English translations of the novel: Hawkes and Minford, 5 vols., 1973–1986, Yang Hsien-yi and Gladys Yang, 3 vols., 1978.

and sociological document than as a literary work[5] and called for a radical change in the approaches to the novel, a change that he compared to a paradigm shift in Thomas Kuhn's conception. (Yu 1974, 6) Yu's pungent critique and vehement call has had profound significance for the field of Chinese fiction studies. They effectively ushered in a radical shift from the time-honored textual scholarship preoccupied with identification of authorship, searching for sources and influences, and verification of dating, editions, emendations and the like to a truly literary scholarship concerned with the novel as a literary masterpiece. This shift has had a great impact on *Hongloumeng* scholarship in particular and on the scholarly work of traditional Chinese fiction in general.

Ying-shih Yu is a historian by specialization. It is up to literary scholars to reflect on the changing view of fiction and to complete the shift with substantial scholarship. In 1988, another Mr. Yu, Anthony C. Yu, addressed the relationship between history and fiction in his essay, "History, Fiction, and the Reading of Chinese Narrative." With the conceptual acumen and critical sensitivity of a literary scholar, he identifies a revolutionary moment in Chinese fictional development which is typified in the self-reflexivity of the *Hongloumeng*, emphasizing the necessity for a change not only in the study of the *Hongloumeng* but also in the study of Chinese fiction and narrative in general: "It is high time to search for a different mode of reading Chinese narrative, whether historical or fictive." (Yu 1988, 19) His widely acclaimed study of the *Hongloumeng*, *Rereading the Stone*, is a landmark in the changes in reading modes and conceptions of fiction studies. The preface to his book informs us that his study goes "beyond the customary verdict on the virtue of the eighteenth-century Chinese masterpiece of prose fiction [...] as that of the most vivid and comprehensive reflection of late imperial culture and social institutions." (Yu 1997, vi) Instead, it proposes a thesis that had received little systematic treatment: "the narrative's merit as verbal art lies in its reflexive and innovative insistence, made through myriad occasions and devices, that it is a work of fiction. The novel, in other words, is as much a story about fictive representation as it is about human life." (Yu 1997, xi)

Anthony C. Yu's theoretical reflections and scholarship represent the completion of the first shift, which is one from a view of fiction as a way of telling stories to a notion of fiction as a form of language art that weaves stories into a verbal fabric. Accompanying the first shift is a second shift in critical methodology from thematic criticism to a formalist analysis of fictional works.

---

[5] Ying-shih Yu points out, "[I]n the mainstream scholarship of the novel that has spanned over a hundred years, it has never truly attained its rightful status as a novel. On the contrary, it has always been processed as a historical document." (Yu 1978, 15).

In this shift, scholars of fiction have laid more emphasis on fictional techniques than on fictional themes and paid as much attention to what the literary work represents as to how it presents what it wishes to present. This shift was marked by several landmark studies. It may be said to have started with Andrew Plaks's *Archetype and Allegory in the Dream of the Red Chamber* (1976), continued with Patrick Hanan's *The Chinese Vernacular Story* (1981) and Plaks's *Four Masterworks of the Ming Novel* (1987), and culminated in Anthony C. Yu's *Rereading the Stone: Desire and the Making of Fiction in Dream of the Red Chamber* (1997). The distinctive feature of this shift as found in these representative studies is their self-conscious preoccupation with the values of forms and techniques of representation in the making of fictional art. This is especially clear in Anthony C. Yu's study of *The Story of the Stone* (*Hongloumeng*). In his study of the novel, he declares, "the narrative's merit as verbal art lies in its reflexive and innovative insistence, made through myriad occasions and devices," and "the narrative is as much a story about a piece of stone (Stone as one protagonist) as it is about what that story is (Stone as script, as linguistic representation and fictive writing) and how it is to be received (the effect of reading Stone)." (Yu 1997, 111) While the shift is tacitly critical of the tendency in Chinese fictional studies that continues to regard formal techniques as merely a means of organizing materials in a given fictional work, A. C. Yu explicitly calls on scholars to regard techniques as the means of exploring and defining the themes and values of presented materials.

A third shift is one from traditional literary approaches predicated on philological, historical, biographical, sociological methods to post-structuralist approaches informed by New Historicism, Feminism, Deconstruction, Postcolonialism, Gender studies, and Cultural Studies. This shift may be said to have started with Jing Wang's *The Story of Stone: Intertextuality, Ancient Chinese Stone Lore, and the Stone Symbolism of Dream of the Red Chamber, Water Margin, and The Journey to the West* (1992) in fictional criticism, and with Ming Dong Gu's *Chinese Theories of Fiction: A Non-Western Narrative System* (2006) in the field of Chinese narrative theory, and to have continued by a few studies of individual fictional works, like Wai-yee Li's *Enchantment and Disenchantment: Love and Illusion in Chinese Literature* (1993), Martin Huang's *Literati and Self-Re/presentation: Autobiographical Sensibility in the Eighteenth-Century Chinese Novel* (1995), Maram Epstein's *Competing Discourses: Orthodoxy, Authenticity, and Engendered Meanings in Late Imperial Chinese Fiction* (2001), and numerous short studies in the form of essays and articles published in various scholarly journals. This shift is still in the initial stages in the field of classical fiction, which can be seen from the curious fact that for unknown reasons, Jing Wang, who has, in a way, pioneered a new approach to Chinese fictional studies, eventually left the field of traditional Chinese fiction. In the field of modern Chinese fiction, the shift has been completed. But for classical Chinese fiction, the potential is great. With the aid of contemporary theories, it will open up new vistas in fictional studies.

These shifts, whether completed or in the initial stage, have given us a great deal of food for thought in the study of Chinese fiction. In a way, they have compelled us to consider whether studies of Chinese fiction are in the process of undergoing a paradigm shift in Thomas Kuhn's conception. "In its established usage," notes Kuhn, "a paradigm is an accepted model or pattern." (1970, 23) It sets forth models for replication. In his appropriation of the term for the study of scientific revolution, Kuhn argues that "a paradigm is rarely an object for replication," but rather "is an object for further articulation and specification under new and more stringent conditions." (1970, 23) His reconception of paradigm has broadened its denotations and made it useful for disciplines of research. Kuhn's examination of how paradigms gain their status is of special significance for us. Paradigms come into being because "they are more successful than their competitors in solving a few problems that the group of practitioners has come to recognize as acute." (Kuhn 1970, 23) A paradigm is established upon recognized "achievements that for a time provide model problems and solutions to a community of practitioners." (Kuhn 1970, viii) An established paradigm is defended by members of a given community and when further research finds it unable to provide a model for solving problems, it is challenged by other members of the community who grope to posit a new paradigm. A new paradigm is resisted because it may not be as good as the old one. But one thing is sure: "The success of a paradigm [...] is at the start largely a promise of success discoverable in selected and still incomplete examples." (Kuhn 1970, 23–24) Once the incremental successes accumulate to a critical point, the old paradigm gives way to a new paradigm which proves to be more successful in providing models for problem solving.

Kuhn's conception of paradigm, the role of paradigm in research, and paradigm change may offer us valuable insights into fiction studies. Personally, I think that we are in the process of completing a paradigm shift, which has the promise of pushing Chinese fiction studies beyond the boundaries of Sinology to be merged with the international and interdisciplinary studies of narrative in the global context. The rise of Chinese *xiaoshuo* or fiction is rather late in Chinese literary history in comparison with the dominant genre of poetry, but in the worldwide context, the rise of Chinese fiction was not belated. If European fiction could trace its origins to the medieval romance (*roman*) in the twelfth century and short stories in prose that did not appear until the fourteenth century,[6] Chinese fiction as a literary genre appeared in the Tang (seventh–tenth century), and fiction in the modern sense of the term dates to the Six Dynasties (220–589) or even earlier. (Lu Xun 2005) In its evolution and development, Chinese fiction shared many common characteristics with its European counterparts and eventually merged into the same narrative genre in modern times. But in methodologies, Chinese fictional studies are still preoccupied with traditional approaches without enough interest in poststructuralist and postmodern approaches, especially in the study of established classical works. Without a paradigm shift, Chinese fiction and fictional study cannot engage in genuine dialogues with the international trend of fiction studies, still less contributing to international narratology.

Three Anxieties and a Paradigm Shift

I venture to call for a paradigm shift in the study of Chinese fiction, especially in pre-modern fiction. I make this call partly in response to the changes that I have observed in the field, and partly as an attempt to tackle three related concerns or anxieties. The first anxiety is what Harold Bloom calls the "anxiety of influence." (Bloom 1973, 5–7) In the study of classical fiction in Chinese literature, the anxiety of influence, which often troubles scholars in the field, can be boiled down to a question: how can one generate new and interesting readings of the classical texts that have been examined and reexamined by scholars for generations? The time-honored perspectives, which focus on historical context, author's biographical data, philological exegeses, sociological inquiries and the like, and the favorite methodologies, which explore the genesis, authorship, composition, redactions, editions, transmission, and thematic concerns of a text, have been utilized over and over again before us. In reusing these approaches and methodologies, we the latecomers cannot help but produce "twice-cooked meat," a Chinese culinary term for restatements of or variations on old scholarship.

The second anxiety may be called the "anxiety of marginalization." Studies of Chinese literature or literary Sinology as a branch of scholarship has had a long history in the West, but it has not yet entered the mainstream literary studies despite protracted efforts by several generations of scholars,

---

6 "In literary history, one of the earliest dates it [*roman*] appears is 1140, when *roman* denoted a story in verse adapted from Latin legends. Originally, *roman* referred to imaginative works in the vernacular; mainly the medieval French verse epics. By the 16th c. it was applied to works in prose." (Cuddon 1991, 802).

Chinese and Western. Since the rise of postmodernism, there have been visible indications that, except for studies of modern Chinese literature, literary Sinology as a whole has been pushed even further to the margins of general literary studies. And even in the bright spot of modern Chinese literary studies, instead of bridging the gap between Chinese literary studies and general literary studies, it has ironically brought about a rift between classical Chinese literature and modern Chinese literature, causing the former to be further marginalized. Evidently, this tendency is contrary to the international trend of fictional study.

The third anxiety may be termed the "anxiety of aphasia." Since the introduction of Western literary discourse, especially postmodern theories, present-day Chinese theoretical discourse has been so westernized that the time-honored Chinese system of literary theory has practically lost its voice in the confrontation between the East and West. In a study of ancient Chinese literary theory, one scholar of Chinese literary thought laments: "In literary creation, criticism, and appreciation, some concepts and categories of ancient Chinese literary theory still have a certain amount of life, but Chinese literary theory as a theoretical system has ceased to exist." (Sun 1996, 3) In spite of repeated calls by Chinese and Western scholars for two-way dialogues between Chinese and Western literary theories, most of the attempts at dialogues have ended up in pseudo-dialogues, or disguised Western monologues. Although Chinese fiction arose earlier than Western fiction, theoretical studies of Chinese fiction lag far behind Western inquiries, and theoretical assumptions and critical terminology are mainly borrowed from Western fictional study. Long overdue are studies that treat Chinese fiction on its own terms and in relation to the theoretical and critical achievements of world fiction.

These anxieties represent questions that have occupied my mind and the minds of many scholars, especially young ones, for a long time: 1) How can we avoid producing restatements and variations of old scholarship? 2) How can we advance studies of Chinese fiction so that it will no longer wander along the margins of general literary studies? 3) How can we conduct meaningful dialogues between Chinese and Western theoretical discourses that would constitute a genuine two-way exchange of ideas? These are hard questions and have no readily available answers. Here, I venture to offer an opinion. For answers to the first question, we need to go beyond existent scholarship to create new paradigms and methodologies. For answers to the second question, we need to situate Chinese fiction in the global context of fiction studies and conduct studies in a discourse modernized by the infusion of contemporary theories. For answers to the third question, we need to create a critical language that results from the fusing of traditional Chinese thought and contemporary literary theories. In my opinion, a possible key to finding answers to these questions may be obtained by reinvigorating and rejuvenating the old legacies with new ideas and approaches. In the process of reinvigoration, we may use contemporary theories as food for our thought. By digesting introduced theories, we may reap creative inspirations to create new paradigms and methodologies that are appropriate for the study of Chinese fiction, especially canonical texts. In the postmodern era, the explosion of new theories may be dazzling to the eye and daunting to the spirit. But now, the age of theory is definitely over. In the age after theory, many once fashionable theories no longer dominate theoretical discourse or are simply *passé*. As the dust of the theoretical turn has settled, we have more reasons to believe that some theories or aspects of theories have stood the test of time and proved to be useful for conceptual and critical studies. New Historicism, postcolonialism, feminism, gender studies theory, semiotics, deconstruction, psychoanalytic criticism, reader response criticism, theories of representation and others – all can supply us with inspirations for constructing new paradigms and methodologies as well as producing new readings.

People may ask: Since contemporary theories are derived from studies of Western literature and culture, can they be integrated into studies of Chinese fiction, which was produced in entirely different cultural conditions? This doubt has been debated by scholars in the field of Chinese literature for a long time. A notable debate was carried out at a round-table panel at the 1990 Asian Studies Annual Conference.[7] The debate ended inconclusively. Now, two decades after the debate, the situation has not changed much in the field of traditional Chinese literature. By contrast, impressive achievements have been made in the field of modern Chinese literature. The introduction of postmodern theories into that field has drastically enlarged the horizons of modern Chinese literary studies. A series of innovative and fascinating studies have proved that the introduction of contemporary theories works and is effective. I believe that it may work equally well in traditional Chinese fiction so long as we open our minds and have the resolve to make it work. Twenty years after the debate, the question now is no longer one of whether we should integrate contemporary theories into our discourse but one of how we can do a good job of it.

We need to seriously consider this issue because we have come to a time when the boom of Theory is already over. Some scholars claim that "the great era of theory is now behind us and that we have now entered a period of timidity, backfilling, and (at best) empirical accumulation"; others reject speculative theories and insist on the "practice of theory" in the present; still others simply pronounce the end of Theory and call for rollbacks to earlier paradigms

---

[7] See *Chinese Literature: Essays, Articles, Reviews*, 13, 1991, 77–82.

and "returns" to traditional methodologies based on formalism and aesthetics. (Mitchell 2004, 330–331) But for traditional fiction studies, we have not yet fully embraced methodologies with formalism and aesthetics as their underpinning. Here, I will just analyze one facet of this issue: the content versus form approach. In literary studies, there is a tendency to divide a literary work into two related conceptual categories: the content (subject matter), and the form (ways of representation). It is the same in narrative studies. The two conceptual categories form a kind of dualism which refers to a two-level model of narrative that is the central hypothesis and assumption of a number of narratological theories. Seymour Chatman, in his *Story and Discourse*, analyzes fiction as a dualism, which is variously couched in a series of binary terms: "deep structure" and "surface manifestation," "content plane" and "expression plane," "*histoire*" and "*récit*," "signifier" and "signified." All of these dual terms, according to Chatman, may be regarded as more or less equivalent distinctions of two terms: "a story (*histoire*)," the content, and "a discourse (*discours*)," the expression, the means by which the content is communicated. (Chatman 1978, 19) This structuralist conception describes a common mental process in the reading of fiction: "story, the content element, and discourse, the form element, are posited as constructs separable by easy mental operations from stories actualized in concrete representations." (Chatman 1980, 261) Of the two categories in the dualism in fictional studies, the reader generally pays more attention to the content plane than to the formal plane. The same is true in studies of Chinese fiction. The dominant tendency is to focus on the content of a particular text or what it means, rather than on its form or how it means. By contrast, there are only a few studies which focus on how a particular fictional work generates its meanings.

In the study of Chinese fiction, I argue, the time is more than ripe for us to shift our attention from the subject matter and content to formal issues that are intrinsic to the making of verbal art. This shift is necessary not just because enough critical work concerning the content of a text has been done but also because the "science of literature can never be a science of content, but only of the conditions of content." (Barthes 1967, 87) Although I am not entirely sympathetic to the notion that the aim of literary criticism is not to discover meanings but to understand how the institution of literature functions,[8] I do believe that "to discover the structures and conventions of literary discourse which enable them to have the meanings they do" (Culler 1977, 8) would open our minds and deepen our understanding of literature. "The virtue of the mod-

---

[8] The French school of literary theory holds this view, see Jonathan Culler's "Introduction" to Todorov 1977.

ern novelists," Mark Shorer said half a century ago, "from James and Conrad on down – is not only that he pays so much attention to his medium, but that, when he pays most, he discovers through it a new subject matter, and a greater one." (Schorer 1967, 72) For this reason, I think we should take heed of the insights in A. C. Yu's *Rereading the Stone* and emphasize a shift from what a text means to how it means. The shift from *what* to *how* is concerned not only with interpretations of a text but also with the poetics of making, the purpose of which is not only to enrich and illuminate critical practice but also to discover the structures and conventions of literary discourse which will help us find ways to produce new and multiple interpretations of canonical texts.

In the Chinese and Western traditions, both modern and pre-modern, there is the tendency to view fiction as a reflection or refraction of life. A fictional work is supposed to be a series of windows on life, with words as transparent panes through which a reader can see a world represented. But the world represented is not a picture or series of pictures reflected in a mirror. It is an artifice constructed with language through the fiction writers' technique. Words are *not* transparent panes. A fictional work's language is not just a medium for carrying the intended meanings and significance of the author. The windowpanes are opaque and are inscribed with designs that are noticeable only through textual analysis. The materiality of sign is often implicitly or explicitly manipulated to convey subtle meanings and implications that are not expressed by thematic structure and subject matter. This is possible because language is used "not just as a device for formalistic analysis capable only of tracing the outline, texture and contours of a text, but as a mode of analysis which can suggest interpretations of structural form. Choice of words and sentence-types possess conventional reverberations, associations, for members of a reading community." (Fowler 1977, 4) From the writer's point of view, there is another reason why we should approach fiction by way of technique, and preferably by way of semiotics. In the West, fiction has become the major medium for technical innovations in modernist and postmodernist literature, and the innovations are generally conducted in linguistic creativity. In this respect, we can easily recall such famed experimental writers as James Joyce, Henry James, Marcel Proust, Virginia Woolf, William Faulkner, and Ernest Hemingway, who made technical innovations to allow language to carry more than surface meanings.

Crossing Divides of Fiction Studies

In the present-day era of globalization, the study of Chinese fiction is still largely a subject within Sinology. There is a series of divides within literary

Sinology between pre-modern and modern fiction, between fiction and other genres, between Chinese fiction and world fiction, between traditional and postmodern approaches, and between fictional and non-fictional studies. Theoretically, no one has drawn these demarcations, but in practice, these divides have effectively constituted invisible but powerful barriers that few scholars are willing to break. In the domain of periodization, C. T. Hsia may be the first to cross the divide between pre-modern and modern Chinese fiction with his two studies, *A History of Modern Chinese Fiction* (1971) and *The Classic Chinese Novel* (1968). Still, the two books each focus on two different historical periods and therefore do not constitute a real breakaway from the barrier between pre-modern and modern literature. David Wang is another scholar who challenges our perception of him as a scholar of modern Chinese literature and ventures into the pre-modern period with his book *Fin-de-Siècle Splendor: Repressed Modernities of Late Qing China* 1849–1911 (1997). Again, his book deals with analytic data taken wholly from the historical period before the rise of modern Chinese literature. Wai-yee Li's *Enchantment and Disenchantment: Love and Illusion in Chinese Literature* (1993) is a rare study that breaks the divide between fiction and other genres. By examining a range of genres including lyric poetry, classical essays, historical texts, drama, and fictional works of different periods from high antiquity to late imperial China, Li is one of the few who cross the barrier between different genres. Her second book, *The Readability of the Past in Early Chinese Historiography* (2007) continues her bold move of boundary-crossing, but she stops at the divide between pre-modern and modern literature. Martin Huang's book *Negotiating Masculinities in Late Imperial China* (2005) not only shows the visible influence of contemporary gender theories but also employs analytic data from different cultural sources, poetry, fiction, historiography, classics, political treatises, and books on moral conduct. Wei Shang's *Rulin waishi and Cultural Transformation in Late Imperial China* (2003), breaks the barrier between fiction and non-fictional materials, but it is again a study that focuses on a historical period. I have yet to see a study that crosses the divide between Chinese and world fiction and situates the study of Chinese fictional works within the international context of fiction studies.

In my opinion, these divides are imagined barriers humanly constructed because of the academic need for specialization and have remained intact due to critical inertia. Rigid observance of these divides overlooks the inherent interrelatedness of literature, history, and culture, the mutual interaction between different types of discourses produced in a historical period, the overt and covert impact of early discourse upon later discourse, and the reciprocal process through which the past has shaped the present and the present reshapes the past. Not a few scholars in the Sinological circles have felt the restricting strain by these divides and are making some preliminary efforts to change the situation. Here, I will only cite a few examples. In her current research on the relationship between the fall of the Ming dynasty and literary representation in seventeenth-century China, Wai-yee Li proposes to "examine aspects of late-Ming literary, aesthetic, and cultural sensibility and their representation, continuation, and transformation in early Qing writings."[9] What is refreshing in her on-going research is that she undertakes to "juxtapose cultural self-perception and self-definition before and after the fall of the Ming dynasty in various discourses (on things, on women, on the self, and on history), while noting shifts and differences within the conventional period designation of 'late-Ming' and 'early-Qing.'" Martin Huang is a recognized fiction scholar of late imperial China, but he professes to have a strong interest in modern Chinese literature. In one of his on-going projects, he proposes to "break the invisible 'barriers' between the scholars of 'traditional Chinese literature' and those of 'modern Chinese literature.'"[10] In his current book-length project, "*Jin Ping Mei Cihua* and Commercial Publicity: Narrative Construction of the Everyday World in Late Imperial China," Wei Shang seems to attempt to break the barrier between fictional and non-fictional materials.[11] Thus, beneath the calm façade of willing adherence to the requirements for specialization, there lurks the motivating force to cross the divides. Leading scholars in the field have encouraged the crossing of the invisible divides. Wai-yee Li, for example, professes: "I wanted to write about something as different as possible so I wouldn't repeat myself. I find that if you work in different periods, it forces you to ask different questions."[12] Stephen Owen warmly praised Wai-yee Li's versatility in an interview: "Although she always works with a deep grounding in a contemporary context, one hallmark of her work is to see connections between texts across 2000 years, and she is probably one of the few scholars at Harvard whose areas of particular specialization are separated by two millennia – antiquity from roughly 400–100 BCE and the late-imperial

---

[9] Wai-yee Li, Fellow of Radcliff Institute for Advanced Study, Harvard University. Information quoted from http://www.radcliffe.harvard.edu/people/wai-yee-li. (15 March 2011).
[10] Martin Huang, Professor of Chinese literature at the University of California-Ervine. Information quoted from http://www.faculty.uci.edu/profile.cfm?faculty_id=2743 (20 May 2005).
[11] Wei Shang, Professor of Asian Humanities and Chinese Culture at Columbia University. Information quoted from http://www.columbia.edu/cu/weai/faculty/shang.html (20 May 2005).
[12] Quoted from Ken Gewertz, "Divining the dreams of lost worlds," Harvard Gazette Archives. http://www.news.harvard.edu/gazette/2001/01.18/03-lostworld.html. (15 May 2011).

period from sixteenth to eighteenth century."[13] Conceptually, the enforcing power of the barriers comes from critical inertia, especially in ways of reading fiction. Reading fiction is a pleasure for those who enjoy reading fiction. It can be addictive, not just in the mere act of reading but also in ways of reading. The conventional mode of reading tends to be a consumptive mode in which the reader adheres to the accepted patterns of reading and passively consumes what he reads, often in a mindless fashion. The same is true for writers and critics of fiction. In China nowadays, fiction writing is still mainly occupied with telling an enthralling story; the general reading public is still mainly interested in reading a good story with traditional narrative structure and techniques. This habitual way of reading and writing arises from long-term social and psychological conditioning. Robert Scholes views traditional narrative structures as "part of a system of psycho-social dependencies that inhibit both individual human growth and significant social change." (Scholes 1980, 208) In his opinion, conventional modes of reading and criticism are like an "opiate" which should be renounced as "a prelude to improvement in the human situation." (1980, 208) For this purpose, he suggests that we should introduce postmodern anti-narrative theories, "because they ultimately force us to draw our attention away from the construction of a diegesis according to our habitual interpretive processes." (Scholes 1980, 207) The function of postmodern anti-narrative theories is to "problematize the entire process of narration and interpretation" and to force us to go out of interpretive and hermeneutic inertia and to open up new hermeneutic space. (1980, 207)

A change in perspective and theoretical orientation will open up new vistas and new avenues to literary Sinology, especially in Chinese fiction studies. With a change in perspective and theoretical orientation we can also see that the traditional and the postmodern are not as separated as one thinks. On the contrary, what appears to be new in modernist and postmodernist fictional works in the West may simply be something that has been neglected or consigned to oblivion in traditional Chinese fiction. Conversely, fictional works that seem to conform to the Western principles of realism, turn out, on close analysis, to violate the tenets of realism on a massive scale. Because of the impact of Western literary theory and critical inertia, realism and its variations, critical realism and naturalism, are undoubtedly the most frequently used concepts to describe Chinese fictional works, often to the complete neglect of a large number of Chinese prose fictional works, including short stories, novellas, or novels, that are composed with patently non-realistic elements, supernatural motifs, fantastic details, and mythical narrative frames.

---

13 Quoted from Ken Gewertz, "Divining the dreams of lost worlds," Harvard Gazette Archives. http://www.news.harvard.edu/gazette/2001/01.18/03-lostworld.html. (15 May 2011).

Critical inertia also affects creative writing of fiction and blinds Chinese fiction writers to the precious fictional legacies from China's past. Let us take magical realism for example. As a postmodern technique of fiction writing, it has exerted a great impact upon present-day Chinese writers. Quite a number of eminent Chinese writers writing today admit that they have come under the influence of Latin American writers who are masters of magical realism. But few of them have paused to consider the fact that the magic, the fantastic, and the supernatural not only constitute the narrative elements in Chinese fiction but also become overt and covert structural designs. In generally accepted realistic novels, there are numerous instances of miraculous and fantastic happenings that simply violate realistic principles in literary creation and the law of probability in life. This is especially true in the field of the Chinese novel. Among the six commonly acknowledged masterpieces, the *Sanguo yanyi* [Romance of the Three Kingdoms], *Xiyou ji* [Journey to the West], *Shuihu zhuan* [Water Margin], *Jin Ping Mei* [The Plum in the Golden Vase/The Golden Vase], *Rulin waishi* [The Scholars], and *Hongloumeng* [The Story of the Stone/Dream of the Red Chamber], only the *Rulin waishi* can rightfully be viewed as an extended prose fiction written in realistic, critically realistic mode, and free from unrealistic elements of the supernatural, the grotesque, magical realism, and the fantastic. Due to the explicit descriptions of the characters' sex life and a focus on mundane details of every day life, *The Plum in the Golden Vase* has been characterized as a realistic or naturalistic novel. But the realistic view cannot accommodate the unrealistic and supernatural elements: Immortal Wu's prediction of the major characters' fates, Daoist Priest Pan's exorcising of ghosts, Star-Gazer Liu's devising of charms and spells for Pan Jinlian, Pu Jing's supernatural act of intercession for all the dead characters, the reincarnation of Ximen, the anti-hero, as his own son, and some other episodes with supernatural and surrealistic elements. In addition, Li Ping'er's dying dream of her ex-husband's ghost, Ximen's dreams of Ping'er, Yueniang's nightmare on the night before she wants to put her family in the care of Yun Lishou and so on – these episodes are narrated in a mode which can be said to be surrealistic and grotesque. In a way, the whole novel was implicitly structured on a similar design to that of *The Story of the Stone* (*Hongloumeng*). In Chapter 29, after all the characters have appeared in the novel, the author invokes Immortal Wu to appear on the scene, employing his fortune-telling as a structuring ploy to hint at the development of the rest of the novel. As for other extended Chinese fiction, the *Romance of Three Kingdoms*, despite its being a historical novel, is full of supernatural and fantastic elements. *The Water Margin*, interspersed with fantastic and supernatural elements, is also structured on a mythic frame of a stone tablet. Wu Cheng'en's

Journey to the West is a pure fantasy based on the pilgrimage of the monk Xuanzhuang in history, who made light of numerous hazards and risked his life to travel to India for Buddhist scriptures. Pu Songling's *Liaozhai zhiyi* [Strange Tales from the Leisure Studio], another recognized masterpiece of Chinese fiction, is a collection of stories that are fictional works of magical realism, the fantastic, and the absurd par excellence, because most of its protagonists are simply ghosts and animal spirits who interact with human characters to perform human dramas of life.

An overview of Chinese fiction informs us that one can rarely find a classical Chinese fictional work that contains no fantastic and supernatural elements, be it historical fiction based on the imitation of official histories or pure fiction imagined out of the blue. The ample use of the uncanny and supernatural is not intended solely as allegorical ploys, but meant as an unconventional manner of representation, the implications of which remind us of those of fantastic and magic realism. Todorov defines the fantastic: "the fantastic is based essentially on a hesitation of the reader – a reader who identifies with the chief character – as to the nature of an uncanny event. This hesitation may be resolved so that the event is acknowledged as reality, or so that the event is identified as the fruit of imagination or the result of an illusion." (Todorov 1975, 156) But in the Chinese tradition, the fantastic elements cannot be adequately explained in terms of a hesitation on the part of the reader; nor can they be resolved as the results of imagination or illusion. For in Chinese novels like *The Water Margin*, *The Plum in the Golden Vase*, and *The Story of the Stone* (*Hongloumeng*) the fantastic happenings are neither the results of the reader's hesitation nor the characters' illusion but are part and parcel of the plot development. They are so prevalent that I may call them instances of "magical realism" because they conform to the characteristic features of magic realism: "the mingling and juxtaposition of the realistic and the fantastic or bizarre, skilful time shifts, convoluted and even labyrinthine narratives and plots, miscellaneous use of dreams, myths and fairy stories, expressionistic and even surrealistic description, arcane erudition, the element of surprise or abrupt shock, the horrific and the inexplicable." (Cuddon 1991, 522)

But to a large extent, even magic realism is not adequate for explaining the fantastic in the Chinese tradition. In most fictional works of magic realism, fantastic details, despite their relations to myths, legends, and fairy tales, are largely the effects of the transformations of reality by the subconscious or unconscious mind. In Chinese fiction, fantastic details are treated as though they were realistic details. Moreover, they are woven into mythic or supernatural frameworks that may be taken from mythology, legends, folklore, or simply invented by the fiction writer. A typical example is the use of the stone lore in the three great classical Chinese novels: the excavation of an enigmatic stone tablet that releases 108 stars of heavenly spirits and earthly fiends who are reincarnated as the legendary Robin Hood-like bandits in the *Water Margin*, the miraculous birth of a monkey out of a stone who becomes the hero in the *Journey to the West*, and the reincarnation of a mythic stone whose vicissitudes becomes the subject matter and plot of *The Story of the Stone*.[14] The magic representation of the stone in the last novel is especially unusual. It is a creation by Nüwa, the legendary progenitor of human beings in the Chinese mythology; it reincarnates into the male protagonist; it can change in size freely; it can be a gigantic block and yet it can become as small as a sparrow's egg to be carried in a baby's mouth at birth. Its appearance and disappearance coincide with the male protagonist's ups and downs in life. It launches the protagonist into life and eventually brings him back to its mythic origin. These kinds of miraculous happenings do not simply constitute intriguing details; they form overt and covert structures that control the unfolding of the plot, characterization, and the imparting of hidden themes. They cannot be explained away by realism; nor can they be understood by recourse to surrealism, magical realism, and the fantastic. Like the modern fiction of surrealism and magical realism, Chinese fictional works with miraculous happenings were not entirely meant as intriguing details to cater to the popular taste but intended as ways to understand life and reality above or beneath their surface meanings, and their manner of presentation suspends the normal faculty of consciousness and logical reasoning with the aim to express subconscious and unconscious ideas and feelings and to reveal the true nature and conditions of history, society, life, and the human soul. Thus, it is no exaggeration to say that the epistemology of Chinese fiction anticipated the rise of surrealistic and magically realistic novels in modern times.

The Totality of Fiction and Multiple Critical Approaches

My brief examination of Chinese fiction in terms of magic realism suggests that contemporary theories of fiction/narrative are not as recent as many scholars tend to think, and that the study of narrative should not be limited to one period or one critical approach. In fiction studies, a separation of one approach from another is both theoretically untenable and practically limiting.

---

14 For an excellent study of the relation of the stone lore to Chinese fiction, see Wang 1992.

The continued separation of approaches hinders the development of fiction criticism and theories in the Chinese tradition. We need a paradigm that integrates different perspectives and approaches. In its methodology, this paradigm should combine as many approaches as possible: historical, philological, philosophical, psychological, linguistic, semiotic and so on. In terms of perspectives, an integrated approach seeks to explore the study of fiction, not only from the critical perspective of reading and interpretation, but also from the creative perspective of writing and representation. The critical perspective is, of course, the reader's perspective, which seeks to treat a fictional work as a verbal construct growing out of the integration of themes (content, subject matter), and forms (achieved content, techniques). The creative perspective is the author's perspective, which is based on a view of fiction as a result of mimesis, semiosis, and simulation. Just as reading is inseparable from writing, so the critical perspective should not be divorced from the creative perspective.

I have mentioned the usefulness of Kuhn's theory of paradigms for addressing the changes and challenges of Chinese fiction studies. In existent theories of literary studies, there is a tendency that seems to have fallen under the influence of Kuhn's theory of paradigm formation. Proponents of a new theory will almost always take issue with an existent theory and reject its conceptual underpinnings and methodologies, thereby antagonizing established scholarly paradigms and approaches. As a consequence, there has been a split among scholars of literary studies, which has by now developed into a clearly demarcated divide between traditional and postmodern approaches to scholarship. It often seems that the older paradigms and newer paradigms can no more co-exist than fire and ice do in the same stove, to use a Chinese saying. An important question then arises: Are older and newer paradigms destined to be exclusive of each other? My answer is a resounding "no." I argue that not only can they coexist but they also complement each other. The crux of the matter is how to mediate between approaches and integrate them. A brief examination of the controversy over the New Historicism will give us some insights into how to formulate paradigms that address the changes and challenges in fiction studies, how to patch up the split between pro-theory and anti-theory advocates, and how to bridge the gap between traditional and postmodern approaches to scholarship.

New Historicism grew out of a reaction against the old historicism and the ahistorical tendency in poststructuralist theory and an attempt to restore a historical dimension to literary studies. Initially, some of its proponents rejected both formalist criticism and the earlier ways of reading literature in its historical context. In so doing, it "offends against a number of orthodoxies in both literary and historical studies." (White 1989, 294) J. Hillis Miller criticizes the reorientation in literary studies to cultural studies spear-headed by New Historicism as a "universal turn away from theory in the sense of an orientation toward language as such" and as a "turn toward history, culture, society, politics, institutions, class and gender conditions, and the social context, the materials base." (Miller 1987, 283) In their turn, the New Historicists criticized Miller's criticism as a "categorical opposition of 'reading' to cultural critique, of 'theory' to the discourses of 'history, culture, society, politics, institutions, class and gender,'" which "seems [to them] not only to oversimplify both sets of terms but also to suppress their points of contact and compatibility." (Montrose 1989, 15) Criticized by both the left and the right, the New Historicists made adjustments to their intellectual venture and their acknowledged leader, Greenblatt, eventually abandoned the name in favor of "cultural poetics."

We may benefit a great deal from the debate and from the reorientation of literary study to cultural study. In response to critiques, the New Historicists have taken an integrated approach to literature in relation to history, society, culture, and other discourses, and simultaneously criticize and incorporate aspect of traditional and contemporary theories. Although they criticize the formalistic interpretation of New Criticism, which conceives of the literary text as a self-contained, well-wrought "urn" that contains immanent meaning, it retains some of the close reading techniques of New Criticism. In their relations to structuralism and deconstruction, while it objects to the ahistorical tendencies of structuralist and deconstructive reading, they accept the structuralist and deconstructive conception of literature as systems of representation, and employ structuralist and deconstructive strategies to read texts. Refiguring the relationship between literature and history, the text and the world, and adopting alternative reading strategies, New Historicists argue that different forms of discourse, be they fictional or factual, popular or elitist, interact with other discourses and are overdetermined by communal and institutional practices in a particular historical context. They also emphasize the rhetorical conditions of a text's making and relate literary theories of the text to the constitution of historical objects as well as to the reading of them. As Louis A. Montrose puts it in a saying of chiasmus, New Historicists presuppose both "the historicity of texts" and the "textuality of history." (Montrose 1986, 8) By the former, he means "the cultural specificity, the social embedment, of all modes of writing – not only the texts that critics study but also the texts in which we study them." (1989, 20) By the latter, he means two points. First, "we can have no access to a full and authentic past, a lived material existence, unmediated by the surviving textual traces of the society in question – traces whose survival we cannot assume to be merely contingent but must rather presume to be at least partially consequent upon complex and subtle social processes of preservation and effacement." (1989, 20) Second, "those textual traces are themselves subject to subsequent textual mediations when they are construed as the 'documents' upon which historians ground their own text, called 'histories.'" (Montrose 1989, 20) As a whole, it exhibits a tendency to embrace different theories and approaches rather than privileging one over the other. As Montrose summarizes, the theoretical, methodological, and political assumptions and implications of the New Historicist endeavor focus on "refiguring the socio-cultural field within which canonical Renaissance literary and dramatic works were originally produced" and "resituating them not only in relationship to other genres and modes of discourse but also in relationship to contemporaneous social institutions and non-discursive practices." (1989, 17) This totalizing approach has had a great impact on cultural studies. Nowadays, "the prevailing tendency across cultural studies is to emphasize their reciprocity and mutual constitution: On the one hand, the social is understood to be discursively constructed; and on the other, language-use is understood to be always and necessarily dialogical, to be socially and materially determined and constrained." (1989, 15)

The totalizing inclusiveness is what we need when formulating a paradigm for Chinese fiction study. Clearly, each theory, or each approach has its strengths and weaknesses. An integration of different approaches and methodologies should help us in our attempt to cross the divides in Chinese fiction studies. I have observed an emerging trend in the studies of Chinese fiction toward an integrated approach to fiction study. In some aspects, it really exhibits the characteristic traits of the New Historicism and cultural materialism. It is explicitly or implicitly exemplified in recent studies, David Wang's *Fin-de-Siècle Splendor: Repressed Modernities of Late Qing China 1849–1911* (1997) and *The Monster That Is History: Violence, History, and Fictional Writing in 20th Century China* (2004), Martin Huang's *Negotiating Masculinities in Late Imperial China* (2005), Wai-yee Li's *The Readability of the Past in Early Chinese Historiography* (2004), Wei Shang's study of *Rulin waishi and Cultural Transformation in Late Imperial China* (2003), Liangyan Ge's *Out of the Margins: The Rise of Chinese Vernacular Fiction* (2001), Zuyan Zhou's *Androgyny in Late Ming and Early Qing Literature* (2003), Qiancheng Li's *Fiction of Enlightenment: Journey to the West, Tower of Myriad Mirrors, and Dreams of the Red Chamber* (2004), and in my own study, *Chinese Theories of Fiction: A Non-Western Narrative System* (2006). This trend stresses the interrelationships of society, the subjectivity of politics, the textuality of history, the social symbolism of artifacts on the one hand, and on the other hand, the politics of economic conditions, the discourse of desires, the materiality of language, and the historicity of text. Moreover, it advances strategies of reading that emphasize the inclusion of analytic data, literary and historical, artistic and documentary, popular and elitist, fictional and non-fictional, and the use of contemporary theories. As an emerging trend, it is still fairly young, but it has the potential of not only bridging "the structural, experiential, and conceptual gap between the public and the private, between the social and psychological, or the political and the poetic, between history or society and the 'individual,'" identified by Fredric Jameson (1981, 20), but also bridging the series of divides that I have identified: those between pre-modern and modern literature, between traditional and postmodern approaches, between traditional and modern literary studies, and between Chinese fiction and world fiction. In its comprehensive and all-encompassing manner, this trend may give us insights to formulate a new paradigm, which comes close to the "cultural poetics" advanced by Stephen Greenblatt (1989, 1–14). In his reconception, Greenblatt defines "cultural poetics" as "the study of the collective making of distinct cultural practices and inquiry into the relations among these practices." (Greenblatt 1988, 5) Its main concerns are "how collective beliefs and experiences were shaped, moved from one medium to another, concentrated in manageable aesthetic form, offered for consumption [and] how the boundaries were marked between cultural practices understood to be art forms and other, contiguous, forms of expression." (Greenblatt 1988, 5)

Fiction is a totalizing genre in many ways. Ontologically, it is a totalizing entity that represents and simulates both the natural world and the human world. What the world has, it can present; what the world has not, it can simulate. In the minds of Chinese fictional writers, they implicitly conceived of fiction as a form of writing that could be reasonably compared to the all-encompassing and self-generative Dao (Tao). A fictional work generates multiplicity of meanings or open readings precisely in the way the Dao generates myriad things in the universe through the interaction of *yin* and *yang*. Epistemologically, fiction is predicated on an epistemology of totality that behooves the writer and reader to approach the multifaceted worlds in a fictional work from heterogeneous perspectives. In fictional creation, a fictional work is a medium that inscribes the author's totality. In fiction reading, a fictional work implies the reader's total self. Metaphysically, fiction is a textual system of totality. The totality of the system presupposes a network of narrative whose self-generative mechanism of meanings is comparable to that of the Dao or Taiji, the supreme principle in Chinese thought, which is also called the One. The One is not just a unifying principle; it is also a structuring and life-giving force. Lao Tzu [Laozi] said, "Heaven in virtue of the One is limpid; Earth in virtue of the One is settled; Gods in virtue of the One have their potencies; the valley in virtue of the One is full; The myriad creatures in virtue of the One are alive; Lords and princes in virtue of the One become leaders in the empire. It is the One that makes these what they are." (1963, 100) I may add that an extended fictional work in virtue of the One is able to get its myriad characters, details, scenes, episodes, and narrative threads organized, structured, and emplotted. In analytic terms, we may call the One "theme," "central thesis," "controlling idea," "intrinsic structure," or "intrinsic pattern." But, aesthetically, it is a kind of mysterious, ethereal pneuma, a creative force of totality like the indescribable and unnamable Dao that give a fictional work its being and distinguishes a masterpiece from a mediocre work.

Toward a Transcultural Poetics of Fiction Study

The totality of fiction defies divides and barriers. To cross those visible, invisible, cultural, and other humanly constructed divides, we are in need of a transcultural poetics of fiction study that integrates all available perspectives and approaches in fiction studies. In view of this need, I suggest that for Chinese fiction study to contribute to the emergency of a transcultural poetics of fiction, we need to overcome two opposite tendencies in Chinese fiction studies: a conservative attitude that refuses to engage post-structuralist and postmodern theories; and the other that tends to impose Western-centric theories on Chinese fiction and to remain insensitive to distinctive characteristics of Chinese fiction.

In his theorizing on fiction studies, although Scholes has called for postmodern anti-narrative theories, he admits that the traditional narrative processes "are too deeply rooted in human physical and mental processes to be dispensed with" by postmodern anti-narrative. We cannot and should not abandon traditional approaches. A purely traditional approach or a purely postmodern approach will be counterproductive in one way or another, but creative integration will open up new vistas and new avenues to literary Sinology. With an integrated approach, we can also see that the traditional and the postmodern are not as separated as one thinks. In conclusion, I propose a new paradigm in fiction studies. This paradigm is characterized by a refusal to observe strictly demarcated boundaries between modern and pre-modern literature, fictional and non-fictional texts, and fiction and other literary genres; an equal emphasis on formal and content approaches to fictional texts; a dialogic interaction between the formal analysis of verbal discourses and the ideological analysis of discursive practices; and an integration of traditional and postmodern methodologies. Because it assimilates the insights of cultural materialism, New Historicism, post-structuralism, postmodern forms of Marxism and psychoanalysis, theoretical advances in studies of fiction and narrative as well as achievements in practical criticism, we may call it the cultural poetics of totality in fiction studies.

Bibliography

Barthes, Roland. "The Structuralist Activity." *Partisan Review* 34.1 (1967): 82–88.
Beijing University Chinese Department, ed. *Zhongguo xiaoshuo shi* [History of Chinese Fiction]. Beijing: renmin wenxue chubanshe, 1978.
Bloom, Harold. *The Anxiety of Influence: A Theory of Poetry*. Oxford: Oxford University Press, 1973.
Chatman, Seymour. *Story and Discourse: Narrative Structure in Fiction and Film*. Ithaca, NY: Cornell University Press, 1978.
– "Reply to Barbara Herrnstein Smith." *On Narrative*. Ed. William J. T. Mitchell. Chicago: Chicago University Press, 1980. 258–265.
Chen Meilin and Feng Baoshan. *Zhanghui xiaoshuo shi* [History of the Chaptered Novel]. Hangzhou: Zhejiang guji chubanshe, 1998.
Cuddon, John A. *A Dictionary of Literary Terms and Literary Theory*. Oxford: Blackwell, 1991.
Culler, Jonathan. "Foreword" to Tzvetan Todorov. *The Poetics of Prose*. Ithaca and New York: Cornell University Press, 1977. 7–13.
Epstein, Maram. *Competing Discourses: Orthodoxy, Authenticity, and Engendered Meanings in Late Imperial Chinese Fiction*. Cambridge, MA: Harvard Asian Center, 2001.
Fowler, Roger. *Linguistics and The Novel*. London: Methuen, 1977.
Ge, Liangyan. *Out of the Margins: The Rise of Chinese Vernacular Fiction*. Honolulu, HI: University of Hawaii Press, 2001.
Gewertz Ken. "Divining the dreams of lost worlds." Harvard Gazette Archives. http://www.news.harvard.edu/gazette/2001/01.18/03-lostworld.html (15 May 2011).
Greenblatt, Stephen. *Shakespearean Negotiations: The Circulation of Social Energy in Renaissance England*. Berkeley, CA: University of California Press, 1988.
– "Towards a Poetics of Culture." *The New Historicism*. Ed. H. Aram Veeser. New York: Routledge, 1989. 1–14.
Gu, Ming Dong. *Chinese Theories of Fiction: A Non-Western Narrative System*. SUNY series in Chinese philosophy and culture. Albany, NY: State University of New York Press, 2006.
Hanan, Patrick. "The Early Chinese Short Story: A Critical Theory in Outline." *Harvard Journal of Asiatic Studies* 27 (1967): 168–207.
– *The Chinese Short Story*. Cambridge, MA: Harvard University Press, 1973.
– *The Chinese Vernacular Story*. Cambridge, MA: Harvard University Press, 1981.
Hawkes, David and John Minford. Trans. *The Story of the Stone*. 5 vols. Harmondsworth, England: Penguin, 1973–1986.
Hou Zhongyi. *Zhongguo wenyan xiaoshuo shigao* [A Draft History of Chinese Classical Language Fiction]. Beijing: Beijing daxue chubanshe, 1990.
Hsia, Chih-ts'ing [C. T Hsia]. *The Classic Chinese Novel: A Critical Introduction*. New York and London: Columbia University Press, 1968.
– *A History of Modern Chinese Fiction*. 2nd ed. New Haven and London: Yale University Press, 1971.

Huang, Martin. *Literati and Self-Re/presentation: Autobiographical Sensibility in the Eighteenth-Century Chinese Novel*. Stanford, CA: Stanford University Press, 1995.
– *Negotiating Masculinities in Late Imperial China*. Honolulu, HI: University of Hawaii Press, 2006.
Jameson, Fredric. *The Political Unconscious: Narrative as a Socially Symbolic Act*. Ithaca, NY: Cornell University Press, 1981.
Kuhn, Thomas. *The Structure of Scientific Revolutions*. 2nd ed. Chicago, IL: University of Chicago Press, 1970.
Lao Tzu [Laozi]. *The Tao Te Ching [Daode jing]*. Trans. Dim Cheuk Lau. Harmondsworth, England: Penguin, 1963.
Li, Qiancheng. *Fiction of Enlightenment: Journey to the West, Tower of Myriad Mirrors, and Dreams of the Red Chamber*. Honolulu, HI: University of Hawaii Press, 2004.
Li, Wai-yee. *Enchantment and Disenchantment: Love and Illusion in Chinese Literature*. Princeton, NJ: Princeton University Press, 1993.
– *The Readability of the Past in Early Chinese Historiography*. Cambridge, MA: Harvard University Council for East Asian Studies, 2008.
Li Xiusheng and Zhao Yishan, eds. *Zhongguo fenti wenxue shi – xiaoshuo juan* [History of Chinese Literature by Genre: Fiction Volume]. Shanghai: Guji chubanshe, 2001.
Lu Xun. *Zhongguo xiaoshuo shilüe* [A Brief History of Chinese Fiction]. Beijing: Renmin wenxue chubanshe, 1973.
Lu Xun. "Zhongguo xiaoshuo de lishi de bianqian" [The Evolution in the History of Chinese Fiction]. *Lu Xun quanji* [Complete Works of Lu Xun]. Beijing: Renmin wenxue chubanshe, 2005. 317–322.
Martin, Wallace. *Recent Theories of Narrative*. Ithaca and London: Cornell University Press, 1988.
Meng Zhaolian and Ning Zongyi. *Zhongguo xiaoshuo yishu shi* [History of Chinese Fictional Art]. Hangzhou: Zhejiang guji chubanshe, 1998.
Miller, J. Hillis. "Presidential Address 1986. The Triumph of Theory, the Resistance to Reading, and the Question of the Material Base." *PMLA* 102 (1987): 281–291.
Mitchell, William J. T., ed. *On Narrative*. Chicago, IL: Chicago University Press, 1980.
– "Medium Theory: Preface to the 2003 Critical Inquiry Symposium." *Critical Inquiry* 30 (2004): 330–331.
Montrose, Louis A. "Renaissance in Literary Studies and the Subject of History." *English Literary Renaissance* 16 (1986): 5–12.
– "Professing the Renaissance: The Poetics and Politics of Culture." *The New Historicism*. Ed. H. Aram Veeser. New York: Routledge, 1989. 15–36.
Moretti, Franco. "The Novel: History and Theory." *New Left Review* 55 (2008): 111–124.
Plaks, Andrew, ed. *Archetype and Allegory in the Dream of the Red Chamber*. Princeton, NJ: Princeton University Press, 1976.
– *Chinese Narrative: Critical and Theoretical Essays*. Princeton, NJ: Princeton University Press, 1977.
– *The Four Masterworks of the Ming Novel*. Princeton, NJ: Princeton University Press, 1987.
Rolston, David, ed. *How To Read the Chinese Novel*. Princeton, NJ: Princeton University Press, 1990.
Scholes, Robert. "Language, Narrative, and Anti-Narrative." *On Narrative*. Ed. William J. T. Mitchell. Chicago, IL: Chicago University Press, 1980. 200–208.

Schorer, Mark. "Technique as Discovery." *Theory of the Novel*. Ed. Philip Stevick. New York: The Free Press, 1967. 65–84.
Shi Changyu. *Zhongguo xiaoshuo yuanli lun* [On the Origins and Sources of Chinese Fiction]. Beijing: Sanlian shudian, 1994.
Sun Yaoyu. *Zhongguo gudai wenxue yuanli* [Ancient Chinese Literary Theory]. Nanjing: Jiangsu jiaoyu chubanshe, 1996.
Todorov, Tzvetan. *The Fantastic: A Structuralist Approach to a Literary Genre*. Ithaca, NY: Cornell University Press, 1975.
— *The Poetics of Prose*. Ithaca: Cornell University Press, 1977.
Veeser, H. Aram, ed. *The New Historicism*. New York: Routledge, 1989.
Wang, David. *Fin-de-Siècle Splendor: Repressed Modernities of Late Qing China 1849–1911*. Stanford, CA: Stanford University Press, 1997.
— *The Monster That Is History: Violence, History, and Fictional Writing in Twentieth-Century China*. Berkeley and Los Angeles: University of California Press, 2004.
Wang, Jing. *The Story of Stone: Intertextuality, Ancient Chinese Stone Lore, and the Stone Symbolism of Dream of the Red Chamber, Water Margin, and The Journey to the West*. Post-Contemporary Interventions. Durham, NC: Duke University Press, 1992.
Wang Rumei and Zhang Yu. *Zhongguo xiaoshuo lilun shi* [History of Chinese Theories of Fiction]. Hangzhou: Zhejiang guji chubanshe, 2001.
Shang, Wei. *Rulin waishi and Cultural Transformation in Late Imperial China*. Cambridge, MA: Harvard University Council for East Asian Studies, 2003.
White, Hayden. "New Historicism: A Comment." *The New Historicism*. Ed. H. Aram Veeser. New York: Routledge, 1989. 293–302.
Wu Gongzheng. *Xiaoshuo meixue* [Aesthetics of Fiction]. Nanjing: Jiangsu renmin chubanshe, 1985.
Yang, Hsien-yi and Gladys Yang, trans. *A Dream of Red Mansions*. 3 vols. Beijing: Foreign Languages Press, 1978.
Ye Long. *Zhongguo xiaoshuo meixue* [Aesthetics of Chinese Fiction]. Beijing: Beijing daxue chubanshe, 1982.
Yu, Anthony C. "History, Fiction and the Reading of Chinese Narrative." *Chinese Literature: Essays, Articles, Reviews* 10 (1988): 1–19.
— *Rereading the Stone: Desire and the Making of Fiction in Dream of the Red Chamber*. Princeton, NJ: Princeton University Press, 1997.
Yu, Ying-shih. "The two worlds of the Hongloumeng." Trans. Diana Yu. *Rendition* 2 (1974): 5–21.
— *Hongloumeng de liangge shijie* [The Two Worlds of the Hongloumeng]. Taipei: Lianjin, 1978.
Zhou, Zuyan. *Androgyny in Late Ming and Early Qing Literature*. Honolulu, HI: University of Hawaii Press, 2003.

Göran Rossholm
General Beliefs from Fiction

This essay attempts to clarify the notion of general truth with regard to narrative fictional literature; the natural starting point is some remarks in the ninth chapter of Aristotle's *Poetics*:

> [...] a poet's object is not to tell what actually happened but what could and would happen either probably or inevitably. [...] poetry is something more scientific and serious than history, because poetry tends to give general truths while history gives particular facts.
> By a "general truth" I mean the sort of thing that a certain type of man will do or say either probably or necessarily. [...] A particular fact is what Alcibiades did or what was done to him.[1]

General truth, in contrast to particular truth, is a very common theme in the history of Western literature and poetics. I believe that the idea that fictional literature may be a vehicle of general truth occurs in different shapes in different parts of the world; that is, I take it to be a rather global matter in the study of fiction and fictionality. In particular, its importance is striking in explicitly didactic literature – here exemplified by the sad ending of an illustrated story taken from Heinrich Hoffman's *Der Struwwelpeter* (see image below).[2] The general truth we are supposed to grasp is that playing with matches is very risky.

There are two basic problems in this context. First, why do we consider these generalizations to be true? We do not believe that the fictional stories we read are true. Of course, sometimes we recognize some moral that we do not agree with, but if the readers never believed the general statement expressed by the made-up story, we would not have didactic fictional literature. The second problem is: Why do we produce narratives to convey general truths? Why not just say: "The sinner succumbs, but the good guy does very well."? In addition to these two questions, I will address a few more specific ones: What role does a certain idea play in this context, the idea that readers of narratives – fictional or not – experience the narrated events and states of

---

[1] I quote from W. Hamilton Fyfe's revised translation from 1932 in Loeb Classical Library. It differs from Stephen Halliwell's more recent version (1995) in some respects. The most important variant in the present context is that Halliwell has "philosophical" instead of Fyfe's "scientific."
[2] The copied page, here and at the end of the essay, presents Hoffman's original drawings from the 1844 edition, see http://www.lyrikheute.com/2012/06/morgen-hier.html (24 February 2013).

Fig. 1: Illustration from Heinrich Hoffmann's *Der Struwwelpeter* (1844).

affairs as unmediated, as directly shown to them?[3] Does this kind of experience increase the credibility of the general statement or not? Finally, I will discuss the question of the kinds of general beliefs the reading will most probably induce in its reader. Everything I say on this subject must be taken with a certain reservation: the reader is an adult. What humans take as true and why they do so changes with age.

Let me begin by making a few preliminary remarks about general truths in fiction.

There are at least three kinds of general phenomena generated by fictive narratives: general terms, general statements and general imperatives. The first, general terms, may be exemplified by what Aristotle says about appropriateness and character in his *Poetics*. In Chapter 15, he requires that a fictive character shall be "appropriate," and he illustrates his requirement in this way: "A character may be manly, but it is not appropriate for a woman to be manly or clever." (Aristotle 1932)

Classical comedy supplies an array of examples in the wake of this idea of appropriateness: the wealthy, stupid father, the clever slave, later the clever servant, the lovely and innocent young woman, the wasteful young man and so on. In Horace's version, in the *Ars Poetica*, this last type is spelled out:

> The beardless youth, free of tutors at last, delights
> In horse and hound, and the turf of the sunlit Campus,
> He's wax malleable for sin, rude to his advisors,
> Slow in making provision, lavish with money,
> Spirited, passionate, and swift to change his whim.
> (Horace 2005, 161–165)

Horace describes – and prescribes, but that is not the point just now – a general type, not a particular human creature. A particular character occurring in a Roman comedy may be said to exemplify this type. However, generalized terms do not have to be stereotypes, as in classical comedy, nor do they have to be prescribed by an aesthetic system. One category of general terms derived from fiction illustrates the link between the particular and the general in a more drastic way. Don Quixote, Hamlet, Don Juan, Raskolinkov and Pippi Longstocking are five particular, though fictive, persons, but they are also the basis of generalized types: someone, in fiction or reality, may be characterized

---

[3] I believe that this is one of the defining features of narratives in general (Rossholm 2004, 2010, 2012). However, in the present context of this essay, the reader doesn't have to subscribe to anything stronger than the thesis that fiction readers sometimes experience their reception as direct, not in the sense of being the victim of illusions, only that directness is an apt metaphor for characterizing their reading experience.

as *a* Don Quixote, *a* Hamlet, *a* Don Juan, *a* Raskolinkov or *a* Pippi Longstocking, that is, an instance of a general term. Finally, the general terms in this context do not have to refer to different kinds of human individuals; they can stand for objects of all sorts, events, states affairs and whatever. In literary analyses, they may often be identified with what the literary scholar would call themes or motifs.

The second kind consists of general sentences. These are statements derived from the narrative, or from a close paraphrase of the narrative, by substituting singular terms of the text with general ones, terms applicable to the same events, states of affairs and objects, and by prefixing the sentence with a quantifier, that is, with phrases such as *all* young men, *most* young men, *many* young men and so on. Such generalizations have, of course, truth-value.

Term-generalizations, on the other hand, are neither true nor false. They apply, or they fail to apply. And term-generalizations may easily be transformed into statements, more precisely into the statements from which they so to speak come. The fact that the young man in Roman classical comedy exemplifies the character-types "malleable for sin," "rude to his advisors," and "lavish with money" is motivated by the presumed truth of the general statements that young men are ready to sin, rude to advisors and lavish with money.

Finally, general imperatives are neither true nor false, but like general terms they are motivated by generalized statements. A friend of mine once suggested that the essence of the works of Bertolt Brecht could be expressed in two words: *Be smart!* This imperative is given its force in Brecht's literary world by the general fact that the less smart succumb in his plays; in particular, the persons who try to live by higher moral standards, such as *Be brave*, *Be honest*, *Be good*, have less chance of surviving than the ones who live according to the device *Be smart*.

Thus general statements are often implicitly present in both general terms and general imperatives.

*

The first two questions mentioned – Why believe in the general lessons we derive from made up stories? And why not state these lessons directly? – are focused on in an article by Staffan Carlshamre (2004). Carlshamre also describes the process by which the reader goes from the particular, the story, to the general, in contrast to inductive reasoning in the empirical sciences, the route from observation to empirical law. A description in a fictional text exemplifies a certain general label, a motif, a theme or character-type. This semantic relation – exemplification – is similar, but certainly not identical, to the epistemic relation between evidence and law.[4] The similarity to scientific practice is further stressed by the readers' propensity to apply the general truth to particular instances, for instance themselves, or the author. (The novel *One Day in the Life of Ivan Denisovich* discussed below may be taken as an example of the latter, and didactic literature in general as an example of the former). This fits well with Aristotle's idea (cited above) that "poetry is something more scientific and serious than history."[5] As an answer, or a partial answer, to the questions why we believe in the generalization inferred from fiction, Carlshamre suggests that we, the readers, confuse the step from fictive character to general type (or from fictive state of affairs to theme or motif) with the step from observation to general law. (Carlshamre 2004)

The parallel between generalization from fictional narrative and scientific law-making may be taken a little further by the distinction between report and observation. Reports, that is, statements to the effect that an A is B, may be generalized to statements, for instance that all A's are B. But also observations such as my seeing that A is B may be generalized, and only in this latter case do we have an instance of what I called directness above. Generalizations following from observations appear stronger for the observer than generalizations from reports – they do not have to rely on the credibility of the reporter. This, if correct, points to an answer both to the second question, why authors present general truths by telling stories instead of simply directly stating these truths, and to the third question, about the role played by the reader's impression of being directly informed about the content of the narrative.

Is this the basis of a satisfactory answer to the questions why we accept generalizations from fiction as true and why authors choose to narrate in order to convey general truths? An example that at first may appear to support this thesis is Hitchcock's movie *The Birds*. The movie, any movie, is an excellent example of a medium of directness: we experience that we ourselves are directly watching the events, and sometimes also that we are directly involved

---

[4] Two parenthetical points. First: The step from the fictive and particular to the factual and general is not a mechanical process. The appearance in a Roman comedy of a particular young man who is rude to advisors and lavish with money can be generalized in many different directions; here are only three: 1) All men who are rude to advisers and lavish with money are young. 2) All entities that are rude to advisers are young men who are lavish with money. 3) All males who are rude to advisors are young and lavish with money. Second: if the term exemplification is used in accordance with Goodman (1981), which I recommend, a literary description does strictly speaking not exemplify a theme but a theme-description. However, in informal contexts the term "exemplify" may be used to cover exemplification across different levels.

[5] However, Carlshamre does not mention Aristoteles' *Poetics* in his article.

in the situation represented. When we leave the cinema, we have – some of us, at least – the uncanny feeling that birds, all birds, are evil and dangerous. And this feeling is certainly much stronger than our reaction would be to the flat declaration "Birds are evil and dangerous."

However, on second thoughts we realize that the example shows us that the thesis is wrong. We may feel that birds are dangerous, but that is not the same as believing that this is a fact. The movie may even cause a serious phobia: we react with fear when we see birds, we avoid them and have nightmares about them. All these are behavioural signs of the belief that birds are dangerous. But as long as we recognize our bird phobia as a phobia, we know that our reaction is irrational because we know that birds are not evil and dangerous. Our bird-fearing state of mind is at most belief-like.[6]

So we have to look for other sources of our willingness to accept generalizations from fiction as true than the similarity to scientific induction and the sense of directness. Here are three more candidates: verisimilitude, the game of reading fictional literature, and the author's intention.

The term "verisimilitude" is like "appropriateness" and "general truth," a term firmly rooted in the classical tradition of Western poetics. In the chapter on character (Chapter 15), Aristotle formulates a principle of verisimilitude in this way:

> In character-drawing, just as much as in the arrangement of the incidents, one should always seek what is inevitable or probable, so as to make it inevitable and probable that such and such a person should say or do such and such;

Is verisimilitude, or probability, or credibility, the key term in the present context? Do we believe in general statements derived from fictional narratives because the incidents and the characters are like incidents and persons we meet in real life? Maybe, but this explanation seems to put the cart before the horse. It does not explain why the spectator of a Roman comedy takes the general statement, derived from the spectacle, that young men are rude to advisors as true. It presupposes that the spectator already believes that young men are rude to advisors. By the criterion of verisimilitude, readers, or viewers, do not arrive at any new beliefs, they do not become informed about anything.

So let us look at the second candidate, "the game of reading." By this phrase I refer to an idea that the readers of fictional literature engage in a game regulated by some rules, among them one expecting the reader to infer general truths from the story. I do not argue that this idea is correct, that we always play this game when we read fictional narratives. At least, it is obvious

---

6 Cf Gendler's concept – and examples – of "alief" (Gendler 2010).

that we expect that some narratives, for instance animal fables, exempla, parables, should be read in this way.

Most probably, like the criterion I called verisimilitude, this game would rarely give us new general truths; on the contrary, the general truths we would construct based on fictional stories would be truths we already believe in. When we watch Hitchcock's *The Birds*, we might conclude that it confirms our belief that our daily environment may contain dangers that we are not aware of before they threaten us. We are not informed about anything, we are only reminded of general truths we hold as true before our reading or watching.

However, the two criteria suggested, verisimilitude and reading as a game aiming at general truths, give us some distinctions which may be helpful when we try to clarify generalizations from fiction. The first distinction is between being informed and being reminded. It should be emphasised that the second option, reminders, does not mean that readers are in the same belief state before and after reading. The diffuse belief just mentioned about our everyday environment is probably not something we constantly pay attention to. When we are reminded of it, this belief becomes an *occurrent* belief. This in turn may change our attitudes and even strengthen our belief. And this is the second distinction, actualized by these two alternative proposals, the distinction between occurrent and non-occurrent beliefs.

Finally, we have cases which fall between reminders and new information. This can be illustrated with a small change in the example just presented, the movie *The Birds*. After having seen Hitchcock's thriller, I may inductively infer the general statement – note, I say statement, not truth – that "Our everyday environment contains threats that we are normally completely unaware of." I may never have formulated anything equivalent to this before, but now this general thought makes me reinvent my beliefs – consciously or, more probably, unconsciously – and conclude, like the hero in a detective story, yes, now all the pieces come together, now I see it clearly: Our everyday environment does contain threats that we are normally completely unaware of. This general conviction is new – I have never been aware of it before – and, at the same time, it is not – all the premises have been with me all the time. Like recalled beliefs, it is "from within." This is my third distinction, between beliefs from outside and beliefs from within.

How does the third alternative – the author's intention – relate to these distinctions?

We may be convinced that a general statement is true partly because of the author's intentions – her/his intention that she/he believes in this general statement, or that she/he wants us to do so, or both. When this happens, when we acquire new general beliefs from outside partly by recognizing or guessing the author's intention, our reading either adds some new convictions to our pre-existing body of beliefs or revises pre-existing firm convictions. I guess that the former occurs more often than the latter, but we may imagine a fictional hospital novel, which makes a very credible impression with respect to medical data – the writer seems to be a medical expert. However, some general statement is at odds with our layman medical convictions, and this conflict may well be solved by letting the fictional novel win. Since my general impression is that this writer does not make up medical data, I conclude that my previous belief is wrong.

Still, I believe that the three standard cases of general truths derived from fiction and believed to be true by readers are: firstly, that readers are reminded of something they already know, or, secondly, that the story prompts them to infer something from their previous convictions, or, thirdly, that they come to believe in a general statement that fills a gap in their body of beliefs. Alexander Solzhenitsyn's novel *One Day in the Life of Ivan Denisovich* (1963) may be used as an illustration. This book comprises, as the title says, just one day, more specifically one day in a prison camp in the Gulag system. The protagonist Ivan Denisovich is serving ten years' imprisonment – a fact mentioned at the end of the book. By describing Ivan's miserable health, his pain and the humiliations he is subjected to, the novel of course describes the health conditions, the pains and so on in general for Gulag prisoners. Further, the description of one day in the camp suggests how life is during a much longer period, more than three thousand days. This generalized information adds one more kind of suffering to the ones explicitly described: the monotony and feeling of hopelessness of camp life. The picture of being a prisoner in the Gulag system is most probably meant by Solzhenitsyn to be taken as true, literally true, and many readers are, I imagine, convinced that the relevant background is true. This generalized belief may for some readers only confirm either well-established convictions or previously unconscious conclusions from known premises, and for some it may fill gaps in their body of beliefs. The novel may even have forced some readers to revise their beliefs about the Soviet justice system. I believe that the first three options are the most common: that readers are reminded of something, that they are made aware of something following from what they hold to be true, or that a gap in their body of beliefs is filled. But, against the background of beliefs about the writer and his personal experiences, other readers' beliefs about the trustworthiness of the book, the reactions of the Soviet authorities and, of course, a belief about Alexander Solzhenitsyn's intentions, and, finally, the realistic form of the novel – its verisimilitude –, against the background of all this, the reading might bring new general truths from outside to some readers, truths in blatant conflict with views held up to then.

Thus if we believe in a general statement derived from a fictional narrative partly because we recognize or make a certain guess about the author's intentions, we might arrive at a new general belief. But the intention is usually not enough; the credibility of the author has to be evidenced, as in the example just given. Even if presented with reliable information that Alfred Hitchcock himself believed that birds were a real threat to humanity, or that he intended to induce such a belief in his audience, most of us would still not believe that this is true. We would change our beliefs about Hitchcock, but not about birds. Most general truths derived from fiction are truths we already know, maybe only implicitly, or truths that fill gaps in our body of beliefs.

But if this is true, how do we explain the vitality of didactic traditions of fictional narrative? Why do writers convey their ideas, their assumed general truths, by writing animal fables, a highly non-realistic genre? According to my presentation, they seem to be limited to conveying mostly already acquired beliefs.

The kind of general truths I have characterized as "from within," but still more than just recalled beliefs, affects the degree of consciousness and the structure of the reader's body of beliefs. The reader becomes aware of the general truth by reflection – a reflection that may be instantaneous – and the logical structure of her/his beliefs is reorganized. With respect to the recalled general beliefs, I suggest that part of the answer should be sought in the fact that the general belief inferred from fiction is occurrent. The reader is aware of a truth she/he already holds as true but usually does not pay much attention to. When a belief is repeatedly made occurrent, it is likely that it becomes stronger. Further, the story makes the general truth easier to remember, since stories, in particular good ones, are easy to recall. Moreover, the narrative may deepen a belief we already hold. When we have difficulty in presenting illustrative applications of a general conviction, our belief is shallow, and contrarily, when we can explain what we mean by presenting detailed illustrative material, we have a deeper understanding of the general statement and an enhanced capacity to apply the statement to new instances. It does not matter whether these illustrations are fictive or factual. They do not constitute evidence for the truth of the statement, they testify to our fuller understanding of what we are talking about, they prove that we are not merely paying lip service to our stated belief. Fictional narratives provide such illustrations. A text reference, 2 Samuel: 11–12 in the Old Testament, borrowed from Tamar Gendler (2010, 129–130) fits in here.[7]

---

[7] Gendler uses the Bible text to illustrate what he calls "first-person exceptionalism," a position that points to the paradoxical fact that most people believe that they are better than most people (2010).

King David sends Bathsheba's husband Uriah to the war so that he will be killed and will then no longer stand in the way of David's and Bathsheba's matrimonial union, a conduct that understandably irritates God, who delegates Nathan to formulate the reproaches. He does so by telling David the parable about the poor man, who owns nothing more than one lamb, and the rich man, who takes this lamb to serve to a visiting traveller. David is very upset by the behaviour of the rich man, but he does not understand that the general moral – which he obviously approves of – also applies to himself and Uriah until Nathan points to him and says: "Thou art the man." King David then recognizes his own conduct in the parable: "I have sinned against the Lord." Without any new information from outside, just an ostensive gesture, David comes to realize a shocking fact. (Gendler, 2010)

Finally, the aim of didactic literature is not necessarily to have an influence on the reader's beliefs – it may be to change the reader's behaviour. One more illustration from *Der Struwwelpeter* below may serve as an example: the boy Konrad promises his mother to abstain from his bad habit of sucking his thumb while she is out; however, he fails ("Fort geht nun die Mutter und / Wupp! den Daumen in den Mund"), and the tailor enters and cuts off both of Konrad's thumbs with his enormous scissors. (The two final pictures and verses are given below). The imperative moral is clear: Don't suck your thumb! But do we really believe that there is risk that a tailor will rush in and cut off our thumbs if we disobey? Probably not, but we might feel less comfortable when we secretly put our thumb in our mouth because of this brief story. Something unpleasant is associated with thumb-sucking, but not necessarily any belief, and this unpleasantness may influence our behaviour. Hitchcock's movie might illustrate the same effect. We all recognize this kind of manipulation from present-day commercials.

Turning to the question of the role of the readers' sense of immediacy – that they experience their reading as direct, not mediated, reception – I have already said that I do not believe that this quality by itself usually makes us convinced about the truth of the general statements we derive from fictional narratives. But immediacy may be crucial for what I called belief-like states, and it may also influence behaviour. The iconic examples mentioned above, the movie *The Birds* and the illustrated book *Der Struwwelpeter*, might serve as examples. I also think that there may be one other kind of link between deriving general statements from fictional narratives and immediacy. As already mentioned, the reading of fiction (not only explicitly didactic fiction) proceeds along lines close to inductive reasoning: firstly, observing particular incidents corresponds to reading about particular events; secondly, generalizations forming hypotheses is the next step in both activities, and thirdly, these

Fig. 2: Illustration from Heinrich Hoffmann's *Der Stuwwelpeter* (1844).

hypotheses are applied to new instances. Only the first step – observing and reading what is literally stated – differs. It may well be so that the isomorphy between inductive reasoning and fiction reading may have the effect that the quality that characterizes only the first activity – direct observation – colours the latter. Reading becomes more *like* direct perception.

*

I will end by commenting once again on the quote (above) from Aristotle about the scientific character of the general truths expressed by literature. One of my conclusions is that beliefs in general statements inferred from fiction are, more often than not, beliefs from within, beliefs we already had, in one sense or another, before our reading started. This seems to be at odds with Aristotle's emphasised analogy with the laws of empirical science. Valuable and interesting natural laws are discovered, that is, they are new, and they are from outside. Is he wrong about the similarity between generalizations from fiction and generalizations in scientific reasoning? Maybe not from his own vantage point – maybe Aristotle's conception of the validity of inductive proof and of the natural laws resembles more the beliefs from within I have been talking about than the probabilistic view of modern science. Anders Wedberg summarizes Aristotle's position with respect to inductive generalizations as follows:

> In some passages, he also shows awareness of what we today call induction, viz. inferences from "all known" to "all." The type of "induction," however, to which Aristotle attributes a really important role in his theory of demonstrative science, is what nowadays is sometimes referred to as "intuitive induction." By considering a number of particular A's that are B, we come to perceive the universal connection between A and B: "All A's are B." When we have once, through *epagoge*, become aware of the connection, it becomes the object of a rational intuition. (Wedberg 1982, 88–89)

Wedberg's formulations may be interpreted as indicating a stronger kinship between Aristotle's conception of scientific induction to fictional generalizations "from within" than to modern ideas of empirical law making. The choice of words – perception, awareness of general connections, object of rational intuition – is certainly not in tune with contemporary ideas of how to validate empirical generalizations, the step from "all known" to "all"; they rather point to an insight similar to recalling something forgotten, or half-forgotten, or some other mental act within the repertoire I have called "from within."

Bibliography

Aristotle. *Poetics*. [*Longinus: On the Sublime. Demetrius: On Style*]. Trans. W. Hamilton Fyfe. Loeb Classical Library, 199. London: Heinemann, 1932.
– *Poetics* [*Longinus: On the Sublime. Demetrius: On Style*]. Trans. Stephen Halliwell. Loeb Classical Library, 199. Cambridge, MA: Harvard University Press, 1995.
Carlshamre, Staffan. "Vad berättelser betyder" [What stories mean]. *Tidskrift för litteraturvetenskap* 3–4 (2004): 38–54.
Gendler, Tamar Szabó. *Intuition, Imagination and Philosophical Methodology*. Oxford and New York: Oxford University Press, 2010.
Goodman, Nelson. *Languages of Art. An Approach to a Theory of Symbols*. Brighton: The Harvester Press, 1981.
Hoffman, Heinrich. *Der Struwwelpeter oder lustige Geschichten und drollige Bilder*. Leipzig: Insel, 1844.
Horace *Ars Poetica, or: Epistle to the Pisos*. Transl. Anthony S. Kline. http://www.poetryintranslation.com/PITBR/Latin/HoraceArsPoetica.htm. 2005. (24 February 2013).
Rossholm, Göran. "Now's the Time." *Essays on Fiction and Perspective*. Ed. Göran Rossholm. Bern, Berlin and New York: Peter Lang, 2004. 199–221.
– "Fictionality and Information." *Fictionality-Possibility-Reality*. Eds. Petr Kotatko, Martin Pokorny and Marcelo Sabatés. Bratislava: Aleph, 2010. 19–31.
– "Mimesis as Directness." *Mimesis: Metaphysics, Cognition, Pragmatics*. Eds. Gregory Currie, Petr Kotatko and Martin Pokorny. London: College Publications, 2012. 14–39.
Solzhenitsyn, Aleksandr. *One Day in the Life of Ivan Denisovich*. Trans. Thomas P. Whitney. New York: Fawcett Publications, 1963.
Wedberg, Anders. *A History of Philosophy, 1: Antiquity and the Middle Ages*. Oxford: Clarendon, 1982.

Mari Hatavara
Historical Fiction: Experiencing the Past, Reflecting History

The conference theme is fiction, its nature, forms and functions. My paper discusses these issues through the genre of the historical novel, where questions of referentiality, truth-value and cultural identity are thematised. Historical fiction has lately aroused interest for its potential to deepen and widen the scope of historical writing. (Fay 2002, 1; Adhikari 2002, 43, 47; Demos 2005, 329–330; Harlan 2005, 143) On the other hand, the historical novel has been condemned as an impossible genre due to the inevitable friction between artistic composition and historical verisimilitude. Some theorists, like Harry E. Shaw (2005), say historical fiction is problematic because historical narrative can never be complete. Others, such as Ann Rigney (2004), focus on how historical fiction can play a significant role in the formation of cultural memory. While Shaw emphasises the role of serious realist fiction in representing historical reality, Rigney suggests that creatively reworked artificial memories may prove more accessible in practice than those strictly adhering to the facts.

An analogical discussion about realism and truth-value can be found around traditional historical fiction and historiographical metafiction. Historical fiction in its traditional form is considered referential, having a bond with past reality (Maxwell 1998). On the other hand, the first and also more recent definitions of the postmodern version of the historical novel emphasise its involvement in the epistemological problems present in representing the past, and on the constructed nature of reality and history. (Hutcheon 1988; Nünning 2005) In the former definition, the story and its referentiality distinguish the historical novel as a genre, whereas in the latter definition, historical metafiction is characterised by the emphasis on the discursive formation at the expense of the referential function.

In these definitions, it is either content or form, story or discourse, that dominate, and the realistic representational mode is connected with referentiality. To me, it seems that both disputes build on partially false presuppositions as they emphasise one side of the historical novel but overlook the other. To my mind, the "traditional" historical novel is also at least somewhat self-conscious and highlights its own textuality, whereas historiographic metafiction does apply and highlight referentiality even when concentrating on the constructed nature of history. Thus realism and artificial reworking are not opposites but rather constitute a vital liaison in representing history. That is why historical fiction – traditional and postmodern – is able to discuss and thematise history both as an account of what happened in the past and as a cognitively constructed view of those events as history.

The main question in my paper asks how historical fiction participates in discussions on history in both these meanings. How, specifically, do fictional forms and modes of representation enable the reader to engage in understanding and evaluating the past as history? The specificity of fiction I want to stress here is its multi-layered narrative structure, based on the necessary separation of the author and the narrator in fiction. Furthermore, narrators as well as characters often come in several layers. (Genette 1993, 69–78; Cohn 1999) As Tamar Yacobi argues, fiction is a system of quotations, of embedded discursive levels. (Yacobi 2000, 713–718) The textual level is governed by the implied author; the narrative level involves one or more narrators, and the story in inhabited by characters. These layers of discursive agents allow the transgression of the temporal and epistemological limits involved in historical writing.

In this paper, I study the textual and narrative arrangement and storyworlds of two historical novels. My examples are from Finnish fiction written in Swedish, namely Fredrika Runeberg's *Sigrid Liljeholm* from 1862 (= SL) and Lars Sund's *Colorado Avenue* from 1991 (= CA) – the former among the first historical novels in Finland, the latter an example of historical metafiction, a tradition that began in Finland in the late 1970s. I will demonstrate how both traditional and postmodern forms of historical fiction utilise fictional modes of narration and offer the reader interpretative positions that enable engagement in historical discussion.

Sigrid Liljeholm has a third-person narrator situated in the time of the writing of the novel who often comments on past events. The narrator starts the novel with a frame narrative disclosing the origin of the story, which is set in Southern Finland at the end of the 16th century, when King Sigismund and Duke Charles were struggling for power over the Swedish throne. Besides historical events, the novel relates an unhappy love story of a young maiden, Sigrid Liljeholm, a daughter of a follower of the Finnish-Swedish Admiral Clas Fleming.

Colorado Avenue consists of three parts and an epilogue. The title page of each part gives the time and place of the events, which span from 1893 in Colorado, U.S.A., to 1928 on the Finnish seashore of Quarken. The epilogue extends the time line to 1929, and is also set on the coastline of Quarken. The main character is Hanna Östman (Näs after her marriage). She emigrates to the U.S. as a young woman, marries trade-unionist Edvard Näs, and has two children with him. After Edvard's premature death, Hanna returns to Ostrobothnia and starts a successful store. The narrator uses both first and third person forms of himself, and metaleptically moves back and forth from the time of writing to the time and place of the events.

In this paper, I will firstly study the textual arrangement, especially paratextual features like titles and frame narratives, secondly analyse the narrators and narrative structures, and thirdly look at how the storyworld is made available to the reader. As will become evident, these features are separable only for analytical purposes, but work together in the interpretation. As Dorrit Cohn states, "a work of fiction itself creates the world to which it refers by referring to it." (Cohn 1999, 13) This entails the synchronicity and interdependence of text, narrative and story. In historical fiction, however, this synchronous story-discourse relation is supplemented by the intertextual link the reader builds between the story and the previously encountered representations of the same historical events, which become subtexts for the novel.

Cohn points out that fiction – not only historical fiction – often includes references to real places and events. She does, however, disregard this phenomenon by stating that in fiction these references need not correspond with reality, and for this reason they are not significant. (Cohn 1999, 13–15) I, however, want to stress a qualitative difference of these references in historical fiction. Firstly, when a historical novel refers to a certain known historical time and place, the reader has prior knowledge from historiography. Secondly, as the past is approached from the time of the writing of the novel, a tension builds up between the characters experiencing the storyworld and the implied author reflecting it. The reader needs to interpret this temporal and epistemological tension in order to understand the historical nature of a novel. This is where historical novels differ from other kinds of novels, even if they all rest on the assumption of a minimal departure from the known reality: in historical fiction, the facts corresponding with reality are more specific and their interpretation is based on the tension between the time depicted and the time of writing.

Textual Frames and Layers

Frame narratives and particularly prologues were typical in novels of the 19th century. Their functions were often to express the narrator's authorial positioning to the story. (Arping 2001) In historical fiction, they connect to the poetics of writing and commenting on history, and also to the balance between referentiality and self-reflection. Corrections, definitions and further details provided in paratexts like forewords and footnotes may be judged a negative feature, disturbing the reading process and breaking the illusion of coherence of the storyworld. At the same time, they are part and parcel of the historical novel's link to the historiography proper, and essential in building the historical illusion. (Schabert 1981, 23) Richard Maxwell understands them as means to justify mixing fiction with history. (Maxwell 1998, 543) In any case, it is important to look at their role and functions in a novel; as Gérard Genette maintains, paratexts serve the interpretation of the text itself and provide opportunities to guide the reading process. (Genette 1997, 12–13, 197, 287)

Sigrid Liljeholm's frame narrative seems to provide a rather direct instruction on how to interpret the novel. The frame narrative is about a manuscript the narrator received decades ago as a young girl. The narrator openly declares the manuscript, and her own narrative based on it, to be more about little incidents than about the big events of history. At the same time, the narrator discusses her doubts about the portrayal of Clas Fleming in both the manuscript and in some historical sources she has used for comparison. She mentions a few history books, and comments on one written by Johan Gabriel Werwing. The narrator suspects that King Charles XI – a descendant of Duke Charles who became Charles IX – had influenced the book at the expense of Clas Fleming:

> Stundom föreföll det mig som om jag såge gubben Werving småle i sin själ, när han med mycken salfvelse utfar mot Flemings grymhet, blodtörst och framför allt hans uppstudsighet emot hertig Carl, men tillika icke försummar att anföra bref och bevis på huru Fleming handlade alldeles i enlighet med sin konungs befallningar och icke utan förräderi eller svek kunnat förfara annorlunda. De der beskärmelserna se ut temmeligen som sand, strödd i den kungliga censurens ögon. (SL, v–vi)

> At times, it seemed to me that I could see the old man Werwing smile inwardly when he vigorously ran Fleming down for his cruelty, bloodthirstiness, and above all for his insubordination to Duke Charles, and yet at the same time he had not neglected to mention letters and proofs of how Fleming acted precisely according to the orders of his king and could not have done otherwise without resorting to deceit or fraud. Those complaints look like sand thrown into the eyes of royal censorship. (All translations mine)

It can be argued that the novel *Sigrid Liljeholm* is structured in a similar manner, and the reader needs to be aware of the possible deceitfulness of the explicit commentary. Even though the narrator modestly argues that the novel is not about the important events of history, it does relate the battles and intrigues of the Cudgel War, and has cardinal historical figures like the Fleming family and Duke Charles as some of the main characters.

The frame narrative of *Sigrid Liljeholm* builds a strong connection to both the historical era depicted and the former representations of it by the discussion on what parts of history the story is about, by mentioning real historical figures and, furthermore, by the reference to contemporary historiography. Several subtexts are mentioned: besides real history books and the fictional manuscript, the novel is said to be based on a play by the author of the novel. The frame narrative begins with a description of the narrator's younger self burning this tragedy about Clas Fleming. The narrator ironizes her former teenage self by indicating that young writers by definition want to produce something sublime and grand ("högt och stort." SL, iii). The other participant in this discussion is an old aunt of the narrator, who immediately starts to guess the details of the play being burnt. The aunt mentions several clichés that in the contemporary literary criticism were associated with popular, melodramatic literature of lower quality. (Cf. Wallace 2005, 21) Against this backdrop, the narrator provides references to contemporary historiography, which indicates that the novel at hand belongs to a more serious tradition.

Runeberg's use of contemporary historiography is clearly visible in some parts of the novel where the text is virtually quoted from other sources. These quotations are not marked, even though they are almost verbatim. Several passages are from Anders Fryxell's *Berättelser ur Swenska historien* (Tales from Swedish history [1830] 1837). The example is from a conversation between Johan Fleming, Clas Fleming's son, and Arvid Stålarm, another Finnish nobleman.

> Fleming swarade: Jag för min del will icke ens förråda min konungs hund än minder hans slott och land. Kan min person något göra, skall jag nog stanna qwar och wåga mig med finnarna i den farlighet, som dem af hertigen tillstunda kan. (Fryxell 1837, 324)

> Förråda ens min konungs hund, ville jag ingalunda, mycket mindre hans slott och land. Kan jag, med min ensamma person, göra någon nytta, så vill jag gerna qvarstadna och med finnarne våga mig i den farlighet, som dem af hertigen kan förestå. (SL, 254–255)

> [Fryxell:] Fleming answered: I, for my part, would not want to betray my king's dog, even less his castle and his land. If my person may be of any help, I shall surely remain here and with the Finns face any danger the Duke may cause.

> [Runeberg:] I would not choose to betray my king's dog, even less so his castle and land. If I, a single person, can be of any help, I shall gladly remain here and with the Finns face any danger the Duke may bring about.

This quotation, then, repeats the words of a historical character documented in a history book. In *Sigrid Liljeholm*, passages like this falsify the frame narrative's overt statement not to engage with significant historical events, but fulfil the covert one of partaking in a historical discussion of the past events and their interpretation. This is also put forward in sections commenting on and quoting documents like letters; it is mentioned, for example, that many letters exist from a certain period testifying to Clas Fleming's activity, one of which is quoted. (SL, 90)

Lars Sund's *Colorado Avenue* does not have a frame narrative but an episode-titled epilogue at the end. This epilogue, however, is a direct extension of the main story and does not introduce another narrative layer. Neither does it directly comment on the textual or narrative arrangement of the novel, and is mostly vital for the plot. *Colorado Avenue's* textual layers come in quotes from fictional letters and claims of genuine quotes from excerpts of old newspapers. The narrator, for example, describes going through editions of the papers *Vasabladet* and *Hufvudstadsbladet*.

The most interesting textual feature in *Colorado Avenue* is a section in which a film manuscript is quoted and the making of a silent movie is reported. Chapter 14 in the first part of the novel starts with a description of a scene from a black-and-white silent movie. A small boy on a porch, who turns out to be Hanna's son Otto, is depicted running happily towards some approaching men only to find out they are carrying his father, shot in a demonstration. This is a crucial turning point in the novel, where, with the young lovers parted by death, Hanna decides to return to her home country, and Otto reluctantly leaves his country of birth at the age of seven. The fictional film is the only form in which the reader gets information of the events.

The representation of the movie is a series of described scenes and quoted texts from the screen, and finally a description of the actors and directors on the set making the movie. Whereas all fiction is, as I argued, a system of quotations, quotations like these involving another medium bring this system of quotations to a head, since they involve a modification from one medium to another, in this case from visual to verbal. (Cf. Yacobi 2000, 712–717) The textual and artistic nature of the novel is highlighted as this description of an emotional event is represented with one more remove from the main plot, through the description of a movie.

Like the frame narrative in *Sigrid Liljeholm*, this quotation from a fictional movie evokes generic context. The first text quoted from the screen gives the genre of the movie: "En ballad med 4 akter och tre mellanspel med verklighetsbakgrund." (CA, 110; "a ballad with 4 scenes and three intermissions, based on a true story.") A ballad is a tragic love story often featuring a couple with different social statuses. This generic model fits Hanna's and Ed's story, even though the tragic end is more a result of their differences in character than in their social background.

Both novels use intertextual references to historical documents and sources in order to build historical credibility. Both also discuss the generic tradition of literature with allusions to drama and film. These allusions to fictional practices do not, however, diminish the illusion of referentiality but rather maintain it by setting the novels against a background of more melodramatic and less serious genres. Thus, both references to historical sources and references to renounced genres aim at building historical liability. Next, I will analyse the narrative levels of the novels and their discursive practices.

Narrative Levels

Mise en abyme-structures, narratives within the narrative, have been called mirrors of the text. (Dällenbach 1989) They function much like frame narratives, since both offer parallel, possibly analogous stories to the main story. They are also special cases of narrative, since a character takes the role of a narrator for a while. In *Sigrid Liljeholm*, Sigrid tells a fairy tale – about a king with a son and a daughter – to the children of Fleming. The tale shows how women are overlooked but powerful actors in history. The struggle between sexes and female oppression in history is an overall theme in the novel (Hatavara 2006), but not particularly significant to the history/fiction-discussion.

Colorado Avenue has narratives within the main narrative as well. They are not, however, positioned like *mises en abyme*, since they are not located inside the storyworld. They are an example of the various forms of metalepsis in the novel, as the characters narrating them temporarily move to the same narrative level as the main narrator. In many cases, the traffic between the narrator's retrospective position and the past storyworld goes in both directions. After Johannes Smeds has denied his younger son his wish to become a cantor, the narrator addresses the son directly:

> Ja, Gustav: mycket hade kanske gått annorlunda om du fått skola dig till klockare! Om du hade fått ut den där musiken som spelade och klingade inuti dig.
> Men nu vart du som hållen i reserv. [...]
> – Nå en jag då!
> Den gälla och uppfordrande pojkrösten avbryter berättarens sentimentala betraktelser över Kommunalarins-Gustav. Och rakt in i denna berättelse kör en flakkärra, runt vilken det står en spetsig arom av dynga. (CA, 197)
>
> Well, Gustav – much would have been different had you had the chance to become a cantor! If you had gotten out the music that rings and chimes inside of you.
> But you were ever kept in reserve. [...]
> – What about me then!
> A shrill and insistent voice of a boy interrupts the narrator's sentimental musings on Gustav, the commissioner's son. And right into this story drives a truck, around which there is a sharp aroma of dung.

It is unclear whether Gustav and the narrator really communicate, but when Otto yells out "What about me then!" and demands to be part of the narrative, the narrator and a character clearly share the same discursive space. This unsettles the position of the narrator, who has acted mostly like a historian, gathering information from historical sources. Then again, most parts of the novel do not provide any explanation of how the narrator has gained access to the information. Thus, the epistemic motivation that such an explanation would reveal is not shown. In this respect, the novel does not follow the pattern of historiographical metafiction, reflecting and contesting given information. Rather, it highlights the existence of the story itself, without the mediation of the narrator. Genette has maintained that metaleptic blending of the discourse and story levels frequently confuses the readers' expectations. (Genette 1980, 234–235) In *Colorado Avenue*, these kinds of narrative metalepsis do clearly cross the narrative boundaries, but not at the expense of the storyworld, rather the opposite. Before looking more closely at how the novels offer the storyworlds to the reader, I will analyse another phenomenon on the borderline between story and discourse, namely the mixing of the narrator's and the characters' voices.

Free indirect discourse (FID) is a mode most often claimed to be possible only in fictional narratives, since it mixes the voices of agents on two different narrative levels and thus entails knowledge of and access to a mind of another agent. (Cohn 1978, 112–113) Additionally, the mixing of a narrator's seemingly objective language with the subjective language of a character results in interpretative difficulties which in all likelihood should not exist outside fictional literature, that is, in factual literature where the origin of an utterance and its intentions should be clear. Furthermore, FID as a dual-voice discourse often lingers between an ironic and an emphatic standpoint towards a character, and in both cases is regarded as being highly subjective and emotive. (Cohn 1978, 116–117; McHale 1978, 275 and passim; Teilmann 2000, 77; Tammi 2006)

The fictional specificity, like everything else about FID, has been under dispute for decades. (McHale 2005) I will not participate in this discussion here, but study how FID is used in these novels in relation to their historical nature. What is important in this case is that FID conforms in person and tense to the third person narrator's speech, but in style and deictic adverbs to the character's speech. Since the narrator telling and reflecting the story assumes a retrospective view of the events, and the character is experiencing them as her present, the mixing of these two discursive and temporal positions is of interest here. As Cohn has pointed out, FID enables the presentation of past minds in the discursive present, for example, by using the adverb "now." (Cohn 1978, 126–128)

Sigrid Liljeholm portrays the opinions and feelings of characters on both sides of the power struggle between Duke Charles and King Sigismund, the latter side represented mostly by Fleming. Besides individuals, collective thoughts of the larger masses are sometimes represented in the novel, for example the peasants' decision to revolt against the troops led by Fleming under King Sigismund's command:

> Men vördnaden för konungen och hans befallningshafvande, höll ännu bönderna tillbaka, ehuru redan på flere håll blod gjutits.
> Nu var det annorlunda. Nu hade de hertig Carls eget ord på, att de ägde rättighet till sjelfförsvar emot knektarne. Fleming egde ingen rätt att beherrska, än mindre att förtrycka folket. Bonden behöfde icke föda knektarne, då de icke höllos till rikets tjenst, utan endast till Flemings upproriska afsigters befrämjande. (SL, 28)
>
> But the obeisance towards the king and his representative still constrained the peasants, even if blood had already been shed in many regions.
> Now things were different. Now they had Duke Charles's own word that they had the right to defend themselves. Fleming had no right to rule, even less to oppress the people. They did not need to feed the soldiers, since the soldiers were not in the service of the kingdom, but were only there to support Fleming's rebellious aims.

The subjectivity of the people is clearly present here: repetition of the temporal adverb "now" designates the time of the characters experiencing the past, and the choices of words indicate possible thoughts and words of the characters themselves ('Now we have Duke Charles' own word that we have the right to defend ourselves. Fleming has no right to rule, even less to oppress the people. We do not need to feed the soldiers, since the soldiers are not in the service of the kingdom, but only here to support Fleming's rebellious aims.') These kinds of collective thoughts are possible in FID, since it does not necessarily follow any one original utterance but may convey preverbal or incoherent thinking. (Cohn 1978, 103; McHale 1978, 277)

From a historical point of view, it is remarkable that these words seem to have an authentic source, even though they were necessarily not verbalised by the peasants in the exact form given in the novel. Before the quotation, the novel relates how certain leaders of the peasant rebels, like the historical figure Jacob Ilkka, have just given speeches with the same content and with the aim to agitate the peasants. Whereas in fiction it may be a fundamental error to try to assume an original utterance by the character somewhere "behind" FID, since the text in the novel is the only verbalisation of the world it creates (McHale 1978, 256), in historical fiction these historically significant opinions do have a prior existence. What is more, it is important for the historical interpretation to designate the origin of any opinion that led to historical events. In the case quoted, two possible interpretations, not mutually exclusive, can be discerned: that the novel *Sigrid Liljeholm* shows how the peasants were misled by their leaders and aims at arousing the reader's sympathy towards them, or that *Sigrid Liljeholm* suggests history is driven by intentions with no single, discernible source, to the effect that all origins seem lost in layers of subjects and discourses, much as in a game of Chinese whispers.

In both cases, the intentions of the peasants are brought into a discursive present, as they think they "now" have the right to defend themselves. *Sigrid*

Liljeholm uses FID to mediate between the discourse time and the story time. *Colorado Avenue* uses a more open mode of metalepsis. Both transgress the temporal boundary between the narrator reflecting history and the characters experiencing the past. This enables the reader to partly access the storyworld as the characters experience it. I will now look closer at the ways in which the two novels make their historical storyworlds accessible to the reader.

Historical Storyworlds

Storyworlds have gained much theoretical attention in recent narratology. Cognitively inspired narratology studies and elaborates on the processes of immersion (Ryan 2001), readerly orientation within the storyworld (Herman 2002, 2009a), and perceptual positioning on the levels of storyworld, narration and the actual reading process. (Jahn 1996) David Herman has argued that the reader understands narrative worlds by mapping discourse cues into WHAT, WHERE and WHEN dimensions of a storyworld. This allows the reader to situate him/herself in the storyworld, and to adopt the temporal and spatial position in the fictional reality. (Herman 2002, 14–15; 2009b, 71) Relying partly on Marie-Laure Ryan's argumentation, Herman names two basic strategies the reader uses in approaching the storyworld: the process of accommodation and the principal of minimal departure. (Herman 2009b, 80–82) The reader's imaginative relocation to the storyworld may be studied at the beginning of *Colorado Avenue*.

Whereas *Sigrid Liljeholm* begins with the frame narrative, *Colorado Avenue* takes the reader right into the middle of the storyworld with a description of a character and her recollections.

> Dollar-Hanna hade ett särskilt förhållande till dynamit.
> Lukten av sprängd dynamit var henne oupplösligen förknippad med kärlek och sorg. Från det att hon återvände hem till Finland och ändå till sin död många år senare skulle hon förmå återkalla denna lukt så tydligt att hon faktiskt kunde känna den sticka i näsan – en från blandning av svavel, upphettad metall och ozon. Luktförnimmelsen frammanade i sin tur bilden av en karl, som långsamt kommer vandrande längs en dammig gata, bärande på ett par sadelväskor och ett winchestergevär och med hatten neddragen i pannan; i fonden tornar berg upp sig, deras spetsiga, snöklädda toppar skimrar som stora glasskärvor mot den djupblåa himlen.
> Mannen var min morfars far.
> Från Telluride, Colodaro hade Dollar-Hanna burit hem dynamitlukten. (CA, 7)

> Dollar Hanna had a particular relationship with dynamite.
> The smell of detonated dynamite would always for her be inextricably linked to love and sorrow. From the moment of returning home to Finland until her death many years

later, she would always recollect this smell vividly enough to feel it burn her nose – a pungent mixture of sulphur, heated metal and ozone. This sensory recollection in turn evoked an image of a man who slowly comes walking down a dusty street carrying a pair of saddlebags and a Winchester rifle, a hat pressed down on his forehead; in the background rise the mountains, and their pointed, snow-covered tops sparkle like large shards of glass against the deep blue sky.
The man was my mother's grandfather.
From Telluride, Colorado, Dollar Hanna had brought home the smell of dynamite.

A subtitle page precedes this beginning, giving the information: "Del 1. Rödskärs-Hannas stora kärlek. Telludire, Colorado. 1893–1905." ("Part 1. The big love of Hanna from Rödskär. Telluride, Colorado. 1893–1905.") This provides the reader directly with the information on what (the big love), where (Telluride, Colorado) and when (1893) needed to accommodate herself within the storyworld. Moreover, since the character is named "Hanna from Rödskär," Rödskär being a real place on the Åland Islands west of the Finnish mainland, it is evident that Hanna is one of the many immigrants from Finland to the U.S.A. around the turn of the 20th century, thus giving a historical background. The theme of being abroad is further emphasised in the third and last sentences of the quotation, where Hanna's return home is mentioned.

Besides the coordinates in a storyworld, cognitive narratology understands that human experientiality lies at the core of narratives. Monika Fludernik understands that readers narrativise, making sense of texts by applying real world understanding through the perspectival schemata of ACTION, TELLING, EXPERIENCING, VIEWING and REFLECTING. (Fludernik 2003, 244–247) These perspectival schemata give the reader an access point to the storyworld and an experiencing subjectivity in it, much the same way as Herman understands that the reader navigates using the coordinates offered. At the beginning of *Colorado Avenue*, the perspectives of viewing, experiencing and reflecting are activated: the narrator reflects on ("a *particular* relationship") the character Hanna's experience ("the *smell* of detonated dynamite," "*love* and *sorrow*"), which conjures up a view ("an *image* of a man"). It is evident that *Colorado Avenue* explicitly offers the reader coordinates to, and an experience of, the storyworld.

From the point of view of fictionality and historical representation, two features of this opening are especially interesting: the narrator's positioning in relation to the storyworld and the perspectival schemata of viewing. At the beginning, the narrator seems to be a third person narrator located outside of the storyworld, with at least some of the privileges of an omniscient narrator, capable of relating the minds of the characters and moving in space and time. (Cf. Royle 2003, 261–262, 269–272; Culler 2004, 22–23; Nelles 2006, 119–121) But then, in the third paragraph, the narrator turns out to be a person in the story, a descendant of the man described. This makes the narrator part of the fictional world described one of the characters there. Cohn has argued that a historian is actually rather a character narrator than a narrator outside of the storyworld. (Cohn 1999, 122–123) According to her argumentation, however, this results in the narrator being restricted to the narrative abilities of a natural person, not able to know or depict the minds of the others. I would argue, however, that in historical fiction – as in *Colorado Avenue* – the narrator may both assume the role of a historian, reflecting past story on the basis of documents and the like, and utilise fictional narrative liberties like telepathy. This offers the reader an audience position inside the fiction, where the storyworld is the actual world which the characters experience as their present and the narrator and the audience reflect as their past. Still, despite this assumed role as a historian, the narrator is able to read and relate to the minds of the (other) characters in the story.

The different perspectival schemata in the opening of *Colorado Avenue* first seem to follow each other logically, as the narrator reflects on the experience of the character. The third frame of viewing, however, does not readily fall into the same continuum. The change from past to present tense highlights its nature as an image rather than a part of the narrative. It is offered, and may be interpreted, as a mental image of the character Hanna, her visual recollection. The temporal order of the narrative layers is reversed. In the passage quoted, it is not only the narrator but also Hanna who assumes a retrospective view of the narrated events, since they are her memories: first her memories of the smell of the dynamite, then the mental image conjured up by this memory. The description of the oldest and deepest layer of her mind is, however, offered to the reader through the schema of viewing with coordinates of what, where and when in the present: in the present tense and with a perspectival position in the described view, the foreground and the background of the image given. What is more, the tense in the third sentence of the quotation is in the form of "would always" ("från [...] ända [...] skulle hon förmå"), which indicates a prolonged, repetitive action. In this way, the scene, even though mentally at three removes (the narrator, Hanna recollecting, Hanna's mental image) is brought close to the reader, and the past world made accessible. Immediately after that, in the third paragraph, the narrator's retrospective view and his personal relation to the story is given, as he uses the past tense and identifies the man described as his forebear.

Throughout the novel, the narrator moves between his position as a historian relating the story to a contemporary audience, and offering more direct glimpses of the storyworld like the image in the last quotation. Even metaleptic passages are informative with respect to historical timing and placing:

> Med den suveränitet över tid och rum som tillkommer mig i egenskap av berättare kastar jag dig nu, tålmodiga läsare, trettio år framåt i tiden och snurrar samtidigt jordklotet ett drygt halvt varv åt öster räknat från Telluride, Colorado!
> Ve hamnar då i Siklax skärgård.
> På Rödskär närmare bestämt. I den stora sommarvilla min morfar Otto Näs byggde på holmen. Tidpunkt: senhösten 1928. Året när luftskeppet *Italia* störtade i packisen vid Nordpolen, Loukola, Nurmi och Andersén gav Finland en trippelseger i hinderlöppningen vid Olympiska spelen i Amsterdam, Nurmi blev professionell och hamnarbetarna strejkade. (CA, 78)

> With the sovereignty over time and space I have as narrator, I dash you now, my patient reader, thirty years ahead in time and, at the same time, spin the globe a bit more than half a turn east from Telluride, Colorado!
> We end up in the archipelago of Siklax.
> On Rödskär, to be more exact. In the summer house my grandfather Otto Näs built on the islet. Time: late autumn, 1928. The same year the airship *Italia* crashed into pack ice at the North Pole, Loukola, Nurmi and Andersén gained a triple victory for Finland in steeplechase at the Amsterdam Olympics, Nurmi turned professional and the dockworkers were on strike.

The narrator openly plays with his double role as omniscient narrator and historian, declaring his ability to take the reader to whatever time and place he chooses while at the same time giving historical details connecting the storyworld to history. This indicates that the narrator, despite his ability to move in time and place and to telepathically read the minds of the characters, does not adopt the fourth feature of omniscient narration, the omnipotent ability to make anything happen in the storyworld. (Nelles 2006, 120) This goes together with the role of a historian: the narrator wants to assure the reader that although the past world is accessible to him, it is not changeable, since the events have actually taken place.

As mentioned, *Sigrid Liljeholm* begins with a frame narrative which gives the reader the coordinates of the storyworld. It also introduces an authorial narrator, who claims to have written the text to come and is now sending it to a friend to read. The narrator holds her temporal distance to the storyworld throughout the text, but does describe visiting the places where the story is set. The following is about Qvidja, one of the mansions of Clas Fleming.

> På Qvidja reste sig ett högt gråstenstorn; det qvarstår der än i dag som en skepnad från forntiden, och talar om den tid, då Klas Fleming och hans ädla maka brukade vistas derinom. Men i de rum, derifrån ofta Klas Fleming, enväldigare än mången konung, styrde Finland, der gnaga nu råttorna på de rika sädesförråderna från Qvidjas vidsträckta åkrar.
> De första årtiondena af detta sekel stodo ännu de tvänne rum, som utgjorde tornets tredje våning, i gammaldagsdrägt. I de djupa fönsternischerna funnos stolar med Adam och Eva broderade, jemte kunskapens träd, på hvarje dyna. Färgerna voro urblekta, och

det hela såg ut som om det kunnat vara en återstod af dessa rums utseende för 200 år sedan.

Gerna älskade man då att tänka det här, i dessa rum, en gång vistats den mäktige Klas Fleming, den stolta Ebba Stenbock, deras unga, glada döttrar och den riddarlige, ädle, unge Johan Fleming; han, hvars korta lefnads sorgliga slut blifvit en af de sägner, som barnet redan hör med andlöst deltagande, och som sedan bo i hjertat, så länge det kan klappa varmt. (SL, 165–166)

In Qvidja stands a high stone tower; it remains to this day, a reminder of times past and speaks of when Clas Fleming and his noble spouse stayed there. But in those rooms, from where Clas Fleming ruled over Finland, more autocratic than many a king, rats now gnaw the rich grain stores from the fields of Qvidja.

During the first decades of this century, there remained two rooms which made up the tower's third floor, still in the costume of the old days. The deep window niches had chairs with Adam and Eve and the tree of knowledge embroidered on each cushion. The colours had faded, and the whole setting looked as if it could have been the remnants of what the room had looked like 200 years before.

It was nice then to think that here, in these rooms, there once lived the powerful Clas Fleming, the proud Ebba Stenbock, their young, merry daughters and the chivalrous, noble, young Johan Fleming; he, whose short life had a sorrowful end, one of those stories which even a child listens to with breathless attendance, and which from then on stay in one's heart as long as it keeps warmly beating.

Käte Hamburger has analysed a similar passage in Adalbert Stifter's essay "Der Hochwald" (1842), in which the narrator concretely uses the temporal perspective of the time of the writing in respect to the storyworld. According to Hamburger, a narrator in a passage like this assumes the temporal position of a real subject, and the deictic references are to be interpreted as if the narrator were a real person. (Hamburger 1993, 79–80) In this case, temporal references originate from the middle of the 19th century, from the time Runeberg wrote the novel. The tenses used confirm the interpretation, since the time of the writing is depicted in the present but both the time of the narrator's visit and the time of the story use the past tense.

The passage quoted demonstrates the multiple ways in which fictionalised historical characters can be portrayed in relation to fictional characters. The last paragraph indicates the perspective of both the writer and the reader of a historical novel since the past characters are imagined from the present perspective. When the narrator describes her own visit and the Fleming family's stay in Qvidja in the past tense, she positions them both in the same temporal continuum even though they occur at different points. Also, the narrator has shared the same space with the Fleming family. Thus the past storyworld is presented as a concrete place, still existent, and as a concrete time in the same historical continuum where the authorial narrator and her audience are situated.

As Rigney has pointed out, historical fiction is characterised by the interplay between story elements that are historical and those that are invented. (Rigney 2001, 19) In historical fiction, historical characters referred to and depicted become fictionalised. This process, according to Cohn, makes correspondence to real events and circumstances optional, not mandatory. (Cohn 1999, 13–15) It is, however, crucial to the genre that the reading process requires prior knowledge of these events. Even if Fleming in *Sigrid Liljeholm* is not *the* Fleming, the character is certainly associated with the historical person and evaluated on the basis of this knowledge. Both *Sigrid Liljeholm* and *Colorado Avenue* build and maintain the illusion of the depicted storyworld, its events and characters as past reality by building links between the history reflected and the past experienced.

Making Past History

"All historical events are past events but not all past events are historical events," writes Markku Hyrkkänen in his evaluation of R.G. Collingwood's philosophy of history. (Hyrkkänen 2009, 263) He emphasises that history always changes according to the concerns and interests of today. This is, of course, also true in the case of historical fiction: the time of the writing affects the view of the subject matter. The two novels analysed here participate in many contemporary discussions: *Sigrid Liljeholm* is deeply involved in women's emancipation as well as discussions on the nature of war. *Colorado Avenue* depicts immigration to the U.S., revisits the painful civil war and discusses national identity.

In these novels, the referred past events are paired with invented ones. Still, the connection with history is maintained through intertextual allusions to known past events. What is more, the novels openly highlight and discuss their textual and narrative structure, and the truthfulness of the events depicted. This self-referentiality does not, however, diminish the reader's engagement with the historical material portrayed. Rather, it makes her/him conscious of the nature of history both as past events and as a representation of them, and in doing so encourages involvement in the discussion on history.

Both novels analysed here create and maintain the illusion of writing history by using representative and discursive modes mostly associated with fiction. Many of them, like metalepsis between the narrator and a character, or the mixing of the voices of the narrator and a character in FID, mediate the temporal positions of experiencing the past and reflecting history. The multilayered textual and narrative structure of fiction allows both the portrayal of several temporal positions and travel between them in a manner that invites and encourages historical understanding. The narrators in these novels employ fictional liberties associated with omniscience, like telepathy and freedom to move in time and place, but still present the storyworlds as if they really happened in the past. These novels show how historical fiction may offer readers a possibility to become immersed in the past world while maintaining the awareness of it being part of history – a history they themselves participate in and reflect upon.

Bibliography

Adhikari, Madhumalati. "History and Story. Unconventional History in Michael Ondaatje's *The English Patient* and James A. Michener's *Tales of the South Pacific*." *History and Theory* 41.4 (2002): 43–55.

Arping, Åsa. "'Men vi måste nödvändigt ha ett företal.' Författare och förord i svensk 1830-talsprosa." *Carl Jonas Love Almqvist – diktaren, debattören, drömmaren*. Ed. Lars Burman. Hedemora: Gidlunds, 2001. 81–94.

Cohn, Dorrit. *Transparent Minds: Narrative Modes for Presenting Consciousness in Fiction*. Princeton, NJ: Princeton University Press, 1978.

— *The Distinction of Fiction*. Baltimore, MD: Johns Hopkins University Press, 1999.

Culler, Jonathan. "Omniscience." *Narrative* 12.1 (2004): 22–34.

Demos, John. "Afterword: Notes From, and About, the Fiction/History Borderland." *Rethinking History* 9.2–3 (2005): 329–335.

Dällenbach, Lucien. *The Mirror in the Text*. [French orig. 1977: *Le récit spéculaire: essai sur la mise en abyme*] Trans. Jeremy Whiteley and Emma Hughes. Oxford: Polity, 1989.

Fay, Brian. "Unconventional History." *History and Theory* 41.4 (2002): 1–6.

Fludernik, Monika. "Natural Narratology and Cognitive Parameters." *Narrative Theory and the Cognitive Sciences*. Ed. David Herman. CSLI Lecture Notes, 158. Stanford, CA: CSLI Publications, 2003. 243–267.

Fryxell, Anders. *Berättelser ur svenska historien. D. 4, Innehållande Lutterska tiden, Afd. 2, Johan III och Sigismund*. [Tales from the Swedish history, 4. On the era of Luther] Stockholm: Hjerta, [1830] 1837.

Genette, Gérard. *Narrative Discourse*. [French orig. 1972: *Discours du récit*] Trans. Jane E. Lewin. Oxford: Basil Blackwell, 1980.

— *Fiction & Diction*. [French orig. 1991: *Fiction et diction*] Trans. Catherine Porter. Ithaca, NY: Cornell University Press, 1993.

— *Paratexts: Tresholds of Interpretation*. [French orig. 1987: *Seuils*] Trans. Jane E. Lewin. Literature, Culture, Theory, 20. Cambridge: Cambridge University Press, 1997.

Hamburger, Käte. *The Logic of Literature*. [German orig. 1957: *Die Logik der Dichtung*] 2nd rev. ed. Trans. Marilynn J. Rose. Bloomington, IN: Indiana University Press, 1993.

Harlan, David. "In This Issue." *Rethinking History* 9.2–3 (2005): 141-145.

Hatavara, Mari. "Fredrika Runeberg's Strategies in Writing the History of Finnish Women in *Sigrid Liljeholm*." *Scandinavian Studies* 78.2 (2006): 153–166.

Herman David. *Story Logic: Problems and Possibilities of Narrative.* Lincoln, NE: University of Nebraska Press, 2002.
— *Basic Elements of Narrative.* Oxford: Wiley-Blackwell, 2009a.
— "Narrative Ways of Worldmaking." *Narratology in the Age of Cross-Disciplinary Narrative Research.* Eds. Sandra Heinen and Roy Sommer. Berlin and New York: De Gruyter, 2009b. 71–87.
Hutcheon, Linda. *A Poetics of Postmodernism: History, Theory, Fiction.* New York and London: Routledge, 1988.
Hyrkkänen, Markku. "All History is, More or Less, Intellectual History: R. G. Collingwood's Contribution to the Theory and Methodology of Intellectual History." *Intellectual History Review* 19.2 (2009): 251–263.
Jahn, Manfred. "Windows of Focalization: Deconstructing and Reconstructing a Narratological Concept." *Style* 30.2 (1996): 241–267.
Maxwell, Richard. "Historical Novel." *Encyclopedia of the Novel I.* Ed. Paul Schellinger. Chicago: Fitzroy Dearborn, 1998. 543–547.
McHale, Brian. "Free Indirect Discourse: A Survey of Recent Accounts." *Poetics and Theory of Literature* 3 (1978): 249–278.
— "Free Indirect Discourse." *Routledge Encyclopedia of Narrative Theory.* Eds. David Herman, Manfred Jahn and Marie-Laure Ryan. London & New York: Routledge, 2005. 188–189.
Nelles, William. "Omniscience for Atheists: Or, Jane Austen's Infallible Narrator." *Narrative* 14.2 (2006): 118–131.
Nünning, Ansgar. "Historiographic Metafiction." *Routledge Encyclopedia of Narrative Theory.* Eds. David Herman, Manfred Jahn and Marie-Laure Ryan. London & New York: Routledge, 2005. 216.
Rigney, Ann. *Imperfect Histories: The Elusive Past and the Legacy of Romantic Historicism.* Ithaca, NY: Cornell University Press, 2001.
— "Portable Monuments: Literature, Cultural Memory, and the Case of Jeanie Deans." *Poetics Today* 25:2 (2004): 361–396.
Royle, Nicholas. *The Uncanny.* New York: Routledge, 2003.
Runeberg, Fredrika [with the pseudonym –a –g.]. *Sigrid Liljeholm.* Helsinki: Theodor Sederholm, 1862.
Ryan, Marie-Laure. *Narrative as Virtual Reality. Immersion and Interactivity in Literature and Electronic Media.* Baltimore, MD: Johns Hopkins University Press, 2001.
Schabert, Ina. *Der historische Roman in England und Amerika.* Darmstadt: Wissenschaftliche Buchgesellschaft, 1981.
Shaw, Harry E. "Is There a Problem with Historical Fiction (or with Scott's *Redgauntlet*)?" *Rethinking History* 9.2-3 (2005): 173–195.
Sund, Lars. *Colorado Avenue.* Helsinki: Söderströms, 1991.
Tammi, Pekka. "Exploring *terra incognita*," *FREE language INDIRECT translation DISCOURSE narratology: Linguistic, Translatological and Literary-Theoretical Encounters.* Eds. Pekka Tammi and Hannu Tommola. Tampere: Tampere University Press, 2006. 159–173.
Teilmann, Stina. "Flaubert's Crime: Trying Free Indirect Discourse." *Literary Research/ Recherche littéraire* 17 (2000): 74–87.
Wallace, Diana. *The Woman's Historical Novel: British Women Writers, 1900–2000.* Basingstoke: Palgrave Macmillan, 2005.
Yacobi, Tamar. "Interart Narrative: (Un)reliability and Ekphrasis." *Poetics Today* 21.4 (2000): 711–749.

The Frontiers of Fiction: Recent Developments

Stefan Helgesson
Unsettling Fictions: Generic Instability and Colonial Time

Paratexts may come and go, but in South African literature there is one preface that is enduringly famous. It is in the second edition of her celebrated first novel *The Story of an African Farm* that Olive Schreiner elegantly dismisses what she sees as fanciful and deceptive British narratives about Africa. Here we find Schreiner's realist credo, contrasting "the stage method," according to which "each character is duly marshalled at first, and ticketed; we know with an immutable certainty that at the right crises each one will reappear and act his part, and, when the curtain falls, all will stand before it bowing," with what she calls "the method of the life we all lead" and by which "nothing can be prophesied." (Schreiner 1975, 23) The barb of her remarks, we soon learn, is directed at the imperial romance and all-too colourful colonial travelogues:

> It has been suggested by a kind critic that he would better have liked the little book if it had been a history of wild adventure; of cattle driven into inaccessible "kranzes" by Bushmen; "of encounters with ravening lions, and hair-breadth escapes." This could not be. Such works are best written in Piccadilly or in the Strand: there the gifts of the creative imagination untrammelled by contact with any fact, may spread their wings.
>
> But, should one sit down to paint the scenes among which he has grown, he will find that the facts creep in upon him. Those brilliant phases and shapes which the imagination sees in far-off lands are not for him to portray. Sadly he must squeeze the colour from his brush, and dip it into the grey pigments around him. He must paint what lies before him. (Schreiner 1975, 23–24)

The interesting complication is that Schreiner writes this in defence of what is obviously a *fictional* narrative with characters ranging from the flat and farcical (such as Bonaparte Blenkins and Tant' Sannie) to the complex and credible (such as Waldo and Lyndall). In other words, she invokes veracity and plausibility as the bedrock of her poetics – so as to legitimate her story about named individuals that have no referential counterparts.

This is, of course, entirely in keeping with a British and European conception of fictional narrative in the nineteenth century. What is less typical – and here we should recall that Schreiner's novel was published in London – is how this conception is employed from a colonial vantage point as a corrective to *other* fictions. One type of fiction, which remains close to empirical truth, is to be preferred to another, which is "untrammelled by contact with any fact." In Schreiner's view, the value of fiction hinges on its own undoing: it is when it tempers the imagination that it can perform its epistemological task of producing new and valid knowledge about the world.

Truth claims and referential claims enter the equation, in other words, and this is where I wish to place the emphasis in my discussion: on how late colonial (and early post-colonial) texts negotiate the tension between fiction and reference. Both aspects of writing are frequently engaged at one and the same time, even as attempts are made – as in Schreiner's preface – to consolidate a generic division of labour between them. This generic instability in colonial texts is, I contend, an index of two interrelated problems: 1) the inevitability of mediating social reality through language and 2) the struggle to reshape imported genres and discourses in response to the historical conditions of the (post-)colony. To explore this, and with the intention to add modestly to our understanding of the development of fiction on a world literary scale, I enlist the contrasting examples of Schreiner's *The Story of an African Farm* and Euclides da Cunha's *Os sertões*. Both are foundational texts in the literatures of South Africa and Brazil respectively. But whereas *Farm* is a fiction that makes truth claims, *Os sertões* can be described as a documentary that uses fictional devices to make its point. Being generic hybrids produced in conflictual historical circumstances, both works substantiate Brian G. Caraher's claim – with regard to the development of genres – that "a crisis in significance precipitates an initial and faltering attempt at refocusing the meaning jeopardised or lost in already established social and cultural forms." (Caraher 2006, 31) Schreiner and Da Cunha, working in colonial and postcolonial spaces in the late nineteenth century, are in other words engaged in the task of producing new meaning for which no satisfactory precedents exist. This could perhaps be generalised as the condition of all writing, but it is exacerbated under conflictual historical conditions.[1]

Of crucial importance to my argument is the notion that fiction affords ways of ordering time. More than so, fictionality provides these writers with a qualified freedom imaginatively to explore and produce temporalities that question or ironize the dominant version of time as Europe-centred progress. Here I approach Ricoeur's argument that narrative should be understood as actively shaping the human experience of time as meaningful. Although I

---

[1] Applying a more systemic world literary perspective, these texts could thereby also be seen as test cases for Franco Moretti's hypothesis about the "formal compromise" that drives literary development. Moretti understands this compromise in terms of a three-way negotiation between "foreign plot," "local characters" and "local narrative voice" – a model which is in fact *not* sustained by Schreiner's and Da Cunha's works. Rather than reproducing foreign *plots*, I would claim that it is imported epistemological frameworks – regarding history, fiction, cultural value, salvation– that they depart from and grapple with (Moretti 2000, 65).

agree that fiction and narrative are two distinct concepts, I put aside the finer points of that debate and take them instead to be cognate phenomena implicated in a comparable operation of meaning-construction. (Ricoeur 1980) Of greater consequence – and this runs counter to Ricoeur – is, however, the way in which Schreiner and Cunha produce *conflicting* notions of time, a feature which could be described in the purely formal terms that Ricoeur calls "surface grammar" (1980, 177), but for which a fuller explanation needs to be sought in terms of how such instability is formed by and speaks to the historical situatedness of the two writers.

With these remarks in mind, I am in other words arguing for a historical – as opposed to a universalising – understanding of fiction. Here, I am in agreement with Catherine Gallagher, who has compellingly traced the historically distinct emergence of fiction in Europe. Focusing on the rise of the novel, Gallagher makes a crucial distinction between flights of fancy and fiction proper. It may seem that there exist universally "stories that apparently do not make referential truth claims, such as fables and fairy tales," but are these really what we mean – or rather what the nineteenth-century novelists meant – by fiction? (Gallagher 2006, 337) The issue here, it seems, concerns the risk of *mistaking* fiction for truth. The sixteenth-century poet Sir Philip Sidney defended fanciful stories on the grounds that they "nothing affirmeth, and therefore never lieth." In other words, Gallagher argues (2006, 337), it was the very *unbelievability* of fanciful stories that legitimated their existence. If a reader was convinced that the events presented had actually occurred, this was tantamount to deception. When Daniel Defoe tried his best to pass off *Robinson Crusoe* as a true story, this should therefore be read as an attempt at *concealing* the deception. In early eighteenth-century England, there had not yet emerged a generic space in the literary system for a narrative that was believable but made no referential truth claims. This space would soon emerge, however, motivated in part by the need for writers to evade charges of libel. The result was what Gallagher terms the "discovery" of fiction as a discursive resource that paradoxically narrowed the scope of the imagination to the plausible while at the same time broadening fiction's appeal and public acceptance.

The suspension of disbelief – to use Coleridge's term – that fiction in this sense required of the reader was accompanied by the cultivation of scepticism. The qualified make-believe of a fictional narrative enabled the reader to imagine situations that *could* happen, and to do so by way of heroes and heroines that often made the "wrong" choices by proxy and placed the reader in a superior position vis-à-vis the fictional world.[2] Disbelief, which then becomes

---

[2] Gallagher is of course well aware that already Aristotle spoke of poetry's capacity to speak of what *can* happen, rather than what has happened. But her point is that it is only in eigh-

suspended in an attitude of "ironic credulity," is thereby a condition of fictionality in this sense.³ Such scepticism, which requires a continuous cognitive negotiation between the plausible, the false and the real, goes hand in hand with an emergent secularist, empiricist and capitalist modernity that relies not least on the imaginary-yet-real form of transaction known as credit. "Modernity," as Gallagher puts it, "is fiction-friendly." (2006, 345)

Does this also apply, one may then ask, to *colonial* modernity in the late nineteenth century? It would seem so. If anything, the social conditions of colonial societies, with their long-distance ties to an overseas European culture and to metropolitan centres of banking and state power, relied even more on the establishment of imaginary – indeed, fictional – relations with the world. This obtains even in the case of Euclides da Cunha's Brazil, which had been independent since 1822 but remained, eight decades later, in thrall to what Da Cunha disparagingly called a "civilização de emprestimo," a borrowed civilisation, or in Putnam's translation "a civilization which came to us second hand."⁴

If, however, the historical condition of creole populations in Latin America and Africa favoured fictionality as a *cultural* attitude – and transformed the "realism" of European novels into fanciful tales of faraway places – it must be added that European colonial discourses imposed a fictionalising understanding of the cultures, languages and, indeed, the civilisational value of the colonial other. In early modern Europe, the lack of knowledge about what lay beyond Europe was richly compensated for by flights of fancy, such as we find in Shakespeare's *The Tempest*; in the full-fledged modernity of the nineteenth century, as numerous postcolonial scholars have shown, we find on the one hand an excess of knowledge, serving to order humanity and its cultures hierarchically along a scale of development and progress, and on the other, in the literary realm, a rich production of adventure stories, mysteries and romances with remote settings such as Africa and India. (Pratt 1992; Chrisman 2000; Boehmer 2005, 13–57)

This is what makes fiction ambiguous to writers such as Olive Schreiner and Euclides da Cunha. By insisting on the need to dip the brush "into the grey pigments," Schreiner adopts the restricted notion of fiction as plausible

---

teenth-century Britain that fiction acquires the widespread cultural acceptance that lays the ground for our contemporary understanding of it.
3 Gallagher draws on Martinez-Bonati's use of the term "ironic credulity." (Gallagher 2006, 346).
4 Da Cunha 2005, 172, cf. 1994, 231. There is no space here to elaborate on the problem of Brazil's European cultural legacy, which loomed large in the literary and intellectual production of the late nineteenth and early twentieth century – witness for instance Graça Aranha's *Canaã* (1902), or the satirical depictions of "Europeanists" in Machado de Assis's novels.

but non-referential on behalf of her own colonial position. Her aesthetic choice is, in fact ethically motivated: it is a matter of relating responsibly to those facts that "creep in" upon her but are obscured by the British texts that supposedly *refer* to her life-world, which complicates the understanding of fiction considerably. Reference of some kind, as I claimed at the outset, is therefore involved in Schreiner's fictional undertaking. The fact that her novel is generically "impure," mixing allegory and philosophical speculation with more straightforward realistic narration, adds to the conundrum.

Before attempting to answer this riddle, it may be of help to posit Da Cunha's *Os sertões* as a counterpoint to *The Story of an African Farm*. Contrary to Schreiner, Da Cunha's project is explicitly non-fictional. "Written in the rare intervals of leisure afforded by an active and tiring [career]," as he says in his preface, his books aims at providing "for the gaze of future historians" a full account of the Canudos conflict as well as "the most significant present-day characteristics of the subraces to be found in the backlands of Brazil." (1994, xxxix) Da Cunha is beholden to the scientific horizon of his day, notably positivism and social Darwinism, including the racist forms of anthropology associated with these discursive formations. That much is evident, but so is his propensity to contradict himself when actually portraying individuals from these "subraces" who constitute, in his view, the very "bedrock" of the Brazilian nation. (1994, 695) The motive behind Da Cunha's undertaking was in fact, as many critics have asserted, to speak the truth about the Brazilian republic's massacre of the *sertanejos*, to counter the fictions and fantasies about the uprising that were bandied about in the urban press. (Andrade 2002, 59–182) Taken as a whole, *Os sertões* is nonetheless a beehive of contradictions and even more generically impure than Schreiner's novel, switching from geological and anthropological vocabularies to journalistic and – significantly – novelistic modes of narration. Intriguingly, there are critics who claim that even in his most "scientific" mode, when describing the geological and botanical features of Brazil, Da Cunha in fact exceeds established knowledge, thereby providing a partly fictionalising account of the land. (Maia 2008, 129)

One conclusion to be drawn from this is that both Schreiner's and Da Cunha's texts manifest certain limitations of the discursive tools at their disposal. The European novel and European science and scholarship provide them with their vocabularies, but these vocabularies fall short of accounting for their entangled, disjunctive experiences of colonial time. This, I claim, is where Schreiner's ethical appeal to veracity in representation, but with recourse to fictional modes of writing, gains traction. It is precisely because temporal experience is inarticulate and elusive, and hence not verifiable according to the standards of positivistic rationalism, that it must be approached discursively by way of an imaginative, fictional engagement.

In *The Story of an African Farm*, we can register this imaginative engagement by following how Schreiner allows various temporal rhythms to clash within the domestic space of the farm. Beginning with its famous opening sentence – "The full African moon poured down its light from the blue sky into the wide, lonely plain" (Schreiner 1975, 29) – the passing of time is continuously thematised throughout the novel. The first chapter is called "Shadows from child-life"; its first section, "The watch." The philosophical-allegorical first chapter of the second part of the novel is called, significantly, "Times and seasons."

The concern with time is often articulated through the consciousness of the fictional characters, but can also, as in "Times and seasons," be expressed in an entirely different, impersonal register. In the first pages of the novel we find young Waldo, the devout child of the German overseer Otto, listening in awe to the ticking of the watch:

> At the head of his father's bed hung a great silver hunting watch. It ticked loudly. The boy listened to it, and began mechanically to count. Tick – tick – tick! one, two, three, four! He lost count presently, and only listened. Tick – tick – tick – tick – tick!
> It never waited; it went on inexorably; and every time it ticked *a man died!* He raised himself a little on his elbow and listened. (Schreiner 1975, 30)

The boy, impressed by the words from the Bible that his father had read him that evening – "For wide is the gate, and broad is the way, that leadeth to destruction, and many there be which go in thereat" – has visions of how multitudes from ages past as well as now, from the ancient Greeks and Romans to "the countless millions of China and India," go over the dark edge of the world to their own eternal damnation. In a curious combination of mechanical and sacred time, Waldo now hears the watch saying "Eternity, eternity, eternity!" (Schreiner 1975, 31)

This transcendent view of time has what may be called a negative significance for the novel as a whole. *Farm* is an agnostic narrative, and Waldo will eventually reject his fervent Christian beliefs. This can be read as the outcome of Schreiner's appropriation of Herbert Spencer's thinking – but this agnosticism does not cancel the importance, in the novel, of the clash between sacred and secular temporalities. The distinctiveness of the novel draws mainly on its secular registers of time, which follow the diurnal/nocturnal and seasonal rhythms of the colonial farm, and the colonial society's gendered constraints on the individual's development. Whereas Tant' Sannie, as she is lured into marrying the devious intruder Bonaparte Blenkins, strives for a comedic resolution to the passing of her time, and while the rebellious Lyndall makes what could be read as an existentialist bid for freedom when she leaves the farm as an unmarried woman, the ultimate outcome of the narrative is tragic, leaving both Waldo and Lyndall dead.

To return to my main argument, it is here, in the disjunctive representation not only of different characters' passage through time but also by invoking the discrete registers of quotidian, sacred, evolutionary and historicist time, that the significance of fictionality should be noted. If the narrative as a whole is shaped by the frustrated quest for individual freedom – the right for young Lyndall to be master of her own time – in a harsh environment, then the imaginative testing of different views of time could be read as attempts at relativising them vis-à-vis each other. "The farm by daylight was not as the farm by moonlight," we read. (Schreiner 1975, 32) The waking hours make the harshness and drudgery of the farm life all too apparent. The only date that is ever mentioned in the novel is directly connected to the daily struggle for survival: "At last came the year of the great drought, the year of 1862. From end to end of the land the earth cried for water." (37) In that same chapter, we find the children Em, Waldo and Lyndall reiterating not just a master narrative of European history – the story of Napoleon, as remembered from "the brown history" in school – but also the new-fangled evolutionary, geological time conveyed by the "Physical Geography." This is Waldo speaking: "what are dry lands now were once lakes; and what I think is this – these low hills were once the shores of a lake; this 'kopje' is some of the stones that were at the bottom, rolled together by the water." (41) What captures Waldo's imagination is to think "of the time when the strange fishes and animals lived that are turned into stone now, and the lakes were here." (42) The story of Napoleon's rise and fall – "He was one, and they were many, and they were terrified of him," Lyndall says admiringly – seems like a distant fairy-tale. The even remoter deep time of evolution, however, is more immediately relevant to their surroundings. It exercises the imagination, but is also strangely pertinent to Waldo, to think of the drought-stricken Karoo as having been covered with water.

All of this can be read as diverse attempts at coming to terms with the "thrownness" – to use a Heideggerian term – of white creole life in the Cape Colony, a concern which the novel codes in terms of "the soul's life" in the "Times and seasons" chapter: "The soul's life has seasons of its own; periods not found in any calendar, times that years and months will not scan, but which are as deftly and sharply cut off from one another as the smoothly-arranged years which the earth's motion yields us." (Schreiner 1975, 127) This chapter, with its philosophical tone, constitutes Schreiner's attempt at reconciling not only an inner striving with the impersonal facticity of the world, but also a Christian outlook – consonant with her own upbringing on a mission station – with what she had learnt from her formative encounter with Herbert

Spencer's *First Principles*. (Schreiner 1884) Tracing a dialectical trajectory from childlike faith to agonising atheism, "Times and seasons" arrives at a Spencerian synthesis, a developmental view of being:[5] "This thing we call existence [...] Not a chance jumble: a living thing, a *One*. [...] the earth ceases for us to be a weltering chaos [...] all is part of a whole, whose beginning and end we know not." (Schreiner 1975, 143)

The tragic outcome of both Lyndall's and Waldo's strivings renders this conciliatory view of time impotent, however, and what is above all noticeable in *Farm* is Schreiner's conspicuous inability to accommodate the colonised other within this vision of the "One." Granted, the German overseer Otto does articulate a radically egalitarian view of humanity, which includes the colonised, and Tant' Sannie, who is a figure of ridicule and scorn, is a mouthpiece for racist prejudice towards the "Kaffir" servants – "[she] held they were descended from apes, and needed no salvation" – but there is never any attempt by Schreiner in this novel to extend her fictional exploration of colonial time beyond white creole society.[6] (She does so in later works, such as the novella *Trooper Peter Halket of Mashonaland*, but that lies beyond the purview of this essay).

Euclides da Cunha's *Os sertões* differs from *Farm* precisely in this respect: it constitutes a monumental attempt at accommodating the *sertanejo*, the "internal" other of the Brazilian nation. His documentary ambitions notwithstanding, Da Cunha had only personally experienced the last of the four campaigns against the backlands rebels, and never saw the town of Canudos until it had been reduced to rubble. When setting out to write the full story of this rebellion, therefore, Da Cunha could not simply report what he had witnessed but had to construct an account out of whatever material he had at his disposal. And this he did, from a vast number of angles. *Os sertões* is a monstrous work, impossible to address adequately in a short essay, but I will begin by simply listing some of the ways in which Da Cunha approaches this task – notably by inscribing different temporalities into his narrative.

Part one, "The land," is a geological and botanical account of the Brazilian landmass, the backlands in particular. Here Da Cunha's time-frame extends millions of years back, and he appropriates in effect geological time on behalf of the fledgling Brazilian republic. Part two, "Man," offers a description of the

---

[5] On Schreiner's agnosticism, see Kissack and Titlestad 2006.
[6] Schreiner 1975, 62. The discussion about whether or not Schreiner held racist views is an old one. My take on the issue is that Schreiner's position evolved and became increasingly anti-racist, with the Anglo-Boer war as a decisive moment which radicalized her. *Farm*, her precocious first work, does not question the racist ordering of colonial society as such, but neither does it condone it.

backlands population, freezing in characteristic ethnographic fashion "the" *sertanejo* in the present tense, as though the habits described were endlessly repeated and never developed or adapted.[7] It is also here that Da Cunha explicitly racializes and temporalizes the *sertanejo*, in Spencerian evolutionist fashion, as being "three whole centuries" behind the modern, European civilization of coastal Brazil. (Da Cunha 1994, 231) Part two, however, also closes in on the settlement of Canudos and its leader, Antônio Conselheiro. Here Da Cunha switches from the role of ethnographer to historian by providing a reconstructed version of Canudos as it had been before its destruction. As I will show, it is here that fictionality in a distinctly novelistic sense begins to be employed as a discursive resource.[8] Part three, "The conflict," is the longest and gives a thorough description of the four campaigns as well as the national hysteria fuelling the war. The deep temporal vistas of Part one have here been exchanged for the short time frames of distinct events – sometimes in a minute-by-minute narrative, sometimes with broad panoramic overviews, but always, it would seem, couched within the "meanwhile" that Benedict Anderson (1983) sees as definitive of the time of the nation. If *Os sertões* can be said to have a plot, which in Ricoeur's understanding is what confers meaning upon temporally isolated events (1980, 177–178), this plot is nothing less than the fractured emergence of Brazil as a nation.

The brevity of this essay limits me to presenting just two examples of how fiction and reference are intertwined in *Os sertões*. The examples provide a study in contrasts: the first relates a scene which Da Cunha could not possibly have witnessed; the second brings us as close as possible to Da Cunha's own experience.

Towards the end of Part two, after a rambling discussion of the "ethnological problem" of Brazil, of the customs of the "jagunços" (bandits) and "vaqueiros" (cowboys), of the racial composition of the "mestizos" in the backlands, of the impact of missionaries, and so on, Da Cunha focuses on the short-lived rebellious community of Canudos itself. A long section is devoted to a description of the evening prayers, which enables Da Cunha in a cinematic style *avant la lettre* to draw a collective but also individualised portrait of the rebels.

> Now and again, the bonfires dying down, barely smoldering beneath a cloud of smoke, would suddenly flare at a puff of the night breeze, lighting up the faces of the throng. At such times the closely huddled masculine group stood out, affording the same identical

---

[7] Which, following Johannes Fabian's analysis, is characteristic of an older style of ethnography (Fabian 2002, 81).
[8] Fernandes (2006) argues something similar, but ultimately maintains a much stricter and conventional division between fiction and scientific discourse.

> contrasts: rude, strong cowboys, who like fallen heroes had exchanged their fine leathern armor for an ugly canvas uniform; well-to-do cattle-breeders, happy at having abandoned their herds and stables; and, less numerous but more in evidence, the vagabonds of every description, hardened criminals of every offense. (Da Cunha 1994, 225)

This anonymous throng is then individualised, providing in effect a cast of characters for the ensuing narrative:

> There is José Venâncio, the terror of Volta Grande [...]. Alongside of him is the audacious Pajehú, with his bronzed face and high cheekbones, his athletic but slightly stooping frame. [...] Behind him is his adjutant and inseparable companion, Lalau, whose attitude is likewise a most humble one, as he kneels bent over his loaded *trabuco*. (Da Cunha 1994, 225–226)

And so the chapter continues, naming more than a dozen additional male individuals with distinct histories and physical characteristics, and enfolding this description in an evocative account of the evening prayers led by Antônio Conselheiro.

The implications of this fictional reconstruction of the Canudos community are ambiguous. At the moment of writing, Canudos is reduced to rubble and almost all of the named men have been killed. They are, therefore, at the mercy of Da Cunha's pen. Besides such a general "violence of representation" noticeable in the emphasis on criminality, for example, Da Cunha also reverts now and then to his racist and pseudo-medical vocabulary. He describes the beauty of a face in Canudos in terms of "the Jewish type"; he speaks of the "collective neurasthenia" of the religious rites. (Da Cunha 1994, 224, 229, cf. 2005, 168, 171) But this symbolic violence is countered by what we might call Da Cunha's sympathetic imagination. By presenting the reader with a fiction of Canudos, Da Cunha is reaching out beyond what his scientific discourse allowed him to know "for a fact." Along similar lines, the portrait of the community becomes an act of remembrance of what Da Cunha himself could not remember personally, and of which virtually no survivors remained. In an outright contradiction of the symbolic violence of placing the *sertanejos* in the past, as inferior and degenerate others, the fictional reconstruction of the Canudos community and the subsequent narration of the conflict place the *sertanejos* in what Ricoeur calls the "public time" of the narrative (which is clearly comparable to but not necessarily coterminous with Anderson's notion of the homogeneous time of the nation). Public time is shared time; it is the time that is produced *in* interaction – even violent interaction – and is hence a powerful refutation, within the bounds of *Os sertões* itself, of Da Cunha's social Darwinist notion of time which explicitly separates the *sertanejos* from the modern, coastal inhabitants. (cf. Ricoeur 1980, 175) This is all the more evident if we consider Da Cunha's sardonic account of how the Rio de Janeiro press fuelled a national hysteria over Canudos by promulgating what was really a fiction about the uprising. (Da Cunha 2005, 272–273) He dismisses in other words the hegemonic "public time" of Rio – which conforms to Anderson's emphasis on the press as the key expression of national, homogeneous time – in favour of the *disjunctive* public time intimated, with the help of fictional devices, by his own narrative. Much like Schreiner in her preface, Da Cunha presents his narrative as a *corrective*, not to imperial but to urban, republican flights of fancy.

This reading – lest it seem too pat – can be supplemented by looking at a contrasting section right at the end of *Os sertões*, where Da Cunha highlights the uncertain referential status of what is supposedly the least fictional part of the narrative. The reader has by now followed the detailed and exhaustive account of all four campaigns against Canudos. Right towards the end, however, comes a section called "Notes from a journal." It is prefaced like this: "Let us transcribe, without altering a single line, the concluding notes from a 'Diary' written as these events were taking place." (Da Cunha 1994, 701) To this Da Cunha himself added a footnote: "These notes, jotted down in the course of the day, in camp, and completed that night, on Mount Favella, however lacking in accuracy they may be, have the value of spontaneity, reflecting the tumult amid which they were written." (1994, 714) This is Samuel Putnam's translation; Da Cunha's original is rather more striking and concise: "Estas notas, esboçadas durante o dia no acampamento e completadas à noite, no alto da Favela, têm o valor da própria incorreção derivada do tumulto em que se traçaram." (2005, 435) Rather than "the value of spontaneity," they have here "the value of the very lack of accuracy."

What follows after these preliminary remarks is, among other things, a moving account of how the surviving women and children of Canudos are led as prisoners into the camp. The moment when the soldiers are confronted with their defeated enemy and "the longed-for victory suddenly lost its appeal," mirrors the earlier fictional account of Canudos and its inhabitants and ties the entire war narrative together. Retrospectively, one might say that Da Cunha's witnessing of the prisoners is what enabled and necessitated his fictional response (written *after* the diary) to these "others" as something more than prisoners. By doing so, rather than restricting himself to documentary evidence, Da Cunha allows *Os sertões* to disrupt the temporal regime of social Darwinism and include the time of the others (the *sertanejos*) in the shared public time of Brazil.

One may add to this observation that nothing clearly distinguishes the style of the five pages of diary notes from the rest of the narration in this section of *Os sertões*. All that we have to guide us is Da Cunha's own signposting that the notes are different, and that they are different in two contradictory respects: they are closer in time to the related events, and hence more authentic; yet being closer in time, they are less accurate, marked by the confusion of the moment. This confusion is in no way evident as we read the actual notes, but the self-reflexivity of Da Cunha's remark is significant. If the diary allows us to come as close in time as possible to the moment when he witnessed these events, he likewise makes no particular claim for the superior referential value of witnessing. The event of witnessing is only ever piecemeal and momentary. The diary, being both authentic and inaccurate, is thereby – paradoxically – quite close in kind to Gallagher's understanding of fiction as separate from fact but not deceptive. Just as paradoxically, the rest of Da Cunha's war narrative, having been revised and presented as factually correct – but with the help of fictional devices – would then be closer to deception and further from fiction in Gallagher's sense. A rift opens here, it would seem, between Da Cunha's explicit claims and his textual practice.

It is not my intention here to resolve this instability but rather to highlight it as a central and meaning-making quality of *Os sertões* – different yet comparable to the generic instability pervading Schreiner's novel. We find here an example of Caraher's developmental logic of genre which I referred to at the outset, according to which social crises prompt the refocusing of meaning in generic forms. It is also related to Franco Moretti's notion of the "formal compromise" typical of the global emergence of the novel, but it does not confirm his tripartite division of the compromise into "foreign plot," "local characters" and "local narrative voice." (Moretti 2000, 65) The compromise that I have investigated has more to do with the negotiation between the fictional register as a discursive resource and the conflictual experience of colonial time.

The references to Caraher and Moretti should not be taken to imply that Da Cunha's and Schreiner's works are "incomplete" or "imperfect" in comparison with some supposedly consummate European model, which would be to misunderstand my point entirely. It is rather that the shifting relationship between fictional and referential registers is deeply implicated in creating meaning out of temporal experience. Such a reading bears out Ricoeur's understanding of narrative as that which does not simply repeat or reproduce the experience of time but which actively creates, through repetition and the unity of plot, its meaning. I part ways with Ricoeur, however, when it comes to his repeated emphasis on the conciliatory capacity of narrative. This is not supported by the empirical record. In Schreiner's and Da Cunha's writing, it is rather the fissures, gaps and contradictions in their deployment of fiction –

that is, the way in which they fall short of producing a single coherent meaning – that speak to their historical moment of emergence.

Bibliography

Anderson, Benedict. *Imagined Communities: Reflections on the Origin and Spread of Nationalism*. London: Verso, 1983.
Andrade, Olímpio de Souza. *História e interpretação de* Os sertões. Rio de Janeiro: Academia Brasileira de Letras, [1960] 2002.
Boehmer, Elleke. *Colonial and Postcolonial Literature*. 2nd ed. Oxford: Oxford University Press: 2005.
Caraher, Brian G. "Genre Theory: Cultural and Historical Motives Engendering Literary Genre." *Genre Matters: Essays in Theory and Criticism*. Eds. Garin Dowd et al. Bristol: Intellect, 2006. 29–39.
Chrisman, Laura. *Rereading the Imperial Romance: British Imperialism and South African Resistance in Haggard, Schreiner, and Plaatje*. Oxford: Clarendon, 2000.
Da Cunha, Euclides. *Os sertões*. Rio de Janeiro: Lacerda, [1902] 2005.
– *Rebellion in the Backlands*. Trans. Samuel Putnam. London: Picador, [1944] 1994.
Fabian, Johannes. *Time and the Other*. New York: Columbia University Press, [1983] 2002.
Fernandes, Raúl C. Gouveia. "Comentários sobre a 'moldura' de Os sertões." *Luso-Brazilian Review* 43.2 (2006): 45–62.
Gallagher, Catherine. "The Rise of Fictionality." *The Novel*. Vol. 1. Ed. Franco Moretti. Princeton, NJ: Princeton University Press, 2006. 336–363.
Kissack, Mike and Michael Titlestad. "Olive Schreiner and the Secularization of Moral Imagination." *English in Africa* 33.1 (2006): 23–46.
Maia, João Marcelo Ehlert. *A terra como invenção: o espaço no pensamento social brasileiro*. Rio de Janeiro: Jorge Zahar, 2008.
Moretti, Franco. "Conjectures on World Literature." *New Left Review* 1 (2000): 54–68.
Pratt, Mary-Louise. *Imperial Eyes: Travel Writing and Transculturation*. London: Routledge, 1992.
Ricoeur, Paul. "Narrative Time." *Critical Inquiry* 7.1 (1980): 169–190
Schreiner, Olive. Letter to Havelock Ellis, 28 March 1884. http://www.oliveschreiner.org/vre?view=collections&colid=18&letterid=3. (24 February 2013).
– *The Story of an African Farm*. Johannesburg: Ad Donker, [1883] 1975.

Stephan Larsen
Whose Magic? Whose Realism? Reflections on Magical Realism in Ben Okri's *The Famished Road*

In her very useful and informative survey, *Magic(al) Realism*, Maggie Ann Bowers has, among other things, the following to say about Ben Okri's famous novel, *The Famished Road*:

> West African magical realism often incorporates local influences to produce a cross-cultural literature that emulates the situation of many West Africans today. As the critic Brenda Cooper notes: "African writers very often adhere to this animism, incorporate spirits, ancestors and talking animals, in stories, both adapted folktales and newly invented yarns, in order to express their passions, their aesthetics and their politics" (1998: 40). She claims that these stories are still prevalent due to the superficial influence on the local culture of colonialism in West Africa (Cooper 1998: 40). Because of this, although Okri is a British Nigerian who has lived in London for most of his life, his novel *The Famished Road* ([1991] 1992) is told predominantly from a West African perspective. The novel follows the struggles of an *abiku* child (a child attached both to the spirit world and the living world, who is born again only to die and return again) and the child's attempt to negotiate between the two forces from the living and the dead that seek to dominate him. The traditional West African mythological content and narrative perspective of the narrative lead some critics to question whether this is indeed a magical realist novel. The question of whether the mythological aspect is considered to be real or magical depends strongly on the cultural perspective of the reader. If the reader lives within a cultural context where magical happenings of the type portrayed in the novel are considered to be a possible aspect of reality and not magical at all, then the reader may not recognize the magical realist element of the narrative. (Bowers 2004, 56–57)

That type of statement seems to me to give rise to several questions, for instance:

1. Is not the notion that supernatural events are not considered magical by people living in cultures where there are no clear borders between the natural and the supernatural at the very root of magical realism? Why should African magical realism be different from, say, Latin American or Indian magical realism in this respect?
2. Are not the reactions of the characters in the story, and/or the attitude of the narrator, to supernatural events of greater importance when it comes to deciding whether or not a text is representative of the magical realist mode than the supposed reactions of a supposed reader?
3. What reasons have we to assume that the novel is chiefly, or exclusively, intended for West African readers only superficially influenced by colonialism? And even if this were the case – does it really matter?

However, perhaps the first question we should ask ourselves is: What arguments can be presented in favour of regarding *The Famished Road* as a magical realist text, and how convincing are these arguments when compared to the arguments against this classification?

In this context, it would be of great use to us to have a generally accepted definition of the term "magical realism" by which to measure the novel. Unfortunately, such a definition is nearly impossible to find, as "magical realism" is one of the most hotly debated terms in the world of literary studies, and notoriously difficult to define. I choose the definition suggested by Wendy B. Faris in her essay "Scheherazade's Children: Magical Realism and Postmodern Fiction" as my point of departure, not because no objections could be raised against it, but because it seems to me more detailed and more analytic than most of the possible alternatives. (Cf. Hart 1989, 27–28, Coppola 1998 and Alstrum 1999)

Faris divides her definition into five "primary characteristics" and nine "secondary or accessory specifications." (Faris 1995, 167 and 175) The first of the five primary characteristics is: "The text contains an 'irreducible element' of magic, something we cannot explain according to the laws of the universe as we know them." (167) That this criterion fits *The Famished Road* is clear from the very first page of the novel, where we can read:

> In the beginning there was a river. The river became a road and the road branched out to the whole world. And because the road was once a river it was always hungry.
>
> In that land of beginnings spirits mingled with the unborn. We could assume numerous forms. Many of us were birds. We knew no boundaries. There was much feasting, playing, and sorrowing. We feasted much because of the beautiful terrors of eternity. We played much because we were free. And we sorrowed much because there were always those amongst us who had just returned from the world of the Living. They had returned inconsolable for all the love they had left behind, all the suffering they hadn't redeemed, all that they hadn't understood, and for all that they had barely begun to learn before they were drawn back to the land of origins.
>
> There was not one amongst us who looked forward to being born. We disliked the rigours of existence, the unfulfilled longings, the enshrined injustices of the world, the labyrinths of love, the ignorance of parents, the fact of dying, and the amazing indifference of the Living in the midst of the simple beauties of the universe. We feared the heartlessness of human beings, all of whom were born blind, few of whom ever learn to see. (Okri 1991, 3)

Here, it appears as a matter of course that the world of the spirits exists, and interacts regularly with the world of the living. It is also self-evident that a river can turn into a road, and that both the river and the road are living, sentient beings, capable, for instance, of experiencing hunger. None of this can be either explained or denied.

The second characteristic is: "Descriptions detail a strong presence of the phenomenal world [...]." (Faris 1995, 169) This criterion, too, fits *The Famished Road* very well, as the novel is replete with descriptions of the everyday life of simple people, its smells, tastes and sounds. The following paragraphs from the tenth chapter may serve as an example:

> When the meat was cooking, on another fire, a great pan was sizzling with oil. The whole compound smelt of aromatic stew, peppers, onions, wild earthy herbs, and frying bushmeat. When everyone could be seen salivating in anticipation, Mum made me go and bathe. I wore a new set of clothes. Visitors and compound-dwellers came one by one to our room. They took their seats. Mum combed my hair and gave me a parting. Dad also had a parting. Mum bathed. In the bathroom she dressed up in her fine clothes. She did her hair and made up her face in the passage.
>
> Soon our little room was crowded with all kinds of people. Many of them were from our compound, one or two of them were from our previous habitation, a few of them were total strangers, and a lot of them were children. It was hot in the room and everyone sweated. All the chairs were filled and all the floor space taken. A woman struck up a song. A man struck up a more vigorous song. The children looked on. Mum came in with a plate of alligator pepper seeds, a saucer of cigarettes, and breadfruit. (Okri 1991, 41)

Faris' third characteristic seems more problematic. It reads: "The reader may hesitate (at one point or another) between two contradictory understandings of events – and hence experiences some unsettling doubts." (Faris 1995, 171) This criterion seems to be based on Tzvetan Todorov's division of the fantastic into two sub-categories in the third chapter of his study *The Fantastic*. Todorov says:

> The fantastic, we have seen, lasts only as long as a certain hesitation: a hesitation common to reader and character, who must decide whether or not what they perceive derives from "reality" as it exists in the common opinion. At the story's end, the reader makes a decision even if the character does not; he opts for one solution or the other, and thereby emerges from the fantastic. If he decides that the laws of reality remain intact and permit an explanation of the phenomena described, we may say that the work belongs to another genre: the uncanny. If, on the contrary, he decides that new laws of nature must be entertained to account for the phenomena, we enter the genre of the marvelous. (Todorov 1973, 41)

There are several reasons to question whether this criterion really belongs in a definition of magical realism at all. Firstly, it appears to invalidate the first characteristic as regards the irreducibility of the magical. Secondly, it seems to call for a great deal of speculation and guess-work, or an extensive survey of reader responses, the result of which would probably be open to different interpretations anyway. Faris admits that "some readers in some cultures will hesitate less than others." (Faris 1995, 171) How, then, can we solve that problem? What type of readers should be given the prerogative to decide what is what – those who hesitate or those who do not? And on what grounds should such a prerogative be based? The question returns: shouldn't the decision whether or not a text should be regarded as magical realist be based on the attitude of the characters and/or the narrator to supernatural events? In other words, shouldn't the solution to the problem be sought inside rather than outside the text under discussion? In a note, Faris makes it clear that she is aware that these and similar questions may arise, but nevertheless insists that "we readers' investment in the codes of realism is still so strong that even the narrator's acceptance does not overcome it." (Faris 1995, 188) But who are "we readers"? Do possible readers of texts written in English really constitute a category so homogeneous that such a generalisation can be defended? And isn't "the willing suspension of disbelief" the most fundamental difference between reading fiction – *any* kind of fiction – and texts that lay claims to describing actual reality? Shouldn't we, when reading fiction, let ourselves be guided by "poetic faith," so that, as long as we are reading, we regard as true whatever the text describes as true, irrespective of whether we are dealing with telepathy and levitation in some magical realist novel or unlikely coincidences in a novel by Balzac or Dickens? In *The Famished Road*, the supernatural elements are described neither as figments of the imagination nor as hallucinations – what our protagonist/narrator sees actually does exist, even though nobody else may be able to see it.

Faris' fourth characteristic is: "We experience the closeness or near-merging of two realms, two worlds." (Faris 1995, 172) That this criterion fits *The Famished Road* is easy to verify, as exemplified by the following quote from the third chapter:

> I watched crowds of people pour into the marketplace. I watched the chaotic movements and the wild exchanges and the load-carriers staggering under sacks. It seemed as if the whole world was there. I saw people of all shapes and sizes, mountainous women with faces of iroko, midgets with faces of stone, reedy women with twins strapped to their backs, thick-set men with bulging shoulder muscles. After a while I felt a sort of vertigo just looking at anything that moved. Stray dogs, chickens flapping in cages, goats with listless eyes, hurt me to look at them. I shut my eyes and when I opened them again I saw people who walked backwards, a dwarf who got about on two fingers, men upside-down with baskets of fish on their feet, women who had breasts on their backs, babies strapped to their chests, and beautiful children with three arms. I saw a girl amongst them who had eyes at the side of her face, bangles of blue copper round her neck, and who was more lovely than forest flowers. (Okri 1991, 15)

Here we can see that the distance between the world of the living and that of the spirits is literally just the wink of an eye, and they are both real, both described in great detail. The notion that the whole thing could be dismissed as a dream or a hallucination is contradicted by the fact that the spirits seem to be able to see Azaro as clearly as he sees them. One of them points at him and exclaims: "'That boy can see us!'" (Okri 1991, 15)

The fifth characteristic is: "These fictions question received ideas about time, space, and identity." (Faris 1995, 173) This criterion, too, fits *The Famished Road* very well, as observed by several critics, for instance by Christopher Warnes in his study *Magical Realism and the Postcolonial Novel*, particularly the chapter entitled "The African World View in Ben Okri's *The Famished Road*." As regards space and time, Warnes says:

> There is an abundance of examples of spaces like the road, the bar, the forest and the marketplace being represented in a natural fashion within the code of the real and then "supernaturalised" by that of the fantastic. Although this strategy is not as clear with regard to the representation of the passing of time in the novel, it is still possible to isolate the poles on the reality-esoteric axis on which this representation takes place. For example, when Azaro, in a rare moment of standing back from experience in order to analyse it, notices how the landscape around him is changing, he formulates the change in terms of conventional units of time: "Steadily, over days and months, the paths had been widening" (104). At the other end of the reality-esoteric axis we encounter the fracturing of this conception of time: "as I kept watch I perceived, in the crack of a moment, the recurrence of things unresolved – histories, dreams, a vanished world of great old spirits, wild jungles, tigers with eyes of diamonds roaming the dense foliage" (176). As the moment "cracks", it reveals a deeper level of temporal meaning which had been concealed by the apparent unity of the concepts of "days" or "months." It appears that Okri is gesturing towards the possibilty that behind the objective facade of linear conventional time lies a mythical time of return, recurrence, cyclicality. (Warnes 2009, 137–138)

A similar duality can be observed in the delineation of character, a fact described and exemplified by Warnes in the following manner:

> [...] Azaro himself is simultaneously a young child of the ghetto and a spirit child. Dad is a worker, a family man, a resident of the compound and is simultaneously "Black Tyger" a fighting hero of mythical status who defeats ghosts and can make lightning flash from his fist (301). [...] Madame Koto, like Dad, is also the bearer of a double load of signification. On the one hand, her successful entrepreneurship suggests in microcosm the roles played by capital in the modernising postcolonial state. On the other hand, she is constantly identified with witchcraft, either through her actions or by the attitudes she evokes in others. (Warnes 2009, 137)

In none of these cases is one half of the dual identity presented as more real, or more true, than the other.

The purpose of the nine "secondary or accessory specifications" on Faris' list is, according to what she herself says, "less to distinguish magical realism from the rest of contemporary literature than to situate it within postmodernism" (1995, 175), and perhaps one should bear this in mind when discussing them. However, these criteria, too, seem relevant, as magical realism is not infrequently described as a branch of postmodernism. (Cf. D'haen 1995, 191–208)

The first criterion is: "Metafictional dimensions are common in contemporary magical realism: the texts provide commentaries on themselves [...]." (Faris 1995, 175) Of this, we see nothing in *The Famished Road*. However, the text does remind us of its literariness in another way, namely by means of elements of intertextuality, of dialogue with other texts. Even the title of the novel is an echo from a well-known poem by Wole Soyinka, "Death in the Dawn," where we find the following lines:

> The right foot for joy, the left, dread
> And the mother prayed, Child
> May you never walk
> When the road waits, famished.
> (Soyinka 1967, 10–11)

Robert Fraser has commented on the relevance of these lines to Okri's novel in the following way:

> Here you have the elements of a situation: a mother, a child, the road with its hunger, the lurking danger of death. In the first volume of "The Famished Road" sequence, Azaro, the boy narrator and protagonist, helps his mother to avoid the swerving peril of a truck (*FR* 9). After getting lost during a riot, he finds himself in the house with seven spectral policemen. His mother finds him, and bears him home in triumph. Later, she chafes her foot against a cooking pot. She sits down murmuring "The right foot is supposed to be lucky" (*FR* 78). Soyinka's grand premonition has turned into an informal, private moment. (Fraser 2002, 67)

It should also be pointed out that the name of the protagonist, Azaro, is a slightly distorted form of Lazarus, the name of the man who is raised from the dead by Christ in John, 11:43.

When Azaro's Dad decides to become a boxer, fighting strenuous battles with opponents both from the world of the living and from that of the spirits, he assumes the name "Black Tyger." The spelling of the word "Tyger" inevitably brings to mind William Blake's poem "The Tyger," from the collection *Songs of Experience*. Like "the Tyger," Dad, in his role as the champion of the poor against all kinds of evil, is both frightening and impressive, and his natural habitat certainly seems to be "the forests of the night." (Erdman 1988, 24) As Robert Fraser has pointed out, Blake's song is "an expression of awe at some elemental source of energy. It also, however, refers to a particular event: the

September massacres of 1792 during the French Revolution when the revolutionary mob in Paris left a decisive mark on the mind of Europe. Okri's novel is set at a time of similar political disruption in the development of Africa. Black Tyger stands at the vortex. He is history in the making." (Fraser 2002, 74)

The second criterion is: "The reader may experience a particular kind of verbal magic – a closing of the gap between words and the world, or a demonstration of what we might call the linguistic nature of experience." By way of clarification, Faris goes on to say: "this magic happens when a metaphor is made real," for instance, when "in *Midnight's Children*, we hear that Saleem is 'handcuffed to history' and then witness the invasion of his head by the voices of his compatriots." (Faris 1995, 176) In a manner of speaking, Azaro, too, is handcuffed to history, but he never explicitly says so, and I find it hard to detect any petrified metaphors being brought back to life in *The Famished Road*.

The third criterion is: "The narrative appears to the late-twentieth-century adult readers to which it is addressed as fresh, childlike, even primitive. Wonders are recounted largely without comment, in a matter-of-fact way, accepted – presumably – as a child would accept them, without undue questioning or reflection: they thus achieve a kind of defamiliarization that appears to be natural and artless." (Faris 1995, 177) I take exception to the word "primitive," but otherwise, this description could very well serve as a summing-up of the narrative in *The Famished Road*, where the narrator, as we know, actually is a child. The fact that Azaro is also a centuries-old spirit hardly seems to matter in this context as neither Azaro the child nor Azaro the spirit appears to feel the need to explain or comment on the supernatural, but simply accepts it as an aspect of everyday existence.

The fourth criterion is: "Repetition as a narrative principle, in conjunction with mirrors or their analogues used symbolically or structurally, creates a magic of shifting references." (Faris 1995, 177) *The Famished Road* is replete with repetitions, leitmotifs and symmetries, and its basic structure may definitely be described as circular rather than linear. Where the mirror effects are concerned, much hinges on to what extent we want to take the word "mirror" at face value. Faris seems to be prepared to accept a metaphorical interpretation, as evidenced by her example: "Saleem's life in *Midnight's Children* mirrors that of the new Indian nation with which he was born." (Faris 1995, 177) Something similar could be said concerning Azaro's relationship to the recently independent African nation into which he is born – what Saleem and Azaro have in common is the paradoxical combination of carrying great hopes for the future and at the same time being marked for death. This is how Azaro sums up his Dad's insights in the final chapter of *The Famished Road*:

> In his journeys Dad found that all nations are children; it shocked him that ours too was an abiku nation, a spirit-child nation, one that keeps being reborn and after each birth

come blood and betrayals, and the child of our will refuses to stay till we have made propitious sacrifice and displayed our serious intent to bear the weight of a unique destiny. (Okri 1991, 494)

The fifth criterion is: "Metamorphoses are a relatively common event [...]." (Faris 1995, 178) When he is born into the world of the living, Azaro metamorphosizes from spirit into human. Azaro's Dad metamorphosizes from night soil man into a boxer of mythical stature, with the purpose of providing a better life for his family, perhaps even for the entire nation. As a result of his fights with all kinds of spirits, he also undergoes a rebirth of consciousness, which may be seen as another kind of metamorphosis. Perhaps Okri wants to show that in order to change the world one has to be reborn in one sense or another, able to view life through "new" eyes. In spite of the fact that Dad almost has to sacrifice his life in his fight against evil, his metamorphosis into a boxer is described as essentially a good thing. Madame Koto, the bar owner, undergoes a considerably more frightening metamorphosis. At the beginning of the story, she is depicted as the kind of woman who is glad to help her less fortunate neighbours in their hour of need, but after she comes into contact with greedy and power-seeking politicians, she quickly becomes as bad as they, and worse, turning her back on the poor. If Dad is turned into a champion of the good, both in the world of the living and that of the spirits, Madame Koto is turned into what can best be described as a witch. Dad fights evil spirits, Madame Koto draws them to her, filling her bar with them. Her metamorphosis is so thorough-going that Azaro makes the following observation: "She had changed completely from the person I used to know. Her big frame which had seemed to me full of warmth now seemed to me full of wickedness. I didn't know why she had changed." (Okri 1991, 251)

The sixth criterion is: "Many of these texts take a position that is antibureaucratic, and so they often use their magic against the established social order." (Faris 1995, 179) There is no explicit antibureaucratic tendency to be found in *The Famished Road*, nor, for that matter, in very many other magical realist novels. However, it is true that magical realist texts often question the established social order, and stand up for those in the most exposed social positions against those who possess, and abuse, political power. According to Carlo Coppola, "[p]ostmodern critics often emphasize that this type of writing has flourished at times of considerable political turmoil, unrest, and stress." (Coppola 1998, 797) That is exactly what the political situation in *The Famished Road* looks like – there really is no established social order of any kind, but only a chaos of violence, fraud, and corruption, where most politicians don't seem to be interested in anything but seizing and keeping power for its own sake, and for those material benefits that go with power. The political battle is fought between The Party of the Rich, which Madame Koto joins, and The Party for the Poor, which Azaro's Dad joins, soon becoming its foremost champion. The names of the parties may seem obvious enough, but to describe The Party of the Rich as evil and The Party for the Poor as good is to misrepresent the political message of the novel. Okri's attitude is far more disillusioned. On a closer scrutiny of how the two parties and their activities are depicted, the difference between them seems well-nigh negligible, as can be seen from the following excerpt:

> The air was full of noises. The politicians' vans rode up and down, blaring their party music, making their interminable announcements and promises. It became quite confusing to hear both parties virtually promise the same things. The Party of the Rich talked of prosperity for all, good roads, electricity, and free education. They called the opposition thieves, tribalists, and bandits. At their rally, they said, everyone would be fed, all questions would be answered.
>
> That evening the van of the Party for the Poor also paraded our street. They too blared music and made identical claims. They distributed leaflets and made their promises in four languages. When the two vans, each packed with armed bodyguards, passed one another, they competed with the amount of noise they could generate. They insulted one another in their contest of loudspeakers; and the heated blare of their music clashing created such a jangle in the air that the road crowded with spectators who expected a tremendous combustion. The two vans clashed twice that evening. We kept expecting some sort of war to break out, but both parties seemed restrained by the healthy respect they had developed for one another. The truth was that the time hadn't yet arrived. (Okri 1991, 390)

It is easy to agree with Brenda Cooper's interpretation of the political, and moral, message of the novel:

> How does the novel explain this rash of greed, cruelty and corruption, disfiguring the country which, like the *abiku* babies, is still in the womb, only about to be born? The image embodies the answer. When the spirits of old inhabit the politicians of new, and become indistinguishable from them, the political disintegrates under the burden of the grotesque, imprisoned within the cage of the universal human cycle of greed, the monster who endures under the road, the wicked *abiku*, who imprisons its mother in a cycle of despair. (Cooper 1998, 90)

This explains why Madame Koto, who starts out as human being, even a good and decent human being, turns into a grotesque monster of greed, lust and selfishness after giving in to the temptations of politics. It also seems to provide a political dimension for Azaro's persistent efforts to break the vicious circle of *abiku*-hood.

The seventh criterion is: "In magical realist narrative, ancient systems of belief and local lore often underlie the text." (Faris 1995, 182) That this is true of *The Famished Road* seems so obvious that no further comments are called for.

The eighth criterion might pose more of a problem. It reads: "[...] a Jungian rather than a Freudian perspective is common in magical realist texts; that is, the magic may be attributed to a mysterious sense of collective relatedness rather than individual memories or dreams or visions." (Faris 1995, 183) At first glance, this seems rather self-evident – if supernatural elements in a novel can be explained away as dreams, figments of the imagination, or the hallucinations of some mentally disturbed character, it seems reasonable to assume that the novel in question is within the scope of conventional realism. It seems equally reasonable to stipulate that a novel should be regarded as magical realist only on condition that all – or at least the majority – of its characters, and the narrator, agree that the supernatural really does exist and plays an important part in the everyday life of people. However, problems may arise if the "mysterious sense of collective relatedness" is assumed to include not only the fictive characters but the reader as well – *any* reader from *any* culture. Renato Oliva's essay "Re-Dreaming the World. Ben Okri's Shamanic Realism" may be regarded as an example of the dangers pertaining to this type of Jungian reading. This essay constitutes an attempt to read *The Famished Road* and its sequel, *Songs of Enchantment*, "solely," to quote Christopher Warnes, "as performances of Yeatsian and Jungian ideas, erasing entirely all traces of Yoruba culture, Tutuola and Soyinka." (Warnes 2009, 129) Even in the first few pages of his essay, Oliva expresses himself in a manner that could, at worst, be construed as neo-colonialist:

> While magical realism certainly affords Caliban the opportunity to "write back" and reject some of the cultural paradigms of his colonial heritage, it is no less true that Caliban is our Shadow, and that magical realism is founded in our unconscious. Archaic man, with his primitive mentality and tendency to magical thinking, survives in each of us. (Oliva 1999, 172)

Oliva goes on to say:

> A dream never expresses itself in a logical or abstract way, but, rather, in figurative language that is a survival of an archaic mode of thought. The imaginal form of communication is primary and comparable to that of the child, of primitive cultures, and of the poet. (Oliva 1999, 173–174)

Warnes dismisses these formulations as dangerously close to the language of Victorian anthropology, and continues:

> Though Oliva is influenced by the ideas of analytical psychology rather than social evolutionism, when he reads Okri's magical realism as comparable to the language of "the

> child, of primitive cultures and of the poet," he does so in order to extract from it truths about the human condition that have become obscured for Westerners. In Oliva's hands, Okri's text becomes a vehicle for journeying into the unconscious, the pre-logical, the archaic. Like the armchair anthropologist who found everywhere he looked the evidence for his particular informing assumptions, Oliva extracts from Okri those parts of the narrative that concur with particular configurations of thought he wants to emphasise and then, like Jung or Yeats, asserts these to be universally valid observations about history or the human psyche. (Warnes 2009, 130–131)

Warnes criticism can be summarised thus: "Oliva's is a magical realism that has been sundered from its historical roots in order that it can be utilised in the excavation of the collective unconscious." (130)

Oliva is, of course, quite right in saying that magical realism is not "the exclusive prerogative of certain cultures" (1999, 172) – after all, the mode does occur in texts from all parts of the world. This, however, does not mean that we are free to disregard the fact that each and every magical realist text emanates from its own particular conditions, historically, politically, and culturally. The problem with Oliva's line of reasoning is not only that it can be considered eurocentric but that it takes the realism out of magical realism, which certainly does not consist of dreams alone.

The ninth and final criterion is: "A carnivalesque spirit is common in this group of novels." (Faris 1995, 184) "Carnivalesque" is a very complex concept, and its connection(s) to magical realism could, and probably should, be made the subject of a study of its own. (Cf. Cooper 1998, 24–28) Faris defines the carnivalesque in magical realism as the "use of magical details, especially, details which are often not allegorically significant or clearly referential at first glance (even if they become so on reflection)" and "a generally extravagant, carnivalesque style." (Faris 1995, 184–185) If we use this definition as our point of departure, we need not hesitate to regard *The Famished Road* as permeated by a "carnivalesque spirit."

*

To sum up: if we make use of Faris' definition of magical realism in discussing *The Famished Road*, we find that four of her five "primary characteristics" and (at least) six of her nine "secondary and accessory specifications" are applicable to Okri's novel, which seems to enable us to make a strong case for regarding it as belonging to this mode.

Where the questions "whose magic?" and "whose realism?" are concerned, I would like to make the following suggestions:
1. In *The Famished Road*, both the protagonist/narrator and all the other characters obviously regard the supernatural as an integral part of every-

day existence, which means that to them, malevolent spirits are as real as, for instance, corrupt politicians.
2. As long as the reading goes on, the reader, irrespective of his/her personal opinions on the subject, should regard the magical elements of the story as real, thus accepting the point of view of the characters and the narrator.
3. However, unlike the characters and the narrator, the reader, irrespective of what culture he/she belongs to, may choose to regard the story as an allegory. To himself – as well as to Mum, Dad, Madame Koto and others – Azaro is an *abiku*, a spirit-child doomed to be reborn over and over again. To the reader, however, he may also function as a symbol or metaphor, "a literal expression of a figurative truth" (Hart 1989, 27), about conditions in his country, and in several African countries during the years immediately following independence. Perhaps he may also be regarded as a metaphor for the human condition, with all that this involves of the irrepressible will to live as well as the awareness of the inevitability of death, a line of reasoning not to be confused with the Jungian interpretation discussed earlier. As Patricia Hart has it: "the apparently impossible event leads to a deeper truth that holds outside the novel." (Hart 1989, 27)
4. To some readers, the magical realism of *The Famished Road* may seem to assume "a vatic function, calling upon the reader to suspend rational-empirical judgements about the way things are in favour of an expanded order of reality." (Warnes 2009, 12) In other words, the supernatural elements are taken at face value. To some, the magical elements may be seen as seeking "to critique the claims to truth and coherence of the modern western world view by showing them up as culturally and historically contingent," which means that the supernatural elements are interpreted as metaphors, and the text as concerned with "discourse about reality rather than reality itself." (Warnes 2009, 13) To my mind, the wonderful thing about *The Famished Road* and, really, any magical realist novel, is that is succeeds in achieving both these goals at the same time, thus, hopefully, changing "the reader's prejudices about what reality is." (Hart 1989, 27)

Bibliography

Alstrum, James J. "Magic Realism." *Encyclopedia of World Literature in the 20th Century*. Ed. Steven R. Serafin. Farmington Hills, MI: St. James Press, 1999. 157.
Blake, William. *The Complete Poetry and Prose of William Blake*. Ed. David Erdman. New York: Doubleday, 1988.
Bowers, Maggie Ann. *Magic(al) Realism*. London: Routledge, 2004.

Coppola, Carlo. "Magic Realism." *Encyclopedia of the Novel*. Ed. Paul Schellinger. Chicago, IL: Fitzroy Dearborn, 1998. 795–797.
Cooper, Brenda. *Magical Realism in West African Fiction. Seeing with a Third Eye*. London: Routledge, 1998.
D'haen, Theo L. "Magic Realism and Postmodernism: Decentering Privileged Centers." *Magical Realism. Theory, History, Community*. Eds. Lois Parkinson Zamora and Wendy B. Faris. Durham, NC: Duke University Press, 1995. 191–208.
Faris, Wendy B. "Scheherazade's Children: Magical Realism and Postmodern Fiction." *Magical Realism. Theory, History, Community*. Eds. Lois Parkinson Zamora and Wendy B. Faris. Durham, NC: Duke University Press, 1995. 163–190.
Fraser, Robert. *Ben Okri: Towards the Invisible City*. Tavistock: Northcote House, 2002.
Hart, Patricia. *Narrative Magic in the Fiction of Isabel Allende*. Diss. Rutherford, NJ: Fairleigh Dickinson University Press, 1989.
Okri, Ben. *The Famished Road*. London: Cape, 1991.
Oliva, Renato. "Re-Dreaming the World. Ben Okri's Shamanic Realism." *Coterminous Worlds. Magical Realism and Contemporary Post-Colonial Literature in English*. Eds. Elsa Linguanti, Francesco Casotti and Carmen Concilio. Amsterdam: Rodopi, 1999. 171–196.
Soyinka, Wole. *Idanre and Other Poems*. London: Methuen, 1967.
Todorov, Tzvetan. *The Fantastic. A Structural Approach to a Literary Genre*. Trans. Richard Howard. A Volume in the CWRU Press Translations. Cleveland, OH: Press of Case Western Reserve University, 1973.
Warnes, Christopher. *Magical Realism and the Postcolonial Novel. Between Faith and Irreverence*. Basingstoke: Palgrave Macmillan, 2009.

Christian Kupchik
Confessions of the Hydra: Variations on the Concept of Fiction in Latin America

It was in 1492 that Christopher Columbus sailed from Palos with great expectations, for he planned to find a shortcut to the end of Asia.[1] He returned with the certainty of having attained his goal. This, however, was not the only thing he would be firmly convinced of. For in the proximities of the Dominican Republic he believed he had seen a group of those mythical mermaids – later confirmed to have been manatees – that "rose up from the seas," though he was disappointed in finding out "they were not as beautiful as those in portraits or descriptions." He also mentioned there were "cannibals that look like monsters: single eyed and with snouts, like dogs." A number of chroniclers also came up with narratives about the wonderful reality of the New World. In a version by Friar Marcus from Nice, he states that "further to the north of New Spain, tremendously rich Indians lived in the Seven Cities of Gold: houses were eleven floors high, with facades decorated with turquoise stones"... (Marco da Nizza 1926, 57) Antonio Pigafetta, from Vicenza in Italy, who chronicled the journeys of Magellan, reports that they found a place peopled by giants who wore animal skins, "with the heads and ears as large as those of a mule, the neck and body of a camel, the legs of a deer and the tail of a horse. They utter sounds like horses' neighs, as well." (Pigafetta 1998, 184)

Whenever it becomes impossible for us to comprehend or get to know the Other, our first remedy will be to exploit the mythical as an apt description of that helpless feeling, generated by a reality that is beyond what we know: something strange or unfamiliar to us. This has, from the earliest of times, led to the perception of Latin American reality as a translation into fiction, labeled as "delirious," "a wonder," or else, as magical.

Whenever we discuss fiction, our first feeling is that of being immersed in the atmosphere of mystery. This atmosphere belongs to a universe in which the flavor of words – our love for words – will rule. For words will then be free from the strong restraints of theory and concept to become fertile soil for the seeds of the symbolic or allusive. They might form a space-image that prioritizes sensitivity over knowledge, an imaginative realm that makes use of prophecies, memories or crystals, challenging established concepts of truth. This is a space for figurative language, for allegorical sense, for paraphrasing – not in order to explain, clarify or describe what we expect from this world,

---

1 All translations in the following essay are, if not otherwise stated, the author's.

but to beautify it. Borges would summarize it: a language of hurried dreams, of dreams in suspension among immortal wanderings. Condensation and displacements.

Words bring light, not to separate and give us the ability to tell the difference between false or true, but to dazzle. The connection or link between every word and its referred meaning will always bring a light that is its own, the flame of a style, not of truth (even though what is understood as subject is what we understand as "real"). In this sense, the essentials of fiction involve the appeal of that *atmosphere* created and provoked by words. The power of fiction is the power to harvest signs, to add up or hoard voices: in this world, a cloud, a color, a name, a bell, are so much more than just a cloud, a color, a name or a bell. And they are so much more because they are a part of that atmosphere, of that environment. In terms of science, the cloud, the color, the name or the bell will always refer to given meanings, to something that is or belongs to a given field of signification. However, they would never refer to an environment or an atmosphere.

This environment strives to become assembled into the intensity of a word that, in turn, will always seek to represent more than what is only actual or real, with the purpose of re-locating it in a wholly different setting. Speech, *lengua, parole*, can never operate in its narrative function if it does not question frontiers, reaching further and building its own, new horizons in a dynamic, permeable, fluctuating sense. The message of fiction is to the fullest possible extent a poetic message and – in the words of Paul Zumthor in *La lettre et la voix* – an abyss: built with signs that mark a *decalage* attracting our eyes to a slope drawn between mirrors and prolonging it into the infinite.[2] Fictions seem to be, ultimately, the work of a language that has gone on an eternal pilgrimage, the work of differed communications and polyvalences conceived as seeds.

Du côté de chez Swann by Proust (1913) tells us of that essential character of fictions, in clear words but not at odds with refinement: within the context of narrative, an hour is not an hour but a garden with a plethora of perfumes, sounds, focuses and plans, that is, environments and climates. Among other things, the climate or environment makes it possible for a miracle to suddenly break in, though not as the *factum divinum* held by St. Thomas in his *Summa contra Gentiles*. That is, not as the *virtus* or strength to overcome the power of

---

[2] "This slope is fiction. Or, better said, fiction is this state of language, that flowing mode of existence. It conjures up the word of Adam as he names creatures, though he will never complete the task for the names he gives them always lack a letter, a sound, a sure proof of identity." (Zumthor 1987, 175).

Nature. No. Proust does not think of the miracle as a remedy against lack of belief but as a phenomenon that pertains to fiction, as a place through which emotions and psychological evocations may be channeled, for instance: the phenomenon of transformation, of eclipse, the disappearance of temporal structures. *Portenta et prodigia*. The experience of that most celebrated passage of the Madeleine clearly illustrates this: the taste of the Madeleine is that point in which physical senses and memories merge. It is the point at which the physical imprint releases the memory, the place at which what is material can take our mind back in time to update it to this here and now. There is a complex time web that Proust perceives as "disappearance of time." To the narrator, the taste of the Madeleine involves nothing less than the miracle of being able to abstract oneself from the chronology and restrictions of time. That calm peace of understanding that the word "death" produces – and that anguish its meaning generates – makes no sense to him, not any more. It is under the umbrella of fiction and of playful metaphors that prodigy can emerge. *Portenta et prodigia*, we said: we stand eye to eye with an amazing, two-fold miracle, because it is both secular and firmly oriented towards certain goals. This means that it lacks innocence. The literary battle against death is Proust's battle for life and for what links life to fiction.

We all live immersed in the fluidum of language where, as in Marcel's Madeleine, fragments of truth are soaked. *Ceci n'est pas un pipe* was René Magritte's warning before the close-up image of a smoking pipe, to show that images may betray us. This idea was also exploited by Michel Foucault, in his essay on the painter (1973), to back up his theories about the weak illusion linking words to things. Nevertheless, the fact of focusing upon fictions in their own natural field – that of aesthetics – does not necessarily imply sailing along the river with no banks of truth in sight. In one of the major contemporary philosophical conceptions of this compliance to truth, the *Tractatus logico-philosophicus*, Ludwig Wittgenstein states that the world is but a picture (*Abbildung*) of reality. This proposition, which presupposes a structural similarity between the picture and what is pictured, suggests a condition not always in accordance with the nature of fiction. (Wittgenstein 1981) Fiction and truth, however, can never be represented as foes, as two armies in battle, but as the mythological hydra that can speak with many tongues, each in a different head.

The Paraguayan writer Augusto Roa Bastos, in his novel *Yo, el Supremo* (*I, the Supreme*), turns Patiño – the scribe and amanuensis of the dictator Francia – into an ideal of transparency between writing and the spoken work, between language and reality: he copies everything the Supreme says and thinks, and even copies as he speaks. The underlying attitude of the Supreme's pronouncements is, to a certain degree, the extension of his idea of writing history, based on two major principles: first, that remembering the past means you must have lost touch with it; and secondly, that "facts and events are impossible to narrate and even less so, if told by different people" ("que los hechos no son narrables, y mucho menos aún por distintas personas," Roa Bastos 1974, 189). For writing, in a sense, makes reality impossible. Writing not only makes reality inaccessible to the readers; it will also falsify it. It will stop objects in motion by artificially making them static. Writing destroys what the Supreme calls the utterable-visible: "Writing inside the language makes all object, present, absent or future, impossible." ("Escribir dentro del lenguaje hace imposible todo objeto, presente, ausente o future.") It is only the Supreme who is able to see and comprehend reality, by means of a crystal ball that is incrusted in his pen. This ball, he states, allows him to "see things outside of language" ("ver las cosas fuera del lenguaje," Roa Bastos 1974, 204).

We wander. Our wandering takes us around a desert, in turn surrounded by words of sand. A possible oasis arises against the horizon: the promise of sugar cathedrals and the photograph of what is invisible. Deceit and truth, fiction and reality. Proust's Madeleine is not what we sense in our mouth, it is not even a Madeleine. Everything original has a double dimension, that of what is imminent and that of what is past: the present has no presence. Once again: *Outopia*. Why can it not be? Because it has already been. The uterine place is this place, and even so it is a placeless place: all of us live here, and come from there, but nobody can put that experience into words. The stage our body infers is a utopia, for it was never a part of the visible world and the sensitive will find its expression in what is not seen.

What is real? How can we "name" the core of that outside world that stops talking as soon as language gives it a name? How can we recover what is hidden, when it seems forever lost? How would it be possible to restate that literature is an epiphany that makes the world appear in a new light, as the unforeseen or as the unperceived? In 1939, Jorge Luis Borges published an article in *El Hogar* [The home], a magazine for female readers. Its title might provide an answer to our questions: *Fiction feeds on fiction*. And then, starting from *The Arabian Nights*, Borges sets off to show and prove there is no such thing as original fiction: for all fiction in literature will emerge from a tradition holding pre-existing works of fiction. (Borges 2005, 433–434)

He made no mistake. Christopher Columbus took with him, among other works of reference for his voyage (such as *Naturalis Historia* by Pliny the Elder, the *Etymologies* by Isidore of Seville, *Imago Mundi* by Pierre d'Ailly, or *Il Milione* by Marco Polo), the chronicles written by Sir John of Mandeville, a deceiver, the traveler who never traveled but who said he had reached the mythical kingdom of Prester John, and that he could not get to know Heaven because he did not have enough time. His work, conceived in 1360 and in a style that three centuries later was praised by Dr. Samuel Johnson, fed on the chronicles of clergymen who had traveled to the lost heart of Asia (Guillaume de Roubruck, Giovanni del Pian Cardine, Odorico da Pordenone), and on Greek and Latin mythology. As a matter of fact, that was the source of many descriptions of the New World, setting out to name a space where reality rules only through wonder. In this intertextual space, nothing is what it seems to be: fictions do have ways of access to the cognitive language of truth and – by reciprocity – trustworthy language might well recognize its sources in fictional discourse.

I would like to take us back here to an episode in the novel *Respiración artificial* [Artificial respiration] by the Argentinian writer Ricardo Piglia, operating in this sense. Piglia had already published, among other writings, *Nombre falso* [False name], an excellent collection of stories. He released *Respiración artificial* in 1980, at a time when Argentina's cultural stage was obscure due to the dictatorship that had seized power with much bloodshed in 1976. This work was a main event in Argentinian literary production, for it clearly drew a line and whatever was written or read after it never remained the same as before. On the other hand, the contents, by means of an innovative style conjugating the form of a crime or police story with the tradition of philosophical novels, or of novels based on ideas, focus on a highly lucid analysis of the political, social and cultural history of Argentina, through a time-span of one hundred years.

Apart from these and other evident achievements of this novel, the episode I want to mention now is based on a *uchronia*, of time outside of time, a resource the author skillfully introduces by merging actual and fictitious facts in a single unit, without clearly defining where one or the other begins and ends. In brief, there is a character, Tardewski, who tells the main character of the story in a very small town in inland Argentina that he has found a very good critical work on *Mein Kampf*, written by an anti-fascist historian, Joachim Kluge. This work enables him to learn about what Adolf Hitler did between 1905 and 1910, that is, between the ages of 18 and 23. At that time, referring to Kluge, Tardewski says, Hitler wanted to become an artist, more specifically, a painter. He would go to the bars and bohemian quarters of Vienna at the turn of the century, though he found no sympathy for his ambitions. It seems he was a very bad painter. Or, in Piglia's words: "Worse than very bad, he was *kitsch*" ("Peor que pésimo: era kitsch," Piglia 1994, 195). However, that is not what actually matters here. What does matter and was recorded is that Hitler mysteriously disappeared from public view between October 1909 and

August 1910. And this was because he was a deserter who would not comply with his duty to do mandatory military service. This comes as a surprise to the reader, and might even be regarded as a parody. Apparently, Hitler spent that time as a refugee in Prague, where he continued to live in the bohemian style of a low-quality, poor painter. He habitually visited the *Arcos* coffee shop on Meiselgasse Street, a meeting point for German-speaking intellectuals, frequented by Franz Kafka in those days. Tardewski quotes a letter to Max Brod, written in January 1910, in which Kafka states: "I feel happy because at long last I am learning something, so this week I will continue to hold my position at the table in Arcos, the coffee shop." ("Estoy contento porque por fin aprendo algo, de modo que esta semana seguiré conservando mi puesto en la mesa del Arcos," Piglia 1994, 199).

Tardewski finds, presumably, two more letters in which Kafka talks about an Austrian exile also in the habit of frequenting the *Arcos*. In the first letter, dated November 24, 1909, addressed to his friend Rainer Jauss, the writer tells about a strange guy who calls himself a painter and who has fled from Vienna, though the reasons for his exile have not been made clear. "His name is Adolf," Kafka writes, according to Tardewski, and again, according to Piglia, "he speaks German with a strange accent, though stranger still are the stories he tells us. They are strange, at least, coming from someone who calls himself a painter, because painters are usually mute." ("Se llama Adolf y su alemán tiene un acento extraño, aunque no más extrañas son las historias que cuenta. Extrañas al menos para alguien que se dice pintor, porque los pintores son mudos," Piglia 1994, 200).

The other letter, written to Max Brod about a manuscript on which the Czech author is working, says, "Yesterday, while talking about the manuscript, I was still under the effects of my conversation with Adolf, someone I did not mention to you at that time. He had said a number of things I was pondering, and it is very possible that as I was thinking of them, I may have made some clumsy mistake, uttered some phrases that, confidentially speaking, would be strange." ("Ayer al discutir el manuscrito yo me encontraba todavía bajo los efectos de mi conversación con Adolf, de quien en ese momento no te hablé. Él había dicho ciertas cosas y yo pensaba en ellas y es muy posible que debido al recuerdo de esas palabras se haya deslizado alguna torpeza, alguna sucesión que sólo en secreto sea extraña," Piglia 1994, 201).

Interestingly, Piglia worked out a theory applied to the crime or police literary genre, a theory he named *paranoid fiction*:[3] "Everyone's a suspect,

---

[3] "Paranoid fiction" was a subject at a seminar held at the University of Buenos Aires and later published as an article, under the same heading, in the Buenos Aires newspaper *Clarín* 5 October 1991.

everyone feels chased. The criminal is no longer an isolated individual but a band, with total power. Nobody understands what is going on. Clues and witnesses are contradictory, and suspicions float in the air as if they might change according to the interpreter." (Piglia 1991) Now, this fiction develops into such an obsession – the author's, the narrator's, but also the reader's – that it ends up materializing as real.

This case has a real Kafka, a real Hitler, and a real Arcos. Of course, the meeting was not held in *the real*, though Piglia perfectly describes the Kafkaesque perturbation of totalitarianism and the anguish this possibility causes in the author. We should remember that Piglia wrote *Artificial Respiration* from a place of silence, a place of fear, a place where writing was not allowed. In fact, he wrote against the impossibility of writing. In other words, his writing emerged in "the Process" (this is how the dictators in Argentina defined their government: as a National Reorganization Process, usually known as the Process). And he also wrote, of course, from the standpoint of Kafka's *Process*.

Coming back to *the* artificial respiration, to the *false name*, and the imposed real, Piglia, and Roa Bastos before him, and Borges before them, and Joyce before all of them, and perhaps even Plutarch or – why not – Homer, wrote (or perhaps, in the case of Homer, created) fictions that know of no outsides, impossible to tell beyond themselves. For instance, "Pierre Menard" by Borges, or *I, the Supreme*, or *Artificial Respiration*, relegate us to the order of meta-phantoms: an endless, neurotic lecture on the impossibility of telling ourselves, and of the impossibility of not telling about this impossibility.

From the notion of the text as a whole, there emerges one of the fundamental utopias of our modern times: the definition of a text with no outsides. *The Book* by Mallarmé, *Le livre à venir* by Blanchot, Borges' dreams, are all images of a text that might contain all the stories to be told, in addition to all the combinations we might devise between two or even all of them. In Piglia, this utopia is, at the same time, reaffirmed and questioned. It is impossible to think outside of it, or without it: somewhat like the map Borges imagined, covering the whole land.

Modern fiction, then, draws up an ambitious objective: multiplying the objective potentials of language, confronting objective reality, recognizing its complexities, eluding all gullible pretense of knowing beforehand the structure of what is real, without ever vindicating what is false. The two faces of Janus in fiction are, anyway, even present in those fictions that deliberately include fireworks: false sources, false qualities, confusing historical data with imaginary data and so on. And these tricks are not implemented to confuse the reader but to indicate that double nature of fiction, inevitably mixing the empirical with the imaginary. This mixture dominates certain types of modern fiction, as in the case of some stories by Borges or of some novels by Thomas Bernhard, but in fact it is present, to a greater or lesser extent, in all works of fiction, from Homer to Beckett. Western literary history abounds in examples of fiction's great paradox: if these stories present us with an impressing gallery of things made up, of what Ibsen famously called "lies and accursed stuff," it does so in order to make itself more credible.

Piglia confronts those critics who accuse Borges of being detached from reality as a writer and of being aloof and unaware of political contexts: "Literature will always work with what is real. The problem lies in that the realistic version is not the only representation that may be conceived." (Piglia 2000, 172) The poetics of Borges, Piglia reminds us, promotes the struggle of readings: to what extent are all allusions understood, to what extent are references true? What is genuine, and what is apocryphal? By bringing out this aspect of Borges' literary work, the "unsolved crime," Piglia does no more than lend his voice to the literary tradition that includes him as well. In it, he says, texts provoke a paranoid reaction, for they conjure up the illusion of a message that eludes us and promotes the delirium of trying to decipher it (and, more often than not, this is also true of history). This is why Borges' works demand to be interpreted. From this point of view, the link between fiction and reality, or between imagination and history, must not necessarily be subjected to philosophical criteria of truth or falsehood.

The "turbulences of sense" (so called by Juan José Saer in his brilliant *El concepto de ficción* [The concept of fiction] 1997, 154) work as obstacles to the process of erecting a pure structure for truth, as proposed by Wittgenstein in the *Tractatus*, and as greater obstacles still to the radical de-construction of the concept of truth, supposedly paving the way for unbridled imagination in search of its Eden. *There is no paradise of truth without a forbidden fruit: fiction. There is no paradise of pure imagination, deprived of the episode of the Fall involving the forbidden fruit: the control of truth.* This means that there is no language absolutely clear of truth, nor absolutely clear of fiction.

We err. We are still sentenced to the Paradise Lost, the place-without-a-place, that space where the unknown fruit is still awaiting, where there are so many stories still to be written. Where nothing is true, and nothing is a lie ...

Bibliography

Borges, Jorge L. *Obras Completas. Vol. IV: 1975–88*. Buenos Aires: Emecé, 2005.
Foucault, Michel. *Ceci n'est pas une pipe*. Scholies, 5. Montpellier: Fata Morgana, 1973.
Marco da Nizza [Marcos de Niza]. *Discovery of the Seven Cities of Cibola*. Ed. and trans. Percy M. Baldwin. Historical Society of New Mexico, Publications in History. Albuquerque: El Palacio Press, 1926.

Pigafetta, Antonio. *Noticia del primer viaje en torno al mundo*. Ed. Ana García Herraez. Valencia: Grial, 1998.
Piglia, Ricardo. "La ficción paranoica." *Clarín* (Suplemento "Cultura y Nación") 10 October 1991: 4–5.
— *Respiración artificial*. Biblioteca breve. Buenos Aires: Seix Barral, [1980] 1994.
— *Crítica y ficción. Entrevistas*. Buenos Aires: Seix Barral, [1986] 2000.
Proust, Marcel. *Du côté de chez Swann*. Le Livre de poche. Paris: Gallimard, [1913] 1954.
Roa Bastos, Augusto. *Yo, el Supremo*. La Creación literaria. Buenos Aires: Siglo XXI Editores, 1974.
Saer, Juan José. *El concepto de ficción*. Buenos Aires: Ariel, 1997.
Thomas Aquinas. *Summa contra gentiles; On the Truth of the Catholic Faith*. 5 vols. Trans. Anton C. Pegis *et al*. Image Books. New York: Doubleday, 1955–1957.
Wittgenstein, Ludwig. *Tractatus Logico-Philosophicus*. Trans. Charles K. Ogden. International Library of Psychology, Philosophy and Scientific Method. London: Routledge and Kegan Paul, 1981.
Zumthor, Pierre. *La lettre et la voix de la "littérature" médiévale*. Collection Poétique. Paris: Seuil, 1987.

Coda: Fiction, Translation & Interaction

Göran Malmqvist
Fiction in Global Contexts: Translation, the Universal Language of Literature

Someone has suggested that World Literature – Literature in a Global Context – is Translation. Without translation, no World Literature. In this talk, I shall address three topics: the craft of translation, the double responsibility of translators, and the role of translation on the international book market.

The craft of translation and the double responsibility of the translators

In his magnificent work *After Babel: Aspects of Language and Translation* (1975), George Steiner points out that translation, among other things, is a work of self-denial, demanding that the translator serve the original, rather than imposing him- or herself on it. But he also points out that translation, like all reading and even all listening, is a work of editing, a work of interpretation, determined by subjective and contextual factors. If the writer is a Maker and Creator, then the translator is ideally a highly skilled craftsman. But as the task of translation also involves editing and interpreting, the translator must also serve as actor. The translator must *imitate* the author of the original work, and his translation should ideally be a *likeness*, a representation, of the original work.

The translator must be keenly aware of his or her double responsibility, to the writer of the original work and to the readers of the translation. Normalizing and leveling are at the very core of the problem of all literary translation. These terms refer to the trimming and smoothing out the text, cutting off its edges and neutralizing its very effects. The author, the creator of the text, may allow himself or herself the freedom to deviate from norms, forging new words, distorting syntax and playing with the multiple senses of words and nuances. The translator, the craftsman, must do his or her utmost to convey such deviations in the translation. The worst cases of leveling are cutting out segments of the text, and adding what is not present in the text.

Cultural leveling is equally reprehensible. Any source language expresses a particular world vision which may be quite different from that of the target language. The translator should be aware of the fact that the translation of a text at the same time is a translation of a culture. Such elements as may seem strange to the readers of the translation must be elucidated to them, not in footnotes (which I abhor as they tend to interfere with the flow of reading) but preferably in an introduction to the translation.

A translator who wishes to guard against the normalization threat should bear in mind that only empathy will guide him or her onto the right path. Empathy, not necessarily with the author, but with the work, will give rise to a common sensitivity which in turn will, at best, result in a stylistic identification of the original work and the translation.

The notion of empathy leads me to the extremely important distinction between two kinds of translators: the professional translator and the amateur translator (I refer you to the second definition of the term "amateur" in the *Oxford English Dictionary*: "One who cultivates anything as a pastime, as distinguished from one who prosecutes it professionally"). While the professional translator may not enjoy the privilege of selecting the work to be translated, the amateur translator translates only works which he or she considers to be of high literary quality. Considerations of remuneration are as a rule of lesser importance for the amateur translator than for the professional translator. This fact has an important bearing on the relation between the translator and the publisher.

Having read a fair number of translations into English of Chinese literary works published in the US, I have been struck by the frequent occurrence of severe instances of leveling and normalization, such as cutting out segments of the text, and even rewriting entire chapters that are considered to be unacceptable to or not easily understood by the American reader. In several instances, the translators of these texts have informed me that these changes were made on the expressed demand of the publisher. I would like to believe that no amateur translator would be prepared to give in to such demands.

The role of translation on the international book market: Some examples from Sweden

In the half century during which I have had contact, as a writer and translator, with the publishing world in Sweden, great changes have occurred. A few old establishments in the trade have grown too large and have swallowed up a number of minor and formerly independent publishing houses, originally run by people motivated by a keen interest in literature. It would seem that an MBA degree carries much more weight than love of literature does. It is at the same time encouraging to note that in the last few decennia a number of small publishing houses have appeared, run by literature-loving enthusiasts, eager to make available to the Swedish readers translations of literary works, often from non-European countries, works that established publishing houses would not touch with a pair of tongs.

Translations occupy a dominating part of the Swedish book market. The following statistics show the ratio of translated works of fiction versus original works published in Sweden in the following three five-year periods:[1]

	1866–1870	1926–1930	1986–1990
Original works	187	1120	1500
Translations	213	1490	5500
From English	68	814	4400
From French	55	196	260
From German	50	178	140

In the five-year period 1986–90, only 700 translations were from languages other than English, French and German. The great majority of these 700 translations were from other European languages. Translations from the languages of Asia, Latin America and Africa were utterly few.

In our modern societies, internationalization, tourism, borders open for goods, capital and labor are considered important steps toward globalization. But in spite of this, in Sweden, as in many other European countries, an opposite tendency is clearly manifested in the field of non-European literature.

A publishing friend of mine has provided me with the following statistics: in the years 2005 to 2007, 9,000 titles of "pure" literature (in Swedish: *skönlitteratur*) were published in Sweden. 25 of these works, a few per mille, came from Africa. The situation for translations of literature from Latin America and Asia (including the Arab world) is about the same. Of all translations into Swedish published in the years 2005 to 2007, 74% came from the US and the UK. Surprisingly little was translated from the Continental European languages: from French 3.6%, from German 2%, from Spanish 1%; from Arabic 0.3%. Someone has said that the gaps in Chinese literature translated into Swedish are so large as to be hardly visible.

Having checked the stocks in Stockholm's largest bookstore in the year 2001, my publisher friend found 53 titles from Asia, Africa and Latin America in a total stock of 100,000 titles.

About 20% of the population of Sweden is of non-Swedish extraction. And yet immigration literature is almost invisible. A small communal library in a

---

[1] The statistic material of this table and in the remaining part of this section was kindly provided by Mr. Styrbjörn Gustafsson, Bokförlaget Tranan, Wollmar Yxkullsgatan 5B, 118 50 Stockholm; e-mail: info@tranan.nu.

borough close to Stockholm, densely inhabited by immigrants, stocks 25,000 titles, 125 of which from non-European continents.

One publishing house that to a higher degree than all others has tried to remedy this imbalance is Tranan, established in 1991. Tranan's publication list includes the following numbers of titles of literature translated from non-European languages: Arabic (21), Chinese (13), Vietnamese (12), Korean (6), Japanese (2), Mongol (1), New Persian (4), Malayalam (4), Tamil (3), Bengali (2), Hindi (2), Kannada (1), Assamese (1), Oriya (1), Kirewe/Swahili (1). In addition, Tranan has published 27 titles by African writers, written in English (18), Portuguese (8) and French (1); 31 titles by Latin American writers, written in Spanish (15), Portuguese (15) and English (1); and 11 titles by Asian writers, written in English (7), Portuguese (3) and Hebrew (1).

Nobody would be prepared to argue that the scarcity of translations of non-European literature has to do with considerations of literary quality. The cause of this lack of balance must be sought elsewhere. It seems to me that the leading media (Press, Radio and Television) have a special responsibility in this regard. Competent surveys and presentations of newly published literature from distant and ignored language areas would no doubt be instrumental in promoting an increased awareness of these literatures.

Reviews of translated literature, published in newspapers and journals, rarely comprise comments built on qualified analysis. As a rule, qualified analysis only applies to scholarly reviews of translations of canonical works, and particularly to re-translations of classical works. In most instances, reviews are written by people who do not necessarily have command of the language of the original work, or who, even though they may know that language, do not have access to the original text, or have neither the time nor the inclination to undertake a thorough comparison of the two texts. It is therefore quite natural that reviewers of translated works rarely devote much attention to the quality of the translation, unless it happens to be particularly excellent or particularly poor. Severe criticism of a poor translation may indeed serve a highly useful purpose: it may make the translator decide either to give up translating or to seek to improve his or her performance. It may also impress upon the publisher the necessity of seeking competent translators.

Institutional support in Sweden and in the Baltic area

It is quite obvious that the advance of a truly global literature would need support from a number of quarters, both governmental and non-governmental.

In Sweden, the Swedish Academy, the Swedish Arts Council, the Swedish Authors' Fund and the Swedish Writers' Union in various ways contribute to the support of translation. To the Swedish Academy, responsible for the award of the Nobel Prize in Literature, access to eminent translations of contemporary literature is, of course, of paramount importance. All members of the Academy are able to read works in at least three European languages (English, German and French); some members have a good command of one or more other European languages, such as Russian, Polish, Italian, Spanish, Portuguese and Greek. One member has a command of Chinese. When judging literature written in languages other than these, members of the Academy have to rely on translations. The Academy spends a great deal of both energy and funds in order to gain access to the best possible translations of literary works which are deemed to be relevant for its deliberations on the Prize. In order to establish forums for discussing fundamental aspects of literary creation and translation, the Academy also organizes Nobel Symposia, attended by writers, scholars and literary critics from all over the world. Each year, the Academy awards four prizes of about 5,000 Euro each to translators translating into and from Swedish. Considerable sums are also spent each year in support of translations of Swedish literature into other languages.

The Swedish Arts Council supports the translation of foreign literature into Swedish. In 2011, grants were given to support the translation of 314 titles in 28 different languages; 116 of the 314 titles were in English, 33 in French and 37 in German, which means that 63% of the total support was given to translations from those three languages. Here is a list of other European languages, with titles in descending order: Danish 15 titles, Norwegian 13, Italian, Spanish and Russian 10 titles each, Finnish 8, Icelandic, Portuguese and Greek 3 titles each, Dutch, Polish, Czech and Hungarian 2 titles each, Catalonian, Romanian, Serbo-Croatian and White Russian 1 title each. Support was given to five titles in Arabic. Only a handful of titles on the list were written in other non-European languages, such as Japanese, Chinese and Tibetan. No support was given to translations from African languages.

The Swedish Authors' Fund awards grants for "test translations," amounting to a measly 5,000 Swedish Crowns. In 2008, a total of 28 grants were awarded, at a cost of 140,000 Swedish Crowns. The Swedish Authors' Fund also administers the payment of the so-called "Library Compensation" (*Biblioteksersättning*), awarded to writers and translators and calculated on the basis of book borrowing in Swedish public libraries. For each loan, the Government pays the Fund SEK 1,26 (ca. Euro 0,15), SEK 0,76 öre of which is paid to the author and SEK 0,38 to the translator.

The Swedish Writers' Union administers a great many stipends for both writers and translators. The activities of the Union had an interesting offshoot in the establishment of The Baltic Centre for Writers and Translators, an international residential workplace and meeting point for writers and translators, located in the city of Visby on Gotland, a large island off the eastern coast of Sweden. Since its establishment in 1993, the Centre has become an internationally recognized institution, operating under the auspices of UNESCO. It focuses on multilateral literary activity and cultural exchange and has since its start accommodated a great number of writers and translators from all over the world. The Centre arranges annual international festivals, translation workshops, seminars and meetings and has also hosted some major international conferences, some in cooperation with UNESCO. In the European Union context, the Centre has been in the avant-garde in questions concerning the enlargement of the Union and has been developing long-term, east-west cultural exchange. The Centre is governed by a Board, with representatives of the Swedish Writers' Union, the county and the municipality of Gotland and the Baltic Writers' Council, a multinational, non-profit, non-governmental organization open to all Writers' and Translators' Unions in the Baltic area, defined as Denmark, Estonia, Finland, Germany, Iceland, Latvia, Lithuania, Norway, Poland, Russia and Sweden.

The Baltic Centre for Writers and Translators provided the impetus for the establishment of a Literary Translation Seminar at Södertörn University close to Stockholm, one of the younger Swedish universities. Since its establishment in 1998, this seminar has provided highly successful courses in literary translation into Swedish from Polish, Russian, German, French, Finnish, Czech, Turkish and Estonian. These courses have been offered by some of the most eminent translators in Sweden.

Recent setbacks in Sweden

In order to economize, the relevant authority within Södertörn University has decided to shut down the Literary Translation Seminar. The decision to discontinue one of the most successful seminars in literary translation offered by a Swedish university has aroused severe criticism from a number of quarters, among them the Swedish Academy, which, in a letter to the Rector of Södertörn University of May 10, 2012, responded as follows, in my translation into English:

> It has been said that the common European language is translation. This is true not least of a small country like Sweden. From the translation of *The New Testament* in 1526 to the renderings of works by Proust, Kafka, Mann and Joyce in the last century, Swedish culture has depended on eminent translators who have enriched the language and given readers access to priceless worlds of ideas.

But translation has, of course, not been confined to the cultural sphere of Europe. In recent years competent translators have given the cultural life of Sweden important incentives through translation of works by Chinese, Japanese, Arabic, Persian and Turkish writers, as well as essential works produced in the United States and Latin America. Competent translators have been of vital importance for Sweden's participation in international dialogues.

The Seminar in Literary Translation, with emphasis on pure literature, which has for a number of years been provided by Södertörn University, is an important feature in this context. Here, older and experienced translators have been able to transmit their skills to their future colleagues and in that way preserve an unbroken tradition of an important enterprise that has served our country well. Södertörn University ought to be proud of that achievement. Instead, the University actually – for narrow, economic reasons – wishes to discontinue the Translation Seminar.

Many of us members of the Swedish Academy are thoroughly acquainted with the importance of translations as well as the problems connected with it, and the Academy has also arranged an international Nobel Symposium addressing these questions. In these circumstances, we strongly protest against the ingenuous wastefulness that this saving would result in. We wish most strongly to advise Södertörn University against a discontinuation of the Seminar in Literary Translation that in the long run will prove disastrous.

Competent translation requires competent translators and competent translators require a mastery of their own language and an excellent command of the language or languages into which or from which he or she translates. It is therefore of paramount importance that the integrity of the Swedish language be preserved and that the study of foreign languages be well provided for in our schools and universities. In recent decennia, the Swedish language, the integrity of which, since July 1 of 2009, has been protected by a special language law, has suffered rather severe domain losses, partly as a result of the increased use of English in media and as a language of instruction in certain university courses. It is particularly worrying that certain influential players on the Swedish mercantile market openly try to counter-check the statutes of the language law of 2009. One such example is the demand of Svenskt Näringsliv (the Swedish Trade and Industry Association), expressed in a letter to the Government on August 18, 2009, that documents relating to patent rights be worded in English instead of in Swedish. Government acceptance of that demand would cause the Swedish language a very severe domain loss. It is also exceedingly worrying that the place in Swedish universities' curricula of various major European languages is threatened. The latest casualty is Italian, the teaching of which has been discontinued at Gothenburg University.

A possible solution? An International Centre of Translation Literature

The decisions to discontinue the Literary Translation Seminar at Södertörn University and the teaching of Italian at Gothenburg University are indicative of a general trend among the holders of purse strings to belittle the value of endeavours in the realm of "pure" culture. This leads me to the question: How can we create, among the shapers of cultural policy, the political awareness and will to encourage more translation? In order to seek ammunition to help me answer this question, I approached the publishing firm Bakhåll (The Ambush) in the city of Lund, established by two literature loving brothers in 1980. Since the start, Bakhåll has published some 400 titles, 196 of which are translations (110 from English, 38 from German, 26 from French, 9 from Russian, 6 from Spanish, 3 from Danish, 3 from Arabic, 1 from Dutch, 1 from Greek, 1 from Chinese and 1 from Japanese).[2]

There are several beautiful feathers in the cap of this tiny publishing house: the complete works of Kafka, of which fourteen volumes have been published, together with three important works *on* Kafka, retranslations of eight works by Dostojevski, works by Hesse, William Blake, Heinrich von Kleist, Rilke, Rimbaud, T. S. Eliot, Gertrud Stein, Rafael Alberti, and others. Bakhåll also publishes works by Swedish writers of serious novels, some of whom are as yet unknown to the reading public. This is especially important, as much of the Swedish literature published by the large publishing houses consists of detective novels and works by celebrities of limited literary value.

The Ambush publishers replied to my query as follows: while they are keen on publishing translated literature, they are up against hard economic conditions. They would welcome an international centre, to which they could apply for financial supports of, say, 5,000 Euro for a novel of some 400 pages. This sum would, of course, not cover the whole expense for the translation, but would be of great help. They suggest the following procedure: the publisher submits the original work, together with an assurance that the translation would be undertaken by a qualified literary translator. The centre would be expected to provide a binding commitment of support before the project is launched.

The Ambush publishers also suggest that it would be excellent if an International Centre of Translation Literature could be established somewhere, to

---

[2] The statistic material here and in the remaining part of this section was kindly provided by Bokförlaget Bakhåll, Box 1114, 221 04 Lund; e-mail: staff@bakhall.com.

serve publishers and translators on a world-wide basis. Presently, this is the concern of literary agents, but they are mainly interested in bestsellers and operate mostly at Book Fairs. As a rule, they are not interested in odd and advanced literature from "minor" language areas. Both publishers and writers experience great difficulties via agents in drawing attention to their books.

A web-based Centre for the Exchange of Literature could be operated without great administrative costs. With a minimum of staff, such a Centre could serve as a web to which publishers from the whole world could turn, to show books which they are prepared to offer other publishers to translate and publish, and also to find books which they themselves would like to translate and publish.

The establishment of such a Centre would hopefully constitute a step toward realizing the truth of the following statement by Horace Engdahl, former Permanent Secretary of the Swedish Academy:
THE UNIVERSAL LANGUAGE OF LITERATURE IS TRANSLATION

Bibliography

Steiner, George. *After Babel: Aspects of Language and Translation*. Oxford: Oxford University Press, 1975.

Gregory Currie
Afterword: Fiction as a Transcultural Entity

There is some reason to take the pessimistic view that warfare is a universal of human social and psychological affairs.[1] This does not mean that everyone is always at war, or that war may never be avoided. It means that warfare is a recurrent feature of human kind in a great variety of circumstances, that avoiding it is difficult, and that war between groups of humans goes back into the distant, prehistoric past.[2] Of course warfare has changed a great deal: in how it is conducted, with what weapons, on what scale, according to what rules. But a thing may change in many ways without ceasing to be, and without transmuting into something else. We could not truly say "Over the millennia, warfare has changed radically" if it were not the same thing – warfare – then as now.

In all these respects fiction is like warfare. Fiction has undergone radical and intrinsic change. But it is still fiction – what else could it be? We have had fiction as immemorially as we have warfare, for all the change that fiction has undergone. That is the suggestion I put forward here.

Actually, there are two suggestions, though they go together rather naturally. The first is that we should understand fiction in a way which allows for a great deal of variation in how it is exemplified. Warfare can be exemplified by small groups of people conducting violent campaigns for territory or other advantages using stones and clubs, by huge mechanised armies and by intergalactic star fleets. Fiction is exemplified in camp fire stories, oral traditions telling of gods and heroes, courtly tales inscribed on parchment, staged drama, movies, and mystery stories downloadable to your Kindle. But merely allowing for such multiple realisation does not ensure that there is actually a vast expanse, spatially and temporally, of fiction. The claim that there actually is such an expanse – the second suggestion I am making – is an historical one for which we must, at some stage in the argument, bring forth evidence. But at present I simply want to place before you the two proposals and to fend off some objections to them which have been voiced.

While these two suggestions are formally independent, there is a good deal of motivational connection between them. People who favour cross-cultural

---

[1] I am grateful to Anna Ichino for detailed comments on an earlier version of this paper, which led to substantial rewriting and, I hope, to some modest improvement.
[2] For the hypothesis that warfare goes back into the evolutionary past sufficiently to help account for the emergence of altruism, see Bowles 2009.

comparisons (who think, at least, that not all such comparisons are misleading) look for signs that, despite the evident differences between groups of people, there are important, explanatory uniformities. To do that they need to have an account of fiction which allows for great variation in its realisation. Those on the other side who wish always to show that cultural generalisations mislead and who sometimes think that even the attempt to make them is immoral find much more to admire in concepts with narrow, local application.[3] I don't at all deny the reality of difference, which I believe I can accommodate very well, but I worry that focusing exclusively on difference misses something important.

The idea that there might be objections to the claim that fiction is universal in the sense described above is made vivid by some of the other essays in this volume. Thus Marcia Sá Cavalcante Schuback raises the question "how the notion of world literature changes the very concept of fiction," while Margalit Finkelberg asks "whether the idea of fiction as crystallized in ancient Greek literary theory, first and foremost, in Plato and Aristotle, may be considered universally valid" and goes on to speak of Aristotle's "rather idiosyncratic idea of fiction" being given "an aura of universality."[4] Fritz Peter Knapp notes the contrast between those who think of fiction as a more or less universal category and those who argue for its specifically historical character, with claims to the effect that fiction was "discovered" by Chrétien de Troyes in the latter half of the 12th century.[5] He concludes that "fictionality thus remains a very rare special case within romance production, which was otherwise dominated by pseudo-history." Wim Verbaal claims that "In many literary cultures, fiction does not have any right of existence, one of these being [...] Latin literature," while Stefan Helgesson argues "for a historical – as opposed to a universalising – understanding of fiction."[6]

A lot of this sounds rather anti-universalist. But I'm not absolutely sure that any of these writers would, when my view is explained in all its rationality, disagree with me. There are ways to understand what is being said in these

---

[3] The debate here is one familiar from social anthropology; see Currie 2012.
[4] Cavalcante Schuback, "The Fiction of the Image," and Margalit Finkelberg, "Diagnosing Fiction: From Plato to Borges," both in this volume. For comment on some of Finkelberg's work from a perspective I find appealing, see Rutherford 2000.
[5] "Historicity and Fictionality in Medieval Narrative," this volume, citing Haug 1992.
[6] Verbaal, "How the West was Won by Fiction," and Helgesson, "Unsettling Fictions: Generic Instability and Colonial Time," both in this volume. Helgesson refers approvingly to the argument of Catherine Gallagher, which I will discuss further on. Of the contributors to this volume my own approach is perhaps closest to that of Ming Dong Gu who calls for a "better understanding of fiction as a transcultural genre" in his article "Toward a Transcultural Poetics of Fiction."

essays that avoids a direct conflict, and the issue of conceptual change which some authors focus on is a particularly difficult issue. For one may think that our concept of a thing may change while that thing continues to be. Much here depends, predictably, on what we mean by "concept." There is no doubt that we think about fiction in new ways; we have changed expectations of it, and we see relationships between works that were unavailable to earlier readers. Still, I say that it makes sense to specify a "core concept" of fiction which has not changed. To satisfy our requirement of realisability that core concept needs to be thin: it picks out what is common and distinctive to fiction throughout all the change that fiction undergoes. That core concept will always need supplementation from history, for no fictional work is merely fiction; it is fiction of a certain kind, in a certain context, for a certain audience.

What, then, is that core concept? I will give it directly. But to avoid the impression that mine is an obscure philosophical intervention, unhelpful to the literary project, I give the version of someone deeply immersed in the history of literature and without, so far as I know, any controversially philosophical commitments. Dennis Green, in his study of literature in the twelfth century, says this:

> Fiction is a category of literary text which, although it may also include events that were held to have actually taken place, gives an account of events that could not conceivably have taken place, and/or of events that, although possible, did not take place and which, in doing so, invites the intended audience to be willing to make-believe what would otherwise be regarded as untrue. (Green 2002, 4)[7]

There is not much I would disagree with here, and indeed Green acknowledges the influence of a formulation I gave some time ago. (Currie 1990, Chapter 1) I will, however, highlight an implication of this for the relations, particularly relations of trust, between authors and readers. The first is that, since the aim of fiction is pretence, the author of fiction is not committed to the truth of everything he or she says. When we understand people to be asserting things, we understand them to be putting them forward as true, and their claim that what they say is true carries with it potential costs. If the one who asserts is wrong she is liable to disappoint the hearer, perhaps to mislead and hence to inconvenience him, hence to lose his good will and her own good reputation, since the error may be reported to others. When we speak seriously we have an

---

[7] This concept of fiction seems to correspond well to that discussed in connection with *Genji* in Gunilla Lindberg-Wada's essay: "Murasaki Shikibu and *The Tale of Genji*": "the term fictional tale, *tsukurimonogatari* [invented tale], goes back at least to the latter half of the twelfth century." (This volume).

interest in being reliable, unless some unusually countervailing consideration makes lying the better option. Fiction cancels these commitments, because it invites not belief but make-believe, or pretence, or imagining.[8] Fiction allows authors to say things they are not committed to without fear of misleading their readers and of reputational loss, for they know that readers know that they are not committed to them, and hence that readers do not expect their utterances to correspond to how things really are.

Now one objection that will be raised here is that such an account of fiction's nature cannot explain how seriously we take fiction. And we certainly do take it seriously. In this volume we are told that the seventeenth century Chinese playwright Hong Sheng composed his drama *Changshengdian* "In order to elaborate upon the ideal of 'true love,'" for which purpose the author "purifies the historical Emperor Ming Huang and Lady Yang, making them into pilgrims of true love." "Purifies" here implies, I take it, "falsifies," though the additional implication is that the falsification is done for an artistically and perhaps morally good cause. But the play did not find favour with the then Emperor, Kangxi (r. 1662–1722) who "was infuriated by what he considered Hong Sheng's deliberate use of historical events to provoke Chinese nationalistic sentiments."[9]

When fiction and our concerns about the real world collide in the way they do here, things can get difficult.[10] Sensitivity about the historical context of a narrative, or about its fidelity to the record, is common enough today, and plays, novels and other fictions become objects of contention (though rarely involving royalty) when they are thought to mislead. Michael Crichton's 2004 novel *State of Fear* describes a (thwarted) attempt by eco-terrorists, keen to persuade the public of the reality of global warming, to create a tsunami which will devastate California. The book received a generally critical and sometimes angry response from the scientific community, citing widespread misrepresentation of the evidence despite apparently meticulous attention to the science in the novel and accompanying statements. But Crichton had his defenders; he was invited, on the basis of the novel, to testify before the Senate Committee on Environment and Public Works by its Chairman, who had previously described global warming as "the greatest hoax ever perpetrated on the American people" declaring the novel "required reading" for the committee.[11]

---

[8] One might in certain contexts want to distinguish these three categories quite sharply; here I understand them, as is often the case in the philosophical debate over fiction, as roughly synonymous.

[9] Ayling Wang, "Interaction Between the Reader, the Critic and the Author," this volume.

[10] For reflections on contemporary fictions which incorporate history, see Mari Hatavara, "Historical Fiction," in this volume.

[11] See the interview with Crichton in *New York Times*, September 29, 2005.

As I said, fictions, then and now, are often treated as very serious objects, not merely in the sense that they can be supreme examples of human imagination, style and invention, but because they can provide important information on the real world. They inflame nationalist and ethnic passions, and can produce false or at least unreliable beliefs on a variety of subjects. Recent work on the psychology of fiction reading confirms a tendency on the part of readers to be influenced by fiction. People who read a brief story about a girl who is taken to a shopping mall for a pleasant day out and who is murdered there by an escaped psychiatric patient will be more inclined thereafter to agree with the idea that the world is a dangerous place, to show pessimism about the possibility of justice and to worry about the restraint of psychiatric patients. Interestingly, the effect is pretty much the same whether people think they are reading fiction or a truthful newspaper report. (Green & Brock 2000)

Any reasonable account of fiction's nature must allow for this, and mine does that. (I emphasise that I draw here only on the rough account quoted from Dennis Green, and reserve the right to introduce complexities and qualifications as the debate goes on). Unsurprisingly, what I say will not cover everything that everyone calls fiction, for many uses of that term are metaphorical, ironic or hyperbolic. Lies are sometimes called fiction but lies belong in the category of assertion and so are not fiction from the point of view of the present discussion, as we shall see. And when Lars-Erik Berg says that "My identity is fiction, because it is *not me* that I see, but *Other's reactions to me*," I can only assume that a point is being made about the unreality of the self (as the subject understands it, perhaps), and not about its fictionality.[12]

How can we square the idea that fiction is pretence with the fact, already noted, that fictions are often taken seriously as the potential cause of unwanted shifts in opinion and outlook? This is a complex question with no single answer, but let me highlight two factors. The first is that people have a strong tendency to want to police imagination and pretence as well as belief and action. We would be troubled if our children's games focused on the pretence of murder, theft and fraud; there are things we don't want to imagine about ourselves and others, and things we would be troubled to hear that others were imagining about us. The extent to which these worries are well-grounded is debatable, but the present point is that placing fiction in the domain of pretence does not suggest that fiction will never be a source of anxiety.[13]

---

[12] See "Photons of the Human Mind" in this volume.
[13] This debate, pursued further, would take us into philosophical territory currently labeled "Imaginative resistance"; see Currie 2010, Chapter 6.

These anxieties concern the supposed effects of imagining various things; they are not dependent on assumptions about the communicative intention of the author. But if we think of fictions as sources of cognitive change it is natural to ask whether this is in part due to the fact that they are often taken as intentional expressions of the author's opinions. And so the second thing to say is that the account given by Dennis Green's formulation is not in any conflict with the idea that fiction sometimes serves an important communicative purpose. Admittedly, we currently lack a comprehensive theory of the ways in which serious, or at least seriously meant ideas are communicated, often implicitly, by fictional stories, but there are a number of suggestions about how this can happen.

Here it is helpful to distinguish between what is said and implied concerning the plot, which we can think of as within the domain of pretence, and what the saying and implying of these things in the way they are said or implied suggests about the author's motivation for doing these things. Ideas can be communicated in many ways, and stating them explicitly is only one of them. As Sperber and Wilson emphasise, we are exquisitely sensitive to the intentions of others, and constantly ask ourselves "Why did she do that?" If my friend leans back rather deliberately on the park bench where we sit I will assume that she had a reason for doing so and that it is likely that she wants to communicate something to me; if her leaning back reveals a figure in the distance who is a mutual acquaintance of ours I will naturally and effortlessly assume that she wanted to communicate to me his approach. None of this involves anyone saying anything. She might have said "Have you noticed that delightful tree to the left?" counting on me then to notice the figure in that direction. This time something is said, but what is said and what is most significantly communicated are not the same.

Encouraged by this, one might then see merit in the idea that fiction sometimes works on the model of parable; we, like the disciples, understand that Jesus' parable of the prodigal son is supposed to represent to us important ideas about the extent of God's capacity for love and forgiveness. We understand that the plot is pretence; Jesus is not trying to convince us that there is some real family whose activities he is reliably describing. But our imagining of that story can be expected to make vivid to us something else – something which Jesus wants to convey to us concerning God's relation to human kind. We assume that Jesus had some serious point in telling his story; given what his audience knew of him, his demeanor and concerns, it is highly unlikely that he would have taken the trouble to tell the story merely for entertainment. We seek relevance in his utterance, and given the context of the Gospel, a very obvious hypothesis about the relevance of this discourse is that it is intended to encapsulate, in concrete form, the somewhat more abstract and difficult notion of God's infinite love.[14] And if we treat Jesus as a reliable informant on this topic we shall then be likely to form beliefs corresponding to the ideas suggested. We may not treat Proust and Tolstoy as reliable in quite the way some of us are inclined to regard Jesus as reliable, but there is a strong human tendency to treat testimony seriously, especially when the testifier manifests such admirable qualities as the capacity to construct a moving and well-structured narrative, though these may also be qualities unrelated to reliability on the topic in question. The extent to which reliance on such testimony is rational is therefore questionable at this stage, and there are doubtless other mechanisms at work in fictional communication. But perhaps enough has been said to indicate that there is no improbability in the idea that utterances which are pretended or at least unasserted can have the effect of conveying serious and sometimes complex ideas – true or false ones.[15]

So far I have emphasized how serious but unstated ideas may be communicated via a fiction. Another way is to have the ideas made explicit but to avoid asserting them, putting them instead in the mouth of a character. An author who has a character say "Jews are untrustworthy" has certainly not said that Jews are untrustworthy, and in many fictions such a fictive utterance would not be seen as an invitation to believe that Jews are untrustworthy; one merely ensures that the character who says this is manifestly unpleasant and unreliable. Still, there is a tendency for people to believe what is said within pretence, and that tendency is easily triggered if the character is given a favourable or even neutral representation. We know from psychological experiments that if a character in a story tells another character that eating chocolate makes you slimmer, people who have read the passage are immediately thereafter more inclined to agree with the proposition that it does so, despite this being a rather implausible claim. (Prentice, Gerrig & Bailis 1997)

Up till now I have been working with the idea that works we label fiction consist only of invitations to pretence and do not contain any explicit assertions; that view cannot be sustained for long. Crichton, in writing *State of Fear* is unusual in alternating between fictive mode and assertion, with technical appendices and prefatory material; thus his work as a whole is more than usually a mixture of fiction and nonfiction. But on a smaller scale this is not unusual; we are often justified in seeing some part of a fictional work as asserted. In judging something to be fiction over all we make a rough and ready accounting of the (weighted) ratio of genuinely fictional to nonfictional

---

14 On the idea of relevance in communication see Sperber and Wilson 1995.
15 On this see Gregory Currie & Anna Ichino, "Beliefs from fiction," forthcoming.

material. After all, no one complains when you say you swam in water when in fact there was a good deal of chlorine and of other substances in the liquid. (Currie 1990)

We may now agree that the thin, pretence-based concept of fiction given by Green, is consistent with the idea that fiction is a potent source of cognitive change: change of belief, desire, emotion, mood, perspective and outlook. Indeed the notion of fiction as pretence suggests an intriguing possibility: that there is *more* reason to worry about the effects of fiction on belief and on behaviour than there is concerning non-fiction. For fiction writers are able to influence without being explicitly committed to, and hence without being held responsible for, the ideas which carry this influence; they need not, therefore, meet standards of epistemic responsibility, of evidential and argumentative support, that govern explicit assertion. For that reason the fictional environment is likely to be populated by ideas with an initial plausibility but lacking the real, substantial support that an epistemically more demanding environment would expect.

So it is not surprising that fiction is a source of concern to those who make laws, police morals, possess power or who would simply like to do all these things. That fiction is a sensitive category, socially, politically and morally, is entirely to be expected. Accordingly, we should allow that people's attitudes towards fictions, the social arrangements they put in place to control them, and the kinds of fictions they think it worth producing or reading will vary a great deal across time and culture. Of course we have other reasons to expect that also; on purely aesthetic grounds and given what we know about the plasticity of artistic traditions, we would expect a good deal of variability in the production of fiction. But the manifest cognitive power of fiction and the consequent external forces at work to control it add greatly to this variability.

*

The objection just considered is not the only source of concern to those who would like a more substantial and historical concept of fiction than the one I have endorsed. Some expressions of these worries puzzle me. Catherine Gallagher says in an influential essay that the novel "discovered" fiction. She goes on:

> It used to be assumed that fictions form a part of every culture's life, and if evidence for the assumption were needed, one could point to the seemingly universal existence of stories that apparently do not make referential truth claims, such as fables and fairy tales. It seemed to follow that something resembling the modern acceptance of the word *fiction* must be universally comprehended and the phenomenon at least tacitly sanc-

tioned. A general human capacity to recognize discourses that, in Sir Philip Sidney's words, "nothing affirmeth, and therefore never lieth" (Sidney 1962: 29), made the term appear unproblematically applicable to narratives from all times and places. Recent scholarship has shown, though, that this modern *concept* of narrative fiction developed slowly in early-modern Europe, a development reflected in the changing uses of the word in English. (Gallagher 2006, 337–338)

Gallagher's "though" in the final sentence of the quotation suggests that the universalism she has just described is a complacent view tenable only as long as one fails to attend to the history of the "changing uses of the word [fiction]." Yet there is something odd about the evidence which Gallagher immediately brings forth for this view. She continues:

From its common use to denote, "that which is fashioned or framed; a device, a fabric, ... whether for the purpose of deception or otherwise" (*Oxford English Dictionary*, 2nd ed., s.v. "fiction") or "something that is imaginatively invented," a new usage came into existence at the turn of the seventeenth century: "The species of literature which is concerned with the narration of imaginary events and the portraiture of imaginary characters; fictitious composition." As this sense of the word gained greater currency, mainly in the eighteenth century, an earlier frequent meaning of "deceit, dissimulation, pretense" became obsolete. Although consistently contrasted with the veridical, fictional narration ceased to be a subcategory of dissimulation as it became a literary phenomenon. If the etymology of the word tells us anything, fiction seems to have been discovered as a discursive mode in its own right as readers developed the ability to tell it apart from both fact and (this is the key) deception. (Gallagher 2006, 338)

To me, the new usage and the old do not sound very different. The old meaning, as Gallagher gives it does not imply that fiction is deceit, for it reads "that which is fashioned or framed; a device, a fabric, ... whether for the purpose of deception *or otherwise*" with the further implication that it is "something that is imaginatively invented." In what sense is this idea at odds with "the narration of imaginary events"? However, I think it additionally a mistake to place so much weight on the evidence of usage. Words do, of course, change their meanings but it does not follow that there is no continuity in what is recognised as out there in the world; the view that language is our guide to reality strikes me as one of the worst mistakes of the past forty or so years of literary theory. And fiction is one of the things that *is* out there in the world, though of course it is there through human effort. And it seems to me extraordinarily unlikely that the "nothing affirmeth, and therefore never lieth" notion of fiction was one that people were insensitive to before Sydney encapsulated it so memorably, or that they ceased to be sensitive to it at some point in the eighteenth century.[16] On the contrary, this sounds like a good candidate for a concept possessed at all times by mature, functioning language users, who must understand – on pain of being massively misinformed about the world – the difference between someone's saying something and meaning it seriously in the sense of putting it forward as true and hence as something to be believed, and someone speaking in non-assertive mode. For one thing, basic grammatical forms depend for their existence on this distinction. Conditional sentences – "If that is a lion we had better warn Albert" – could not be understood unless speakers and hearers distinguished between asserted and unasserted parts of utterances; in this case the antecedent and consequent have to be understood as unasserted while the whole is asserted. There would also be no room for ironic utterance – a familiar practice at least as long ago as Socrates and probably long before – unless one could understand that sometimes the person who says "That's a delightful tie George is wearing" does not really mean what she says. Indeed, ironic utterances are paradigmatic fictions on a small scale: the speaker pretends to be someone who, absurdly, believes what she pretends to be asserting. (See Currie 2010, Chapter 8)

The passage I have given from Gallagher ends with another rather puzzling claim: "fiction seems to have been discovered as a discursive mode in its own right as readers developed the ability to tell it apart from both fact and (this is the key) deception." In what sense did readers at some time not possess this ability? I think we need to distinguish between the possession and the refinement of an ability. I possess the ability to ride a bicycle. Unfortunately this does not mean that I ride one very well, that I would be able to weave my way expertly through busy London traffic, or that I could perform juggling and acrobatic feats while riding. My ability, like most abilities, is less than perfect (if there is such a thing as perfect riding of bicycles) and I would say the same about our ability, individually and collectively, to distinguish fiction from non-fiction. The fact that one may not be able always and infallibly to distinguish fiction from nonfiction does not show that one lacks the ability to distinguish them – witness all the trouble caused by Orson Wells' too-realistic broadcast of *War of the Worlds*.

This is particularly important because fiction can, as Gallagher emphasises, be hard to distinguish from non-fiction, especially when one lacks the institutional structures – libraries, book reviews, helpful bookshop classifica-

---

[16] It should be emphasised that "fiction" contrasts not with "fact" but with "non assertion" (I simplify slightly here), for nonfiction can be as false as any fiction. Thus I disagree with Wim Verbaal who speaks of "'fiction' in its modern sense as opposed to 'fact'" ("How the West was Won by Fiction," in this volume).

tions – that nowadays support the distinction. That the language of fiction is simply our ordinary language of assertion makes it especially possible for fiction to be mistaken for nonfiction, and vice versa. The author can say "I really believe the following …" but that could always be understood as the speech of an unreliable fictional narrator or, if we prefer the author's own voice, an ironic utterance. There are no words shielded from or reserved for fictional use: "really," "truly" and "in fact" can be used as much within fiction as outside it. If it was unclear whether you were making an assertion when you said "It's raining outside," saying "I'm asserting that it's raining outside" won't settle the matter. It is possible, of course, for a story to begin with an announcement of its own fictionality, as with "Once upon a time." But even this positive test for fictionality is not decisive: an historian, frightened of the regime, may preface his account of the decades of tyranny with those same words, hoping to confuse the not very intelligent censor but knowing that the intended audience will see through it. One must always trust to uncertain indicators when it comes to judging whether this or that is fiction, and there are times when we rely on the implausibility of the plot, or the presence of narrator who knows more than any real narrator could know to make our judgement.

In situations where readers are used to fictions that declare their fictionality through the fantastical nature of their plots, a story with a naturalistic approach can easily be mistaken for non-fiction – as may perhaps have been the case with some readers of *Robinson Crusoe*.[17] Such readers cannot be automatically convicted of lacking the concept of fiction. And given this ever present possibility, it is not surprising that communities make finer distinctions than the simple fiction/nonfiction distinction I am proposing here. Green himself notes the tendency in Mediaeval commentary to make a tripartite distinction between *historia*, *argumentum* and *fabula*. (Green 2002, Chapter 1) *Historia* is reported truth, though generally understood to be a reporting of events at some time before the reach of present memory. *Fabula* consists of that which is manifestly untrue, describing events which are "against nature," as with much in Ovid. *Argumentum*, on the other hand, is fiction which is plausible, making reference only to kinds of things that could happen. Green suggests a strong but not universal tendency at this time to condemn the two fictive categories, either on grounds that anything other than a strict regard for truth is to be deplored (see remarks above about the tendency to distrust imagination), or as a tactic adopted by story-tellers to discredit the activities of

---

[17] Though I have heard it said (by Remigius Bunia) that even this was well understood to *be* fiction by contemporary readers.

their rivals. Yet at the same time there was a recognition, at least in scholarly commentary, that it was possible to achieve an acceptable harmony with one's audience, as Virgil was assumed to have done by flouting the limits of commonly known historical truth in the episode of Dido and Aeneas. Green sees parallel cases in the *Tristan and Isolde* of Thomas of Britain, and the Latin epic *Ruodliebe*. We would certainly go wrong if we thought that writers of this period worked only with the fiction/nonfiction divide, but Green's discussion, for all the complexity it reveals, strikes me as consistent with the belief that this divide was understood; understanding a distinction is not the same as approving both halves of it.

Of course, if pretence is the key to what fiction is – as I believe it to be – there is much more to be said about the history of the practice of fiction, from a maker's point of view and from the point of view of reception. We owe an enormous debt to people like Ian Watt and to later scholars like Gallagher from whom we have learned about the institutions of fiction, the presumptions of readers, the various means by which author's signalled their fictive intention and the difficulties sometimes encountered by authors who wished to express their fictive intent when developing new genres of fiction. An especially interesting topic is the options open to an author who wishes to create uncertainty about whether their intent was fictive or not, or to speak to two audiences, one of which can be expected to recognise the fictive intent while the other is for some reason insensitive to it. But none of this suggests that fiction itself is an invention of the comparatively recent historical past.

Finally, let me bring to bear on this dispute about the rightness of fiction as an historical category the conclusions earlier drawn, that the pretence-based account of fiction is consistent with fiction's capacity to communicate serious and sometimes troubling messages. Gallagher sees a distinction between fiction as she wishes to understand it and what she calls "libelous allegory," which she illustrates as follows:

> Delarivier Manley ... declared that she had published a mere work of the imagination when she was prosecuted for libeling prominent aristocrats in 1709 (Morgan 1986: 146–51). Her book had all the usual marks of libelous allegory: an imaginary kingdom populated by nobles who are monstrous but nevertheless recognizable exaggerations of well-known government ministers and ladies of the court. The "allegory" lent some legitimacy to Manley's alibi of fiction, but her work was popular mainly because readers believed that it revealed the secrets of the powerful, that it referred to contemporary individuals. (Gallagher 2006, 339, citing Fidelis Morgan 1986)

People may well be tempted to use the fictionality of their work as a defence against prosecution or persecution, but there is in reality no valid or reasonable inference from "this is fiction" to "this is not libel." An accusation of libel requires the accused to have knowingly promoted false or at least unprovable opinions deleterious to the subject's reputation. We have seen that fiction can do that. Perhaps it did that in the case of Manley. That the work was allegory does not merely lend "some legitimacy" to the claim that the work is fiction – it entails that the work is fiction. To admit the legitimacy of the pretence-based concept of fiction is not to grant that the fiction/nonfiction distinction will always or even usually be the most important distinction we can make in this area. In some conversations it will be much more important to decide what kind of fiction we are dealing with – allegorical or merely fantastical, say.

An interesting feature of cases like this – cases of libellous allegory – is that they only work for a community of people who are already sensitive to the fiction/nonfiction distinction as I have drawn it. Readers who lack that sensitivity and who read a story of people with monstrously exaggerated characteristics will either take it to be the ravings of a lunatic or the lies of a deceiver. On neither of those hypotheses is one likely to look for an unspoken allegorical message. This shows, I think, how misleading it can be to read off people's conceptual repertoire from their vocabulary; what is more important is their inferential practices, and in this case inferential practice is all on the side of the proposition that readers of Manley's work understood the fiction/nonfiction distinction. Were we now to ask people to say what is fiction and how it differs from nonfiction, I suspect we would get many different answers, not all of them coherent and many not consistent with the pretence-based account I have offered. The situation would have been the same, I imagine, in 12th century Japan and 18th century England. People are, and probably always were, bad at explicating their own concepts. It is a better idea to see what judgements they make and to decide what mix of concept-attributions best accounts for the pattern of judgements. I have only begun to illustrate such a method here.

Bibliography

Bowles, Samuel. "Did Warfare Among Ancestral Hunter-Gatherers Affect the Evolution of Human Social Behaviors?" *Science* 324 (2009): 1293–1298.

Currie, Gregory. "Art and the anthropologists." *Aesthetic Science: Connecting Minds, Brains and Experience*. Eds. A. Shimamura and S. Palmer. New York: Oxford University Press, 2012. 107–128.

– *Narratives and Narrators. A Philosophy of Stories*. Oxford: Oxford University Press, 2010.

– *The Nature of Fiction*. Cambridge: Cambridge University Press, 1990.

Gallagher, Catherine. "The Rise of Fictionality." *The Novel*. Vol. 1. Ed. Franco Moretti. Princeton, NJ: Princeton University Press, 2006. 336–363.

Green, Dennis H. *The Beginnings of Medieval Romance*. Cambridge: Cambridge University Press, 2002.
Green, M. C. and T. C. Brock. "The Role of Transportation in the Persuasiveness of Public Narratives." *Journal of Personality and Social Psychology* 79.5 (2000): 701–721.
Haug, Walter. *Literaturtheorie im deutschen Mittelalter von den Anfängen bis zum Ende des 13. Jahrhunderts*. 2nd ed. Darmstadt: Wissenschaftliche Buchgesellschaft, [1985] 1992.
"Michael Crichton, Novelist, Becomes Senate Witness." *New York Times*, 29 September 2005: http://www.nytimes.com/2005/09/29/books/29cric.html?_r=2&. (6 August 2013).
Morgan, Fidelis. *A Woman of No Character: An Autobiography of Mrs. Manley*. London: Faber and Faber, 1986.
Prentice, Deborah A., Richard J. Gerrig & Daniel S. Bailis. "What Readers Bring to the Processing of Fictional Texts." *Psychonomic Bulletin & Review* 4.3 (1997): 416–420.
Rutherford, R. B. [Review of] "Margalit Finkelberg: The Birth of Literary Fiction in Ancient Greece." *Classical Philology* 95.4 (2000): 482–486.
Sperber, Dan & Deirdre Wilson. *Relevance. Communication and Cognition*. 2nd ed. Oxford: Blackwell, 1995.

List of Contributors

Lars-Erik Berg is Professor in Social Psychology. He has worked as sociologist at the University of Göteborg in Sweden for thirty years, then as professor in Social Psychology at the University of Skövde, Sweden. His basis is pragmatist social philosophy, the perspective of George Herbert Mead. Empirical fields: identity construction and development – as in the article included in this volume – children and their play process, young adults, computer on-line-gaming and identity construction, and furthermore divorced fathers and their children. In particular, Berg has devoted much interest in the possibilities to develop the theory of Mead. Among his articles in English are "Divorce and Fathering in late Modern Sweden," *Advances in Applied Early Childhood Education, 1.* Oxford: JAI. Elsevier Science, 2001, "Children's stories of parental breakup" in A.-M. Jensen and L. McKee, eds., *Children and the Changing Family*. London: SAGE, 2002, and "Aspects of Identification in Computer Gaming," *HumanIT* 3 (2008).

Anders Cullhed is a Professor in Literary Studies at Stockholm University, a translator and a literary critic. He has published widely on fiction theory, intertextuality and tropes in medieval and early modern literature. His works include *Quevedo: El instante poético*, trans. Marina Torres and Francisco J. Uriz, Zaragoza: Institución "Fernando el Católico," 2005, and *The Shadow of Creusa. Negotiating Fictionality in Late Antique Latin Literature*, trans. Michael Knight, Berlin: De Gruyter, 2015. Cullhed is the President of the The Royal Swedish Academy of Letters, History and Antiquities.

Gregory Currie is Professor of Philosophy and Director of Research in Humanities at the University of Nottingham. From Autumn 2013 Currie teaches philosophy at the University of York. He was educated at the London School of Economics and the University of California, Berkeley. His first posts were in Australia, at the University of Sydney, and in New Zealand, at the University of Otago. He is a Fellow of the Australian Academy of Humanities and a Past President of the Australasian Association of Philosophy. Currie is editor of *Mind & Language*, an Associate Editor of the Australasian *Journal of Philosophy*, a Past Fellow of St John's College, Oxford, and has held visiting positions at Clare Hall, Cambridge, the London School of Economics, the Institute for Advanced Study, Australian National University, the University of Maryland, College Park and the University of St Andrews. His research interests cover the arts, imagination, the nature of delusions, and the role of narrative in our thinking. He is the author of *The Nature of Fiction*, Cambridge University Press,

1990, and his most recent book is *Narratives and Narrators*, Oxford University Press, 2010.

Margalit Finkelberg is Professor of Classics at Tel Aviv University. She is the author of *The Birth of Literary Fiction in Ancient* Greece, Oxford University Press, 1998, *Greeks and Pre-Greeks. Aegean Prehistory and Greek Heroic Tradition*, Cambridge University Press, 2005, and of numerous articles on various topics, especially Homer and ancient Greek poetics. She is a co-editor (with G. G. Stroumsa) of *Homer, the Bible, and Beyond: Literary and Religious Canons in the Ancient World*, Leiden: Brill, 2003, and the editor of *The Homer Encyclopedia* (3 vols.), Oxford: Wiley-Blackwell, 2011. She is a member of the Israel Academy of Sciences and Humanities.

Ming Dong Gu is Professor of Chinese and Comparative Literature at the University of Texas at Dallas and a special consultant to *The Norton Anthology of Theory and Criticism*. His file of interest covers Chinese literature, comparative poetics, Chinese intellectual thought, fiction theory, hermeneutics, and cross-cultural studies. He is the author of four books: *Chinese Theories of Reading and Writing*, New York: SUNY, 2005, *Sinologism: An Alternative to Orientalism and Postcolonialism*, New York: Routledge, 2013, *Chinese Theories of Fiction*, New York: SUNY, 2006, and *Anxiety of Originality: Multiple Approaches to Language, Literature, and Cultural Studies* (in Chinese), Nanjing University Press, 2009; and seventy articles in books or journals.

Mari Hatavara is Chair Professor of Finnish Literature at the School of Language, Translation and Literary Studies, University of Tampere. Hatavara's main areas of interest are narrative theory, historical novels and intermedial relations between word and image. Her recent articles include "Contested History, Denied Past. The Narrator's Failure in Ralf Nordgren's Det har aldrig hänt (1977)" in Göran Rossholm and Christer Johansson (eds.), *Disputable Core Concepts of Narrative Theory*, Bern: Peter Lang, 2012, and "Historical Fiction and Ekphrasis in Leena Lander's The Order" in Leena Eilittä, Liliane Louvel and Sabine Kim (eds.), *Intermedial Arts*, Newcastle upon Tyne: Cambridge Scholars Publishing, 2012. She is currently coediting an interdisciplinary volume on narrative theory, *The Travelling Concepts of Narrative* with Matti Hyvärinen and Lars-Christer Hydén (John Benjamins Studies in Narrative Series, Amsterdam, 2013).

Stefan Helgesson is Professor of English at Stockholm University. His research interests include southern African literature in English and Portuguese, Brazilian literature, postcolonial theory and theories of world literature. He is the author of *Writing in Crisis: Ethics and History in Gordimer, Ndebele and Coetzee*,

University of KwaZulu-Natal Press, 2004, and *Transnationalism in Southern African Literature*, London: Routledge, 2009. He has also edited volume four of *Literary History: Towards a Global Perspective*, Berlin: De Gruyter, 2006, and is co-editor of *Literature, Geography, Translation*, Newcastle upon Tyne: Cambridge Scholars Publishing, 2011. He is on the editorial boards of *English Studies in Africa*, *Safundi*, *French Studies in Southern Africa* and *The Cambridge Journal of Postcolonial Literary Inquiry*. The chapter in the present volume derives from his project within the Bank of Sweden Tercentenary Foundation's research programme "Time, Memory and Representation."

Fritz Peter Knapp is Professor ordinarius emeritus of Ruprecht-Karls-Universität Heidelberg, and a member of the Academies of Humanities and Sciences in Heidelberg and Vienna. His main research fields are: comparative and regional history of medieval literature (Latin, French and German), medieval poetics and stylistics, as well as edition, translation and interpretation of medieval texts. He has published some 120 articles and twelve books, among which are *Historie und Fiktion in der mittelalterlichen Gattungspoetik: sieben Studien und ein Nachwort*, Heidelberg: Winter, 1997, and *Historie und Fiktion in der mittelalterlichen Gattungspoetik: 2, zehn neue Studien und ein Vorwort*, Heidelberg: Winter, 2005.

Christian Kupchik is a poet, literary critic, and translator. He has lived in Paris, Barcelona, Stockholm and Montevideo, whereupon he settled in Buenos Aires. He has published five books of poetry, a book of short stories, *Fuera de Lugar*, (Montevideo: Cal y Canto, 1995, and two anthologies, *En la Vía – Cuentos Desde un Tren*, Buenos Aires: Editorial Norma, 2004, and *Relatos de París*, Buenos Aires: Cántaro, 2005. He also published the essays *Emanuel Swedenborg. La Arquitectura del Cielo*, Buenos Aires: Adriana Hidalgo Editora, 2004, 2nd ed. 2005, and *El Dorado y Otros Prodigios*, Madrid: Nowtilus, 2008. Kupchik has specialized in travel literature as a genre, and has taken part in numerous colloquies and conferences on the subject. He managed the *Planeta Nómada* collection, and as part of it he published four books: *El Camino de las Damas, La Ruta Argentina, En busca de Cathay, and Las Huellas del Río*, Buenos Aires: Editorial Planeta, 1999/2000. He regularly participates in the activities of the Centre de Recherche sur la Littérature de Voyages (CRLV), in París VIII, Sorbonne. At present, he co-chairs the magazine *Siwa – Revista de Literaturas Geográficas* (Magazine of Geographic Literatures) and the publishing house *Club Burton*, devoted to the travel genre. He is currently working as a publisher at Paidós Argentina, where he manages four book collections covering essays related to various human sciences (Philosophy, Sociology, Aesthetics, Communication).

Stephan Larsen is an Assistant Professor of Literature at Stockholm University. His research fields are post-colonial literature in general, and African literature in particular. Larsen received his PhD at Stockholm University in 1983. The title of his doctoral dissertation is: *A Writer and His Gods: A Study of the Importance of Yoruba Myths and Religious Ideas to the Writing of Wole Soyinka*, Stockholm University, 1983. He has contributed to Gunilla Lindberg-Wada, Anders Pettersson, Margareta Petersson and Stefan Helgesson (eds.), *Literary History: Towards a Global Perspective*, Berlin: De Gruyter, 2006.

Gunilla Lindberg-Wada is Chair Professor of Japanese Studies at Stockholm University since 1990 and the leader of a multi-year project for the production of *Literature: A World History* in four volumes, under the auspices of The Stockholm Collegium of World Literary History (to be published by Wiley-Blackwell). She is the author of *Poetic Allusion: Some Aspects of the Role Played by Kokin Wakashuu as a Source of Poetic Allusion in Genji Monogatari*, Stockholm University, 1983, and co-editor of *An Arctic Passage to the Far East: The Visit of the Swedish Vega Expedition to Meiji Japan in 1879*, Stockholm: Royal Swedish Academy of Science, 2002. In 1997 she received the Noma Award for the Translation of Japanese Literature for her translations into Swedish of classic and modern Japanese poetry, modern novels and drama. During the years 1996–2006 Lindberg-Wada was the project leader of "Literature and Literary History in Global Contexts: A Comparative Project," which resulted in the four volume series *Literary History: Towards a Global Perspective*, Berlin: De Gruyter, 2006.

Torbjörn Lodén is a Professor of Chinese Language and Literature, Stockholm University, the Director of the Stockholm Confucius Institute and, 2011–2013, Visiting Professor at City University of Hong Kong. His main field of research is Chinese intellectual history. Among his publications are *Kinas vägval – från himmelskt imperium till global stormakt* [China's choice of road – from celestial empire to global great power], Stockholm: SNS, 2012, "Reason, Feeling, and Ethics in Mencius and Xunzi," *Journal of Chinese Philosophy* 36.4 (2009), *Rediscovering Confucianism: A Major Philosophy of Life in East Asia*, London: Global Oriental, 2006, *Från Mao till Mammon: idéer och politik i det moderna Kina* [From Mao to Mammon: ideas and politics in modern China], Stockholm: Ordfront, 1998, and "Dai Zhen's Evidential Commentary on the Meaning of the Words of Mencius," *Bulletin of the Museum of Far Eastern Antiquities* 60 (1988).

Göran Malmqvist is Professor Emeritus in Sinology at Stockholm University and a member of the Swedish Academy. He has published extensively in the fields of Chinese linguistics and literature, and translated many works of Chinese literature (ancient, medieval, modern and contemporary) into Swedish, for instance *Water Margin* (*Shuihu zhuan*) *and Journey to the West* (*Xiyou ji*), see also http://www.svenskaakademien.se/en/the_academy/members/goran_malmqvist_1.

Janken Myrdal is Professor in Agrarian History at the Swedish University of Agricultural Sciences since 1994. After the publication of his thesis "Medieval Arable Farming in Sweden. Technical Change 1000–1520 CE," he has specialized in philosophy of history and change in global agricultural systems. He has taken a particular interest in the theory focus on the meaning of crisis throughout history, and in how, within these contexts, expansion has a tendency to lead to exaggeration. In addition, Myrdal has been doing research in the history of domestic animals: historical land use, milk production and animal health.

Christina Nygren is Professor of Theatre Studies and holds a position as Visiting Professor at the Department of Oriental Languages at Stockholm University. During the last thirty years she has studied, researched and worked in Asia, mainly in China, Japan, India and Bangladesh, but also in Vietnam and Laos. She graduated in Chinese theatre history and theory from the Central Academy of Drama in Beijing and on Japanese theatre history and aesthetics from Osaka University. Main interests are performing arts and popular culture. Her publications include writings on traditional and modern theatre and dance, festival culture, folk performances and popular entertainments in Asia.

Anders Pettersson is Emeritus Professor of Swedish and Comparative Literature at Umeå University, Sweden. His main areas of research are fundamental literary theory and, increasingly, transcultural literary history. Among his more recent books are *Verbal Art: A Philosophy of Literature and Literary Experience*, Montreal: McGill-Queen's University Press, 2000, *Notions of Literature across Times and Cultures* (ed.), Berlin: De Gruyter, 2006, and *The Concept of Literary Application: Readers' Analogies from Text to Life*, New York: Palgrave Macmillan, 2012. Pettersson is Secretary-General of the International Federation for Modern Languages and Literatures (FILLM) and Vice President of the International Comparative Literature Association (AILC/ICLA).

Göran Rossholm is Professor in Literature at Stockholm university. He has written mainly on theoretical subjects (narrative theory, fiction theory, semiotics and interpretation theory) in articles and in one monograph, *To Be And Not Be. On Interpretation, Iconicity and Fiction*, Bern: Peter Lang, 2004. Rossholm has edited *Essays on Fiction and Perspective*, Bern: Peter Lang, 2004, co-edited *Disputable Core Concepts of Narrative Theory*, Bern: Peter Lang, 2012, and is presently working on a book on narrative theory.

Lena Rydholm is a Professor of Chinese at the Department of Linguistics and Philology at Uppsala University. Her Ph.D. thesis was *In Search of the Generic*

Identity of Ci Poetry, Stockholm University, 1998. Her main research interests are classical and modern Chinese literature and literary theory, and contemporary Chinese media. Among her publications are "The theory of ancient Chinese genres," *Literary History: Towards a Global Perspective. Vol. 2. Literary Genres: An Intercultural Approach*, ed. Gunilla Lindberg-Wada, Berlin: De Gruyter, 2006, "Theories of Genre and Style in China in the Late 20th Century," *Orientalia Suecana* 59 (2011), "China Central Television's Spring Festival Gala: Entertainment and Political Propaganda," *NIASnytt-Asia Insights* 3 (2005), "China and the World's First Freedom of Information Act: the Swedish Freedom of the Press Act of 1766," *Javnost – The Public* 20.4 (2013). She has also co-edited several special issues of journals and anthologies, such as *Media Cultures and Globalization in China*, Stockholm University, 2004, and *Chinese Culture and Globalization: History and Challenges for the 21st Century*, Stockholm University, 2009.

Marcia Sá Cavalcante Schuback is Professor of Philosophy at Södertörn University (Sweden). She has also worked as Associate Professor at the Universidade Federal do Rio de Janeiro (UFRJ) in Brazil. Her field of research is continental philosophy, with focus on phenomenology, hermeneutics, German idealism and hermeneutical readings of ancient philosophy. Her latest monographs are *Lovtal till intet – essäer om filosofisk hermeneutik* [In praise of nothing: Essays in philosophic hermeneutics], Göteborg: Glänta, 2006, *Olho a olho: ensaios de longe* [Between two eyes: Essays from far away], Rio de Janeiro: 7 Letras, 2010, *Att tänka i skisser* [Thinking in sketches], Göteborg: Glänta, 2011, and *Being with the Without, a conversation with Jean-Luc Nancy*, Stockholm: Axl Books, 2013.

Bo Utas is a Professor Emeritus of Iranian Studies at Uppsala University, Sweden. His research covers many aspects of Middle and New Iranian languages, especially varieties of Persian, as well as literary, religious and historical topics connected with the use of those languages. Recently his papers on Persian literature were reprinted in a volume entitled *Manuscript, Text and Literature. Collected Essays on Middle and New Persian Texts* (Beiträge zur Iranistik, 29), Wiesbaden: Reichert, 2008.

Wim Verbaal is Professor in Latin Language and Literature at the Department of Latin and Greek of the University of Gent. He took his Ph.D. at this university in 2000 on the writing strategies of Bernard of Clairvaux, the title of his thesis being "A Divine Tragedy. Triumph and Defeat in the Word by Bernard of Clairvaux." He has published a monograph in Dutch on the conflict between Bernard and Abelard as well as several articles on different aspects of Bernard's works and their reception, e.g. in the Modern Devotion by Gerard Zerbolt of

Zutphen. At present he prepares a book on Bernard's writing technics. In addition, he has published articles on Latin poetry: on the *Hortulus* of Walahfrid Strabo, on Rutilius Namatianus' *De reditu suo* and on Juvencus, but his main field of research remains Latin literature of the Twelfth Century, notably in its poetical aspects (the School of the Loire, fictionality, allegoric narratives). He has co-edited the two volumes *Latinitas perennis* (*1. The Continuity of Latin Literature, 2. Appropriation and Latin Literature*), Leiden: Brill, 2007, 2009.

Ayling Wang is Professor and Chair of the Department of Theater Arts at the National Sun Yat-sen University, Taiwan. She obtained her doctoral degree at the Department of East Asian Languages and Literatures of Yale University in 1992. She became an assistant research fellow at the Academia Sinica, Taipei, in 1993; an associate research fellow from 1998 to 2003; and a research fellow from 2003 to 2013. From 2003–2010 she was acting director, deputy director of the Institute of Chinese Literature and Philosophy, Academia Sinica. From 2008 to 2013, she was Vice President of the Chiang Ching-kuo Foundation for International Scholarly Exchange (CCKF). Professor Wang has been awarded the prestigious Outstanding Research Award by the National Science Council, the highest honor the Council bestows on individual professors. She has also been awarded the Outstanding Young Scholar Research by the Academia Sinica. Her main interests include traditional Chinese drama, literary theory and Ming Qing literature. She has published seven books on Ming-Qing literature and culture, and many articles in Chinese, English and Japanese on her areas of interest.

Index of Names

Abelard, Peter 192, 198 f., 300
Adcock, Fleur 198
Adhikari, Madhumalati 241
Adorno, Theodor 69
Ailly, Pierre d' 292
Akert, Robin M. 96
Alain of Lille 189
Alberti, Rafael 308
Algasel *see* Ghazali, Abu Hamed al-
Allen, Woody 101
Alstrum, James J. 276
An Lushan 115 f., 121 f., 126
Anderson, Benedict 269–71
Andrade, Olímpio de Souza 265
Apuleius 191
Aranha, Graça 264
Aravamudan, Srinivas 168
Ariosto 185
Aristotle 46, 153, 157–64, 181, 186, 227, 229, 231 f., 238, 263, 312
Ariwara Narihira 63
Aronson, Elliot 96
Arping, Åsa 243
Assis, Machado de 264
'Attar, Farid od-din 172
Auerbach, Erich 185
Augoustinos, Martha 98
Augustine, Saint 191

Ba Jin 31, 43, 47
Bai Juyi 55 f., 115 f.
Bai Letian *see* Bai Juyi
Bai Pu 112, 115 f.
Bailis, Daniel S. 317
Balzac, Honoré de 278
Ban Gu 9, 38 f.
Barchiesi, Alessandro 191
Barks, Coleman 175
Barnstone, Willis 87
Barthes, Roland 211
Baudry of Bourgueil 197
Bauman, Zygmunt 98
Beck, Ulrich 98, 104
Beck-Gernsheim, Elisabeth 98
Becker, Howard S. 102

Beckett, Samuel 296
Beda, Saint 181
Bei Dao 45
Berg, Lars-Erik viii–ix, 95, 99, 103 f., 315, 325
Bergman, Pär 14
Bernhard, Thomas 296
Bierl, Anton 161
Birch, Cyril 129
Blake, William 280, 308
Blanchot, Maurice 295
Bloom, Harold 208
Blumenberg, Hans 180
Bodel, Jean 183 f.
Boehmer, Elleke 264
Bond, Gerald A. 194–97
Bonnefoy, Claude 74
Borges, Jorge Luis x, 153, 163 f., 290, 292, 295 f., 312
Bourdieu, Pierre 160
Boutemy, André 198
Bowers, Maggie Ann 275
Bowles, Samuel 311
Boyer, Blanche 192
Branden, Nathaniel 125
Brecht, Bertolt 160, 230
Brehm, Sharon H. 125
Brock, T. C. 315
Brown, Roger 96
Brownlee, Kevin 184
Bruijn, Johannes T. P. de 167
Buddha 55 f.
Bulst, Walther 195, 197
Burns, Susan L. 4, 60

Caddeau, Patrick W. 60 f., 63
Callahan, William A. 25
Cameron, J. M. 4
Campany, Robert Ford 10
Caraher, Brian G. 262, 272
Carlshamre, Staffan 230 f.
Cervantes, Miguel de 185
Chang Weiping 112
Chariton 170
Chatman, Seymour 211

Chen Duxiu 41
Chen Hong 116
Chen Meilin 204
Chen Wannai 112
Cheng, Fangwu 43
Chōken 55
Chrétien de Troyes 180, 184f., 190, 193, 312
Chrisman, Laura 264
Chu Seng 112
Cicero 182
Coetzee, J. M. 88, 326
Cohn, Dorrit 242f., 248f., 252, 255
Coleridge, Samuel Taylor 263
Columbus, Christopher 289, 292
Confucius 8–10, 12, 35, 116, 118f.
Converse, Philip E. 96
Cook, Karen S. 96
Cooley, Charles H. 99, 102–4
Cooper, Brenda 275, 283, 285
Coppola, Carlo 276, 282
Crichton, Michael 314, 317
Cuddon, J. A. 5, 7, 208, 217
Culler, Jonathan 211, 215
Cullhed, Anders iii, vi, viii, 32, 325
Currie, Gregory vii, xi, 21f., 31, 311–13, 315, 317f., 320, 325
Curtius Rufus 191

da Cunha, Euclides 262–65, 268–72
Dällenbach, Lucien 247,
Darwin, Charles 61, 265, 270f.
Davies, David 92
Defoe, Daniel 263
Demos, John 241
Dewey, John 99
DeWoskin, Kenneth 9–11
D'haen, Theo L. 280
Dickens, Charles 278
Diderot, Dennis 179
Didi-Huberman, Georges 76
Doležel, Lubomír 153, 159
Doleželová-Velingerová, Milena 41
Dronke, Peter 197
Du Fu 159
Dumas, Alexandre (fils) 171
Dumas, Alexandre (père) 171

Eagleton, Terry 6
Easterling, Patricia E. 162
Eco, Umberto 153
Eliot, T. S. 308
Eliot, George 61
Emmerich, Michael 60
Empedocles 158
Engdahl, Horace 309
Epstein, Maram 206
Erdman, David 280
Erikson, Erik 98
Ernout, Alfred 70
Ernst, Ulrich 180

Fabian, Johannes 269
Fang Xuanling 10
Faris, Wendy B. 276–285
Faulkner, William 212
Fay, Brian 241
Feng Baoshan 204
Feng Menglong 113
Ferdousi 168
Fernandes, Raúl C. Gouveia 269
Fine, Gary Alan 96
Finkelberg, Margalit 153
Fleming, Clas 242, 244f., 255
Fleming, Johan 245
Fludernik, Monika 251
Foucault, Michel 74, 78, 164, 291
Fowler, Roger 212
Franciscono, Marcel 79
Fraser, Robert 280f.
Freud, Sigmund 284
Freytag, Gustav 121
Fryxell, Anders 245
Fujioka Tadaharu 53f.
Fujiwara Koreyuki 58
Fujiwara no Tametoki 53
Fujiwara Shunzei 56, 57f.
Fujiwara Takayoshi 52
Fujiwara Teika 52, 56, 58
Furberg, Mats 85
Fyfe, W. Hamilton 227

Gallagher, Catherine 92, 263f., 272, 312, 318–20, 322
Gan Bao 10–12, 21f., 39
Gao Xingjian 45

Ge Hong 10, 22
Ge, Liangyan 221
Gendler, Tamar Szabó 232, 235 f.
Genette, Gérard 242, 244, 248
Gentner, Dedre 84
Geoffrey of Monmouth 182, 193
Gerrig, Richard J. 317
Gewertz, Ken 214 f.
Giddens, Anthony 96–98, 104
Giovanni da Pian del Carpine 293
Ghazali, Abu Hamed al- 173, 175
Ghazali, Ahmad 175
Goff, Janet 55, 58
Goffman, Erving 98, 102, 104
Gogol, Nikolai 15
Goodman, Nelson 231
Gorgani, Fakhr od-din 170
Gorgias 161 f.
Green, Dennis H. 180, 192 f., 195, 313, 315 f., 318, 321 f.
Green, M. C. 315
Greenblatt, Stephen 220, 222
Gren-Eklund, Gunilla 173
Gu, Ming Dong viii, x, 6, 14, 18 f., 21, 23, 203, 206, 312, 326
Guan Daru 15
Guan Hanqing 112
Guibert of Nogent 194
Guillaume de Roubruck 293
Guo Honglei 15
Guo Moruo 42
Guo Pu 10
Guo Shaoyu 34
Gustafsson, Styrbjörn 303

Haft, Lloyd 7, 12 f.
Hägg, Tomas 170
Hagiwara Hiromichi 60, 63
Halliwell, Stephen 227
Hamburger, Käte 254
Hamill, Sam 34
Han Tongwen 9–11
Hanan, Patrick 204, 206
Hao Ran 44
Harlan, David 241
Harris, Wendell V. 4, 7, 26
Hart, Patricia 276, 286
Hatavara, Mari viii, x, 241, 247, 314, 326

Haug, Walter 180, 185, 312
Hawkes, David 204
Hayashi Razan 59
Heidegger, Martin 76, 267
Heine, Heinrich 170
Heinrichs, Wolfhart 164
Heinze, Richard 191
Helgesson, Stefan viii, x, 261, 312, 326, 328
Hemingway, Ernest 212
Herman, David 250 f.
Hesse, Hermann 308
Hewstone, Miles 96
Higuchi Yoshimaro 54, 57 f.
Hisamatsu Sen'ichi 60
Hitchcock, Alfred 231, 233, 235 f.
Hoffman, Heinrich 227 f., 237
Hölderlin, Friedrich 159
Holyoak, Keith J. 84
Homer 156–58, 161 f., 295 f., 326
Hong Sheng v, 111–22, 124–27, 129–33, 314
Horace 229
Hou Zhongyi 204
House, James S. 96
Hsia, Chih-tsing 12, 13, 131, 213
Hsia, C. T. see Hsia, Chih-tsing
Hu Shi 15, 41
Hu, Ying 10 f.
Hu Yinglin 40
Hu Zhengrong 18 f.
Huang Lin 9–11
Huang Liuhong 111
Huang, Martin 206, 213 f., 221
Hutcheon, Linda 241
Hyrkkänen, Markku 255

Ibsen, Henrik vi, 296
Ichino, Anna 311, 317
Idema, Wilt L. 7, 12 f.
Ilkka, Jacob 249
Iser, Wolfgang 90
Isidore of Seville, Saint 180 f., 183 f., 185, 292

Jaeger, C. Stephen 194
Jahn, Manfred 250
Jakobson, Roman 5
James, Henry 212
James, William 104

Jameson, Fredric 222
Jami, 'Abd or-Rahman 171 f.
Janko, Richard 157
Jauss, Hans Robert 153
Jay, Paul 21
Ji, Deqiang 18 f.
Jiang Qi 16
Jiao Xun 113
Jin Shengtan 40, 133
Johnson, Samuel 293
Joyce, James 212, 295, 306
Jung, Carl 284–86
Juvencus 191, 331

Kafka, Franz 294 f., 306, 308
Kant, Immanuel 68 f.
Khairallah, As'ad E. 171
Kissack, Mike 268
Kitamura Kigin 60
Klee, Felix 79
Klee, Paul 74–81
Kleist, Heinrich von 308
Knapp, Fritz Peter viii, x, 179, 181 f., 184 f., 312, 327
Könsgen, Ewald 198
Kornicki, Peter F. 59
Kottman, Paul A. 74
Kuboki Tetsuo 54, 57 f.
Kuhn, Thomas 26, 205, 207, 219
Kumarajiva 128
Kumazawa Banzan 59
Kupchik, Christian viii, x, 289, 327

Lacoue-Labarth, Philippe 70
Lactantius 183
Laing, R. D. 102
Lamarque, Peter 90
Lao She 42 f.
Lao Tzu *see* Laozi
Laozi 25, 222
Larsen, Stephan viii, x, 275, 328
Lasch, Christopher 98, 104
Legge, James 10
Lemert, Edwin M. 102
Lenin, V. I. 16, 25
Lewis, David 90
Li Guiqi 16
Li, Qiancheng 221

Li, Wai-yee 206, 213 f., 221
Li Xiusheng 204
Li Yu 121, 123 f., 133
Li Zhi 131
Liang Qichao 14 f., 16, 41 f.
Liang Tingnan 113
Lin, Shuen-fu 5
Lindberg-Wada, Gunilla viii–ix, 20, 51, 53, 313, 328, 330
Liu, James J. Y. 6, 8, 21, 33–35,
Liu Xiaobo 46
Liu Xie 34–37, 46
Liu Zhiji 38
Livius 182
Locke, John 96
Lodén, Torbjörn viii–ix, 7, 31, 43, 328
Lodge, David 3
Lu Hsun *see* Lu Xun
Lu Ji 34 f.
Lu Kanru 36
Lu Xun 15 f., 32, 41, 43, 204, 208
Lucanus 183
Lukács, Georg 185
Luo Genze 34
Luo Rufang 131
Lynn, Richard 33

Machiavelli, Niccolò 169
Magellan, Ferdinand 289
Magritte, René 291
Maia, João Marcelo Ehlert 265
Mair, Victor H. v. 40
Malevich, Kazimir 71
Mallarmé, Stéphane 295
Malmqvist, Göran vii, xi, 301, 328
Mandeville, sir John of 292
Mann, Thomas 306
Manstead, Anthony S. R. 96
Mao Dun 42 f.
Mao Qiling 112
Mao Zedong 16, 33, 44 f., 47, 328
Mao Zonggang 40, 133
Marbode of Rennes 194–97, 199
Marco da Nizza 289
Martin, Wallace 203
Martínez-Bonati, Félix 264
Marx, Karl 16, 25, 43, 47, 74, 223
Mattson, Philip 186

Maxwell, Richard 241, 243 f.
McDougall, Bonnie S. 44 f.
McHale, Brian 248 f.
McKeon, Richard 192
McMullen, James 59
Mead, George H. 98 f., 101–4
Meillet, Antoine 70
Mehtonen, Päivi 191
Mencius 328
Meng Zhaolian 204
Mertens, Volker 180
Mews, Constant 198
Miller, J. Hillis 219 f.
Minford, John 204
Mitchell, William J. T. 203, 211
Montrose, Louise A. 220 f.
Moretti, Franco 203, 262, 272
Morgan, Fidelis 322
Moser Jr., Thomas C. 193, 195 f.
Moos, Peter von 183
Moto'ori Norinaga 60–62
Mou Shijin 36
Müller, Jan-Dirk 179 f.
Murasaki Shikibu ix, 51–56, 61 f., 313
Myrdal, Janken viii, 329

Naser-e Khosrou 171
Nelles, William 251, 253
Newcomb, Theodore M. 96
Nezami of Ganja 170 f.
Nicholson, Reynold 172
Ning Zongyi 204
Nonoguchi Ryūho 59
Nünning, Ansgar 241
Nüßlein, Theodor 182
Nygren, Christina viii–ix, 137, 139, 141–44, 147 f., 329

Odorico da Pordenone 293
Oiticica, Hélio 71
Okri, Ben x, 275–85
Oliva, Renato 284 f.
Ovid 191 f., 194–97, 321
Owen, Stephen 159, 214

Pessoa, Fernando 73
Petronius Arbiter 190 f.

Pettersson, Anders viii–ix, 4 f., 20 f., 83, 88, 90 f., 328 f.
Petzet, Heinrich Wiegand 76
Pigafetta, Antonio 289
Piglia, Ricardo 293–96
Plaks, Andrew 203 f., 206
Plato x, 70, 72, 153–62, 173, 176, 312
Plutarch 161, 295
Pöggeler, Otto 76
Pollitt, Jerome Jordan 162
Polo, Marco 292
Pratt, Mary-Louise 264
Prentice, Deborah A. 317
Proust, Marcel 212, 290–92, 306, 317
Pu Songling 217
Putnam, Samuel 264, 271

Qabus 169
Qian Maiqun 15 f.
Qian Zhongshu 43
Quintus Curtius see Curtius Rufus

Radford, Colin 90
Ratkowitsch, Christine 197
Rauschenberg, Robert 71
Regnier, Claude 182
Richter, Gisela M. A. 162
Ricoeur, Paul 262 f., 269 f., 272
Rigney, Ann 241, 255
Rilke, Rainer Maria 308
Rimbaud, Arthur 308
Roa Bastos, Augusto 291 f., 295
Rolston, David 204
Rossholm, Göran viii, x, 227, 229, 326, 329
Royle, Nicholas 251
Rumi, Jalal od-din 172–76
Runeberg, Fredrika 242, 245, 254
Rutherford, R. B. 312
Ryan, Marie-Laure 250
Rydholm, Lena vi, viii–ix, 3, 9, 17, 329
Rypka, Jan 168, 171
Ryūtei Tanehiko 59

Sá Cavalcante Schuback, Marcia viii–ix, 67, 75, 312, 330
Sa'di 169
Saenger, Paul 194
Saer, Juan José 296

Sana'i 171–73
Sanari Kentarō 55
Sappho 87,
Sauter, Willmar 137
Schabert, Ina 243
Scheff, Thomas J. 102
Scholes, Robert 215, 223
Schönberg, Arnold 68 f., 71 f.
Schreiner, Olive 261–68, 271 f.
Schreyer, Lothar 78
Schulz, Walter 78
Schürmann, Reiner 74
Searle, John R. 4, 85
Servius 183
Seubold, Günter 76
Shakespeare, William 6, 74, 264
Shakyamuni *see* Buddha
Shang, Wei 213 f., 221
Shaw, Harry E. 241
Shen Congwen 43
Shi Changyu 204
Shorer, Mark 212
Sidney, Philip 263, 319
Sjölin, Daniel 107
Slater, Niall W. 160, 162
Socrates 320
Soltan Valad 175
Solzhenitsyn, Aleksandr 234
Sommardal, Göran 9
Sophron 158
Soyinka, Wole 280, 284, 328
Spencer, Herbert 266–69
Sperber, Dan 316 f.
Stålarm, Arvid 245
Stein, Gertrud 308
Steiner, George 68, 301
Sterne, Laurence 179
Stevenson, Robert Louis 101
Stowe, Harriet Beecher 87
Su Dongpo 33
Sun Yaoyu 209
Sun Yu 112
Sund, Lars 242, 245

Tammi, Pekka 248
Tang Xianzu 129, 131, 133
Tao Yuanming 39
Teilmann, Stina 248

Thagard, Paul 84
Thomas Aquinas 180, 290
Thomas of Britain 322
Thomasin von Zerkläre 185
Tian Han 42
Tian, Xiaofei 11, 22
Tilliette, Jean-Yves 197
Titlestad, Michael 268
Todorov, Tzvetan 211, 217, 277
Tolstoy, Leo 159, 317
Truman, Harry S. 84
Tseng Yong-i [Tseng Yong-Yih] 111
Tsubouchi Shōyō 61–63
Tu Long 112
Turner, Ralph H. 96
Tyler, Royall 54

Utagawa Kunisada 59
Utagawa Toyokuni III *see* Utagawa Kunisada
Utas, Bo viii, x, 167, 170, 173–76, 330

Velázquez, Diego 74
Verbaal, Wim viii, x, 189, 192, 198 f., 312, 320, 330
Vermeule, Blakey 91
Virgil 183, 192, 322

Waley, Arthur 10
Wallace, Diana 245
Walton, Kendall L. 5, 21, 31
Wang Ayling viii–ix, 111, 314, 331
Wang Bocheng 112, 116
Wang, David 213, 221
Wang Jia 12
Wang, Jing 206, 218
Wang Meng 17
Wang Rumei 204
Wang Tingmo 112
Wang Yuanhua 36
Wang Zeng 112
Warburg, Aby 71
Ward, Jamie 103
Warnes, Christopher 279, 284–86
Warren, Austin 3
Wedberg, Anders 238
Wehrli, Fritz 182
Wellek, René 3
Wells, Orson 320

Werwing, Johan Gabriel 244
White, Hayden 219
Willett, John 160
William of Newburgh 182
Wilson, Deirdre 316 f.
Wilson, Timothy D. 96
Wittgenstein, Ludwig 291, 296
Wolfram von Eschenbach 183
Wolfzettel, Friedrich 180
Wolterstorff, Nicholas 87
Wong, Siu-Kit 8
Woodman, Anthony 182
Woolf, Virginia 212
Wordsworth, William 159
Wu Cheng'en 216
Wu Gongzheng 204
Wu Jingzi 13
Wu Shimei 112, 122
Wu Shufu 111
Wu Yiyi ix, 111–14, 117–19, 122–24, 126 f., 132 f.

Xenarchus 158
Xenophon of Ephesos 170
Xu Shuofang 129

Yacobi, Tamar 242, 246
Yamagishi Tokuhei 52
Yan Lianke 45–47
Yang, Gladys 204
Yang Guifei *see* Yang Yuhuan
Yang, Hsien-yi 204
Yang Ming 36

Yang Mu 34 f.
Yang Xiaomei 129
Yang Yuhuan 112, 118, 130
Ye Long 204
Ye Shengtao 42
Yoshida Hanbei 59
You Tong 112
Yu, Anthony C. 205 f., 212
Yu Dafu 42
Yu, Ying-shih 204 f.

Zeami 55, 58
Zhang, Longxi 35, 38, 159
Zhang Peiheng 112
Zhang Xuecheng 40
Zhang Yi 19
Zhang Yu 204
Zhang Zhupu 40
Zhao Shuli 44
Zhao Tingyang 24 f.
Zhao Yishan 204
Zhao Zhishen 111
Zhi Yu 34
Zhong Rong 36
Zhou Dunyi 8, 32 f.
Zhou Zuoren 42
Zhou, Zuyan 221
Zhu Xiang 112
Zhu Yizun 112
Zi Xia [Pu Shang] 8
Zumthor, Pierre 290
Zürcher, Erik 7

www.ingramcontent.com/pod-product-compliance
Lightning Source LLC
Chambersburg PA
CBHW070605170426
43200CB00012B/2594